Extraordinary Cities

To Enid
and our grandchildren
Holly, Colette and Christian,
Tom, Ella and Leah

Extraordinary Cities

Millennia of Moral Syndromes,
World-Systems and City/State Relations

Peter J. Taylor

Northumbria University, UK

Edward Elgar
Cheltenham, UK • Northampton, MA, USA

Published by
Edward Elgar Publishing Limited
The Lypiatts
15 Lansdown Road
Cheltenham
Glos GL50 2JA
UK

Edward Elgar Publishing, Inc.
William Pratt House
9 Dewey Court
Northampton
Massachusetts 01060
USA

A catalogue record for this book
is available from the British Library

Library of Congress Control Number: 2012946687

This book is available electronically in the ElgarOnline.com
Economics Subject Collection, E-ISBN 978 1 78195 482 9

ISBN 978 1 78195 480 5 (cased)

Typeset by Servis Filmsetting Ltd, Stockport, Cheshire
Printed and bound by MPG Books Group, UK

Contents

Preface   vii

PART I   SETTING DOWN AND SETTING UP

1   A cities' perspective   3
2   Conceptual toolkits   31

PART II   NARRATIVE I: BEGINNING CONJECTURES

3   City and state beginnings: Western Asia's great creative
    interlude   93
4   Geographies of beginning creative interludes   133

PART III   NARRATIVE II: WORLD-SYSTEMS

5   Normal history   181
6   Making the modern world-system: Western Europe's great
    creative interlude   230

PART IV   NARRATIVE III: PROSPECTIVE
          CONJECTURES – WHERE ARE WE AND
          WHERE ARE WE GOING?

7   Working in an urban world   297
8   Towards green networks of cities for the twenty-first century   349

References   380
Cities index   407
General index   416

Preface

This book has taken a long time. My fascination with cities is long standing but it only began to translate into research curiosity in the 1990s. It coincided with trying to make sense of contemporary globalization as a practice, as everyday work that was enabling and reproducing worldwide economic integration. That work was done in cities, and a literature on 'world cities' and 'global cities' was emerging. This change in scale meant my new research curiosity was to become very different from my initial fascination. The latter consisted of 'walking cities', following in the footsteps, figuratively but perhaps sometimes literally, of Robert Park, the great Chicago urban sociologist of the early twentieth century. Taking in the ambiences, enjoying the 'townscapes', discerning differences – cities really felt like extraordinary achievements. But my research focused on work – I asked of a city 'what work is done here?' – and this could not be read simply from the townscape, however impressive the skyscrapers. The latter in Manhattan had commonly been called 'urban canyons' but this metaphor had been generally misconstrued. Real canyons are also impressive places to visit but their essence is the work that is done to create them, the river incessantly entering and leaving the site. This is also the case with urban canyons, so named as places, their essence is in the flows of work entering and leaving, today largely enabled electronically through cables linked to aerials on the roofs. The latter are hardly visible to the pedestrian enjoying the city below.

The idea that you needed to look outside a given city to understand that city is only dimly realized in the English language in one particular term, NY-LON. Predating contemporary globalization it originally referred to the 'new' first becoming fashionable in the world's two greatest cities of the twentieth century. Latterly, linked to globalization, it encompasses the massive flows that take place between Lower Manhattan and the City of London and not just electronic ones: top executives in financial services and related work are said to have three offices – in New York, in London, and in a plane high over the Atlantic. Of course, today's world-economy consists of much more than this particular city-dyad, albeit that it is the most important one. But LA-CHI, HONG-SING and PAR-FRANK, to suggest just three possible names for other important city-dyads, are words that have not been invented; they cannot be found in the dictionaries of any language. In this case language does not reflect our material world; in globalization there are myriad flows across tens of thousands of city-dyads that constitute a global space of flows. Viewed this way cities appear to be very extraordinary, and very exciting to research. In 1998 I was awarded an ESRC research grant with Jon Beaverstock to investigate the economic links that London had with New York and a few dozen other major cities. From this small beginning we built GaWC (the Globalization and World Cities research network), now generally regarded as the leading website (www.lboro.ac.uk/gawc) and academic thinktank on worldwide links between cities. As a very large topic, researching it required working with people across the world and this book is a product of this exhilarating experience. Too many to mention, it may appear a little invidious to single out a few but here are my main collaborators in this venture; they have varied over time. I list them alphabetically: Jon Beaverstock, Ben Derudder, James Faulconbridge, Michael Hoyler, Paul Knox, Robert Lang, Pengfei Ni, Kathy Pain, Dennis Smith, David Walker and Frank Witlox. In addition Phil O'Keefe and Piet Saey read parts of the work in progress and gave me food for thought. I thank them all and I must also acknowledge the funding agencies that made my research possible: five grants from the ESRC, two each from the Leverhulme Trust, from the EU (Interreg III and ESPON) and from FWO (Flanders), and from the Anglo-German Foundation, the Sloan Foundation, and the Brookings Institution, plus research project work collaboration with the Chinese Academy of Social Sciences (Beijing).

My route into studying cities has been an unusual one. I am a geographer but I had not been a contributor to either urban geography or economic geography. Before embarking on research on cities I had spent a couple of decades or so studying political geography. I devised a 'global' political geography that was always hovering in the background of my cities research. In this book I bring it into the foreground, so that cities are considered not just in their relations to other cities but also to states. I know derivatives have been given a bad name in financial markets in recent years but this is the best term to describe where this book comes from. My ideas are derived from Immanuel Wallerstein as a world-systems political geography derivative and from Jane Jacobs as a dynamic cities urban geography derivative. Put these together in a heady mix with the related works of Giovanni Arrighi, Fernand Braudel, Manuel Castells, Gunder Frank, Henri Pirenne and Saskia Sassen, and the result is the text before you. However, as the main title indicates, cities remain the leading topic, but states have to be included prominently because they are necessary for understanding the impact of cities on humanity.

Some readers will have noticed that *Extraordinary Cities* is in contradiction to recent writings on 'ordinary cities'; I think it unfortunate that the adjective ordinary should be applied to any city. I had more difficulty in formulating my subtitle. When presenting some of these ideas at conferences or seminars I have employed the subtitle 'Ideological Ranting of a Bonehead'. This refers to anonymous descriptions of my work in refereeing situations. For a quantitative paper from which parts of Chapters 2 and 6 are derived, a numerophobic referee advised an editor not to publish such research by a 'bonehead'. In a more theoretical paper from which parts of Chapters 2 and 5 are derived, the work was designated 'ideological ranting' by a concerned reader. Hence my natty subtitle, but though tempted, I decided it was not suitable for the book: given a nudge too many people, perhaps reviewers, might be persuaded to agree with the over-the-top negative assessments! However, fortunately most journal referees have been kinder towards my offerings and have often been instrumental in sharpening and improving my arguments. Therefore I thank editors of the following key journals where both gestation and initial presentation of ideas developed below have been published: *Annals of the Association of American Geographers*; *Cities, Environment and Planning A*; *International Journal of Urban and Regional Research*; *Local Environment*; *Political Geography*; *Regional Studies*; *Transactions of the Institute of British Geographers*; *Urban Geography*; and *Urban Studies*.

During most of the writing the working subtitle has been 'City/State Relations in their Geohistorical Tango to Globalization'. Although I think the tango is a reasonably good metaphor for how I treat city/state relations, I now do not consider it important enough to appear on the title page, despite possibly losing some sales in Argentina. Instead I want to signal derivation from Jacobs and Wallerstein while giving more emphasis to the long time dimension of the work, thus coming up with 'Millennia of Moral Syndromes, World-Systems and City/State Relations'. Not very slick, but that's not necessary for the subtitle, it does let potential readers get an immediate sense of the text's coverage.

In the meantime, my grandchildren have been growing up, all six of them, ranging in age from five to early 20s by the time this is published. I dedicate this book to them, and to Enid, because between all of them they have kept me in the real world through revision upon revision upon . . .

And finally, thanks to Neil Sedaka who revealed to me that the book is actually my dinosaur pet.

Peter Taylor
GaWC Cottage, Tynemouth, UK
June 2012

PART I

Setting down and setting up

1. A cities' perspective

Let me start with an admission: the main title of this book is a *non sequitur*. I do not want to mislead readers who might expect a text on a few exceptional cities. My 'extraordinary cities' does not translate into a select number of 'great cities'; there are important books that deal with such cities – for instance, by Saskia Sassen (1991) in her identification of 'global cities' and, historically, by Peter Hall (1998) and John Julius Norwich (2009) – but this book is not of that distinguished genre. Rather I follow Jane Jacobs (1969) in arguing that the inherent complexity of cities distinguishes them from all other settlements. Hence, for me, *every* city is extraordinary. Unlike 'simple towns', cities are astonishing in their economic growth potential and cultural vitality, and amazing in their societal resilience. Thus the fundamental premise of this book is that *all cities are extraordinary*; my title is just for emphasis.

The corollary of this premise is that if cities are so special then they should be taken *extremely* seriously. By this I mean moving cities to centre stage to create a city-centric, and therefore a very different, geohistorical social science. This book is the outcome of an intellectual experiment in 'putting cities first' that I have been conducting for over a decade. I am interested in macro-social change, a topic dominated by study of the fates of 'nations' and the rise and fall of 'great powers'. I do not argue that these histories are unimportant, far from it, but I will propose that concern for states and their concomitant politics tells only part of the macro-social story of humanity. And it is the underlying thesis of my argument that this political part is less important for understanding macro-social change than the economic part centred on cities. States are about pacifying territory to maintain a social order; they are inherently conservative. Such order might be enabling for growing city economies, but it can hardly be a driver of major change in the sense of being 'world-changing'. You need something extraordinary to change the world; you need cities. In the rather modernist terminology of the economist Edward Glaeser (2011, p. 1):

> Cities, the dense agglomerations that dot the globe, have been engines of innovation since Plato and Socrates bickered in an Athenian marketplace. The streets of Florence gave us the Renaissance, and the streets of Birmingham gave us the industrial revolution. The great prosperity of contemporary London

and Bangalore and Tokyo comes from their ability to produce new thinking. Wandering these cities – whether down cobblestone sidewalks or grid-cutting cross streets, around roundabouts or under freeways – is to study nothing less than human progress.

This book tries to show that cities are indeed extraordinary and have had world-changing effects on the history of humanity. I differ from Glaeser only by taking the story way back before classical Athens to the very origins of cities.

Within history and social science I join Glaeser and others in a minority position that puts cities first; but it is a growing intellectual movement. And it is one that brings together some unlikely bedfellows. I begin this introduction by describing six autonomous 'discoveries' of cities, by which I mean fresh appreciations of the significance of cities. Occurring over the last two decades or so, these recognitions of the importance of cities have provided the backdrop out of which this book has emerged. You might well ask why these acts of discovery have been necessary; cities are hardly shrinking violets hidden away in our modern society. Thus in the second part of this introduction I rehearse the arguments as to how cities seem to have been taken for granted, as it were, in so much social science scholarship. This reveals critical limitations of what I label 'state-centric social science', and leads on to a brief exposition of my experiment in creating a 'city-centric social science' in the third part of the introduction. It involves turning some quite familiar ideas upside down. And such a contrarian programme requires a thorough review of the existing models, theories, techniques and methods, since many are likely tarnished by their use in uncritical acceptance of state dominance within macro-social change. Therefore in the final part of the introduction the idea of new conceptual toolkits is presented and from these the organization of the book's argument is derived and outlined.

SIX RECENT DISCOVERIES OF CITIES

The six intellectual discoveries I detail below are all positive in nature: cities are found to be relevant and useful for the discoverers' wants or needs. But cities are not always seen in a positive light. In the late 1960s and 1970s the word most likely to be associated with cities was 'crisis', both political and economic. From the protests and riots of the 1960s to the difficult fiscal states of cities in the late 1970s, cities were where society's ills were most visible. Thus it is hardly surprising they were viewed negatively; cities equal problems. Go forward a couple of decades and it is all change; cities are seen as solutions. Thus the discoveries described below are recent and current celebrations of cities.

Such about-turns in perception of cities are nothing new; Tristram Hunt (2004) shows a similar changing of ideas from one extreme to another in his charting of the appreciation of the British Victorian city. There may well be 'cycles of dislike and like of cities', so perhaps the discoveries of this section may be better termed 'rediscoveries'. I think not; I stay with discoveries because the new positionings of cities are so very different from what has gone before. There is now a recognition of, or hope for, cities being truly extraordinary. For each of the discoveries below I begin with a quotation that reflects this sentiment. I may or may not agree with each author but for now that is beside the point: they all bring cities to centre stage.

Globalization Discovery

According to Richard Knight (1989, p. 327):

> Now that development is being driven more by globalization than by nationalization, the role of cities is increasing. Power comes from global economies that are realized by integrating national economies into the global economy, and cities provide the strategic linkage functions. Activities related to the creation of global linkages, such as identifying opportunities, advancing and implementing technology, financing and handling transaction flows, structuring and servicing global markets, are located primarily in cities and are expanding rapidly. . . . Not only are the barriers between nations being lowered but the control that national governments have over the flow of capital, technology, ideas and so on is also being reduced. To wit, as global society expands, the role of cities increases and the role of nations decreases.

The last sentence shows this discovery of cities to be part of the globalization discourse that has predicted the demise, or at least diminution, of the role of the state in economic affairs. Most of this literature has focused on territorial states versus transnational corporations but here we have linked cities as alternative protagonists. The quotation comes from a book called *Cities in a Global Society* (Knight and Gappert 1989), and like most discoveries, there were simultaneous discoverers: Anthony King (1990) in his *Global Cities* starts with discussion of new 'global paradigms in urban research', a 'paradigm shift' consequent upon globalization (p. 3); and Saskia Sassen (1991) in her *The Global City* argues the necessity for creating a concept to describe a unique new type of city – the global city – to do justice to cities' new roles in managing global economic dispersal (p. 4). The latter book has become immensely influential charting new research agendas on cities in globalization on which there is now a large and expanding literature (Derudder et al. 2012).

Although all three books suggest or imply that cities in globalization
are transcending their states to create a newly structured, city-centred
world-economy, they did not portend simple predictions of the end of the
state: these global city books were somewhat more subtle in their approach
than a simple 'cities versus states' argument. Globalization is changing the
relationship between cities and states in interesting new ways and it is this
that attracted me to the literature on world and global cities. I derived
a world city network approach to understanding cities in globalization
(Taylor 2001; 2004; Taylor et al. 2011) and, following Manuel Castells
(1996), I interpret cities and states as being implicated in the production of
different forms of social space: spaces of flows through cities and spaces
of places bounded by states. This contrast is clear in the social composi-
tions of these spaces: whereas successful states tend towards and promote
cultural homogeneity (i.e. nation-states), successful cities tend towards
and become cosmopolitan. From another perspective treating globalization as a neoliberal project, Brenner (2004; Brenner and Theodore 2002a)
has also recognized the tension between city and national scales and has
thoroughly investigated its relevance for contemporary governance issues.

The globalization discovery has been largely the work of sociologists
and human geographers but other social scientists have also made their
own discoveries of cities.

Economics Discovery

According to Ivan Turok (2009, p. 14):

> Cities are complex adaptive systems comprising multitudes of actors, firms,
> and other organisations forming diverse relationships and evolving together.
> Frequent face-to-face contact and other cooperative and competitive interac-
> tions enabled by proximity help to increase people's knowledge and skills,
> to improve their capacity to respond creatively to economic challenges, and
> to develop new and improved products, processes and services. Other places
> cannot easily replicate these conditions . . .

These processes are known as agglomeration effects, and although they
have a long and prestigious pedigree – Alfred Marshall's (1890) *Principles
of Economics* is the foundation text – for the most part, the discipline of
economics has neglected location factors, and cities in particular, as it
has pursued national economic modelling. But about the same time that
global cities were being discovered, some economists came to appreciate
cities as a locus for understanding economic growth. The result was the
'new economic geography' (Krugman 1995), as economists excavated
early location models, and a revitalized 'urban economics' (McDonald

1997), with cities moving to centre stage for a small coterie of economic researchers.

The key feature that interested economists was the externalities resulting from concentrations of economic activities as represented by cities. Agglomeration was found to have a critical influence on economic process and was rigorously theorized as such (Fujita and Thisse 2002). Furthermore, economic clusters of firms within cities were found to be particularly important (Porter 1998). In this context Jane Jacobs' (1969) *The Economy of Cities* was discovered and lauded (Nowlan 1997): Krugman (1995, p. 5) refers to her as a 'patron saint of new growth theory'. Edward Glaeser (2000; et al. 1992) in particular has promoted Jacobs' ideas. This is particularly relevant because her oeuvre has a crucial role to play in the argument I develop in this book. However, curiously, this economic discovery of cities has remained largely oblivious to the globalization discovery of cities: it seems economists don't do global cities (Taylor 2009).

Nevertheless I find it relatively easy to combine ideas from both discoveries in my arguments below, since city extraordinariness is common to both. In economics this is most strongly advocated by Edward Glaeser (2011) in his *Triumph of the City* where he begins by pointing out that 'the magic of urban density means that agglomerations of people come together for simple reasons and often achieve amazing things' (p. 1). This is exactly my position.

Political Science Discovery

According to Warren Magnusson (2011, pp. 5, 6–7):

> To see both one's locale and the world as a whole *as a city* is to envision it quite differently. What follow are a different politics, political theory, and a political science from what we have been used to. . . . There are (alternative) concepts to be sure – rhizomes and lines of flight, singularities and emergent properties, cyborgs and networks, übermenschen and dassein – but it is hard to know what to do with any of them in the absence of an alternative ontology of the political. That is why I think it is so important to think the political through the city. The city is difficult to understand, but we can see how it works all around us. It offers a place to begin, both as analysts and as activists. Urban life is as familiar as it is strange and complex. If we look at it carefully, many of the standard political and analytic categories begin to melt before our eyes, and other ones more adequate to the purpose begin to take shape.

At first glance this intervention from a politics scholar is surprising since his discipline has been largely developed to understand the ways that states operate. To be sure, there is an important tradition of study of city government, but this urban politics research focused upon municipal politics as sub-state processes. However, as Magnusson and many others have pointed out, the very word politics comes from the Greek 'polis', which were cities, from whence also comes the term 'citizens', now attributed to nation-states. The potential of freeing modern political discourse from state-centrism was always there and it has come to the fore with recognition of the importance of globalization, and cities therein.

Therefore, unlike in economics, the new research on cities in political science has been inspired by the 'global cities' literature with Saskia Sassen (1999; 2000) as a key contributor. The key text here is a collection of 16 essays in the book *Democracy, Citizenship and the Global City* that explicitly asks 'Does the city have a future in democracy?' because these new spaces have been created in globalization and 'constitute themselves as political and social agents' (Isin 2000, p.i). In addition I have made a modest contribution through bringing cities more to the fore in political geography (Taylor 2000; 2002; 2005). However, new encroachments of cities into political discourses are becoming increasingly fundamental, as Magnusson suggests above. For instance, Bell and de-Shalit (2011) consider city identities, Graham's (2004) 'urban geopolitics' asks questions in the field of security that problematize state sovereignty, and Amen and his colleagues (2011) pursue global governance research through cities as 'new sites for international relations'. In addition there are political historical studies that have searched out city-states and city networks as alternative organization to sovereign territorial states (Tilly 1990; Spruyt 1994; Parker 2004). Clearly research on cities has worked its way into the very heartland of state-centric scholarship.

Public Policy Discovery

According to Michael Parkinson and his colleagues (2006, pp. 9–10):

> These are exciting – if challenging – times for cities. During the past decade many cities in many countries have emerged from a period of decline to find new economic, political and cultural niches. There has been a sea change in how cities are regarded. Governments, the private sector and researchers increasingly see them as the dynamos of national and regional economies rather than economic liabilities. Cities are becoming again 'the wealth of nations'. . . . [A]cross Europe, north America and beyond, cities are moving up the political agenda and have become the focus of many policy initiatives.

This shows that the previous discoveries did not go unnoticed beyond academia. They have led to a discovery of the importance of cities by both national and international institutions that had hitherto not viewed them positively.

This turnaround is clearly seen in the United Nations family of institutions. The UN has long reported the population sizes of cities and the term 'mega-city' was coined to describe the growth of very large cities, many in poorer countries of the world. It is these cities, with their dreadful housing and infrastructure problems, that stimulated the UN-Habitat programme. But from originally being seen as urban problems, cities were redesignated as solutions: in the famous 2003 report *The Challenge of Slums*, the increasing concentration of poverty in cities was now interpreted more positively. The opportunities afforded by cities mean that this is where poverty is best alleviated. Stuart Brand (2010, p. 31) traces this new 'city-boosting position' to Habitat fieldwork starting in 1978 that forced the 'reluctant optimism' of the 2003 report. Earlier the World Bank (2000) had discovered economic agglomeration processes in its World Development report that identified cities as key to reducing poverty through growth. By 2007 the United Nations Population Fund joined the new consensus, with its report entitled *Unleashing the Potential of Urban Growth*.

Running parallel to these UN discoveries, the European Union has similarly come to appreciate the importance of cities. Spatial policy in the EU originally focused upon 'problem regions' with no reference to cities (Berg et al. 2006). Part of the problem was that urban policy was deemed to be a national matter so that there were no policy instruments to develop a European urban strategy. However, in the 1990s cities became highly visible within EU regional policy, and this new official recognition has expanded as the EU has embarked on new priorities to maintain Europe's competitive position in the world-economy: cities as city-regions can no longer be ignored (Hall and Pain 2006).

However bringing something as complex as cities to centre stage in public policy making, and spatial planning in particular, is fraught with new problems (Taylor 2011b), and these will feature strongly in the argument developed below.

Green Discovery

According to David Owen (2009, pp. 10, 13):

> Thinking of crowded cities as environmental role models requires a certain willing suspension of disbelief, because most of us have been accustomed to viewing urban centers as ecological calamities. . . . A dense urban area's greenest features – its low per capita energy use, its high acceptance of public transit and walking, its small carbon footprint per resident – are not inexplicable anomalies. They are direct consequences of the very urban characteristics that are most likely to appal a sensitive friend of the earth. Yet those qualities are

ones that the rest of us, no matter where we live, are going to have to find ways
to emulate, as the world's various ongoing energy and environmental crises
deepen and spread in the years ahead. In terms of sustainability, dense cities
have far more to teach us than solar-powered mountainside cabins or quaint
old New England towns.

As indicated in this quotation, this is the surprise discovery, materializing,
in part, from the UN institutional turnaround. Environmental concerns
have their origins in non-urban realms and have often been explicitly anti-
city as in 'garden city' policies to limit urban growth, negatively designated
'urban sprawl'. And more recently cities have been attacked for the large
sizes of their 'environmental foot-prints'. But this is changing: Owen
(2009, p. 3), in his book *Green Metropolis*, identifies New York as 'the
greenest community in the United States', because its density facilitates
use of far less fossil fuel, notably by cars.

Much has been made of the fact that the majority of humanity are now
urban dwellers. This proportion is sure to increase in the coming decades
– perhaps as much as 75 per cent urban by 2050 – so any green dreams of
a world of sustainable rural idylls is no longer relevant. And most of this
growth is happening in 'mega-slums', a derogatory term to describe the
huge informal settlement growth of mega-cities in poor countries. But,
as noted above through the UN, this great settlement shift is now being
reassessed. For Neuwirth (2005) these 'slums' are the 'cities of tomorrow':
it is not just that denser populations make it easier to provide essentials
for living; it is also that these squatter settlements are so vibrant. They
represent a world of innovations and improvizations that Jacobs (1969)
lauds – as Jeb Brugmann (2009, p. 33) tells it in his *Welcome to the Urban
Revolution*: 'City growth creates problems, and then city innovation
speeds up to solve them', and currently this is especially true for environmental problems.

For Brand (2010, p. 51), cities 'are becoming the Greenest thing that
humanity does for the planet' for another major reason. The great rural–
urban rush is leading to reproduction reductions as large families with
many children change from rural assets to urban liabilities. The result is
that lowering of birth rates consequent upon urbanization has 'defused
the population bomb' (p. 59) that has so excited environmentalists for over
half a century. It seems world population will peak much nearer to eight
billion rather than the doomsday environment predictions of the past:
there is a new problem of 'population crash' in several countries (Pearce
2010). Such is the power of cities; this will be integral to my argument as I
bring this book to a close, where I will link these issues much more closely
into city economic processes.

History Discovery

According to Paul Bairoch (1988, p. xvii):

> The history of urbanization is without doubt one of the most exciting aspects of the adventure of humanity. When and how were cities born? Does each civilization have a distinctive form of city? How large were cities in traditional societies? What was the impact of colonization on urban systems? Did the Industrial Revolution favor urbanization? Has urbanization favored innovation and economic development? Does the urban explosion in the Third World constitute a handicap or an opportunity from the point of view of development? All these questions, and many more like them, bear on matters touching the very essence of world history and for that reason alone merit our attention.

Given the rich literature in urban history, it may count as another surprise to see history included in my list of discoveries. Bairoch's book, from which this quotation has been taken, is entitled *Cities and Economic Development*, a subject that focuses upon multiple cities in the wider world. It is in this sense that there is a discovery of sorts since the dominant tradition in urban history is the study of individual cities.

This discovery has a wider range of perspectives than the previous five, ranging from demographic studies (e.g. Lees and Lees 2007), regional studies (e.g. Clark 2009), city systems analysis (e.g. Chase-Dunn 1985), to what might be called 'multiple individual studies'. The latter consist of a selection of important cities through history and a production of vignettes on their particular prowess during their heyday. Peter Hall's (1998) *Cities in Civilization* and John Julius Norwich's (2009) collection *The Great Cities In History* are exemplary examples. Although they have a chronological order that includes consideration of the nature of cities, especially in Hall's case, the large-scale sweep of Bairoch's contribution is not part of their purpose. There are also comparative city studies of critical episodes in that broad sweep; excellent examples are: Patrick O'Brien's (2001) *Urban Achievement in Early Modern Europe*, which is a collection of essays on Antwerp, Amsterdam and London during their 'golden ages', and James Belich's (2009) *Replenishing the Earth*, which chronicles the settlement of English-speaking peoples across the world in a 'long nineteenth century' (1783–1939), focusing on the explosive growth of cities from Chicago to Melbourne.

It can be noted that have been exceptions to traditional neglect of urban themes, notably historians from the Low Countries who did not need to 'discover' the centrality of cities because this has long been a focus of their research. Furthermore, their work typically features relations between cities, which is the approach to understanding of cities promoted in this book. I draw on some of their findings and interpretations in later chapters.

These six discoveries are by no means a comprehensive portrait of recent and contemporary recognitions of the importance of cities in social change – for a glimpse of the wide range of such city-centric concerns see Allen Scott's (2001) collection of 22 essays on 'trends, theory and policy' in *Global City-Regions*. But we have now enough evidence on the rise of cities to centre stage to recognize the importance of the question: why were multiple discoveries of cities necessary in the first place?

WHY THE DISCOVERIES WERE NECESSARY

If cities are extraordinary, how was such power not widely recognized: why have there been repeated discoveries of the critical importance of cities? This is an intriguing question. The basic answer I have to offer is that in the last two centuries the way we think about our collective selves has been nationalized. Cities, like many other social phenomena, are perceived through state-tinged spectacles. The result is a powerful meta-geography of the world represented by the world political map. This map hangs on the wall of every school geography classroom across the world, but it is by no means a narrow disciplinary icon to be forgotten on leaving education. It is a map for citizens; it shows where her/his country is located within the 'family of nations'. It seems that the ideological power of this map has triumphed over understanding the material power of cities. And this is both a popular effect and an academic outcome: social scientists and historians – the main sources for geohistorical studies – have certainly not been immune to knowledge nationalization.

The above argument has been developed by John Agnew (1993) as the 'territorial trap' wherein national frameworks of social activity remain unexamined as a sort of hidden effect that is broadly ignored. I refer to this neglect as 'embedded statism': mainstream social science and history have configured their studies within state boundaries and thereby uncon-sciously privilege the state in understanding social change (Taylor 1996a). Thus the spatial patterning of economic, political and social/cultural proc-esses are considered to be spatially congruent based upon nation-states as the prime unit of humanity. The embeddedness is clear when the adjectives in 'national economy', 'national politics' and 'national society' are seen to be redundant – all three examples are deemed to be obviously (natu-rally?), national since their respective processes are interrupted sharply at state territorial boundaries. Thus the world is 'international' comprising entities such as French economy, French society and French politics or Nigerian economy, Nigerian society and Nigerian politics, and so on through the list of all countries. This spatial congruence of the variegated processes of social change is a modern construct; it has little or no meaning before the creation of our modern world. It reflects the power of modern governments to grow their functions and move into social arenas previously beyond the ken of states – from security (territorial state) to economics (mercantile state) to cultural identity (national state) to popular governance (democratic state) to social wellbeing (welfare state) (Taylor 1994). In the process all manner of other institutions including religious communities, minority groups, cities, and aristocracies were nationalized, losing important elements of their autonomy to state sovereignty. Understanding macro-social change was also nationalized and came to be called social science.

Geohistory of the Development of Social Science

In the argument below I draw on the work of the Gulbenkian Commission on the Crisis of the Social Sciences (Wallerstein et al. 1996) but the configuration of the interpretation is largely mine.

Understanding macro-social change itself is not, of course, exclusively modern; religious and philosophical discourses had long provided social explanations within wider cosmographies. However, what was modern was the emergence of specialists in the study of social change in the nineteenth century. Specialization was a key feature of the German reinvention of universities as centres of research, the latter requiring focus on connected topics to produce modern disciplines. These research disciplines derived from the traditional faculty of philosophy and were divided into what C.P. Snow (1959) would later call the 'two cultures', the clash between the sciences and the humanities. These differed in two related ways; the sciences constructed knowledge as general laws (nomothetic) within the subject matter of physical and biological dynamics; the humanities constructed knowledge as particular occurrences (idiographic) within the subject matter of people and their relations with each other. Specific 'social sciences' emerged in the late nineteenth century as an intermediary category between the two, cross-cutting the distinction by using the methods of the former on the subject matter of the latter. This social science took many forms but gradually distilled into three leading disciplines: economics, political science and sociology. By the mid-twentieth century most universities across the world had departments with these labels (or something very like them).

Why these specific three disciplines? They are products of their time and space. In the late nineteenth century, social scientists were not study-ing just any macro-social change, they were specifically charting progress within modernity. Accepting Enlightenment rationality meant that under-standing the triumph of modernity was deemed possible through discov-ering 'laws' that could then be fed into public policy in a virtual spiral of cumulative rationality. This fitted a general agenda of reform: economic reform of states to guide economic growth, political reform for popular legitimation of government, and social reform to counter the negative effects of rapid industrialization. Hence the disciplinary trinity – econom-ics, political science and sociology – was born to create useful knowledge for the modern state in its reform practices to aid social progress.

This origin had two important consequences. First, the three disciplines covered all forms of macro-social change; there was no intellectual space for other social sciences. Second, they researched only 'modern' socie-ties, defined as the people living in Europe and European-settler regions. Elsewhere societies were less rational and therefore not susceptible to social science laws. This left a gap for idiographic disciplines – humanities – to fill. In parts of the world with ancient civilizations, their 'unchanging nature' (i.e. lack of progress) was studied as Orientalism, a focus on tradi-tional texts and languages to decipher their exotic nature. In the remaining 'uncivilized' world, anthropology developed to understand 'tribal peoples' through intensive fieldwork to observe and catalogue their particularities. Both groups of societies were deemed to be 'peoples without history', to use Eric Wolf's (1982) famous phrase, because history was about progress. Therefore history emerged as a modern discipline to understand only Europe's past: a Whiggish pursuit to delineate how modernity came about in the countries of Europe through particular national study of unique events. The end result was that the social science trinity's study of modern societies was complemented by these three humanity disciplines to ideo-graphically cover the 'unmodern', past and present. This neat arrange-ment, never quite as tidy as I have summarized here, was soon to break down in the second half of the twentieth century when interdisciplinary, multidisciplinary and later transdisciplinary approaches came into vogue to cope with the actual complexities inherent in macro-social change. I will deal briefly with what this means for twenty-first-century scholarship in a later section of this chapter but in the remainder of this section I explore the more obvious implications of the state-centrism of the trinity.

The power of the trinity can be seen in the history of the modern disci-pline of geography, a subject about the same age as the social sciences but initially quite distinct from them. Geography emerged in universities as a quite contrary discipline in two ways. First it claimed to offer synthesis thereby bucking the trend to increasing specialization. Second it straddled the 'two cultures', encompassing both human and non-human topics. In terms of methodology there were swings between the science and the humanities. Environmental determinism tried to explain macro-social change through the causal effects of environment on society; regional geography attempted an artistic synthesis of physical and human processes unique to every place. In neither case was geography theoretically tied to state-centric thinking, although in practice the discipline operated to provide knowledge-supporting imperialism. But these two conceptions of geography were relatively fragile, resulting in the discipline's university status being perennially under challenge. Survival and adaptation varied across different countries, often related to which associated 'time discipline' (history or geology) practising geographers worked with. However, eventually in the second half of the twentieth century, the discipline became divided in its research programmes, with human geography pursuing social science themes and physical geography environmental science themes. And the former soon conformed to the trinity imperative resulting in three dominant sub-disciplines: economic geography, political geography and social geography. This final conformity was not unique: history and anthropology similarly went adjectival: economic history, economic anthropology; political history, political anthropology; and social history, social anthropology. Orientalism was different, its post-imperial vestiges, especially the emphasis on languages, survived within 'area studies', a new post-World War II development. But the latter belongs to a different strand of the social science story.

All human institutions are created to deal with situations in a particular time and place and, as situations change, they become gradually less fit for purpose. But they do not easily disappear, because in the times and places of their successes they build up a resilience, a continuing insistence on their worth by entrenched vested interests. This has been very much the case for the social sciences. In the second half of the twentieth century the trinity of disciplines was challenged by a plethora of new knowledge categories generally referred to a 'studies'. These often developed in parallel with the established disciplines: business studies appeared alongside economics with focus moving from national economy to the behaviour of firms, international studies appeared alongside political science with focus moving from national government to multi-layered governance, and cultural studies appeared alongside sociology with focus moving from national social structure to personal identities. But these parallels suggest the trinity maintained more power over the changes than it actually had. As university departments, trinity disciplines largely maintained control of teaching programmes right up to doctorate level and hence the socialization of new researchers. This is the disciplines doing what they were designed to do:

discipline knowledge workers. But the latter as researchers were creating new research programmes that go far beyond the trinity; in addition to area studies previously mentioned there are also Afro-American studies, communication studies, development studies, gender studies, information studies, post-colonial studies, regional studies, urban studies, etc., each of which have their own further study divisions. And all claim to be free from basic disciplining through using descriptors such as interdisciplinary and multidisciplinary. They are usually institutionalized not as university departments but as more dissipative organizations centred on new journals (mainly private sector initiatives), research centres and conferences. These allow for an eclectic bringing together of ideas, a feature that distinguishes studies from disciplines.

A key question from my perspective is how far the erosion of disciplines by multiple fields of study has reduced embedded statism in social research. Since state-centric thinking is far broader in its influence than social science thinking, it cannot be assumed that recent studies are necessarily any less under the sway of the territorial trap than the trinity.

State-centric Social Science Practices

It is not part of my brief to answer this question comprehensively across a large range of fields of study. My publisher will probably market this book as 'urban studies'; I think 'development studies' would be a more appropriate label but this label is already taken by a body of knowledge that is the very inverse of my approach. Thus I will treat social science practices in only these two fields of study.

The idea of development as providing help to poor countries became government policy for rich countries in the period after World War II. Partly encouraged by the Cold War rivalry between the 'first world' (capitalist west) and the 'second world' (communist east) to attract allegiances from 'third world' countries (ex-colonial poor south), this changing circumstance had a profound influence on social science. A basic rethink occurred due to conceptual revision; the terminology for macro-social changed from progress to development. The former was a property of civilizations (modern versus the rest), the latter became a property of states: old stagnant civilizations did not progress, but new modern, decolonized, states could develop. In the two decades after World War II decolonization created a large number of new independent states, all ripe for development. In fact initially, development appeared to be the very *raison d'être* of this great flurry of state-making.

Enter the social science trinity. The rationality missing in old civilizations could now be expected to appear in the new independent states so that nomothetic social knowledge would finally be extended to the whole world. Laws and theories that worked in what was now the first world could be transplanted to the new third world. Thus would social scientists mark out a new arena for rational policy advice to governments' development departments. The trinity operated to offer economic development models to aid industrialization of new national economies, political development models to promote liberal democratic constitutionalism for new national polities, and social development models that proclaimed nothing less than paths to the modernization of the new national societies. It was realized that these planned processes would be closely interrelated and therefore development studies became strongly interdisciplinary in nature. But the knowledge remained explicitly state-centric; development was deemed to be something that happened to states. The reaction against this notion is the idea that development transcends individual states, and this has been best articulated through world-systems analysis (Wallerstein 1979; 1983; 2004). This is the position I take in this book.

Urban studies would appear to be a completely different case. Cities were among the institutions that lost political autonomy in the nationalization consequent on the rise of modern states. The study of cities as social nodes with multiple outside connections, such as transport hubs, resulting in places through which rapid macro-social changes such as industrialization occurred, would surely not fall into the territorial trap. But yes, urban studies has been as thoroughly nationalized as development studies: the 'national urban systems' research school was the major research programme on how cities relate to each other from the late 1950s into the 1980s (Bourne and Simmons 1978).

The idea of national urban systems derived from central place theory, a model that posited urban places being hierarchically arranged. Nationalizing this model generated the concept of national urban hierarchy, a simple ordering of cities by population size. The results were interpreted as the spatial organization of the national economy and therefore were offered as policy tools for government (Bourne 1975). Comparative analyses of these city hierarchies across countries produced some quite sophisticated understandings. At one end of the spectrum there were hierarchies where all levels were fully represented within a country (the 'rank-size rule'), and at the other there were countries where one city was very much larger than other cities in the country (the 'law of the primate city'). The former were interpreted as complex fully integrated national economies – in short 'developed' – and the latter as simple national economies – in short 'underdeveloped'. Thus the US and Canada fitted the rank-size rule as befitting developed economies while most Latin American countries were distinctly primate in their city population graph – Asunción, Buenos

Aires, Caracas, Havana, Lima, Mexico City, Montevideo and Santiago
are all classic 'primate cities'. To be sure there were exceptions, but these
could be dealt with as particular contingencies; for instance, the primacies
of London and Paris reflecting past imperial prowess, and India's rank-
size rule reflecting the country's size rather than its development. Thus the
national urban systems school offered both credible theoretical outputs
and relevant policy inputs, the dual ideal of good social science.

But, and it is a big but, there was a basic flaw to this nationalization
of understanding cities. The consequence of this approach is a mosaic
world of inter-city relations: an urban world of about 200 or so separate
urban systems, one for each state. This is because inter-city relations
across state boundaries are generally conspicuous by their absence in this
modelling and are always severely neglected. Thus New York is identified as top of the US hierarchy but with little or no reference to its role
as a major port, the leading gateway between the US economy and the
world-economy. This undervaluing of the 'international' in national urban
systems research came to a head with the growth of economic globalization in the 1980s that, seemingly overnight, made this school of research
theoretically suspect and practically less useful.

I began this chapter with the 'globalization discovery' of the exceptional
importance of cities but this should not be interpreted as urban studies
escaping from the national territorial trap. The global/world cities literature has been led by sociologists abetted by human geographers, but the
other discoveries have been less inclined to ditch ideas from the national
urban systems school. The trinity lives on in economics, the most disci-
plined of disciplines, where the economic discovery makes no references to
the globalization literature, and the history and policy discoveries remain
largely wedded to classic hierarchical views of inter-city relations. In fact
the idea that cities are arranged in hierarchies is the main legacy of the
national urban systems school and this has been commonly accepted in the
globalization discovery: an early and very influential contribution by John
Friedmann (1986) simply up-scaled 'national city hierarchy' to 'world city
hierarchy'. The debate about the nature of inter-city relations – hierarchy
versus network – is discussed in some detail in the next chapter.

State-istics

In the substantive sections of this book I try and make my arguments as
evidence-based as possible. It seems to me important that social science
knowledge should be creatively speculative in the early stages of projects
but final products should be concretely grounded on the best evidence
available. The latter will vary by circumstance but ultimately social science

is only as good as its empirical evidence. Thus if we look at Friedmann's world city hierarchy we find no systematic data collection to support the concept, which is in keeping with his creatively introducing a new hypothesis. But later widespread acceptance of the hypothesis is much more problematic. Subsequently it has been reported as to how he came to configure his world city hierarchy revealing the paucity and poverty of his initial evidence: it seems he used a Japanese Airlines flight map that he perused in-flight (Abu-Lughod 1989, p. 32). What is happening here is that the paradigmatic notion of city hierarchies is being up-scaled – a creative input – with an implicit invitation to others – users of his ideas – to confirm the hypothesis or otherwise. But no such comprehensive evidence-based research was forthcoming; if it was generally viewed as unnecessary this would indicate an immanent paradigmatic power of the idea of city hierarchy. This would seem to be confirmed by Sassen (1991) using the concept of 'global hierarchy' as integral to her global city thesis. Looking more closely at this foundation work on global/world cities, it has been found that in a survey of the evidence she used, fully one-third deals with states rather than cities (Taylor 2004, pp. 36–8). As an iconic text on cities, why should this be so?

Researching my subject matter, the study of macro-social change, is a huge undertaking. Translating this task into the lexicon of the natural sciences would bring up the label 'big science'. In these circumstances, the theory is used to suggest what evidence is required and then a huge data collection exercise ensues (for example, through the CERN particle physics laboratory). But social science research does not command such resources; our funding is minuscule within overall science budgets. However, this does not mean that there is no macro-social change research. This is because massive amounts of social data are collected, not by social science researchers, but by bureaucrats in modern states. As these states took on more and more functions they collected data to organize, justify, and evaluate their new activities. Thus most European countries have conducted decennial censuses for about 200 years. Originally just population counts, they are the clearest example of data collection growing as the state grows. But all departments in state bureaucracies now publish data on their activities as a matter of course, resulting in a real treasure trove of information available for social scientists of every ilk. And this includes Sassen (1991) who uses, for instance, data on states for evidence of foreign direct investment in her argument about global cities.

This has proven to be a good solution to the impossible expense of the 'big social science' data needs but it is only satisfactory for social scientists in a rather narrow sense. It provides us with available data but not necessarily the specific data we would choose to collect. It is data collected by the state for the purposes of the state and that is why such data is referred to as statistics, or state-istics as I like to call it. This is not a minor semantic point; it is not even just a matter of subjects covered: the actual nature of this data is affected by its state provenance. Data comes in many forms but there are two basic types that are generally identified: attributional and relational. Attribute data are descriptions of an object; relational data are measures of links between two or more objects. State-istics have a clear bias towards the former, whereas social science should have a particular preference for the latter. For instance, national censuses provide myriad descriptions of state-defined areas from collection units through administrative districts to the whole state territory: an 'areal accounting' exercise to service myriad area-based policies. Overall, most state-istics are attributional because these serve state purposes – generally administration – best.

Even where the state measures flows and movements, notably for commodities (trade) and people (migration), these are only counted when areal boundaries are crossed, which is a very limited way of obtaining relational data. Comprehensive measuring of relational data requires origin and destination information irrespective of whatever boundaries are crossed. A person moving from one neighbourhood of the city to another, or from one region of a country to another, is in either case a migrant, but not always identified as such in national and international statistics respectively. There is a particularly notorious example of how these 'official statistics' do no favours to our understanding of macro-social change. According to the title of Castles and Miller's (2003) classic text on international migration, we are living in *The Age of Migration*. The authors acknowledge previous large international flows of people but quantitatively, with illegal movements taken into account, contemporary globalization is unrivalled in its demographic upheaval (pp. 4–5). But notice the state-centric thinking: the very term 'international migration' presupposes that states are the appropriate units for measuring migration. This is empirically sensible since such data are readily available, but it is seriously flawed theoretically. Castles and Miller (2003) illustrate the limitations of studying 'international migration' in a spectacular manner: they miss out what is happening within China, the largest flow of people in the history of humanity (see their Map 7.1, p. 156). There seems to be little doubt that the demographic process that will have most planetary effect in the first quarter of the twenty-first century is Chinese migration to Chinese cities. But this is 'only' 'internal migration' (that is, not 'international' like, say, migration between Belgium and Luxembourg), and is missing from their state-centric analyses despite the fact that it is completely reorienting the contemporary world-economy.

Understanding cities is a major victim of state-istics. This is not because cities are in any sense neglected – cities are recognized as the locales of numerous 'social problems', are the basis of local administration through which problems are addressed, and therefore there is myriad data on cities. However, it is the nature of the available data that is at issue. Cities in state-istics are places to be measured; nearly all the data is attributional. But cities are dynamic places whose *raison d'être* is relations, myriad internal links, local links to hinterlands and wider links to other cities and regions. Cities cannot be understood fully without adequate relational data. And this is precisely what is not available. To be sure there is usually data on commuting that provides some indication of a city's economic patterning but there is little else. Thus for London there are reams of data from the census and elsewhere describing a multitude of aspects, but if we ask the question of how London relates to Birmingham – there is migration data but little else. More to the point, how does London relate to New York – what are the flows of commodities, people, information that connects the two cities and what are their natures? This is important because it is generally accepted in the global/world city literature that this inter-city relation is the most important connection in the workings of the contemporary world-economy. It even has a name: NY-LON. We can get some information on relations between the UK and the US – trade, migration, inward investments – but not specifically on NY-LON. And why should there be any state-istics on NY-LON? Who would collect it? Not London or New York City governments, they focus on their own city. Not UK and the US, collecting data on a foreign city can be seen as a violation of sovereignty. Quite simply there is no organization in place with an interest in producing statistics on this city-dyad. And even if there was, what about London–Paris, or New York–Tokyo? The list of dyads is almost endless.

Clearly state-istics are not going to provide anywhere near the comprehensive data needed to understand cities in globalization. And yet this is a very relevant 'big social science' topic for research. Without available data from the state, the only solution is to find a way to collect data for relational analysis as a new project in its own right. Fortunately in an electronically connected world it is relatively easy to organize worldwide networks to spread the work and cost of data collection. In this case the medium for the task has been the Globalization and World Cities (GaWC) Research Network (www.lboro.ac/gawc) that I set up in 1978 and that has provided this service to urban researchers as part of the global electronic commons. I will draw on information from this unique resource in the penultimate chapter when I turn to contemporary globalization. However, the models devised in setting up this measurement tool have proven to be generic and will appear in the next chapter as part of my city toolbox. In this way, I aspire to research beyond state-istics.

A CITY-CENTRIC EXPERIMENT

In this chapter I have been setting down my position with respect to understanding cities through social science, the body of knowledge in which we find most research on cities. The gist of my argument is that social science has been found wanting. In the next chapter I will be setting up a new position that I have found fit for purpose as a means of bringing cities to centre stage. Overall, Part I can be considered a thought experiment in which I try and envisage a city-centric social science.

I conclude this chapter by drawing two implications from my critique of social science that will frame my approach in the rest of the book. First I present my considered approach to the social science disciplines, trinity and others, one that I find quite intellectually liberating. Second, I consider more specifically how I approach understanding cities in relation to states: taking a city-centric position does not mean that understanding states has to be neglected. Rather I begin to ask the crucial question about how cities and states relate to each other.

The Possibility of Indisciplinarity

In the previous discussions there has been the suggestion that the boundaries between disciplines have become more permeable. This is reflected in prefixes to 'discipline' that have become increasingly radical in their implications: multidisciplinary research promotes collaboration, interdisciplinary research insists on engagement, and transdisciplinary research suggests thinking beyond disciplines. But all begin with disciplines; *indisciplinary* research is about discarding disciplines. It is, of course, easy for me as a geographer to entertain the latter because taking disciplines seriously simply eliminates geography from academia: the nature of geography has always been a field of study. But this does not prevent me from appreciating the seriousness of a proposition for indisciplinarity. Disciplines provide intellectual depth to social research, coherent bundles of knowledge building on the insights of esteemed 'founding fathers'. Figures such as Alfred Marshall, John Stuart Mill and Max Weber still have something to say to today's researchers. Fields of study have a far less coherent theoretical basis and their founders are usually much less well known and revered: geography has its founding fathers but none are more than of historical interest today. Thus are 'mere' studies frequently damned for being 'shallow', the ultimate intellectual critique. So why the call for indisciplinarity?

Before justifying shallowness, I will interrogate the depth of knowledge that disciplines have supplied. What is this intellectual depth? As previously described it is theory and practice honed about a century ago that has proven remarkably adaptable and resilient. But all social knowledge is transient; founding fathers can only know what they experience in and through their times and places. Nonetheless being revered means that in hindsight we can see that their ideas have fared much better than those of their contemporaries. But in something as complex as macro-social change there will always be severe limits on how far ideas can travel. According to Wallerstein (1991) the social sciences are now struggling against their confines: he calls for 'unthinking social science' to free ourselves from 'nineteenth-century paradigms'. But this is not indisciplinarity, he advocates uni-disciplinarity through unifying the disciplines that study social change (the trinity plus history) into a single historical social science. And he most definitely does not discard aspiring to intellectual depth as he attempts to bring the very different research traditions of history and social sciences together, a genuine best-of-both-worlds strategy. My position is very close to that of Wallerstein; I add 'geo' to his proposed intellectual construct but this reflects more than just my own geographical background. This 'geo' nudges our thinking towards indisciplinarity not just because geography's founding fathers command little or no contemporary respect but through its literal global connotation that chimes with 'twenty-first century as crisis century', wherein disciplinary boundaries appear as so very trivial.

Let me elucidate this position: why advocate the possibility of indiscipline and shallowness? The argument is that the transience of social knowledge is speeding up; previously experienced transience enabled coherent disciplines to maintain relevance over several generations of researchers. In the twenty-first century this will be a luxury lost. Enhanced transience results from contemporary alterations in the nature of macro-social change. For Wallerstein (1999) the structures underpinning our modern world are themselves reaching their limits; we are entering no less than 'the vanishing guarantees of rationality' (p. 137). In other words the disintegration of old structures of behaviour creates a new situation in which knowledge of current and recent behaviour can no longer be expected to have a salient longevity. From a different perspective, Jane Jacobs' (2004) final book, *Dark Age Ahead*, is similarly doom-laden. In many ways her writing career exemplifies my idea of indisciplinarity: she evaded disciplinary identity although posthumously, in a 'reconsideration' of her ideas, she has been found to be a human geographer after all (Harris 2011). Jacobs' warning of a dire future includes an indisciplinary argument in the form of a devastating critique of contemporary universities for providing students with merely 'credentials' rather than an education (pp. 44–63). This has resulted in what she calls 'science abandoned' evidenced by one 'so-called discipline' (p. 79), after another becoming 'disconnected from the scientific state of mind' so that each 'unfortunate segment of knowledge is no longer scientific' (p. 69). Although derived from very different premises, we can appreciate that Jacobs' 'no longer scientific' approximates to Wallerstein's 'vanishing rationality'. Knowledge is not what it used to be.

I address the issues arising from 'twenty-first century as crisis century' in the final chapter and I describe how I get to there in the final section of this first chapter. But there is one further point to be flagged relating to indisciplinarity. As well as the crisis processes outlined by Jacobs and Wallerstein there is, of course, a very dark cloud hanging over the future of humanity: the real possibility of catastrophic climate change within the next century. This provides another reason for indisciplinarity; the rapid erosion of theoretical relevances and empirical findings makes deep thinking problematic, all thinking becomes strategic. Cities feature in the literature on climatic change in the role of victims – low-lying settlements vulnerable to rising sea levels – and states feature in the practice of combating climatic change as hopeless obstacles – the large number of states leads to seemingly intractable free-loader problems in policy making. I aspire to transcend this unpromising assessment of cities and states. Contemporary experience of globalization has exploded the neat spatial congruence of the nation-state through which citizens voted for governments to generate economic growth and thereby provide for the good life. More and more, the economic futures of countries are determined by processes that transcend state boundaries, which makes promoting and diffusing democracy quite problematic. And, of course, the social science trinity is premised on this very spatial congruence. Specialized disciplines were a product of our modern world; their demise will likely be integral to the disintegration of that world. Indisciplinarity appears inevitable; it will be reflected in this book by my lack of respect for disciplines.

Geohistory as a State/City Tango

I have included reference to states in the subtitle of this book to show that while my starting point is cities, I try very hard not to neglect states. Obviously there is a real danger that reacting against state-centric social science will swing the pendulum too far in the new direction. My view is that it is impossible to properly understand cities without knowledge of states and vice versa. Since these two key human inventions are so entwined, I have chosen to characterize their relation as a tango, that most energetic of dances where the two dancers are prescribed related but distinctive roles.

The tango appears to be a suitable analogy for city/state relations because there is a mixture of rivalry and support between the participants. Further, I am interested in how the city/state relationship changes through time and space, and just such a geohistory is be found in the changing fortunes of the dance. Although there are many different styles of tango, they can be reduced to just two basic positionings. The styles are mostly danced in either open embrace, where lead and follow have space between their bodies, or close embrace, where the lead and follow connect either chest-to-chest (Argentine tango) or in the upper thigh, hip area. This reduction of possible relations works well for the entanglements of cities and states. I will argue in narratives below that cities and states usually have an open embrace whereby they define separate realms of activity but on rare occasions they can have a close embrace, as in the political economy of our modern times. In the open embrace the states are definitely the 'lead' and the cities 'follow', but the close embrace is perhaps more interesting, for there can be different ways to 'connect' and it is less clear where the power lies.

Of course, there are always limits to analogies; a tango involves two people playing roles, cities and states are rather more complex than can be captured as roles. In fact these complexities have always meant that understanding relations between cities and states has been beyond the full comprehension of social science disciplines with their boundaries. Instead of knowledge separations I search out knowledge connections without concern for disciplines. I am always intrigued when key researchers say effectively the same thing while coming at the subject from distinctly different perspectives. Here are some inter-author links from across the twentieth century that are at the very heart of my contemporary thinking. First, the same basic statement has been made by two outstanding urban theorists writing half a century apart: in 1921 Max Weber (1958, p. 65) argued that the city is not simply 'a large locality', and in 1969 Jane Jacobs (1969, p. 129) argued that 'a city is not a large town' – I use this insight as the basis for my understanding of cities in the next chapter. Of course, these theorists subsequently diverge in their respective paths to city definition: Weber focuses on functions, Jacobs understands cities as a process (Jacobs 1969, p. 50). Second, move on another quarter century and we find Jacobs echoed in Castells' (1996, p. 386) influential work on network society: ' the global city is . . . a process'. Although the latter is based upon another quite different theory, drawing on ideas of global cities atop a world urban hierarchy, Jacobs and Castells share the same relational view of cities. This idea of city as process is critically useful in handling the complexity of cities. Geographically, the great advantage of conceptualizing cities as process (a bundle of processes), rather than as a place, is that there can be myriad processes in one place. Thus defining

a city as a global city and listing attributes to be found in such a place
to qualify to this exalted status leaves the researcher open to the accusa-
tion of missing so much more about the city. But defining global city as a
process – global city formation – allows it to be understood as one process
among many that make up a given city. There can still be debate about the
relative importance of the global city process, but there is now no simple
practice of labelling that conceals so much else that is going on in the city.
I extend this methodology to states by treating states as process (a bundle
of processes) – state formation is my subject matter. With both city and
states as processes, the salient complexity is assured because it takes two
to tango.

This geohistorical tango unfolds as depicted in Box 1.1.

My narrative begins as the beginning in prehistory and finishes with the
upcoming environmental catastrophe, possibly ending in 'post-history'
(that is to say, a demise that could mark an end of written records). I use
the term 'normal' for two circumstances that encompass most of the existence of humanity: Normal Prehistory covers most of the experience of our
species across the world; Normal History covers most of the experience
of humanity when city networks existed, commonly referenced by the
written word as historical source, and described as 'civilization'. Normal
Prehistory is the world of hunter–gatherers spreading across the world
as small territorial groups. We know from the artefacts they have left
behind that they were also producers and traders but this was only a small
element in their material reproduction. 'Normal' should not be interpreted
as inferring homogeneity; there is and was much variety amongst hunter–
gatherer bands related, for instance, to the ecology of their territories. At
the extremes of this variety there can be unusual bands developing specialist skills, such as in coastal fishing. I call this Abnormal Prehistory and
focus on just one particular example: concentrations of producer–trader
activities. Where they form trade networks, the trading camps can grow
into small cities to create the first incipient city networks. These seem to
have appeared in several places across the world, perhaps most famously
at Çatalhöyük (Anatolia), Sannai-Maruyama (Japan), Great Zimbabwe
(southern Africa) and Cahokia (Mississippi valley). Successful trading
and production leads to increasing population resulting in the first major
urban problem, how to feed the unprecedented concentrations of people.
Solving this problem reveals the first great expression of city creativity:
the invention of agriculture. This generates city hinterlands to complement city networks in the urban spatial ensemble. But this is initially quite
a fragile invention; sustainability is a further step along a learning curve.
Initially decreasing agricultural returns can be compensated by extending
the hinterland, but this has its own limits in terms of accessibility to the

BOX 1.1   FRAMEWORK FOR A NARRATIVE

Normal Prehistory

Hunter–gatherers with producer–trader activities

Abnormal Prehistory
- Specific concentrations of producer–trader activities leading to first city networks
- Increasing demand for food leading to invention of agriculture in urban hinterlands
- Desiccation of hinterlands leading to city failure, empty quarters and subsistence agriculture

Initial creative interludes
- *Particular concentrations of producer–trader activities leading to resilient city networks*
- *Food problem solved by invention of sustainable agriculture*
- *Large cosmopolitan cities enabling world-changing innovations and the rise of commerce*
- *Large, diverse population concentrations create new demand for order leading to invention of city-states*
- *Competition between states leads to multi-city territorial state as empire and the demise of autonomous cities*

Normal History

Rise and fall of world-empires with dependent commerce reproduced through acquiescent city networks

Abnormal History
- Post-Roman imperial power vacuum in Europe lasts for a millennium
- Vacuum not filled through conquest by non-European world-empire
- Rise of autonomous Europe-wide city network in European commercial revolution

---

The modern creative interlude

- *Divided sovereignty in inter-state relations heralds modern world-system*
- *City-led world hegemonic cycles replace rise and fall of world-empire*
- *This enables city commerce to dominate the system with ceaseless capital accumulation becoming the prime social logic of a capitalist world-economy*
- *Cities in world hegemonic states create world-changing innovations to reproduce an ever-expanding capitalism*
- *World city network underpins contemporary globalization, which heralds the demise of the modern world-system*

Global economic and environmental upheaval

- Leading to . . .?

---

city. The result is that without sustainable agriculture, hinterlands become desiccated, empty quarters, and the city network necessarily collapses after a few generations. Thus these early networks of cities are only partially successful, but farming continues without cities as subsistence agriculture. This is the great legacy of traders and producers in Abnormal Prehistory.

There is a second development of city networks that proved to be much more resilient. Again based upon producer trading activities, in these networks the food problem is solved long-term through the invention of sustainable agriculture. Commonly this has been achieved through the harnessing of river floods renewing the soil. The earliest example is probably in Mesopotamia, usually identified as the locus of the first cities, here reinterpreted as the locus of the first resilient city network. This resilience provided time for the trading and production to grow cities to new demographic levels. This creates the conditions for multiple innovations – including writing – that are usually interpreted as 'world-changing': the invention of civilization, no less. As well as in Mesopotamia, this occurs in several locations across the world including Egypt, the Indus valley, China, West Africa, Mexico and Peru. I call these 'initial creative interludes', periods covering several centuries centred upon self-expanding city networks.

Such interludes come to an end with the invention of the state. This is a city invention to solve the problem of internal conflicts in increasingly large and cosmopolitan cities. The nature of governance transfers from light touch administration to sovereign king in new city-states. This change is indexed by the building of walls: the dominant mutuality between cities in networks is converted into a new condition of rivalry and war between city-states. Victors in this process produce multi-city territorial states that become empires subjugating even more cities in their logic of expansion. The demise of autonomous cities marks the end of the creative interlude and the city/state tango begins.

Normal History now proceeds. Starting at different times in different parts of the world, these are periods of the rise and fall of empires, periods of political centralization interspersed with inter-state rivalries to become the next 'universal' empire. Network formation between cities continues, and their commerce remains important. However they lose their autonomy and thereby their full creative potential. City networks can prosper in Normal History but only in circumstances dictated by states – for instance, in the frontiers between empires or in the 'long peace' that a successful empire achieves. However, in Normal History the largest cities are the capital cities of states as recipients of tribute and war booty, a hierarchical political process separate from city network formation. As with Normal Prehistory, in Normal History there are a wide variety of specific outcomes relating to, for instance, imperial ranges and longevities. There will be some unusual situations and those at the limit can be called Abnormal Histories. I focus on one such example: western and northern Europe. Brought into Normal History by the expansion of the Roman Empire, with the demise of the latter it entered an exceptionally long period without a replacement universal empire, a whole millennium in fact. Such a political void would normally be filled by conquest by a powerful outside empire. This did not happen to Europe and the resulting divided political landscape enabled the rise of relatively autonomous cities culminating in a 'commercial revolution', with a Europe-wide city network in the second half of the millennium without empire.

It is from this particular Abnormal History that the modern creative interlude emerged in the 'long sixteenth century' (c. 1450–1650). The decentralized politics was formalized as the inter-state system (international relations and international law confirmed in the 1648 Treaty of Westphalia) and commerce (including production) becomes concentrated in the new city-rich Dutch republic. The phenomenal economic success of the latter 'merchant state' creates the response of mercantilism whereby economic matters are brought to the centre of state affairs – the modern state is born. Now the relations between economic elites and political elites are fundamentally changed: there is a much greater parity than in Normal History. This is called the modern world-system, which operates as a capitalist world-economy. In this historical system cities are able to recover much of their creative potential: world-changing innovations return. Modern change is dominated by innovations emanating from concentrations of vibrant cities in 'hegemonic states', first the Dutch Republic, then Great Britain, and latterly the United States. In this way hegemonic cycles based upon new bundles of city innovations replace the irregular rise and fall of empires in Normal History. The latter continues in regions outside Europe until they are incorporated into the capitalist world-economy. The demise of the last great Chinese empire through such incorporation marks the global triumph of the modern world-system in the nineteenth century.

In the late twentieth century economic globalization, an intensification of the capitalist world-economy as global economy, seemed to mark a final twist in the city/state tango. This new scale of economic process was enabled by the rise of world city networks that transcended the states. This is not the end of states as advocates of a 'borderless world' have suggested, but it does mark a new city/state relationship that has been brought into the twenty-first century. And therefore this is the situation we are in as we face both an economic crisis in the demise of the modern world-system and an environmental crisis caused by the economic success of the self-same system. My narrative concludes tackling this conundrum.

Finally, let me say how the framework in Box 1.1 fits into the organization of the book. The narrative part of my text is divided into three parts of two chapters each. In Part II arguments covering Abnormal Prehistory and initial creative interludes are interwoven across the two chapters. In Part III I devote a chapter each to Normal History (including Europe's abnormality) and the modern creative interlude in order to contrast them. In Part IV I describe contemporary globalization as the apogee of the capitalist world-economy, a prelude to thinking ahead to the twenty-first century as crisis century. But before we come to this mega-narrative I need to introduce and describe the conceptual toolbox that I employ to specify and justify the story I tell. Thus the second chapter of Part I, the introduction, is about social science but without the usual boundaries. In other words I try and do what I preach in the research of which this book is the outcome.

2. Conceptual toolkits

This chapter is an exploration that attempts to transcend social science's nineteenth-century foundations. Such a purpose can be pursued in many different ways: as indicated in the last chapter, my particular approach foregrounds cities, their interrelations, and their relations with states. This requires a customized suite of conceptual toolkits. I know the idea of 'toolkits' is not always popular in social fields of study, primarily because they evoke mechanical modes of operation. But in this case toolkits are an eminently suitable way of describing my methodology because my later arguments will focus very much on work, on making a livelihood. Concepts are the tools of trade in my line of work and therefore I have decided to start with my research toolkits; the fact that they are conceptual should be enough to allay fears that my thinking is too mechanical. Given my indisciplinary stance, it follows that the toolkits should not be seen as a template for others to use, much less a nascent social theory; they are what they are, a collection of tools that I believe are fit for my specific purposes in this book, no less and no more.

There are three toolkits that I use to build my alternative geohistorical framework. This is a very large task and, given space constraints, I will provide only a basic description and justification of each. No claim is made for methodological originality – I take an eclectic magpie approach – and they are ordered in a very conventional manner. I start with defining my social agents, the people who make geohistory. Although my take on cities is largely economic, these agents are social; they have learned how to behave appropriately in order to make a living. To this end, in the first section I introduce Jacobs' (1992) moral syndromes thinking as a toolkit for understanding the necessary ethics that enable different work practices to be successfully reproduced. But agents do not make geohistory in contexts of their own making; I need structural concepts. Since both cities and states share immanent constitution in both space and time, in the second section I introduce concepts of social time and social space; this is TimeSpace, as Wallerstein (1991) calls their simultaneous constructions. Here I construct a toolkit by combining Castells' (1996) seminal social construction of space with Braudel's (1980) classic ideas on time spans. But geohistory is not a simple unfolding of how agents interact with their

surrounding structures; rather there are myriad institutions that moderate the interaction. And this brings me finally to the particular collective
institutions I focus on: cities and states. The third section searches out the
theoretical literature on both to provide an institutional toolkit, drawing
heavily on Scott (1998) for states and Jacobs (1969) for cities.

Thus the narrative of the book is built through employing three conceptual toolkits: a moral syndromes toolkit, a TimeSpace toolkit and a cities/
states toolkit. Obviously these tools do not cover all aspects of what might
be encompassed by 'geohistory', I have been very selective; my concern
has been to find and use tools fit for my specific purpose. To my way
of thinking methodology is only as good as the results it produces; this
means that judgement should be reserved until after use. Therefore I ask
the reader to be patient when reading this long chapter; the proof of this
pudding (another work metaphor!) is to be found in Parts II, III and IV,
the substantive sections where the toolkits are brought out to use.

SOCIAL AGENTS: THE MORAL SYNDROMES TOOLKIT

My argument is a social one. Jane Jacobs is renowned as one of the great
urbanist thinkers of modern times (Alexiou 2006) and my later discussions
of cities will draw heavily on her ideas. But I start with one of her lesser-
known works in which she explores, in the words of the book's subtitle,
'the moral foundations of commerce and politics' (Jacobs 1992). For
those familiar with the 'urban Jacobs', her intervention into ethics and
moral philosophy is quite a surprise. However she is not in the business of
covering philosophy *in toto*, she carefully narrows her subject down to the
moral bases for making a living. But, as Edward Glaeser (2000, p. 473) has
noted, Jacobs' new scholarly departure had 'no explicit urban element'.
Previously, this has led to doubting whether the new ideas she was developing were in any way related to her seminal urban work (Jacobs 1989a,
p. 238). Jacobs is reported as answering this criticism most rigorously,
claiming her ideas on ethics has 'a great connection with cities' and she
gives this example:

> I got curious about the almost gut-hatred that some people feel for cities, and
> that some classes feel for cities. The English upper classes are just so nasty about
> cities. What is it that is so offensive about cities to them? They do not mind
> London because it has Buckingham Palace and all kinds of great monuments
> and things, but places like Sheffield or Birmingham or Leicester – oh, what
> contempt there is for them. It is the same contempt that there is for trade: any
> dealings with money are dirty, and all that sort of thing. (Jacobs 1989a, p. 239)

Of course, this is not just an English social disease, it is a general aristo-cratic distain for anything bourgeois: 'Tradesmen Use the Back Door' is understood the world over. But philosophers, it seems, have used the grand front door.

Jacobs (1992, p. xi) aspires to produce 'an unconventional approach to moral understanding'. Philosophers' traditional concerns for 'virtuous living' and 'virtuous ruling' have neglected the 'ethics of working life', which remains an intellectual *pot pourri*, a random collection of legal pronouncements and business norms. Thus, according to Jacobs, ques-tions concerning 'the startling moral contradictions in working life and the reasons for them' remain largely unexamined. She begins with the example of two impeccable virtues, loyalty and truth, that are in conflict in the work place when we have to choose between being 'loyal at the expense of honesty or, conversely honest at the expense of loyalty'. Adhering to both virtues is 'good', but in choosing between them we are simultane-ously being 'bad'. This is just the sort of dilemma that Jacobs explores. I give a simple example to provide a hint as to where her argument leads. In my work I have to provide references for candidates applying for jobs. In writing a reference for one of my students I try to be honest with balanced reporting of her positive and negative attributes. I want her to get the job but I have to be fair to other candidates and not just provide celebration of her skills. In contrast, if I were asked to write a reference for a relative, say, my niece, loyalty would rival honesty: I would want her to get the job not just because I hope she is the best candidate but because she is family. Of course, I am not asked to provide references for relatives and if I were I would be expected to 'declare an interest' and remove myself from the recruiting process. But we should not assume that honesty always trumps loyalty in the jobs market. There is an old saying that it is not what you know but who you know in getting the best jobs: the relevant arena here is not a reference letter but the golf course or social club, places where loyalty reigns supreme.

There is a very basic connection between Jacobs' study of ethics and her urban studies: following the 'urban Jacobs' (1969) I will be defining cities as concentrations of work, in other words where people are making a living. Notice that the latter phrase implies work that is reproductive: making a living is for life. This is why Jacobs (1992) calls her ethics book *Systems of Survival*; it is about the moral basis for how individuals survive and thereby how households, social groups and larger social collectives are continually being reproduced. Starting at the individual level, I begin with people making a living who are thereby relating to other people also making a living. This social relation is economic but I have no truck with the concept of 'economic man', the impersonal, all-knowing individual optimizer of economic theory. Making a living cannot occur in a moral vacuum, agreements on ethics – how to properly behave – are needed for successful social reproduction. Thus my social agents are 'moral agents' negotiating interpersonal trust and wider societal work ethics.

Moral Syndromes

Jacobs' (1992) highly original approach to understanding social behaviour focuses on making a living. She distinguishes this from 'having a life', at the very least just as important, but this broader topic is not her subject matter. She limits her concern to work practices because she is trying to figure out how humans have survived and prospered materially. Drawing on previous authorities, not least Adam Smith, she recognizes that human beings are unique in the animal world by having two ways of making a living. All animals, including humans, make use of their local environment through collecting, hunting, protecting, and organizing food and raw materials for reproduction. Survival depends upon maintaining local access, typically ensured through territorial control. However, humans have added an additional way of making a living through exchanging goods – Smith's 'trucking', we now call it trading – which can simply be the exchange of local food and raw materials themselves, or production derived from the food and raw materials. Thus all animal species have access to locally available means of reproduction but humans also have access to non-local means of reproduction. Evidence abounds for trading in early human settlements because, for instance, the geological origins of exotic stones such as amber and obsidian can be traced. Archaeologists call this 'the release from proximity' (Rodseth et al. 1991) which has been, according to Gamble (2007, p. 211), extending human social ties 'for at least the last 60 000 years'. This very basic geography – the local/non-local distinction – is not particularly emphasized by Jacobs (1992) but will reappear frequently in my later arguments. For my argument here it tells us that she is presenting generic ideas for understanding human behaviour.

Today these two different ways of making a living are found in (1) all jobs relating to protecting and governing in security (armed forces, police. judiciary), government (working for executive or legislature), and administration (carrying out state service functions including regulation); and (2) all jobs relating to making and trading commodities in farming, mining, manufacture, transport, wholesaling, retailing, professional and non-professional services, information and logistics. Each of the two types of job is associated with a specific moral syndrome that Jacobs (1992) describes as the ethical foundations for these different ways of making a living. Each moral syndrome consists of a set of behavioural

---

BOX 2.1   MORAL SYNDROME PRECEPTS AS LISTED BY JACOBS

Commercial moral syndrome	*Guardian moral syndrome*
Shun force	Shun trading
Come to voluntary agreements	Exert prowess
Be honest	Be obedient and disciplined
Collaborate easily with strangers and aliens	Adhere to tradition
Compete	Respect hierarchy
Respect contracts	Be loyal
Use initiative and enterprise	Take vengeance
Be open to inventiveness and novelty	Deceive for the sake of the task
Be efficient	Make rich use of leisure
Promote comfort and convenience	Be ostentatious
Dissent for the sake of the task	Dispense largesse
Invest for productive purposes	Be exclusive
Be industrious	Show fortitude
Be thrifty	Be fatalistic
Be optimistic	Treasure honour

---

precepts that enable its respective way of making a living to operate successfully. The interesting thing about the syndromes is that they are not just different: they are contradictory. The two sets of precepts describe behaviours that are quite opposite from one another. In other words what is ethical in the work place is not straightforward, it depends on how you make a living. This means behaving morally is work-dependent: what is right and proper for one type of work is a violation of morality in the other type of work.

Jacobs calls these two ethics the guardian moral syndrome and the commercial moral syndrome and they are shown in Box 2.1.

They both consist of 15 precepts; each list constitutes a syndrome because the precepts are closely entwined to make a consistent behavioural set: violating one precept will endanger the whole syndrome and thereby undermine that way of making a living. Jacobs orders the precepts from simple to increasing complexity. Thus she starts with what is definitely barred in each case: commercial work cannot be successfully accomplished if transactions are forced (extortion); guardian work is violated if trading occurs (bribery). Shunning force in commercial ethics allows voluntary agreements to be made; in contrast, for guardian work transactions are based upon force through exerting prowess. The third precept in the commercial list, be honest, and the sixth precept in the guardian list, be loyal, are highlighted by Jacobs as the 'prime virtues' in each syndrome. I briefly referred to their differences above and they can be further used to best illustrate the moral contradiction between the syndromes here. Trade prospers through honesty on both sides in reaching the best deal. But a trade based upon loyalty is problematic – since it is not chosen as the best deal, continuing such behaviour will lead a business to bankruptcy. In contrast guardian work relies on loyalty; an army disintegrates with increasing disloyalty. Here honesty is problematic: a general signalling his battleground intentions in an open and honest manner would soon get the sack for unnecessarily endangering the lives of his soldiers.

Jacobs (1992, Chapters 3 and 5) describes and justifies each of the precepts in some detail; here, I will present the precepts as clusters of behavioural traits to aid in understanding the syndromes (Table 2.1).

Each syndrome has a 'Basic Cluster' containing the key virtues that define the core of its ethics. These were used in the last paragraph to introduce the syndromes. In Table 2.1 the three guardian premises described previously have three additional basic cluster precepts that all contribute to a stable work environment through combining tradition, obedience and hierarchy. On the commercial side there is an 'Operating Cluster' that promotes cosmopolitanism (collaboration with strangers), competition, flexibility (dissent) with stability hinging on contracts that work. The guardian syndrome has an Action Cluster in which vengeance, deception and exclusivity feature, a very different tone to the commercial Operating Cluster. The latter is followed by an Enterprise Cluster where behavioural traits that advance commercial practices are valued: initiative, inventiveness, efficiency, convenience, productive investment, industrious hard work and thriftiness. In contrast the guardians have a Lifestyle Cluster that aims to impress friend and foe alike in which opulent leisure, ostentatiousness, largess, and defending honour feature. Finally, the two syndromes have contrasting Life Clusters: comfort and optimism versus fortitude and fatalism. These define two very different mindsets. The commercial syndrome is ultimately premised on assuming a better future – why else would you invest? Every freely agreed contract benefits both sides – this is a Win–Win world. But for guardians, change is a matter of life and death (literally in battle, career-wise in elections) – this is a Win–Lose world, a zero-sum game.

Table 2.1   Syndromes by clusters of precepts

Commercial syndrome		Guardian syndrome	
Clusters	Precepts	Clusters	Precepts
'Key virtue'	Be honest	'Key virtue'	Be loyal
Other Basic Cluster	Shun force Come to voluntary agreements	Other Basic Cluster	Shun trading Exert prowess
Operating Cluster	Collaborate with strangers and aliens Compete Respect contracts Dissent for the sake of the task	Action Cluster	Be exclusive Take vengeance Respect hierarchy Deceive for the sake of the task
Enterprise Cluster	Be open to inventiveness and novelty Be efficient Use initiative and enterprise Invest for productive purposes Be industrious Be thrifty	Lifestyle Cluster	Be obedient and disciplined Adhere to tradition Make rich use of leisure Dispense largesse Treasure honour Be ostentatious
Life cluster	Promote comfort and convenience Be optimistic	Life cluster	Show fortitude Be fatalistic

The question arises as to how Jacobs (1992) has identified the precepts and put them together as syndromes. Jacobs claims not to have invented the syndromes (p. xii), rather she has discovered them. Jacobs' methodology is inherently empirical and has been described as a process that begins with 'the observation of sensible data from which questions about the data emerge; gradually, through a self-revising process of question–image–insight–further question, one begins to find clues which point towards true understanding' (Chichello 1989, p. 127). Put more simply, she finds patterns through a '"messy" cycle of trail and error' (p. 132). In this case, she tries to understand ethics in human work places like an animal behaviouralist studying animals in groups through wide-ranging observation of their habits and traits (p. 26). Her observation takes the form of scrutinizing voluminous amounts of textual evidence. These included biographies, business histories, academic writing (notable cultural anthropology), and newspapers. This is how she describes finding precepts:

> I drew on three kinds of evidence. Whenever I ran across behavior that was extolled as admirable, I cast it in the form of a precept. If a businessman was praised because his handshake was as good as his bond, I cast it in the precept 'Respect contracts'. . . . I should emphasize . . . that not one of these precepts is here because it turned up as a unique or even a rare instance. Every one showed up over and over, in varying contexts. If a soldier was extolled for redeeming the honor of his regiment by rallying it when it was about retreat, I cast it as 'Treasure honor', and so on. . . . I did the same with behavior that was laid out as expected or proper, as in job-training manuals . . . My third type of evidence was behavior that was deemed scandalous, disgraceful, or criminal. I identified what was being transgressed, such as honesty; or if extortion, say, was the crime, I cast it as 'Shun force' and 'Come to voluntary agreement'. (Jacobs 1992, pp. 25–6)

At first she admits to having produced just 'a mess of contradictions' (p. 27), but understanding that a species as successful as humanity must have developed consistent and meaningful norms of behaviour she persevered until:

> My first glimmer of order came when I noticed that specific precepts were repeatedly associated with specific others: loyalty with obedience and respect for hierarchy, for instance, industriousness with thrift and efficiency. Aha! Precepts came in linked clusters! Each kind of occupation I'd notice had its clusters, and those clusters overlapped with other clusters. Combining the overlaps resolved the clusters into these two lists . . . they were resolved into two systems, each with its own integrity. (Jacobs 1992, p. 27)

All that she now had to do was to find which occupations were associated with different precepts so as to name the two moral syndromes.

The development of Jacobs' thinking in labelling the moral syndromes is quite instructive and steers us away from interpreting them as simply economic and political. My initial source here is the proceedings of a conference held in Boston in 1987 to discuss her new ideas on ethics (Lawrence 1989a). In an initial interview she reveals that her working title for this work is 'Raiders and Traders', which derives directly from her recognition of humans being unique in having a second way of making a living: all animals, including humans, 'raid' their environment to survive, and humans in addition trade (Keeley 1989, p. 2). But in later discussion, she indicated disquiet over the term 'raiders' (Jacobs 1989a, p. 239), extending it to 'raiding or ruling system' at one point (Lawrence 1989b, p. 199). Since we know that eventually Jacobs (1992) used neither of her original labels it indicates that the syndromes do not readily fit into existing conceptualizations of work.

In the final presentation of the syndromes, Jacobs (1992) initially labels them simply 'A' and 'B' (pp. 23–4). The subsequent text suggests labelling syndrome A as commercial was 'easy' because 'occupations associated with it overwhelmingly concerned commerce, and production of goods or services for commerce' (p. 28). But it is perhaps not quite so simple since it includes 'most scientific work', which is based upon non-commercial exchange (p. 28). Furthermore it excludes 'commercial monopolies', which she places firmly in the B syndrome (p. 28). However, we can agree with her that 'by and large' the precepts 'are classic bourgeois values and virtues' but she avoids using the 'bourgeois' label because as a modern concept it brings with it a notion of 'western values' and accusations of 'Eurocentrism' (p. 28): commercial behaviour is more clearly generic. However the move from trading to commercial in this important labelling exercise was perhaps more difficult than Jacobs admits.

Labelling syndrome B was, according to Jacobs (1992, p. 28) 'more enigmatic', as suggested in Lawrence (1989b, p. 195). Although she finds 'classic heroic virtues and values' in the precepts, there is also a 'lot of humdrum bureaucratic work' included that was anything but heroic (p. 29). She considers 'government or ruling' as labels but these are deemed 'too limited'. And in any case, some government service work is in the commercial syndrome, for example weather forecasting, which subscribes 'like all hard sciences, to the commercial precepts' (p. 29). She eventually settles on guardian although also suggesting it is 'a bit narrow' (p. 31). It seems to me that 'governance', a term that has become widely used in the social sciences since Jacobs' deliberations, perhaps better describes the syndrome but I keep to her terminology for the sake of consistency. The important point is that Jacobs has moved from emphasizing the 'taking' character of Syndrome B as in 'raiding', and finally highlights the positive side of 'stewardship' explicit in the idea of 'guardian'. This will be important for the final chapter of the book.

There is still the question of where these syndromes have actually come from. Jacobs (1992, p. xii) argues that humanity has produced the two syndromes 'during millennia of experience with trading and producing, on the one hand, and with organizing and managing territories, on the other hand'. In other words these are generic to human work practices with humans learning what precepts are needed in different work contexts. Working through successful precepts will generate emulation and further honing of practices as the syndromes evolve in different world regions. The latter point is very important: a cursory glance at the list of commercial syndrome precepts might conclude that these are 'Western' values, closely tied to Enlightenment ideas of progress. Glaeser (2000, p. 488) even calls this the 'capitalist ethic'. But no, such interpretation completely misses the nature of the commercial syndrome:

> This is about concrete, nitty-gritty commercial life. It's about giving honest
> weight, finding customers, and competing successfully with other commercial
> people. These precepts rule wherever commercial life is viable, East or West.
> They apply to Islamic innkeepers, Buddhist batik makers, Hindu brass crafts-
> men, or Shinto brake manufacturers, just as they do to Christian, Jewish or
> atheist auto mechanics and potters. (p. 28)

And the commercial syndrome is most certainly not 'capitalist': in the
next toolkit in this chapter I will show capitalism to be more related to
the guardian syndrome, and furthermore, in my subsequent geohistorical
narratives I will emphasize the importance of distinguishing between commerce and capitalism. I repeat for emphasis, both syndromes are generic.

There appears to be no doubting that the guardian precepts are not
specific in time or place; there is the long-term philosophical tradition of
providing advice to rulers on how to rule that broadly adheres to Jacobs'
syndrome. However, philosophical neglect of commercial work means
that Jacobs' other syndrome does have a very 'modern' feel to it: most
readers of this book are likely to feel more comfortable with the commercial precepts. In fact Jacobs (1989b, p. 274) has herself admitted that she
was initially 'most sympathetic with the trading system'. But in the full
development of her ideas she subsequently realized that both syndromes
are equally necessary for reproducing any and all human societies. This
point is insisted upon again and again (Jacobs 1992: *passim*). Work based
on each syndrome needs the other: guardians provide order; commercial
agents provide change. Properly coordinated, and without violating each
syndrome's moral integrity, they can provide the best of both worlds. But
that is much harder to achieve than might be expected.

Relations Between Syndromes

It is important to understand that the sets of precepts that constitute the
two syndromes are not just different and contrasting, they are inherently
contradictory. This has profound implications given that both are necessary in any functioning society. It follows that how the two syndromes
relate to each other within a given society is potentially fraught with
great difficulties. The basic problem is that social practices based upon
either one of the syndromes threaten the integrity of the other syndrome.
For instance, treason and fraud are criminal actions that undermine one
syndrome by operating through the other syndrome. Intelligence officers
or spies should operate through the guardian syndrome but when they
offer secrets to the highest bidder – commercial syndrome behaviour – the
prime precept loyalty is violated and they become traitors. Investors on
the stock exchange should operate through the commercial syndrome but

when a group use confidential information to gain advantage – 'insider trading' is guardian syndrome behaviour – the prime precept, honesty, is violated and they become fraudsters. Given the guardian penchant for vengeance, the death penalty is more likely for treachery than for fraud.

The norms and values of the two syndromes will be violated in all societies; we should not expect human perfection. What matters is the degree of violation. This can be simplified to just two basic circumstances. First, there are situations where breaching the integrity of the syndromes is so high that the society becomes dysfunctional. Reproduction in making a living becomes effectively impossible. Jacobs (1992, Chapter 6) calls these 'monstrous hybrids'. Second, there are social arrangements where the two syndromes enjoy a symbiotic relationship. Here reproduction in making a living is successful but always under challenge, thus length of survival is an issue. These can range from particular 'syndrome-friendly inventions' to more general societal organization. A brief consideration of relations between syndromes illustrates how the moral syndromes toolkit can be used in social analyses. I will begin by describing monstrous hybrids.

Monstrous hybrids are worst-case scenarios when one syndrome's virtues are transplanted into the heart of activities associated with the other syndrome. For instance, both the mafia (Jacobs 1992, pp. 92–7) and the USSR (pp. 98–102) are identified as monstrous hybrids wherein guardian values are used in commerce:

> Structurally, they do much resemble each other; into an otherwise strong guardian syndrome comes the massive breach of the guardian precept to shun trading. Since the guardian syndrome is neither morally nor functionally suited to carrying on production and trade, the commerce involved is corrupted and its moral foundations ruined. (Jacobs 1992, p. 102)

The result is ultimate economic disaster for places whose economies are at the disposal of guardians either as private extortionists or state planners. Dishonesty rules, and loyalty is not capable of sustaining an economy. Jacobs provides an interesting example of a violation of integrity in the other direction: the introduction of an incentive system to police work to increase productivity (p. 147). The latter was measured by arrests per work-hour and the police responded with a huge increase in the number of arrests, very many of them false. This was a case of trying 'to improve the guardian syndrome by plucking industriousness from the commercial syndrome' (p. 152), thereby creating a corrupted police force.

Today's 'development industry' is perhaps the best example of a monstrous hybrid with truly horrendous consequences for people living in the poorer countries of the world. The commercial syndrome engenders a cast of mind that allows for growth, always searching for win–win deals. Thus,

however we define 'development', it surely must involve economic growth
and therefore development practices should be subject to the commercial
moral syndrome. And, equally, it should be kept out of the hands of
guardians. But just the opposite has occurred, economic development has
been designated a state practice resulting in the monstrous hybrid called
'development planning' (Jacobs 1992, pp. 118–23; Taylor 2006).

It doesn't have to be this way and it is not always this way. In the simplest terms, Jacobs (1992, p. 178) describes 'good symbiosis' between the
syndromes as follows:

> guardians taking political responsibility for enacting policies into law, and
> enforcing them; commerce taking responsibility for innovative ways and means
> of complying.

At the level of the firm Jacobs uses examples of micro-credit banks
(pp. 159–66) that are run by the poor (guardian function) for investment
in the work of the poor (commercial function). The classic example is
Muhammad Yunis's Grameen Bank in Bangladesh (pp. 162–5; Yunis
2007) for which he received the Nobel Prize for Peace in 2006. The key
invention is that decisions on loans are kept local thereby harnessing face-
to-face trust and knowledge; the basic operating units are circles of no
more than ten members (pp. 163–4). This example of a 'syndrome-friendly
invention', as Jacobs calls it, works well because loyalty and honesty are
harnessed together: default rates are spectacularly low, sometimes only 2
per cent. Latterly, outside guardian intrusion – in 2011 the Bangladeshi
government removed Yunis from the bank – may well destroy this
initiative.

At the larger societal scale, Jacobs (1992, pp. 179–90) identifies two
basic ways in which symbiosis between the syndromes has worked to
create societies that are reproduced over relatively long time periods.
These are 'a rigid caste or class framework' and 'knowledgeable flexibility'
(p. 179). The former works by keeping guardian and commercial work
apart through hierarchical social custom. Jacobs uses Plato for her generic
description as follows:

> Plato gives us a pure – even though imaginary – paradigm of the rigid caste or
> class method. His proposed guardian caste was set apart by occupations and
> also in every other way: birth, upbringing, selection of wives, residence, uses of
> leisure, and the ideals with which guardians were inculcated. . . . Internally the
> caste was to be divided by merit. Rulers and administrators were responsible for
> deliberating, reasoning, and making plans. Police and soldiers carried out what
> the rulers and administrators commanded. At the top was the philosopher-king
> of outstanding wisdom, goodness and selflessness. . . . For their part, commer-

cial people were to stick to trading and producing – well policed, well protected, and well ruled by guardians. They were excluded from concerns of government except for their obligations to pay taxes and supply material goods required by guardians. (pp. 179–80)

In practice, societies 'where people know their place' ranged from the classic Indian caste system, with Brahmins at the top and merchants near the bottom, to the famous English class system still reflected in the British Parliament's naming of its two houses as 'Lords' and 'Commons'. Across the English Channel this was the framework of the *ancien régime* before the French Revolution turned the 'three estates' – aristocracy, clergy and commoners – into a single 'national assembly' of citizens. The chief disadvantage of rigid caste/class societies is that there is little social space to accommodate change. The merchant *nouveau riche* can be recruited to the aristocracy, but this inevitably undermines the purity of the hierarchy and encourages corruption: French society before the Revolution might be characterized as an emergent monstrous hybrid.

This is all very different from how Jacobs (1992, p. 179) envisages contemporary society is maintaining syndrome integrities:

> The flexible, knowledgeable method of separating the syndromes doesn't ordain children for occupational destinies that they stick with all their lives. It permits individuals to do either guardian or commercial work without regard to birth or upbringing; also to shift between the two, as when a businessman runs for political office or a former soldier becomes a commercial accountant or a carpenter. (p. 189)

For this to work there must be widespread understanding and critical self-reflection by individuals who cross the divide. For instance, the concept of a public service ethos was invented to describe the work of English industrial leaders who became mayors or other officials in their home cities in the nineteenth century. Attending to the precepts of thrift and industriousness in their private work, they nevertheless were able to be ostentatious in their public role by trying to make sure their city had the most impressive city hall, museum, or other public architecture. And behind them there were numerous other people taking on part-time public responsibilities 'while continuing to make their living in commercial work' (p. 205). Much of this has been put under threat by recent neoliberalism in which guardian work has been commercialized (privatization) while commercial work takes on a more guardian ethos (aggressive take-overs) thereby blurring syndrome distinctions. This is clearly a tendency leading to another monstrous hybrid.

Jacobs 'knowledgeable flexibility' equates simply to 'our society', I consider it more specifically as 'modernity'. In knowledgeable flexibility, guardian work and commercial work are more equal than in past caste/ class societies that are commonly referred to as 'traditional', meaning the obverse of modern. In fact the ethos of modernity is usually seen as eliminating customary hierarchy for equality of opportunities (Taylor 1999a). But this insight cannot be explored through Jacobs' work because she entertains no notion of modernity. As mentioned at the very beginning of this section, she describes generic processes, using examples from all historical eras, without engaging with the specificities of different societies in different times. In her ahistorical approach there are no modern times. To understand the specificities of modernity – 'our society' – and how it seems to have become the only example of successful flexibility, we have to turn to another conceptual toolkit.

SYSTEMIC STRUCTURES: THE WORLD-SYSTEMS TIMESPACE TOOLKIT

My argument is a structuralist one: reproduction of work does not consist only of myriad guardian and commercial agents making decisions adhering, by varying degrees, to the norms and values of their respective syndromes. This would imply that social agents simply carry out their work on a ubiquitous level playing field, as if there were neither past influences nor distant effects impinging on how they are able to make a living. In reality there are always underlying societal structures that mould the actual and limit the possible for all actors from the highest king to the meanest trader. The result is that in any one place at any given time there are important power differentials within human societies that reward various work differentially. We need another toolkit to handle this level of analysis.

As implied when noting Jacobs does not have a notion of historical modernity in *Systems of Survival*, this reflects a more general lack of any sense of underlying structures in her work. Thus we have to go elsewhere to augment Jacobs' moral syndromes and my choice here is Immanuel Wallerstein's (1979; 1983; 2004) world-systems analysis. This is a method of understanding social change that particularly foregrounds the temporal and spatial configuration of large societal structures, which Wallerstein (1979) calls world-systems. Wallerstein defines a modern world-system that is distinctively different from other world-systems. In this way Jacobs' unique knowledgeable flexibility of 'our times' can be interpreted as a structurally embedded set of behaviours in a specific geohistorical context: modernity as the modern world-system (Taylor 1999a).

Geohistorical Social Systems

Geohistorical systems are the basic entities of Wallerstein's world-systems analysis. 'World' in this context does not mean global, it means a distinctive world of activities such as the 'Roman world' or 'Inca world' of past systems. Today's 'modern world' is global but has been so only since about 1900; for most of its half-millennium existence it was a 'non-global' social world like all other world-systems. Wallerstein (1979, pp 155–6) also recognizes 'mini-systems', simple systems – bands of about 150 people – lasting for six generations or so. These are the hunter–gatherers who constitute the vast majority of all human existence since the emergence of the human species some 100 000 plus years ago. Most such local entities have long gone and we will never know of them. However, we understand enough to appreciate the fact that these long forgotten ancestors in different parts of world invented forms of non-local exchanges of materials that eventually developed into trade. Although this exchange was quantitatively not important – non-local items in early artefact assemblages usually constituted less than 1 per cent of the total (Gamble 2007, p. 213) – their ultimate effect on the geohistory of humanity is immense. I argue in Part II that in their exchange activities these social agents found themselves on a steep moral and practical learning curve that eventually produced world-systems and, I argue in Part III, culminated in a modern world-system that developed to become global very late in the human calendar. Despite the temporal and immanent importance of mini-systems, Wallerstein focuses upon world-systems, especially to specify the modern world-system as a unique geohistorical social system.

All social systems are *geohistorical* in the sense that they have a beginning (a rise phase), are reproduced (a normal operation phase) and an end (a demise phase). Thus all world-systems emerge in a specific place and time (there is a transition to the social entity), they have a period of successful reproduction (that will typically involve spatial enlargement), and then there is a transition to a successor system (when it no longer exists as a functioning social entity). World-systems have *systemic* properties defined as how they sustain their reproduction. It is these substantive systemic properties that define the nature of a world-system. Wallerstein (1979, pp. 156–64) identifies two basic forms: world-empires and world-economies. The former are large social entities wherein a political superstructure directs much agricultural production of peasants as 'tribute' to a small ruling class. The basic logic of the system is to expand or maintain territory in order to expand or maintain tribute. For Wallerstein, all world-systems prior to the modern world-system have been world-empires. This is what makes the modern world-system unique, the one and only successful world-economy, which emerged in the 'long sixteenth century' (c. 1450–1650). According to Wallerstein (1979), there had been incipient world-economies in the past but they never became fully functioning before succumbing to the superior political forces of neighbouring world-empires. The world-economy type of world-system is defined by its lack of an overarching political superstructure allowing a specific additional manoeuvrability for commercial agents. Taking advantage of this situation the social logic of the system changes to ceaseless capital accumulation. That is to say, accumulation of capital is the behaviour most rewarded within the system. Thus the modern world-system is a capitalist world-economy.

This is not the only way of defining the concepts of world-empire and world-economy. Whereas Wallerstein (1979) treats them as social entities; Braudel (1984) borrows his terminology and reinterprets them as macro-social processes. As processes they can occur simultaneously. Thus he argues that historically Wallerstein's world-empires have been constituted as dominant world-empire processes but with world-economy processes also operating, albeit in a relatively minor way. It is because the latter are subservient or secondary processes that there has been no transition to a fully-fledged world-economy until the modern world-system. But there are interlocking production and trade networks that evolve systemic reproductive properties to materially support the overarching world-empire. Thus for Braudel, the Roman world was constituted as both a world-empire and a world-economy; the latter actually having a wider geographical scope (p. 25). This interpretation is in keeping with Jacobs' notion that all societies encompass both guardian and commercial work. Therefore, I follow Braudel and interpret Wallerstein's two types of world-systems as being guardian-dominated social entities (world-empires), and world-systems where commercial agents are specifically more important (world-economies). This provides a structural answer to what Jacobs (1992) means when she refers to 'our society' with its knowledgeable flexibility. In *Systems of Survival* she describes only contemporary examples of knowledgeable flexibility whereas all examples of rigid caste/class separation of the two syndromes are historical. Thus we can make a further link between Jacobs and Wallerstein. First, world-empires protect the integrity of the moral syndromes through rigid caste/class social frameworks. This separation strategy I call a *modus vivendi*, a separation between guardian and commercial work. Second, there is a *modus operandi* linking guardian and commercial work in the capitalist world-economy, which is Jacobs' reflexive moral flexibility. Hence Jacobs' 'our society' is Wallerstein's modern world-system. It follows that Braudel's (1982) and Arrighi's (1994) careful tracing of city-based 'modern' commercial behaviour from late medieval northern Italy through the Dutch Republic and consequent French and English/British mercantilism to contemporary state concerns for the economic is basically a revolutionary learning process in moving from 'traditional' caste/class syndrome accommodation to the 'modern' reflexive flexibility solution.

However it is important to understand that the rise of modernity is not a case of commercial syndrome replacing guardian syndrome as the dominant ethics and practice: reflexive flexibility does not prioritize the commercial syndrome but brings it into approximate parity of importance with the guardian syndrome in the modern world-system. This has critical implications for comprehending capitalism because the modern world-system is a capitalist world-economy wherein the dominant ideology argues that markets do or should rule. For instance, neoliberal globalization is sometimes interpreted as market-led capitalism winning against 'the state'. However, as we have seen, Jacobs always argues that every society needs both guardian and commercial practices, and today states remain the locus for concentration of governance. Whether this contradicts the existence of a capitalist system depends on how the latter is defined. For Marx, capitalism was always more than economics; it encapsulated power and inevitably involved the state. This view has been more recently reinforced by Braudel (1981) and Wallerstein (1991, p. 202), who place capitalism as 'the enemy of the market'. This is upside down thinking at its very best (p. 207). Remember that Wallerstein defines the capitalist world-economy as a geohistorical system whose social logic rewards ceaseless capital accumulation. The key point is that markets do not maximize profits, monopolies do. Therefore the necessary accumulation to maintain the system has to include guardian practices that facilitate monopolistic tendencies but without the guardians stifling economic growth as they did in world-empires.

Braudel (1981; 1982; 1984) provides the necessary conceptual framework for understanding this compromise of the syndromes. He models society as a three-storey house with distinctive processes at each level. At the ground level there is the material everyday life of the population, on the second level market activities, and capitalism only at the top level. The crucial contrast is between the top two storeys: transparency of markets creating small profits, and the opaque top level where a small privileged group make huge profits through the anti-market practices of corporate monopolies with state connivance. We might call this making profits versus taking profits; put this way the latter is very much guardian practice. The modern result is two structures in 'perpetual struggle with each other' (Wallerstein 1991, p. 203) and, it seems to me, that half a millennium of successful reproduction has justified the perpetual compromise of reflexive flexibility. That is to say, guardian political economy ensures ceaseless capital accumulation as profit taking, while commercial market work ensures economic development though profit making.

Not unreasonably, Wallerstein (1991, p. 215) considers this Braudellian model to be 'a devastating attack' on modern mythologies:

> If the capitalists are the monopolists as opposed to those operating in competitive markets, then the lines of division in reality have been quite different from those to which we are accustomed to thinking. One can trace out multiple forms of monopolistic controls of production or trade or finance. Large plantations are one such form, large trading companies another, transnational corporations a third, state enterprises a fourth. Arrayed in contraposition to them would be the working populations of the world, rural and urban, who inhabit the zone of the material life but who sally forth into the zone of the market to struggle against the power of the monopolists. (p. 215)

But this argument is similarly devastating for an important alternative position that also overturns accepted wisdom. Frank and Gills (1993) have provocatively argued that capitalism is 5000 years old and they provide numerous examples of successful commerce long before the modern world-system. However, the rise of the modern world-system is not just a matter of expanding commerce, it is about a new *modus operandi* in which sizeable portions of a world-economy are transferred to guardian work to generate the capital accumulation required of a capitalist world-economy. Thus the mere existence of general and widespread commerce based on markets should not be confused with capitalism; this has been cogently argued by Sanderson (1995) for Frank and Gills' 5000 years. This argument is elaborated upon in Part II below. This does not deny that wherever there have been markets there will have been tendencies towards monopoly in various forms, but all this economic work will have been secondary to the primary guardian territorial logics of world-empires. It is only with the modern world-system that the struggle between market (commercial syndrome) and anti-market (guardian syndrome) becomes a key continuous element in the reproduction of the system.

Macro-social Change

I am now in a position to specify types of macro-social change. All the social systems identified by Wallerstein are historical systems in the sense that (1) they have a beginning and an end, and (2) they have recognizable ongoing system-wide processes that enable reproduction of the system between the beginning and the end. With just three types of geohistorical social systems this logically generates nine macro-social changes. Within systems, there are three reproductions: how mini-systems, world-empires and world-economies maintain their social structures. Between systems, there are six potential transitions: from mini-system to world-empire and its reverse, from mini-system to world-empire and its reverse, and transitions both ways between the two world-systems. Wallerstein (1979) briefly describes the three reproduction processes but only two of the transitions: from mini-system to world-empire, and world-empire to world-economy. In this he betrays an incipient evolutionary geohistory of increasing system complexity by giving no thought to mini-system into world-economy, and, because he recognizes only one world-economy, there is no historical consideration of world-economy into world-empire. My selection is slightly different; I will consider all nine macro-changes and briefly justify the focus of my upcoming narrative.

Within-system, macro-social change
There are three modes of reproduction:

- Reproduction of mini-systems: Wallerstein (1979, p.155) defines this as a reciprocal-lineage mode of production. These are ancient hunter–gatherer bands that are not equivalent to contemporary hunter–gatherer bands because of different non-local contexts. For the vast majority of human time most mini-systems could only relate to other mini-systems. Such exchanges, that in hindsight are very important for inventing trade, are very different from usually disastrous contact with world-systems. Because we can know little of their reproduction I will not deal much with this macro-social change in my narratives beyond suggesting an initial *modus operandi* between gender-based production (hunting and gathering) and age-based governance (elders).
- Reproduction of world-empires: Wallerstein (1979, p.157) defines this as a redistributive-tributary mode of production. He describes the reproduction as growth of the empire leading 'to the point where the bureaucratic costs of appropriating the surplus outweighed the surplus that could . . . be effectively appropriated, at which point decline and retraction set in' (p.158). Thus the territorial expansion logic of world-empires is limited by their logistics capabilities. Within this reproduction process I will explore how cities fare under fluctuating empires.
- Reproduction of world-economies: these have the potential to overcome territorial logistic limits; in the modern world-system this has resulted in worldwide globality. But reproduction is anything but smooth. In world-economies there are strong tendencies towards

severe ups and downs, economic cycles. These occur because of the uncoordinated nature of markets. In periods of expansion it is in the interest of holders of capital to invest with the collective result of supply outstripping demand. Conversely, in periods of contraction all will want to disinvest creating underproduction. Hence the volatility of perennial cycles in the development of the capitalist world-economy.

Between-systems, macro-social change

There are three pairs of two-way movements:

- Transitions between mini-systems and world-empires: Wallerstein (1979, p. 158) envisages the rise and fall of world-empire as the key process involving 'perpetual incorporation and releasing' of mini-systems that when incorporated 'formed merely one more *situs* out of which tribute was drawn'. This is a relatively simple dual process of conquest and disintegration, which will not feature prominently in my narrative.
- Transitions between mini-systems and world-economies: as noted previously, Wallerstein (1979) does not consider this possibility. In contrast much of my narrative will consider this transition as involving the invention of cities out of hunter–gatherer trading practices. My discussion takes forward Jacobs' (1969) controversial thesis that cities came before, and in fact invented, agriculture thereby enabling city networks to prosper. There are two possible outcomes. First, the incipient new city-based world-economies reach their demise when the sustainability of the new food production gives out. This results in a reversal to hunter–gathering mixed with vestiges of agriculture in a subsistence form. Second, the new world-economy may prosper where the food production is sustainable enabling a different transition to become possible.
- Transitions between world-empires and world-economies: with only one world-economy, Wallerstein (1979, pp. 8–9, 138–50) can only consider the classic case usually referred to as the European 'transition from feudalism to capitalism'. This is also a major part of my narrative but with an emphasis on the role of cities in the transition. In addition, because I have found city-based world-economies before world-empires I have an earlier possible 'reverse' transition to consider: the way in which world-economies created their own guardian destroyers (world-empires) is a fascinating story.

The key point of these two-way transitions is that simple evolutionary paths towards increasing complexity, as implied by Wallerstein (1979) and imbued in much archaeological thinking (Yoffee 2005), is an over-simplification. Macro-social change is itself inherently complex. This can be revealed in several ways, I use the social production of time and space to begin to unravel macro-social change complexities.

TimeSpace Structures

Wallerstein (1991, p. 139) argues that 'time and space are not two separate categories but one, which I shall call TimeSpace'. He invents this integrative concept to distinguish his ideas from the more commonplace 'time–space' that suggests physical location, where time and space are 'just there – enduring, objective, external, unmodifiable' (p. 136). Rather he treats time and space together as intertwined social constructions. They can be considered separately as social times and social spaces for pedagogic reasons but eventually the focus has to be on their inter-relations. And since they are social, the times and spaces in TimeSpace are socially created together by the very agents whose behaviours they ultimately mould and constrain. I will treat TimeSpace at two levels, generic and specific.

Generic TimeSpace across geohistorical systems

Wallerstein's (1991) TimeSpace is built upon Fernand Braudel's (1980) famous identification of three social times distinguished by their time spans as short-term ('eventism'), medium-term (*moyenne durée*) and long-term (*longue durée*). Through their constructions these 'times' encompass diverse outcomes of social behaviour; that is to say they are not just different by their length, they are specifically different substantively. This is evident in Braudel's terminology, which can be translated as episodic history for short-term, cyclical history for medium-term and structural history for long-term. Braudel's purpose in inventing these times was to challenge traditional political history that focused on events and stayed strictly within episodic historical bounds. For Braudel, there was a longer temporal frame that economic historians used in their identification of ups and downs of economic process in cyclical times. And underpinning both the political and economic there was structural time encompassing the everyday work of ordinary people, which seemed changeless whatever was happening in the events and cycles of the other time spans. For Braudel this was the social time most neglected by historians, and appears to be his favourite; that certainly is the case for his intellectual followers: the original French – *longue durée* – has entered the language of academic English. But like Jacobs, Braudel does not allow his personal preference to influence use of his concepts: he insists that historical understanding has to encompass all three time spans. He argues that 'to choose one of these histories to the exclusion of all others' is a 'cardinal error of historiography' (p. 34). However, in practice Braudel does begin his historical texts by focusing on structural time, and I will do this in showing how Wallerstein develops an equivalent TimeSpace.

Wallerstein (1991, p. 142) relates Braudel's structural time to the historical span of a world-system and defines structural space as the spatial scope of the system. The result is a Structural TimeSpace that encompasses the other times:

> Structural TimeSpace is concerned with actual geohistorical social systems. Insofar as they are systems they persist via the cyclical processes that govern them (i.e. in cyclical time). Thus, as long as they persist, they have some features that are unchanging; otherwise, we could not call them systems. But insofar as they are historical, they are constantly changing. They are never the same from one instance to the next (i.e. episodic time). They are changing in every detail, including, of course their spatial parameters. (p. 146, bracketed text added)

Thus *longue durée* is equated with the 'unchanging' aspect of a system leaving the *moyenne durée* to be the product of system development, the historical changes that represent adaptations necessary for reproduction. The latter is therefore identified with cyclical time but this must be problematic for world-empires given the dominance of political processes that generate a social time that will be more episodic in nature. I will develop this theme in discussing the specifics of geohistorical systems below. In his TimeSpace designations Wallerstein (2001) goes on the equate Braudel's two shorter time spans with smaller spatial scales but I will take a different tack in bringing social spaces into the analysis.

I use concepts from the construction of social spaces in the seminal work of Manuel Castells (1996) in which he designates contemporary globalization as 'network society'. In *The Rise of Network Society* he argues that modernity has moved from an industrial age to an informational age in which 'networks constitute the new social morphology of our societies' (p. 469). This 'new spatial logic' (p. 378) is premised on the growth of information and communication technologies that have enabled a network society to supplant industrial society. These two types of society are distinguished by their social spaces: industrial society was created through 'spaces of places' whereas network society is being created by 'spaces of flows'. In his initial description of this succession Castells (1996) implies spaces of flows have today supplanted spaces of places but he later confirmed the two social spaces being constructed simultaneously (Castells 1999) so that the difference between industrial society and network society is about which of the two spatial constructions dominates. Thus contemporary globalization is a period when spaces of flows dominate social reproduction. This opens up historical uses of the concepts as Arrighi (1994, p. 84) suggested in reaction to Castells' (1989) early presentation of the two forms of social space. I follow Arrighi and interpret Castells' social constructions of space as generic.

Work is a social practice in which space facilitates necessary social relations. In spaces of places this means combining temporal simultaneity with spatial contiguity. An example would be the social practices on 'market day' in a 'market place' that enable buyer and seller to meet and conduct their business. In spaces of flows simultaneity and contiguity are separated and the social relations are facilitated through flows. This requires more sophisticated social arrangements involving constructions of trust within networks. In spaces of flows firms need multiple location strategies in order to ensure that flows of capital, commodities and information are reliable. In medieval Europe, for instance, firms operated by having trusted agents (often extended family members) in all major cities where they did business. Today's multiple location firms – transnational corporations – are a critical and necessary feature of globalization (Dicken 2005).

Although I have used commercial work to illustrate the creation of the two spaces above I argue that in practice these spaces are each particularly associated with a different moral syndrome. This is relatively self-evident in both cases. There are spaces of places at the heart of guardian work that, as noted above, Jacobs (1992, p. 29) defined in terms of 'protecting, acquiring, exploiting, administrating, or controlling territories'. This social construction of space is called territoriality and, as described by Sack (1986), it is a way of simplifying space to control it and mould it. As a strategy central to state formation, guardian behaviour primarily produces spaces of places. Similarly, spaces of flows are at the heart of commercial work derived from and premised on trade. This construction of space includes commodity chains, service networks, circuits of capital and other market-related movement. As a strategy central to market formation, commercial behaviour primarily produces spaces of flows. At this point it must be emphasized that in any social world neither space can exist alone – spaces of flows need anchoring in places; spaces of places are reproduced through flows. It is for this reason that these syndrome–space associations only indicate which of the two space construction dominates in a given work type.

I am now in a position to define basic TimeSpace structures in terms of syndrome behaviour. As discussed previously, Braudel's contingent time (episodic history) is the traditional subject matter of political history and therefore I relate it to guardian work; and cyclical time is the temporality of economic history, and results from commercial work. Combining these with the syndrome–space relations above produces two socially constructed structures:

- TimeSpace I is created by guardian practices through the combination of contingent times/spaces of places;
- TimeSpace II is created by commercial practices through the combination of cyclical times/spaces of flows.

I treat this joint Braudel–Castells conceptualization of TimeSpace as generic, a tool to use across geohistory.

Specific TimeSpaces within geohistorical systems

In moving to specific instances of our generic concepts there are two features that have been previously stressed and should always be kept in mind. First, Jacobs' two syndromes are not exclusive; both are always needed in any geohistorical system. Second, the temporal and spatial elements of TimeSpace are not exclusive; Braudel's times always occur simultaneously, and Castells' spaces are always co-present. It follows that linking concepts needs to be rather more subtle than applying the obvious equating of TimeSpace I with world-empires and TimeSpace II with world-economies. As strong associations they provide a starting point for discussion below but ultimately specifics will mess up such neat generics in the actual variety exhibited by the geohistory narratives that follow Part I.

However let me rehearse my generic expectations for both types of geo-historical world-systems. In world-empires TimeSpace I will predominate as this is a guardian-led form of social system. Contingent time means that the periodicity of world-empires will tend towards irregular spans; both empire building and disintegration can be rapid. The reproduction phase between these events can vary immensely and there will always be a parallel tendency for subordinate commercial practices to generate more regular cyclical times but this will be beholden on guardian activities; generally this is unlikely to be clearly discernable. The reproduction phase will consist of territorial expansion and subsequent retraction. Typically this will consist of two territorial types, the imperial centre as land under centralized control, and an imperial edge of separate client states (kingdoms and city-states), who pay irregular tribute to the centre depending on the fluctuating power of the latter. As 'marcher states' these semi-autonomous polities have the ability to take advantage of prolonged weakness in the centre and take it over; this is the relationship between China and its north-west frontier as famously described in Owen Lattimore's (1962) classic work and which has been generalized as a general feature of macro-social change (Mann 1986; Chase-Dunn and Hall 1997; Dodgshon 1998) to be further discussed in Chapter 5.

In the modern world-system TimeSpace II will be much more important so that cyclical time deriving from commercial practices will be much more important and therefore clearly discernable. Numerous such cycles have been postulated and measured and for the level of analysis I am deploying it is the longer cycles that are of particular relevance: Kondratieff cycles of about 50 years' duration and hegemonic cycles of 100–150 years' duration. There have been just three of the latter and these are directly implicated in the reproduction of the system (Wallerstein 1984; Arrighi 1994). The Dutch in the seventeenth century, the British from the late eighteenth and nineteenth centuries, and the US in the twentieth century, are the hegemonic states wherein new 'prime modernities' are created in the development of the capitalist world-economy: mercantile, industrial and consumer modernities respectively (Taylor 1996b; 1999a). These modernities were created in city-rich dynamic regions of these states, in Holland, northern Britain and the American 'manufacturing belt'. The commercial practices within these three states were so successful that they were emulated in rival states. This city-led emulation is a core-making process and the sum of the states where economic copying is successful, plus the hegemon, constitutes the changing core of the world-economy at hegemonic times. Unequal exchange with the rest of the world-economy generates a core–periphery structure: the economy becomes one huge functional region with value flowing from periphery to core. The result is what Frank (1969) famously termed the 'development of underdevelopment' in the periphery in contrast with the development in the core. This exploitative spatial relation is perhaps the aspect of Wallerstein's world-systems analysis for which it is most known, especially by those who would dismiss it as superficial. For this reason I will describe Wallerstein's contribution to understanding modern spatial structures in a little more detail.

The first point to make is that core and periphery are specified as processes; they occur simultaneously in different balances in various places. Thus core is where core processes dominate, periphery is where peripheral processes dominate. Even hegemonic states had their peripheral regions: northern and eastern provinces in the seventeenth-century Dutch Republic, western Ireland and highland Scotland in the nineteenth-century United Kingdom, and the American South in twentieth-century US. Wallerstein adds the category 'semi-periphery' to describe states where the two processes are evenly balanced; these are able to marshal their political power at strategic times when the core is weak so as to upgrade their position in the world-economy. But this is just one instance of a perennial struggle between commercial and guardian processes in the modern world-system. Wallerstein (1979, p. 162) describes the situation thus:

> The operation of the system, once established, revolved around two basic dichotomies. One was the dichotomy of class, bourgeois versus proletarian . . . the other basic dichotomy was the spatial hierarchy of economic specialization, core versus periphery . . . The genius, if you will, of the capitalist system, is the interweaving of these two channels of exploitation which overlap but are not identical and create cultural and political complexities (and obscurities) of the system. Among other things, it has made it possible to respond to the politico-economic pressures of cyclical economic crises by rearranging spatial hierarchies without significantly impairing class hierarchies.

Of course, the two dichotomies intersect as 'channels of exploitation' in cities: the core is a city-rich zone in the capitalist world-economy and the bourgeoisie are inherently urban (derived from burgesses as city dwellers). However, modern class conflict has been largely fought out within states, of which more in the next section. The states themselves constitute an inter-state system of sovereign territories, the patchwork geography that we all know as the world political map. For Wallerstein (1979) it is this unique divided sovereignty, in contrast to single sovereignty in world-empires, which enables a manoeuvrability of capital essential for economic expansion: spaces of flows circumvents spaces of places.

Creating conceptual toolkits for social agents and social structures still does not exhaust our geohistorical research needs. Cities and states feature prominently in the previous listings of reproductions and transitions and we need conceptual toolkits to handle them. As social institutions they act as intermediaries between agents and structures; they provide the context through which the two previous levels of analysis are articulated.

GEOHISTORICAL TANGO: A CITIES/STATES TOOLKIT

My argument is a spatial one; I ground Jacobs' syndromes through their spatialities as cities and states. All social institutions occupy space but, as the previous discussion has shown, cities and states are different because they are constituted by the spaces they occupy. Also, it has been suggested throughout this chapter that cities will bear a heavy theoretical weight in my narratives. Therefore I will come to cities second in this section; they are privileged to be the final link in my toolkits reflecting their critical status.

Treating cities and states as social institutions means conceptualizing them as processes. Instead of describing their content, cities and states as aggregates of things, I focus on their dynamics, the aggregations of key behaviours in the work through which they are reproduced. Collectively these define two ongoing macro-processes that are cities and states. Thus we are led back to moral syndromes and TimeSpaces to show these two institutions are so very different. This can be immediately appreciated by exploring their relative longevities. As a general rule cities are much older than their states: London is much older than the UK, New York is older than the US, Paris is older than the Republic of France, Berlin is older than Federal Germany, Beijing is older than the People's Republic of China, and so on. There are, of course, new cities younger than their states, sometimes specially built capital cities like Washington and Canberra, or cities in the final settlement expansion of the modern world-system, like Chicago and Los Angeles, but the geohistorical evidence suggests these cities will outlive their current states. Although we tend to think of states as very stable – that's what the static world political map implies – this is far from the truth. As institutions subject to contingent times based upon guardian behaviour, states come and go. In contrast, the elimination of cities has become increasingly rare. Great cities of the past such as Babylon and Carthage are no longer with us and there has been a whole archaeological industry searching for 'lost cities', but it is a long time since a great city has been destroyed once and for all. Through sieges, massacres, mass lootings, and bombings, cities seem nearly always to come back. Their longevity is ultimately related to cyclical times and commercial behaviour; they get larger and sometimes shrink somewhat but rarely disappear. To summarize, states are relatively transient and cities are largely resilient. This is clear from a broad geohistorical perspective but the interesting point is the ongoing relation between transient states and resilient cities. It is this that specifies my geohistorical tango; an inter-relation both complementary – they need each other – and antagonistic – their reasons-to-be are so very different. To understand this provocative institutional dancing requires careful consideration of each partner.

There are, of course, massive literatures on both subjects; my conceptual toolkits are highly selective in content as I attempt to provide vital ideas to support my narratives.

States as process
I introduced the state in Chapter 1 as a spatial organization that was rarely problematized in social science studies: the territorialization of state power was taken for granted so that the state/space relation remained typically unexamined across the social sciences. This is beginning to change as indicated by an important collection of papers that specifically address this neglected relationship (Brenner et al. 2003). *Space/State: a Reader* provides a range of approaches of varying sophistication. However the 18

selected studies are restricted to modern states; there are historical papers but none extend back beyond the sixteenth century. My needs are generic; as well as the sovereign territorial states of the modern era, I am interested in other state forms such as city-states and large land empires.

States are typically treated as entities with concomitant description of (sometimes apparently static) functions and practices. But I will focus on states as process. The state is a governance process that generates and reproduces a territorial centralization of power. This is guardian work that generates Castells' (1996) spaces of places, a world of insides and outsides, of boundaries and frontiers. It is a process that can be rudely interrupted: it is the zero-sum games of guardian work that creates dangerous contingent times. In this political world, a single event can change everything. For instance, losing a battle may have the extreme result of eliminating a state: the classic case is the fall of Constantinople in 1453 and the consequent end of the Byzantium empire. Alternatively, for the state process to continue it is necessary to exert prowess, violence or the threat of violence. This is Max Weber's (1978) famous monopoly of legitimate violence as a key characteristic of the state. Such activity may be the ultimate basis of state power but it is only a part of state process, just one precept in Jacobs' guardian moral syndrome. To develop a broader understanding of the process I use James Scott's (1998) *Seeing like a State*, an analysis of states as utilizing 'radically simplified designs for social organization' (p. 7).

Scott's (1998, p. 1) initial concern is to understand why states invariably treat 'people who move around' so badly. He lists those who 'have always been a thorn in the side of states' as follows: slash-and-burn farmers, nomads, pastoralists, hunter–gatherers, Gypsies, vagrants, homeless people, itinerants and runaway slaves and serfs. In other words, states have problems dealing with people whose lives produce spaces of flows. The typical policy solution is to disrupt the flows, make them stay put through sedentarization. Note, however, that Scott does not include long-distance merchants in his list, presumably because their wealth usually precludes them from becoming obvious victims of states. Nevertheless, they too have a history of undermining state policies. Here the policy to control the flows has included tolls, tariffs, protectionism and even strict autarchy. The key point is that spaces of flows are more difficult to manage than spaces of places. Smuggling is ubiquitous – today it is called transfer pricing, a key instrument in the power of large corporations. Hence movement is a generic problem for states as territorial constellations of power.

For Scott (1998, p. 2), 'legibility is a central problem of statecraft'; the more legible a society, the better a state can carry out its 'classic' functions of 'taxation, conscription and prevention of rebellion'. Quite simply, for these activities, spaces of places are more legible than spaces of flows. To make society legible, states simplify the situation through classification and measurement. Such abstraction creates 'social simplifications' (p. 3) of 'facts' that remain unexamined. People know their place through hierarchy, tradition and exclusiveness and accordingly behave obediently and with fortitude (*à la* Jacobs' guardian syndrome) to facilitate stable rule. The 'facts' are characterized in five ways: they are purposive, documented, static, aggregated and standardized (p. 80). Furthermore, under the right conditions, spaces of places can be redesigned in the image of the state itself as ordered and regimented. Spatially this simplification takes geometric forms such as the Roman Empire's network of straight roads and grid-iron cities, Post-Revolutionary France's equal-size 'hexagonal' departments, the straight-line boundaries common to European and European-settler imperialisms in the Americas, Africa and Australia, and the planning of 'high modernist' cities like Brasília (Taylor 1999b; Scott 1998). Envisaging cities in states as 'national urban hierarchies', as described in Chapter 1, is another manifestation of 'state simplification'.

It is important not to equate this inherent process of state simplification as 'simple-minded'. In their control and manipulation states can be quite sophisticated – we still use the adjective 'byzantine' to indicate complex intrigue as originally found in ruling circles in Constantinople. But outputs from this political process suggest two related ways in which ruled society is made simple: first, by employing a synoptic overview; and second, by focusing on the general to the detriment of the detail (Scott 1998, p. 81). But we all know that the devil is in the detail. Thus are states destined to fail in grandiose schemes based upon social simplification because they ignore 'essential features of any, real functioning social order' (p. 6). Whatever states have in mind, societies remain very complex and function only on the basis of myriad 'informal practices and improvisations'. It is 'the indispensable role of practical knowledge, informal processes, and improvisation in the face of unpredictability' that makes imposition of all state planning so problematic.

The ability of states to make their societies legible has increased massively through the history of the modern world-system (Giddens 1985; Scott 1998, p. 77). However, although techniques have become more sophisticated, political motives are much the same: 'appropriation, control, and manipulation . . . remain the most prominent' (Scott 1998, p. 79). Of course, the differences over time are in what is attempted. For instance, Braudel (1972b, pp. 308–9), after listing the fall of several cities to territorial expansion of states in early modern Europe, makes essentially the same point as Scott on limitations of state power:

> The victorious states could not take control of and responsibility for every-
> thing. They were cumbersome machines inadequate to handle their new super-
> human tasks. The so-called *territorial economy* of textbook classification could
> not stifle the so-called *urban economy*. The cities remained the driving forces.
> States that included these cities had to come to terms with them and tolerate
> them. The relationship was accepted the more naturally since even the most
> independent cities needed the use of the space belonging to territorial states.

In contrast, under the influence of 'high modernism' states have been much
less modest (Scott 1998, p. 343). So much so that states have impinged on
economic processes at historically unprecedented levels. These count as
'monstrous hybrids' in Jacobs' (1992) scheme of things: as noted earlier
she gives the example of the USSR planning itself into oblivion. Scott provides detailed exposition of the specific planned tragedies that were Soviet
collectivization and Tanzanian 'village-ization'.

But it is the democratic liberal state that has come to be recognized as
the authentic modern state, combining a democratic politics with a free
market economy (Taylor 1999a) as famously celebrated by Fukuyama's
(1992) thesis of today's capitalist liberal democracies representing the
'end of history'. In the final chapter I will suggest that these states are
possibly leading us to the end of human history but not at all in the way
Fukuyama suggests. For the moment let us show how this very specific
state form conforms to Scott's (1998) simplification imperative. First note
that modern democracy is wholly different from classical Greek direct
democracy; in our democratic states government is formed using indirect
democracy, we vote for representatives to make political decisions. And
to avoid the cacophony of voices that even this restriction might produce,
representatives are typically presented to the voters as political parties.
This is what Schattschneider (1960, p. 59) famously called 'the great act of
organization' that reduces alternatives 'to the extreme limit of simplification': instead of voters having to investigate every candidate's position on
a range of policies, they just have to choose a party and its given package
of policies. And finally the election result is a zero-sum game; to form a
government you need to obtain more than 50 per cent of the votes (in most
presidential elections) or more than 50 per cent of the representatives (in
most parliamentary elections). Ultimately, as a guardian process there are
only winners and losers, all else is academic.

Of course, such a simple process of either/or outcomes can be considered very dangerous: what if the voters are swayed to support illiberal
politicians? Wallerstein (2011) has provided a very convincing argument
on the development of what he calls the 'centrist liberal state' as a means
of handling the radical potential of citizenship and its implication of
equality of rights deriving from the French Revolution. The means was

to design a new politics based upon a series of simple binaries starting with citizen versus non-citizen (p. 144), specify the former as active versus passive citizen (p. 145) before diffusing this method of oppositions widely across political issues; he lists the following: bourgeois versus proletarian; man versus women; adult versus minor; breadwinner versus housewife; majority versus minority; black versus white; European versus non-European; educated versus ignorant, skilled versus unskilled; specialist versus amateur; scientist versus layman; high culture versus low culture; heterosexual versus homosexual; normal versus abnormal; able-bodied versus disabled; civilized versus barbarian (p. 146). The result is an obfuscation of citizen rights:

> The great socially unifying concept of the citizen thus led to the formalization of multiple cross-cutting binary categories and to the binary tension of political life – the split between right and left, the Party of Order and the Party of Movement – a split that centrist liberalism would devote all its efforts to rendering meaningless. (p. 156)

To be successful this particular process of state formation requires bringing to the fore identity politics in which the locus of power defines the politics:

> The nineteenth century saw the creation of our entire contemporary conceptual apparatus of identities. . . . The identities of the powerful were the most urgent. (Who had the right to rule?) They were, however, relational – that is, they identified not only who they were but who they were not. In creating their own identities, the powerful thereby created the identities of others. (p. 271)

This elite management of mass politics is an example of Schattschneider's (1960) argument that democracies house only 'semi-sovereign peoples' because key conflicts are 'organized out of politics'. In this case the agenda setting reaches to the heart of the politics by defining oppositional political identities as residual categories, leaving no ambiguity as to where the power lies:

> The concept of the bourgeoisie preceded and provoked the concept of proletarian/worker. The concept of White preceded and provoked the concept of Black/Oriental/non-White. The concept of the masculine male preceded and provoked the concept of the feminine female. The concept of citizen preceded and provoked the concept of alien/immigrant. The concept of specialist preceded and provoked the concept of the masses. The concept of the West preceded and provoked the concept of the 'rest'. . . . Of course, all these categories were ancient, but they had not been previously defining concepts of one's identity . . . The new categories were the mark of the new geoculture of the modern world-system. (Wallerstein 2011, p. 217)

The centrist liberal state may not mark the end of history but it has been a great survivor within the inter-state system where it has dominated the politics of the core-zone for about two centuries. For much of the twentieth century this 'moderate' state formation was abetted by the rise of consumer modernity as the hallmark of American hegemony. The consequent rise of the middle class as an acquisitive majority, demographically and democratically, in the core-zone further depressed popular radicalism. The end result appears to be a world led by liberal states that are simply not up to confronting the radical challenge of planetary climatic change in the twenty-first century; this theme will dominate the final chapter.

It should be noted that the relative moderation of democratic liberal states domestically – only sporadic and limited use of coercion – does not extend to foreign policy. In mainstream international relations studies (IR) modern states are not treated as being very different from aggressive states of all ages. In fact, the discipline of IR traces its origins back to Thucydides, a classical Greek founding father, to focus on war and the preparation for war (Steans et al. 2010, p. 55). This dominant 'realist' school of thought (p. 53) also subscribes to Scott's (1998) statecraft as simplification, in this case treating the complex political worlds of competitive states in much the same way as we might describe schoolyard squabbles: the enemy of my enemy is my friend. This common failure to count to more than three can result in some curious war alliances, the most well known being in World War II when liberal democratic states allied with the Soviet Union to combat Nazism. One more recent episode of ideological acrobatics was the alliance operating against the national liberation government of Angola in the 1980s. Supported by the Soviet Union and aided by Cuban troops this politics brought forth a most unholy opposition: Reagan's democratic America, apartheid South Africa and Communist China were hardly ideological bedfellows! The record of democratic liberal states certainly suggests that making the outside world legible – making policy by simplifying – appears to be generic. And this reflects back into domestic politics. For instance, the early twenty-first-century anti-war protests targeted US imperialism and included both progressive liberals and reactionary Islamists. In this case the enemy-of-my-enemy process allowed a blind eye to be cast over narrow misogynist and homophobic views in cosmopolitan London as long as those holding them were anti-American (Cohen 2007).

Whatever the control and coercive abilities of the states, the geohistorical results are relatively simple spaces of places. States are about boundaries or frontiers defining dual social spaces; concretely and figuratively expressed by walls to delimit insiders and outsiders. These occurred within cities as ghettoes for minority ethnicities or stranger traders; around cities to keep out noxious people and production, and at a greater imperial scale as with Chinese and Roman walls to separate the civilized from barbarians. In the modern world-system border controls around sovereign states to manage movement of foreigners and their production (trade) are functionally walls. It is this inherent simplicity of practice and representation that makes states relatively transient, vulnerable to zero-sum guardian games. And all this simplistic ruling and fighting occurs in complex worlds of myriad social relations, not least commercially centred on cities. In my analyses in subsequent chapters I follow Monica Smith (2005; 2007) in her demand to interpret and represent states through complex spaces of flows rather than simple homogeneous spaces.

Cities as Process I: Two 'Master Economic Processes'

In the modern world we are used to thinking about economic process occurring at the state-scale as indicated by the concept of 'national economy'. This is used to describe the sum of economic practices that take place within a sovereign state jurisdiction, hence 'British economy', 'Italian economy' and so on. But to Jacobs (1984) these 'economies' are myths. The familiar spatial congruence between economics and politics, as discussed in Chapter 1, is very specific to the modern world-system (and possibly early city-states), as subsequent narratives will describe. To be sure territories and their boundaries are vital for accounting and collecting state resources in the form of taxes and tariffs but this does not mean simple exchequer realms constitute functioning economies. All historical states have used territory and boundary to fill their coffers but non-modern ones never thought they were managing an economy. Jacobs (1984) is particularly clear on this. She dismisses the idea that 'economies' are co-terminus with states as 'the old mercantilist tautology', an error that afflicts all contemporary schools of economics (p. 31). For Jacobs, states are essentially 'political and military entities' (p. 31) and 'are composed of grab bags of very different economies' within their political boundaries (p. 32). In contradiction, through 'looking at the real economic world' Jacobs (1984) finds that 'cities are unique in their abilities to shape and reshape the economies of other settlements' (p. 32) and therefore it is cities that are the 'primary economic organs' (p. 6).

Jacobs (1969) describes the city/economy link as follows:

> Economic life develops by grace of innovation; it expands by grace of import replacing. These two master economic processes are closely related, both being functions of city economies. (p. 39)

These processes link together two levels of analysis. First, there is the city or city-region in which a local economy operates. This is where the innovation and import replacement takes place. Second, there is the network of cities through which the effects of innovation and import replacement reverberate:

> A city does not grow by trading only with its rural hinterland. A city seems always to have implied a group of cities, in trade with one another. (p. 35)

From these basic propositions Jacobs builds a whole theory of economic development. Or as she more eloquently puts it, it is 'the little movements in the hubs' (the cities) that 'turn the great wheels of economic life' (the city network) (p. 121). These internal and external relations of cities have long been recognized, before and after Jacobs' (1969) work, as being necessarily linked (e.g. from Harris and Ullman (1945) through Berry (1964) and Amin and Thrift (1992) to Bathelt et al. (2004)), but they have been theorized in two largely separate sets of literature. Jacobs (1969; 1984) is the key urban theorist appearing in both literatures (Krugman 1995; Taylor 2004): the beauty of her approach is that she tightly integrates these two strands of work theoretically: agglomeration/clusters and network/ connectivities activities are combined. This is what I term 'city-ness' to emphasize that I am dealing with a process. I will describe Jacobs' seminal contribution to economic development in three steps: first, describing city externalities through agglomeration effects; second, outlining city network externalities through connectivity effects; and third, looking betwixt city networks for dependency effects.

City externalities: agglomeration effects
There is a growing literature in urban economics on agglomeration effects (Fujita and Thisse 2002), which are sometimes called 'Jacobs' externalities'; in this section I return to basics and outline this city process as described by Jane Jacobs (1969; 1984; 2000). Externalities are economic processes that originate beyond the market. They are not initially the product of a supply-and-demand relation; rather they result in new demands and thereby create new markets. In this way the economy grows in a manner that, following Jacobs (2000) I will call development. Development has been facilitated to a large degree by urban population concentrations. As Glaeser (2011, p. 247) tells it: 'Cities enable collaboration, especially the joint production of knowledge that is mankind's most important creation'. Such knowledge-rich milieus create city externalities, an agglomeration effect based upon the clustering of people and their ideas. Glaeser claims this process 'can have magical consequences' (p. 247), and Jacobs

(1969) shows how you can apparently get 'something for nothing' in cities as process.

Both of Jacobs' master economic processes are implicated in generating development. The best way to start to understand how this can happen is to identify two types of work, each of which generates quite different types of economic growth. Old work is constituted by existing jobs that define the division of labour in a city economy at a given point in time. The relation to economic growth is as follows. If a factory in the city doubles its production, resulting in doubling jobs in both the factory and with suppliers, the economy will have become larger. But, for Jacobs (2000, p. 37), this does not qualify as economic development. This is because the composition of the economy remains the same: the division of labour has not changed. For this to happen there has to be new work, not just additional jobs but additional different jobs. It is new work that changes the division of labour through a greater diversity of jobs creating development as a more complex economy. And this is where the master economic processes enter the story: both innovation and import replacing are sources of new work.

Innovations create new work that is often derived from old work as spin-offs from existing production (Jacobs 1969, pp. 53–5). In this way old work is important as the 'parent work' of new work derived from innovation (p. 59). In this context agglomeration effects occur broadly in relation to the size of a city for, as Jacobs tells it, 'the greater the sheer number and varieties of divisions of labor already achieved in an economy, the greater the economy's inherent capacity for adding still more kinds of goods and services' (p. 59). She introduces the process using the example of brassiere manufacture, a New York innovation of the 1920s, whose parent (old) work was dressmaking (p. 51). This innovation solved a fashion problem of making the bodies of clients fit better into new dresses. Such innovations are typically found in cities where there exists much potential parent work, where it is commonplace for problems to arise that require solutions, where there are myriad existing services to support new work, and where the population incorporates myriad potential entrepreneurs. Glaeser (2011, p. 8) neatly sums up this process: 'For centuries, innovations have spread from person to person across crowded city streets'.

Jacobs (1969, pp. 63–8) introduces import replacement through the example of bicycle manufacture in late nineteenth-century Tokyo (p. 63). Following the opening of Japan's economy bicycles became very popular imports and initially local repair shops were set up to service the new consumers. From this simple beginning some of these shops converted into bicycle manufacturers who could undercut import prices and therefore replace bicycle imports. Jacobs (2000, pp. 73–7) argues that this process is always more than just imitation; the key is improvization whereby local entrepreneurs creatively customize production to local conditions.

The end result of both innovation and import replacement is new work, which means an addition of job categories to the urban division of labour. In other words, the city economy becomes more diverse. Vibrant cities experience these master processes and thereby diversity becomes the hallmark of their economies. For Jacobs (2000, p. 37) it is this increasing diversity of cities that defines economic development. She sees this as a qualitative difference: the very nature of the economy is changing. This is the way Jacobs distinguishes between development creating more complex economic life and the simple quantitative economic expansion of old work described earlier.

But the two master processes do not work in the same way to generate development. Innovation is a process that creates new work that grows the economy through an export-multiplier effect (Jacobs 1969, pp. 137–40). This is the way that:

> each additional job created by a city's export work adds other jobs in the city's local economy, to supply and serve the growing numbers of workers and their families. And there may be more work to be done . . . supplying goods and services to producers of the growing export work itself. This growth in the local economy is possible because growing export work earns more imports for the city. (p. 137)

Hence a reciprocating system of expansion is generated through increased exports producing a larger local economy beyond just the extra export production. The result is economic development based upon a relatively slow growth process.

In contrast, import replacement 'is apt to cause cities to grow explosively' (Jacobs 1969, p. 146). Import replacement means that the city's exports can 'earn' new imports in lieu of those being replaced. In other words, import replacement inevitably leads to import shifting away from what is replaced to a different array of imports. These new imports are for additional local consumption. Thus, Jacobs (1969, p. 161) argues:

> Just as export growth creates a multiplier effect, so do replacement of imports. But there is a vital difference between the two effects. . . . the multiplier effect from import replacing is far more potent from the multiplier effect from the growth of exports, because all shifted imports go to swell the local economy. An equivalent amount of imports earned by export growth do not.

The result is economic development based upon a rapid, indeed 'explosive', growth process.

Jacobs (1969, p. 150) describes import replacement as 'a process of immense, even awesome, economic force'. She makes three critical claims. First, import replacement 'enables cities to capture new imports *without drawing upon payments for exports*' (Jacobs 2000, p. 78, italics in the original). This appears to be 'impossible' because a city receives something for nothing (p. 78). I call this the import bonus claim. Second, and as a result of the above, the city economy is 'not only larger absolutely but also *larger in proportion to its exports and imports*' (Jacobs 1969, p. 161, italics in the original). The general result is that the larger the city (more import replacement episodes), the more self-sufficient it is. I call this the city resilience claim and it will be an important argument for the final chapter of the book. Third, the world-economy as a whole is enlarged because there is 'expansion in the sum total of all economic activity' (p. 167). This is because when the individual city economy grows, 'as far as the rest of the world is concerned, its total economic activity (has not) diminished' (p. 148). In this argument import replacement is identified as the 'chief means' (p. 148) or 'chief cause' (p. 167) of growth in a world-economy of multiple cities. I call this the world development claim. These claims will be illustrated using the simplest of diagrammatic sketches.

To facilitate the illustration I draw upon Jacobs' (2000) restatement of economic development as an ecological process. In this work she espouses an 'energy-flow hypothesis of economic expansion' (p. 62) that treats settlements as constituted by three flows: in-flows, through-flows and out-flows. In ecology, complexity is determined by the through-flow, what happens within the conduit of energy flow that is the eco-system. The limiting cases in the natural world are barren deserts and dense rainforests: in the former the energy enters and leaves with little activity in between; in the latter there are innumerable activities in the conduit to multiply the energy in-flow in myriad ways to create immensely complex eco-systems. Jacobs argues that cities equate to rainforests; they are settlements where economic processes are multiplied in the urban conduit to create unique levels of social complexity (p. 61). An important corollary of this position is that it goes against what is common sense and general economic understanding that the growth of economies of settlements derives from 'competitively successful export work' (p. 49). The latter is the goal of innovation promotion. But in the eco-system energy flow hypothesis, exports as out-flows are 'discharged energy' that simply cannot be the 'driving energy' (p. 52). It is this reappraisal of the importance of exports that lies behind Jacobs' three crucial claims for import replacement.

Using this ecological approach I will show different types of settlement within a world-economy and indicate the uniqueness of cities as vehicles for economic development. The argument is made through five diagrams, three non-city situations that do not generate development and two city situations showing innovation and import replacement processes. In each diagram there is a settlement as an inner circle encompassed by the world-economy represented by an outer circle. Arrows indicate exports (out-flows), imports (in-flows) and flows within the settlement (through-flows). The economic process consists of two components, production and consumption, in both the settlement and outside economy; they are specifically identified within the settlement as 'P' for production and 'C' for consumption. Each arrow is a process incorporating three economic activities, production at its origin, distribution in its stem, and consumption at its head. Production includes all goods and services in a commodity chain that are produced from raw materials to retailing; distribution includes all the logistics of getting goods and services from production to consumption; and consumption includes consumption by producers (for raw materials, business services) as well as retail consumption for sustaining the population. Thus each arrow represents three units of economic activity. For the three non-city cases I show basic economic processes by indicating adjustments from an initial state to an outcome state. The two city diagrams have an additional development stage between the initial and outcome states. The diagrams therefore have two purposes: to illustrate how cities have different effects on economic change compared to other settlements, and how the two master economic processes differ from one another in their effects. In discussion of the latter, I will indicate how Jacobs' three crucial claims for import replacement are supported.

The simplest case is a settlement with a basic subsistence economy (production equals consumption), where there are no flows in or out. Jacobs (1984, pp. 124–9) describes such settlements as 'by-passed places'. Of course, nowhere actually experiences no change whatsoever and in the actual example she uses, the isolated settlement is actually regressing as old work skills are being lost with no means of replenishment (p. 127). This is shown in Figure 2.1(a) where there is a reduction in the size of the economy (i.e. from six economic units to three).

Economic growth begins with outside links and Figure 2.1(b) represents the opposite of a subsistence economy, one totally dependent on the outside world. This is a settlement with outside flows but no flows within the settlement. In the real world, company towns can approach this situation; for instance a town on the edge of a conifer forest employing people in a large paper mill that exports all its production while simultaneously importing all its subsistence and raw material needs. Thus in Figure 2.1(b) the economy initially 'earns' two units of consumption from its two exported units of production. When the economy expands, the additional old work produces an extra export unit that earns another unit of import

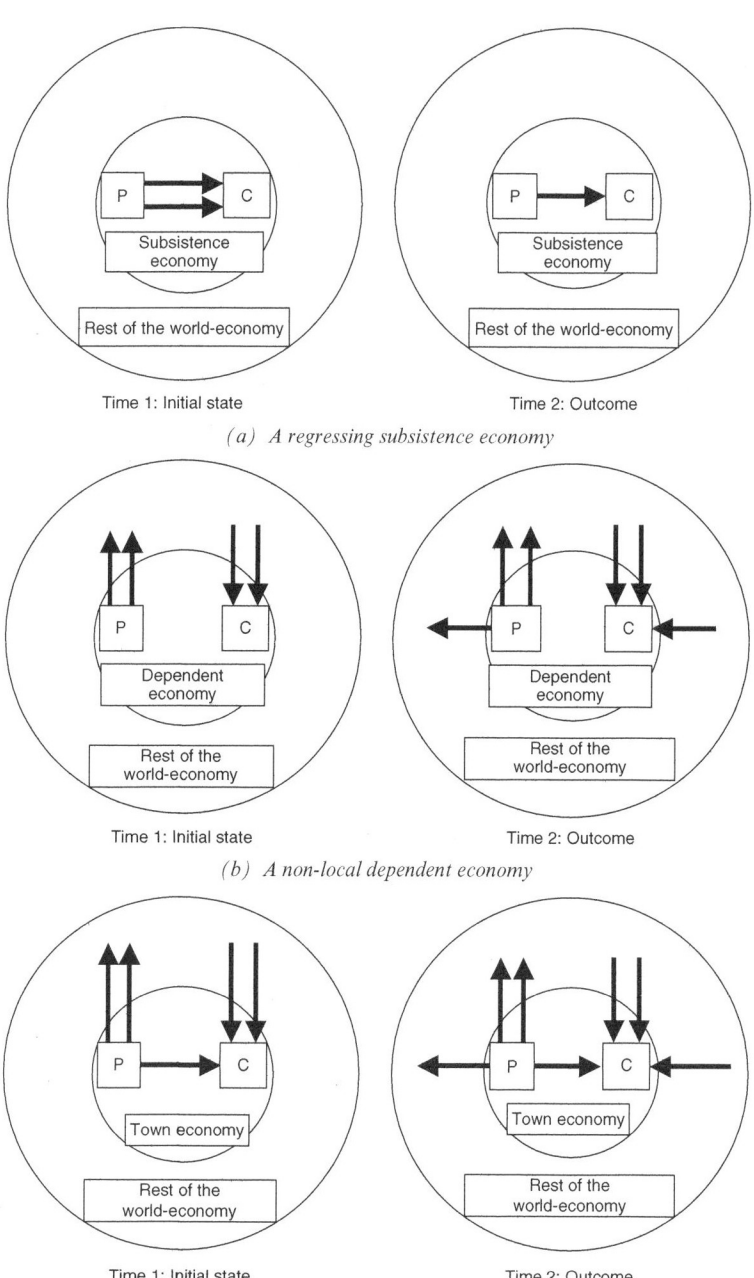

(a) A regressing subsistence economy

(b) A non-local dependent economy

(c) A town economy

Figure 2.1   Non-growth economic processes

for consumption to feed the extra workers. The combined local economy and the enveloping world-economy expand (from 12 to 18 units) but only through old work. This type of economic growth involves no interactions in the urban conduit and the settlement remains a simple economy solely dependent on the outside world. Such settlements are only likely to be sustained to grow into large places with guardian intervention based upon non-market considerations. The Soviet-era cities in the Arctic Circle producing mineral raw materials to keep the USSR self-sufficient constitute the largest class of such 'artificial' urban dependences.

The settlement depicted in Figure 2.1(c) is a much more common occurrence. Here there is the addition of a throughput flow whereby local production contributes to local consumption. This is typical of small urban places such as market towns where, say, some food or raw material from its local hinterland is consumed. I call this a 'town economy' because this local throughput is not linked to the larger outside flows. Thus when there is expansion in production for export, the total economy grows from 15 units to 21 but again this is only due to additional old work. This creates more exports earning more imports, but with no effect on the throughput. That is to say, the economy stays simple in structure – no change in division of labour – despite the increase in size of the overall economy.

In the two diagrams in Figure 2.2 I introduce Jacobs' master economic processes into the argument. The two diagrams depict city economies and in each case the initial phase is the same as for the town economy in Figure 2.1(c). This is to facilitate comparisons. However in Figure 2.2 both diagrams have an additional development stage. Also because I will be comparing change within and beyond each city economy, I divide each distribution stem that connects the city economy to the rest of the world-economy to count one half an economic unit in each sphere.

In Figure 2.2(a) I have included the first of Jacobs' master economic processes, innovation. This is the first condition that introduces new work (indicated as a '+' added to P) and this has two direct effects. First, through solving a local problem the new work generates a more complex division of labour, and the additional production is consumed locally. Thus the throughput in Figure 2.2(a) in the development stage is enhanced. Second, the innovation is not relevant only to the local market, but also new production can be exported as shown in the outcome in Figure 2.2(a). Thus this process creates both extra throughput and an export multiplier effect with increased exporting earning extra imported consumption.

Therefore in total, the city economy as has increased from nine economic units (summing from the Initial State in Figure 2.2(a): a throughput (3) + two other productions (2) + two other consumptions (2) + four half-units in external relations (2)) to 15 units (summing from the

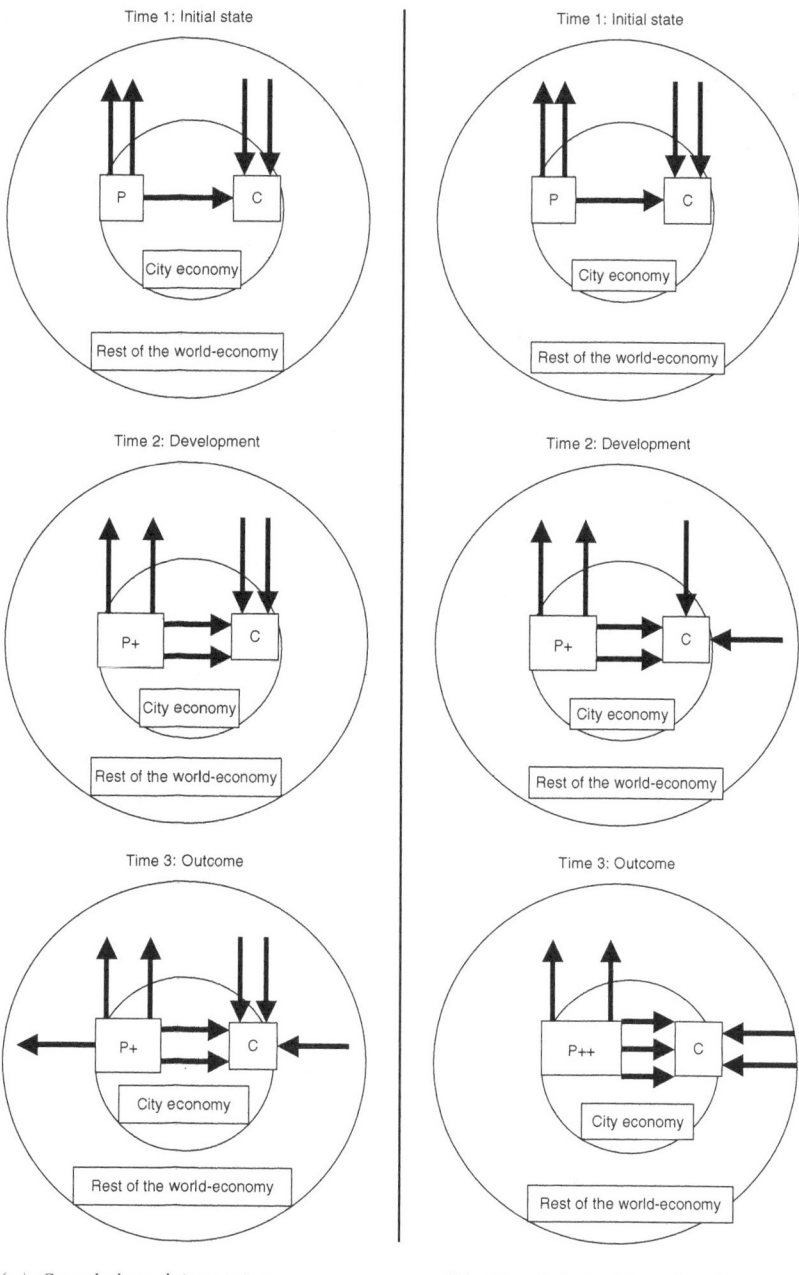

(a) *Growth through innovation*   (b) *Growth through import replacement*

Figure 2.2   Growth economic processes

Outcome: two throughputs (6) + three other productions (3) + three other consumptions (3) + six half-units in external relations (3)). Similarly, the rest of the world-economy has increased from six to nine units. The key point here is that both parts of the economy have grown resulting in a larger world-economy overall from 15 units (9 + 6) to 24 (15 + 9).

In Figure 2.2(b) import replacement occurs. In the development stage one of the import arrows is relocated into the conduit so that at first the city economy has expanded and diversified (new work). However, despite this relocation from the rest of the world-economy, the latter is *not* made smaller because production exports continue to 'earn' equivalent imports for consumption, they have just shifted. But in this case the outcome is dynamic, it is a complex spiral, not simply the next stage. Another import replacement has occurred that will allow a further import shift beginning a spiral of rapid economic development. The key ingredient that makes this possible is the increasingly complex division of labour (new work) that constitutes human capital – the 'skills, information, and experience' that are human potentialities 'cultivated' within the city (Jacobs 2000, p. 56). This is the city acting like a dense rainforest through agglomeration effects: 'In the conduit, human labor and human capital transform the inputs – take them apart, recombine them, pass them around, recycle them, and by all these means stretch imports received into the conduit' (Jacobs 2000, p. 56).

Counting the economic change in Figure 2.2(b) enables us to explicate Jacobs' three critical claims for the import replacement process.

- The import bonus claim: exports remain constant throughout the process while new imports are introduced through import shifting. As cities grow they are able to draw in completely new imports without increasing their exports.
- The city resilience claim: the conduit between P and C has increased three-fold while the number of connections to the rest of the world-economy has stayed the same. As cities grow they become more self-sufficient.
- The world development claim: the city economy has grown from nine economic units to 15, while the rest of the world-economy stays at six units; therefore the total economic activity has increased from 15 to 21 units. As cities grow so to does the world-economy as a whole, that is to say city growth is complementary: it is not a competitive zero-sum game.

For Jacobs (1969, p. 20) a city is defined as any place where new work is added to old work and this includes both innovation and import replacement. The diagrams in Figure 2.2(b) show how important import replacement is, but what about innovation (Figure 2.2(a))? Comparing the two we can see that innovation generates a larger rest of the world-economy than import replacement. Thus the simple sketches in Figure 2.2 show that while import replacements attend especially to the conduit, innovation attends especially to the wider-world economy. To understand the real importance of innovations we need to move on and consider network externalities.

City network externalities: connectivity effects

In Jacobs' treatment of city externalities she argues strongly that it is import replacement that is the more important of the two master economic processes. The previous section has laid out her theoretical reasoning for why this is so. We can add a further quantitative reason: successful import replacements are much more common than successful innovations. This is because one innovation can spawn many import replacements. For instance, the invention of using electricity for street lighting rapidly diffused across cities throughout the world around 1900 replacing old gas lighting. Soon more than the innovation diffused as different parts of the new production also moved – electrical paraphernalia such as light bulbs, safe wires, switches and sockets, and circuit boards were soon to be produced in cities where no electrical innovations took place. Put this way, innovation and import replacement are two sides of the same coin: a mega economic process where every import replacement derives ultimately from an innovation. Thus although the import replacement mechanism is more potent through generating rapid economic growth, in the broader scheme of things the two master economic processes are equally necessary for economic development.

This argument is made clear when we move focus from individual cities to city networks. In fact, innovation is the key process in both the rise and demise of city networks. Beginning with the latter, if the process of import replacement is happening and the innovations dry up then economic development will cease. This is because, left to itself, import replacement homogenizes the economies of cities, like all cities today having electric street lighting. Without the replenishment of new innovations, import replacement creates a set of identical cities with no need to trade with each other: the network is no more. Such complete stagnation has happened historically when cities become isolated. Jacobs (1984, p. 130) uses the example of ancient Ethiopia whose 'long, long period of arrested development' began when its cities lost their ties to 'the urban life of ancient Egypt' as sources of innovation. In contrast new links to established cities enable 'embryonic cities' to grow through exports to a new market, followed by import replacement based on innovations from this new network world. Jacobs (1969) describes how London has acted in this way to stimulate many cities at different times: Copenhagen, New York and Hong Kong are specifically mentioned (pp. 170–71). And more generally she argues that it is Venice's links to the great city of Constantinople in the tenth century that sparked the emergence of the Western European city network that underpinned Europe's medieval commercial revolution (pp. 174–5). These examples are all city network externalities generated by connectivity effects. Their stories will feature prominently in the narrative of Part III below. All of the economic processes above are derived from inter-city connectivities and they constitute network externalities.

Network externalities have been largely ignored by urban economists (Taylor 2009); although they refer to Jacobs' externalities they have focused on externalities within cities, despite the fact that all Jacobs' arguments relate the city economy to the rest of the world-economy as I have previously described in detail. But now we have to move beyond the simple concept 'rest of the world-economy' and consider the geography of this outside economy, something that Jacobs fails to do. This means moving from a basic spatial border relation (imports and exports) to understanding specific configurations of spaces of flows beyond the city (city network). For instance, in the contemporary world city network it is generally accepted that London and New York are the most connected cities. What does this mean? It has to do with the number of flows going into and out of these cities relative to other cities. This may be indexed by numbers of air flights or by numbers of banks overseeing their global finance activities. How is this an externality, an economic bonus beyond the market? Just like city externality, city network externality is to do with advantages in being in a knowledge-rich milieu. The mix of people you are working with or alongside in a city provide a wealth of substantive information, both overt and tacit, on the business being carried out: both New York and London are cauldrons of swirling information about financial markets, their operation and the people who operate in them. But there is also geographical information about finance that is known and constantly being updated in New York and London. These cosmopolitan cities are not just centres of finance, they are crossroads of finance. It is links with other cities across the world that make New York and London such rich sources of worldwide knowledge of the dynamics of finance. Thus a financial worker in New York or London will have a richer source of up-to-date knowledge of what is going on in global finance than an equivalent worker in, say, Atlanta or Hamburg. Historically, the classic case of powerful network externality can be found in seventeenth-century Amsterdam as 'an information exchange': Smith (1984) describes a wide array of network mechanisms that made this city the first great world business knowledge centre of the modern world-system.

Network externalities are recognized by economists studying 'network industries' such as in communications (e.g. Shy 2001). The key point about these industries is their tendency for explosive growth. This is because single additions can have very large impacts. For instance, in non-network industries, adding a new factory will increase production but only in pro-portion to the size of the factory relative to previous production. But the effect of adding a telephone exchange to a telephone network is not to be found by just adding the extra number of people that join the network through the new exchange. Every person newly connected has access to all other people across the network so that the potential growth in flows is multiplicative. This is why network industries 'take off' when they reach a critical mass: recent examples are the fax machine in the 1980s and the Internet in the 1990s (Shy 2001, pp. 3–4). This type of thinking has not been transferred to city networks but it is not too far a stretch of the imagi-nation to link this process to explosive city growth consequent on import replacement. The latter is premised on new work based upon knowledge coming from another city; and every such inter-city link has the potential for introducing further links throughout the network. The resulting new knowledge can be translated into another import replacement and so on multiplicatively. Thus explosive city growth might well be the combined product of city agglomeration and city network externalities.

Cities as Process II: Two Types of External Urban Relations

Before the argument goes any further I need to make a slight digression concerning the nature of the space of flows we are dealing with in inter-city relations. This is another area where Jacobs is exceptional: nearly all geographers, and following them urban economists, planners, historians and archaeologists, emphasize the hierarchical nature of these relations (Taylor 2009). For instance, the national urban systems approach that dominated inter-city research until the 1980s was premised upon urban hierarchy. This research school was treated in Chapter 1 as an example of the nationalization of social knowledge but its importance here is its taken-for-granted notion that as cities grow they create hierarchical con-figurations. This notion was derived ultimately from geography's supreme theory of the time, central place theory (Christaller 1966; Bunge 1966), which gave the concept of urban hierarchy a formal theoretical endorse-ment. This is important for my argument here because if cities did 'natu-rally' relate within simple hierarchies as scripted by state-centric studies, this would be a serious restriction on the diffusion of innovations. Spatial diffusion of innovations was a major theme in national urban systems research and this is part of the research school that has continued to be active through continued postulating hierarchical diffusion (Fujita and Thisse 2002). But with innovations trickling down a hierarchy from top to bottom their potential for promoting economic development is massively decreased and their role in explosive city growth is specifically removed. This is simply because by structuring inter-city relations hierarchically the number of links is tremendously reduced. For instance, a four-tier hierarchy of 25 nodes has 25 links compared to the 600 links in a network of 25 nodes. Thus dissenting from the hierarchy presumption is very important; I think cities form networks and therefore inter-city relations play a much bigger role in economic development than urban hierarchy allows.

My position of assuming a network nature for inter-city relations is justified as follows. I start by using the definitions of Powell (1990) and Thompson (2003) who portray network and hierarchy as contrasting forms of social organization. Networks are based upon cooperative relations, hierarchies on competitive relations. Thus within city networks there is mutuality between cities since, as Jacobs has told us, they need each other. But city hierarchies are there to climb; cities vie with one and other to move upwards. Distinguishing between these two possible processes has been severely hampered by a specific confusion in the study of city hierarchies. Typically, rankings of cities, say by population, or number of firm headquarters, has been used to represent a hierarchy. However, a ranking is merely a list – to show hierarchy there has to be a clear power relation between levels with those above telling those below what to do (Lukermann 1966; Taylor 1997). Of course this happens when cities are used as administrative units by state bureaucracy: national administrations located in capital cities tell local administrations in cities what they can and cannot do reflecting simple territorial power relations. This is a guardian process of state and most certainly does not transfer to commercial relations between cities. For instance, in world city studies London is always ranked higher than São Paolo in the degree of its global commercial activities but to infer that London tells São Paulo what to do on the global stage is nonsensical. Although the notion of hierarchy did enter world cities literature (Friedmann 1986) the concept has proved to be unsustainable.

A research case study will clarify matters (Beaverstock et al. 2001). In the late 1990s the European Union agreed to form a common currency and the euro was launched in 2001. To back up the new currency there had to be a European Central Bank and the question arose as to where it should be located. There were two main candidates: London, Europe's leading financial centre; and Frankfurt, the financial centre of Germany, economically Europe's most successful country. This was a zero-sum game played out in the European Council of Ministers wherein Germany triumphed over the UK and Frankfurt got the bank. The general response to this guardian decision was that Frankfurt would now be in a position to challenge's London's financial leadership in Europe. But this, of course, assumes that the prime relation between London and Frankfurt was one of competition. The latter was true for Germany and the UK arguing their cases in Council of Ministers but inter-city relations are not so formed. Thus when practitioners in leading financial and law firms within both cities were interviewed it was found that competition between the cities was not in their minds at all. Every firm that interviewees worked for had offices in both London and Frankfurt, meaning that all firms in the survey had invested in human, and sometimes real estate capital, in both cities. Therefore they wanted, and assumed, that both cities would be success-ful. In strict commercial syndrome terms they saw London–Frankfurt relations from a win–win perspective; they used each city functionally – London as a global platform, Frankfurt for central European business – and worked accordingly. The conclusion is straightforward: this is a clear case of mutuality: London's growth feeds into Frankfurt and vice versa (p. 8). And this has been borne out subsequently since talk of Frankfurt replacing London – competitive language – has long since faded. More recently Lai (2012) has developed this argument by showing the comple-mentarities between the leading Chinese cities – Beijing, Hong Kong and Shanghai – far outweigh any competitive tendencies.

As noted earlier, the reason the concept of urban hierarchy became popular was because of central place theory, a model of urban places evenly spread and hierarchically arranged. A very neat theory, it was developed to describe urban servicing of rural populations whereby 'central places' each provide goods and services to their local hinterland. The hierarchy arises through larger central places providing more goods and services to larger hinterlands that encompass their neighbouring smaller central places and hinterlands. This produced an interlocking hierarchy of urban places that can be interpreted as different levels of specifically local marketing (Taylor et al. 2010b). Because all inter-urban relations are vertical (up/down) in the theory, even the largest cities within this urban system are restricted in their relations to only other urban places located in their own large, but still local, hinterland. It is this inherent property of hierarchy that seriously restricts inter-urban relations: by ignoring relations horizontally between urban places, the theory is particularly problematic for major cities with important trade relations with other large cities. To accom-modate this vital, inter-urban relation, a central flow theory has been pro-posed. This complements central place theory rather than replacing it. In this argument central place theory is reinterpreted as modelling a process of local (hinterland) city connections, which I call 'town-ness', and central flow theory addresses the process of non-local inter-city relations, which I call 'city-ness' (Taylor et al. 2010b). Thus the question as to whether an urban place is a town or a city is made redundant: as processes, both town-ness and city-ness occur simultaneously within urban places. For instance, nineteenth-century London serviced the world-economy through 'The City', while concurrently servicing consumer needs of its hinterland through the west end, 'always called town' (Kynaston 2011, p. 23) – later, more generally, 'downtown'. Of course, all urban places do differ greatly in terms of the relative balance between the two processes.

Central flow theory is specified as an interlocking network model. It was first derived to describe the contemporary world city network (Taylor 2001; 2004) but has subsequently been interpreted as a generic description of inter-city relations (Taylor et al. 2010b). An interlocking network is an unusual network configuration because it has three layers rather than the usual two. Most networks consist of a nodal level and the network level: social agents are nodes and their interactions generate the network. For instance, in a network analysis of gang behaviour, gang members are nodes and their relations with each other define the social network that underpins the gang. In commercial city networks cities are the nodes but they are not the agents of network formation. In the interlocking model there is a third 'sub-nodal' layer, the firms who are the commercial agents that create both economic agglomerations and economic networks. In this model it is firms who 'interlock' cities through their trading activities.

As described by Pirenne (1969) and Jacobs (1969), trade in early medieval Europe was an individual pursuit by itinerant hawkers who carried all their goods and capital with them as they travelled from place to place. They came together collectively only for protection through travelling in groups. Such small-scale commerce had limited potential for growth but through links to existing urban places it morphed into something very different. Inter-city commerce by merchants was a form of trade that involved transactions at a distance. Such business could only be accomplished by instituting conditions of trust. This was achieved by a merchant house in a given city setting up representation in another city where it does business. This representation can take many forms; family links are a common form with brothers, sons and nephews of the head of family being sent out to do family business across a city network. The key point is that the organizational structure of the merchant house 'interlocks' – facilitates trade between – the cities in which it does business. This is supplemented by supporting institutions such as warehousing to secure goods and transport to transfer the goods. In addition banks are necessary to deal with transfers of capital. And the latter themselves usually operated as banking networks to provide their services across numerous cities. For instance, in the sixteenth century the growing financial centre of Augsberg in south Germany was linked to 18 cities across Europe by the Fuggers, including Leipzig, Rome, Naples, Lyons and Antwerp (p. 47) and by the Welsers to Genoa, Venice, Aquila (south Italy), Milan, Antwerp, Lyons, Vienna and Schackenwald (Bohemia) (p. 48). Notice that two cities, Antwerp and Lyons, appear as links for both Augsburg's great banking families, suggesting that these two cities were particularly important for Augsburg business. This is how the interlocking network model is operationalized: the city network is constituted by aggregating the multiple locations of firms from a range of cities. Of course, the more firms, the more reliable the picture of the network produced – usually analysis only proceeds with more than 20 firms. From such aggregations we can find particular dyads that are important (like the suggestion for Augsburg–Antwerp and Augsburg–Lyons above), and for each city node we can find its total of links with all other cities in the network. This measures a city's network connectivity, which can be interpreted as an indicator of a city's network externality potency.

As mentioned, this model was initially used to describe today's world city network and this research is particularly relevant for showing how a city's network connectivity is linked to its import replacement processes. Following Sassen (1991), the research focused on advanced producer services – business services involving professional, creative and financial work. Firms in sectors such as advertising and commercial law have had to expand their office networks to service their clients as the latter have globalized their businesses. In this way advanced producer services have become a cutting-edge industry; servicing global capital, they have enabled economic globalization to grow through a world city network (Taylor 2004). This work has consistently shown the New York–London dyad to be the most linked pair of cities and both are also the two most connected cities overall as measured by their network connectivities. In other words, it is in London and New York that city network externalities are most potent; these two cities are the major crossroads of economic globalization. Let us see how this works with respect to import replacements.

London has long been the leading centre for commercial law that involves multiple jurisdictions. Thus with the coming of economic globalization, its major law firms were in a good position to consolidate the city's expertise in this rapidly growing area of work. But it was soon found that not all legal work could be done in London; offices were needed in other jurisdictions to tap into essential, tacit as well as formal, knowledge in other leading cities. The result has been that several London law firms have worldwide office networks. Singapore, one of the fastest growing cities through globalization, has been a popular destination for new law offices. These raise that city's network externality through new flows of legal knowledge available in Singapore coming from London and other cities in law firms' office networks. Additionally, a new office opened in Singapore constitutes an import replacement: law previously done in London has been transferred to this other city. A multiplier effect will occur to the degree that the new law work requires and attracts other new work, say, in accountancy or management consultancy. In a very similar matter, New York has been at the centre of the advertising industry since its initial growth in the first half of the twentieth century. Since the 1980s numerous New York advertising agencies have been opening offices in other countries to better serve their clients. Originally, many of these offices were little more than 'post boxes', transits for adverts designed in New York to be minimally customized for a new market. But some of these offices have graduated into being creative centres in their own right: São Paulo now has such creative additions to its economy. Therefore as with law in Singapore, advertising in São Paulo has enhanced this city's network externality and through import replacement it is adding to the city's agglomeration effect (Faulconbridge et al. 2011).

Finally let us return to the question of competition and cooperation in inter-city relations. In the more sophisticated studies of competitive cities, it is accepted that the competition exists alongside cooperative relations (e.g. Begg 1999; Sassen 1999), and in my own promotion of inter-city mutualities I accept that there are competitive processes present (Taylor 2004; Taylor et al. 2010b). We are now in a position to say how these two relations are associated (Taylor 2012a). First, my treatment of the central flow theory as an interlocking network model interprets city cooperation (network) as generic. Second, it follows therefore that city competition is contingent. There are spatial and temporal contingencies. Taking the latter first we can expect competition to be particularly important during downturns in economic cycles. The classic example would be northern Italy in the fourteenth and fifteen centuries when the late medieval downturn led to the inter-city strife known as the Italian hundred years war, which left just four cities maintaining their autonomy: Florence, Genoa, Milan and Venice (Arrighi 1994). Spatially, in a small or medium country, commercial work might only support one major city in the world city network (e.g. Lisbon in Portugal). In this case the city is at the interface of its city-ness in relation to the world city network and its town-ness in relation to its (local) country. In other words, competition arises where the political process creates restrictions on flows through constructing relatively small (local) political spaces of places. Thus has contemporary globalization been marked by São Paulo, Sydney and Toronto pulling ahead of their 'national rivals' Rio de Janeiro, Melbourne and Montréal respectively as 'global cities'. Today's world city network can best be described as a network with hierarchical tendencies.

Cities as Process III: Five Great Economic Forces of Expansion

Thus far I have interpreted the category 'rest of the world-economy' in Figures 2.1 and 2.2 as being linked to the city through city network practices but city networks alone do not comprise all the world-economy. We know from world-systems analysis that there are economic processes linking cities to exploitation of peripheral areas of the world-economy. In other words, linking to cities can be economically positive as described above, but it can also be economically negative; these are generally referred to as dependency relations, which were briefly described in Figure 2.1(b). I can now elaborate on such relations to round off understanding of cities within world-economies.

Jacobs (1984) provides a comprehensive treatment of how the positive mutuality of city as process turns into a negative force of dependence. She argues that the mutuality of a city's links is especially strong in its immediate region, where many cities have enabled vibrant city-regional economies to form: Tokyo is described as an example of this addition to the city agglomeration process (pp. 50–55). These large economies – now called global city-regions (Scott 2001) or mega-city-regions (Hall and Pain 2006) – are a major topic of theoretical and practical importance in urban and planning studies. Jacobs, however, uses city-regions as an economic analytic device to break down the processes involved in the spatial projection of city power and influence.

According to Jacobs (1984), commercial interests in cities mould their immediate geographical surroundings to meet their economic needs. She identifies five 'great forces unleashed by import-replacing cities' (p. 44):

- Enlarged city markets in both size and variety – the rise of market gardening around cities is a typical response to this basic market force;
- Increased transplants of city work (old work) – taking advantage of cheap and available land, old plants move to the edge of the city to expand;
- More and varied jobs in new work – young people move into the city to take advantage of growing opportunities;
- New uses of technology – mechanization of traditional farm work means less work and further migration into the city;

● Growth of city capital – available for building new infrastructure to serve economic transformation of the region.

The key point is that in the city-region the five forces act together to create balanced growth by operating 'simultaneously, massively and in reasonable proportion to one another' (p. 55), so as to create a dynamic, successful economic development. The forces complement each other to mitigate or reverse possible negative impacts: market gardening arises as traditional farming declines; a decline in jobs by both pull and push factors is matched by growth in jobs in the city and in transplanted industry; transplanted industry and market gardening can draw on city capital for added infrastructure needs, which again creates jobs. The end result is that 'the economies of city-regions are incomparably more complex than those of any other types of economies except cities themselves' (p. 57).

In complete contrast, beyond the city-region and outside the city network, these forces create exceedingly simple dependent economies that Jacobs (1984) calls 'economic grotesques' (p. 59):

> It is as if the net of complete economic ties with which a city binds its own hinterland unravels at the borders of a city region. The various strands – markets, jobs, technology, transplants and capital – separate from the mesh and take off by themselves, each in its own idiosyncratic directions. In this fashion, cities shape stunted and bizarre economies in distant regions. (p. 59)

This is a city-based formulation of Gunder Frank's (1969) development of underdevelopment thesis as the basic process of peripheralization in the world-economy. Frank describes one general process; Jacobs specifies five particular negative effects, one for each of the great forces. The result is an economic geography of the periphery divided into five different city supply regions:

1. Primary goods supply regions for agricultural and raw materials responding to market demand. This is a major force for perpetual reorganization of economic relations: for example from English wool-supplying Low Countries textile industries in the late medieval period to the American South supplying cotton for English textile industries in the nineteenth century. The insatiable needs of growing cities create a simple carving up of space into single commodity-supply regions that is a highly efficient arrangement for the cities. This process globalized in the late nineteenth century when different countries and colonies were identified by their product supply: Argentina and beef, Australia and wool, Brazil and coffee, Ceylon (Sri Lanka) and tea, Congo and copper, Gold Coast (Ghana) and cocoa, Ivory Coast and

groundnuts, Malaya and rubber, and South Africa and gold are all well-known examples of this first global commercial geography.

2. Secondary and tertiary goods supply regions for manufacturing and service outsourcing (routine information processing) via transplants. Cities have always been more expensive for labour than rural areas so that the 'runaway shop' is a common historical feature of economic development. This force completely changed the global commercial geography in the late twentieth century with the new international division of labour (Frobel et al. 1980). The core of the world-economy had been distinguished by its concentration of industrial production, but all this changed when multinational corporations devised global strategies to relocate basic manufacturing to cheaper labour locations in the periphery and semi-periphery. From manufacture of traditional textiles to the latest electronic components, industry 'moved South'. Subsequently routine service work has also been outsourced to countries with a surfeit of cheap educated labour, notably India. These examples show that it is the social relations of production that matter, not what is produced: where social relations are ones of dependence the development of underdevelopment does not have to be in primary production. Hence, contra classical development theory emanating from either the US or the USSR in the post-World War II era: industrialization per se does not equal development.

3. Labour supply regions I: labour sheds providing workers via the 'pull' of city jobs. This is the traditional attraction of the city as a place of opportunities – its streets are said to be 'paved with gold'. Although this myth may be far from the truth the key fact is that most migrants from rural areas are better off in the city. These flows are never random, migrant flows expand to create common labour sheds for groups of cities. Since 1950 US cities have attracted migrants particularly from central America; in Europe cities have often attracted migrants from former colonies – British cities from the West Indies and the Indian subcontinent, and French cities from Algeria and West Africa – while the large-scale Turkish migration to Germany reflects past political relations. Today in China, the greatest urban–rural migration in history is providing the labour for Chinese cities to be the new 'workshop of the world'.

4. Labour supply regions II: population clearances providing workers via 'push' factors consequent on technology changes. This has often been the result of new production practices that leave rural populations vulnerable and their lands newly 'overpopulated'. The classic example of this is the Scottish highland clearances of the eighteenth and nineteenth centuries when traditional crofters were thrown off

their land to accommodate more profitable extensive sheep farming. These families finished up in lowland Scottish cities, notably Glasgow, and colonial British cities such as Toronto. Similarly the rural Irish famine/clearance in the 1840s produced migrants for Liverpool and Boston. In the modern world-system this has cumulated into a final contemporary phase that is billed as 'the end of the peasantry' (Vanhaute 2008). It is manifest throughout non-core regions as huge mega-cities in the most unlikely places such as Karachi (15.1 million), Dacca (12.6), Lagos (10.1), Kinshasa (8.2) and Khartoum (5.5) (Taylor et al. 2010a). Although among the fastest growing cities in the world, none of the above cities has a vibrant city economy but dispossessed rural migrants are better off with the slim opportunities they offer compared to where they have come from. I will discuss these cities further in Part IV.

5. Capital realization regions through generating large-scale projects as ways of absorbing surplus capital (for example, building dams). Jacobs (1984, p. 105) describes this as the futility of providing 'capital for regions without cities'. She uses the Tennessee Valley Authority initiative from the 1930s as an example of large-scale infrastructure investment that ultimately failed to create development: its headquarter city, Knoxville, simply did not have the city attributes to lead successful regional and network processes. Instead, the power generated through harnessing the rivers could not all be consumed locally so that the region became an electricity supply region for northern US cities. Since the 1950s, there have been numerous foreign aid packages for poor countries, often featuring new dams for electricity without the cities to productively consume it (Ghana's Volta dam is the classic case), which have failed to create development in the receiving country but have been hugely profitable for firms in the aid-giving country. This general failure of the 'development industry' to produce economic development where it is needed is the subject of the concluding section of this chapter.

The end results of all the above processes are simple economies serving faraway city complex economies; they are poor regions with dependency relations.

An obvious logical solution to this peripheralization is delinking, removing a dependent economy from the world-economy. This has had its proponents within world-systems analysis, notably Samir Amin (1990), who suggests a degree of political and economical disconnect from the rich exploiting countries so as to break dependency relations. Taken to extremes, this idea has led to the attempted elimination of cities as Pol

Pot practised in Cambodia with its concomitant millions of deaths, as city dwellers were forced into an unsustaining and unsustainable countryside (Tyner 2008). Even Julius Nyerere's (1968) much more humane delinking policy for Tanzania involves a self-reliance dictum that undervalues industry and defines development as purely rural: the potentials of Tanzania's historically vibrant cities, Zanzibar and Dar es Salaam, are simply ignored. In contrast, for Jacobs (1984, p.124) disconnection equates to the atrophy of by-passed places (Figure 2.1(a)). From her perspective the way forward is to network in new ways to make connections diverse – as she tells it: 'backward cities need one another' (pp.135, 155). The massive rise in inter-connectivity amongst leading Pacific Asian cities compared to other erstwhile 'third world cities' in other parts of Asia, Africa and Latin America in the decades since 1970 show this can be done (Taylor et al. 2009).

Finally, it can be noted that there are a class of dependent cities with relatively simple economies that are not in exploitative relations with their more complex peers. These are cities that specialize in a single important function within core zones of the world-economy. Unlike the world supply regions above they have a mutual relation with complex cities, whilst still being dependent on them for their economic wellbeing. Here are some of the most common examples.

- The obvious example is urban places that specialize in logistics: hubs for the spaces of flows that are essential to all cities. Seaports and railway towns are the common examples of settlements that have not grown their economies much beyond warehousing and infrastructure maintenance to become complex cities. UK examples are the railway centre of Crewe in the nineteenth century and the port of Milford Haven in the twentieth century.

- University towns are a second category: their perennial 'town–gown conflicts' reflect the traditional domination of the higher education institution at the expense of development work (Taylor et al. 2008). They supply knowledge to more complex cities in the form of training professional and scientific labour. In England, the cities housing the two great traditional universities, Oxford and Cambridge, did not become great industrial cities.

- Officially in Europe all places with cathedrals are 'cities' and some of these can be very small. They supply spiritual services to more complex cities. Their lack of growth (another 'town–gown conflict') is similar to the university situation: in England the two cities housing archbishoprics, Canterbury and York, did not become great industrial cities.

- There are also settlements that specialize in politics: capital cities that are small compared to the other cities they rule. This is common in the US where it is not unusual for a city other than the largest city in a state to be the state capital. This idea of the capital city being a neutral venue, free from vested interests, was the basis for The Hague being made capital of the United Provinces in the seventeenth century: it was not one of the 57 cities having voting rights in the Estates General. Contemporary examples of rich cities designated to be specialist political capitals are Canberra, Ottawa and Washington, DC.
- There are settlements that have developed as centres for leisure/entertainment activities from eighteenth century spas (e.g. Bath in the UK) to nineteenth- and twentieth-century seaside resorts (e.g. Blackpool) to today's heritage places and gambling centres; Venice and Las Vegas are the most successful of this genre. Susceptible to changing fashions, nevertheless these 'one-trick towns' do flourish over generations through the supply of social entertainment.

Despite their economic successes all specialist cities remain vulnerable and it is common for them to pursue policies that diversify them economically. Washington, DC has been successful in this pursuit (Abbot 1999); Cambridge and Las Vegas are examples from other categories that are currently pursuing this end.

The basic points from this long conceptual trajectory on cities as process are summarized in Figure 2.3. This diagrammatic digest can be used as a simple checkpoint when reading about the role of cities in the narratives that follow.

SUMMING UP AND JOINING TOGETHER

The three toolkits have been dealt with separately, and in this concluding section I want to begin to bring them together. Although each is powerful in its own right, and proven to be so, my interest is in how they can be interwoven to draw on the salient bits of each to construct my narrative. I set out four configurations of social organization as ways of thinking about opportunities and obstacles in macro-social change. I develop a generic position on the natures of hierarchy, market, monopoly and network and the interrelations between them. These concepts have figured prominently in the toolkits and they will be vital to the coming narrative; here I consider them together both to confirm their differences and to

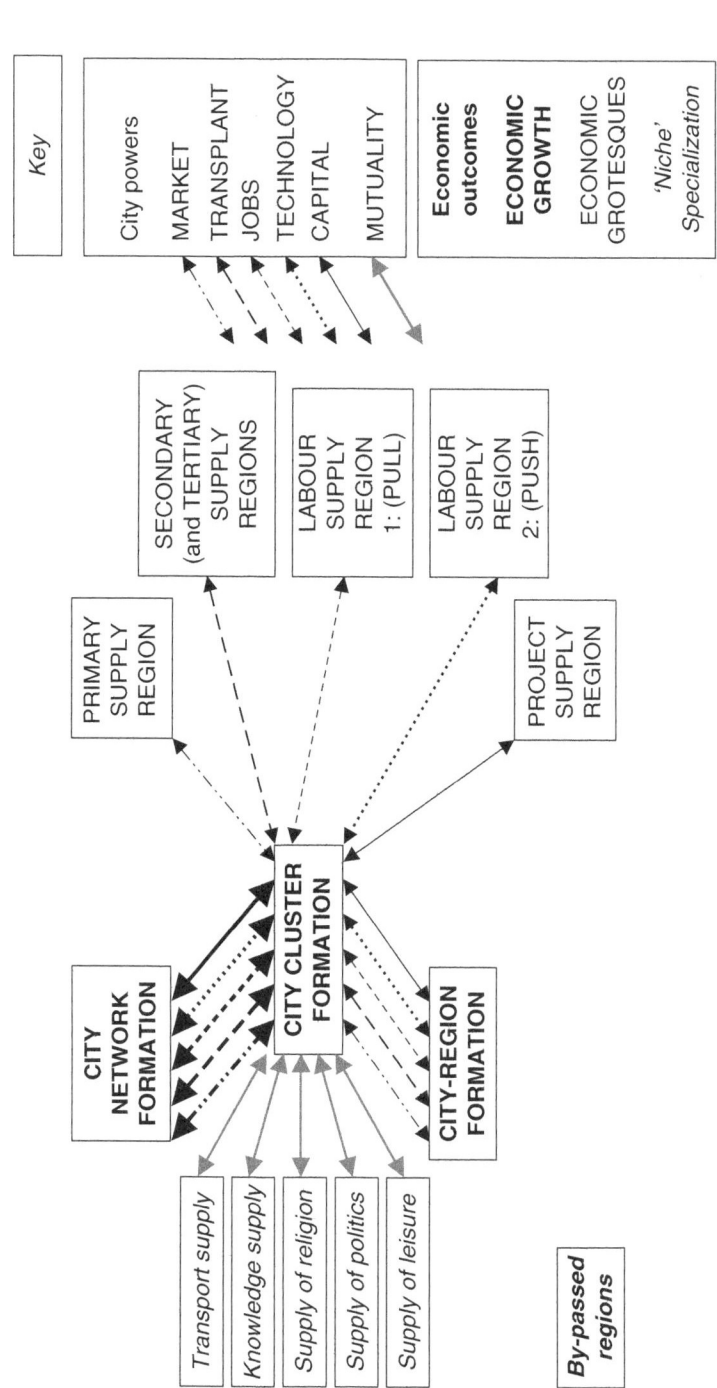

Figure 2.3   *Processes of city-ness*

explore their relations. Typically the literature emphasizes the former; I prepare the ground to treat them as less clear-cut in their actual formations in specific geohistorical situations.

Powell (1990) and Thompson (2003) delineate three different forms of social differentiation: hierarchy, market and network. Thompson (2003, p. 22) treats these three concepts as distinctive logics, coordinating devices and mechanisms of governance in an attempt to provide 'a rationale and case for networks' (p. 237). His purpose means that he uses a comparative approach to the concepts, I will sketch out an additional relational component. In doing so, I add a fourth concept – monopoly. As will have been gathered previously, this is a very important concept within my toolkits because it intersects moral syndrome analysis (guardian monopoly) with world-systems analysis (monopoly in capitalism) and features prominently in state territorial policy and the difficulties in substituting city advantages of agglomeration and connectivity.

Table 2.2 provides a comparison of the four forms of social organization within a schema using Jacobs' moral syndromes.

Thus are market and network associated with the commercial syndrome, and monopoly and hierarchy with the guardian syndrome. The moral precepts in (Box 2.1 and Table 2.1) can be equated with vertical and horizontal practices of power that link them directly to pairs of social organization as indicated. Note however that I relate the concepts to limiting cases of behaviour derived from the moral syndromes; they are 'pure' expressions that we cannot expect to find in practice. Thus we are used to reading about imperfect markets, the use of monopoly to mean oligarchy, disjointed networks, and hierarchies as much more than 'trees'. In other words the concepts are generic processes that need work to be maintained and that work can rarely be expected to create pure forms.

Table 2.2 is a box table and the second scale is an economics/politics differentiation. However I have problematized both dimensions by placing quotes around these labels. This makes a very important point about the difficulties in separating these two spheres of activity. Although treated as 'naturally occurring' by their economics advocates, markets are socially constructed and require an enabling governance to exist. Monopolies may be considered to be severely distorted markets but in reality they commonly involve state engagement. Hierarchy is political in the way it is used in state bureaucracies but in reality this is the usual means of organization in any large unit, public or private. And, of course, networks are political, as in diplomatic relations and popular political movements, but globalization has brought economic networks to the fore. I have been explicit in describing the two moral syndromes which, despite their labels, cannot be simply read as guardian equals politics and commercial equals econom-

Table 2.2   Four configurations in social organization: limiting cases

	'Economic' scale	*'Political' scale*
Guardian limiting cases (Vertical powers)	*Monopoly* Control, secrecy, domination	*Hierarchy* Rule-driven, bureaucratic, strong governance
Commercial limiting cases (Horizontal powers)	*Market* Competition, transparency, self-regulation	*Network* Mutuality, transparency, self-organization

Source: Derived in part from Thompson (2003: 48).

ics. In Table 2.2 I reinforce this key argument. The moral syndrome concepts are much too subtle to be reduced in this way. The most important example of this for my narrative is the Braudel–Wallerstein separation of market from capitalism thereby problematizing economics. Capitalism is linked to monopoly subject to guardian moral precepts, whereas markets are commercial.

In my brief treatment of the world city network above I indicated that this was a 'network with hierarchical tendencies'. This linking of two of the organizational forms is an example of how they can be related rather than separated. Another example is imperfect markets tending towards monopoly.

In Figure 2.4 all six relations between the four forms of organization are identified. These indicate different tendencies in the four processes that we can expect in their 'real world' existence. Thus when cooperation degenerates into conspiratorial behaviour, networks begin to morph into monopolies. When market competition seems more like conflict (coercion), then they begin to resemble Mafia hierarchies. When the latter try to become 'legitimate', then their coercion can be replaced by conspiracy since making money through monopoly is much easier. Clearly these four organizational forms can be deployed to describe more complex patterns of actual organization: that is, moving from the generic to the specifics. And this is precisely what my narratives do in the remainder of this book.

Extraordinary cities

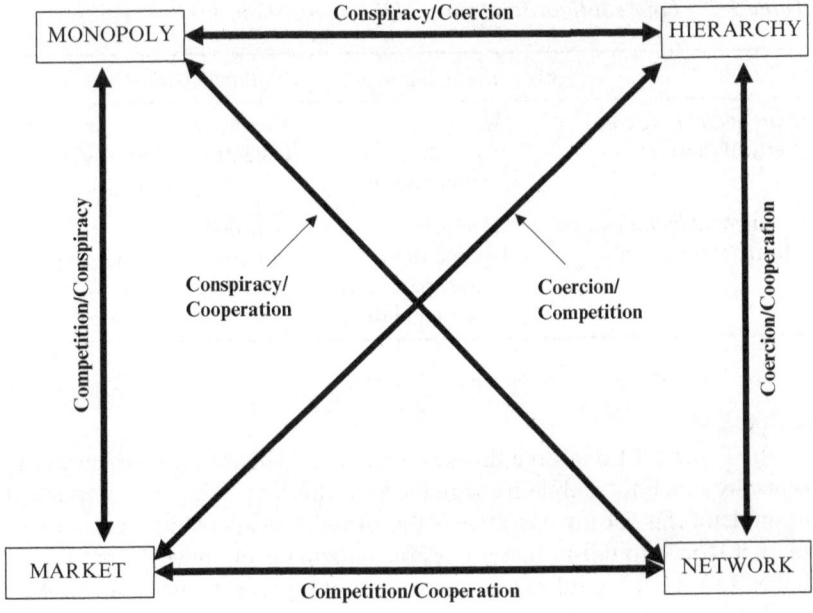

Figure 2.4   Four configurations in social organization: tendency scales

PART II

Narrative I: beginning conjectures

3. City and state beginnings: Western Asia's great creative interlude

INTRODUCTION

This is the first empirical chapter. It applies the previous conceptual toolkits to questions of the origins of cities and states. In particular, my discussions will be firmly located in Wallerstein's (1991) concern for the limits of nineteenth-century paradigms in contemporary thinking. As discussed previously, it is surprising how influential ideas from a century or more ago still predominate in much of contemporary social science. Urban studies provides a classic case; it is necessary to look no further than *The City Reader* (LeGates and Stout 2000), which begins with Gordon Childe's (1950) evocation of a Mesopotamian first 'urban revolution' that is suffused in Victorian progressive (as progression) thought. This otherwise splendid volume offers no alternative to Childe's very traditional ideas on urban origins. It is the purpose of this chapter to do precisely this. Keeping with the focus on Mesopotamia, but adding earlier episodes in my narrative, I draw on Jacobs' ideas on cities and economic development to identify a great creative geohistorical interlude that culminates in the phenomenal innovations of city-rich Mesopotamia in the fourth and third millennia BC. The chapter concentrates on just Western Asia; other equivalent creative interludes in other world regions are introduced in the next chapter.

This particular creative interlude, and the ones described in the next chapter, are traditionally referred to as civilizations. These are distinguished from previous societies by the existence of cities and states. As is commonly pointed out, civilization and city have the same etymological root; thus civilizations are societies containing cities. But this line of thinking can lead to taking cities for granted in the focus on civilization (Price 1978, p. 175): for instance, in a book entitled *The First Cities*, it has been argued that 'to attempt to define more precisely the "city" is pointless; it is "civilization" we must define' (Whitehouse 1977, p. 8). As regards the relation between states and civilization, the latter has also been interpreted 'as essentially coterminous with that of state society' (Webb 1975, p. 158). Yoffee (2005, p. 17) agrees but with a proviso: 'State and civilization, inextricably interlinked, must be kept analytically distinct, because it is possible for there to be several states within the same "civilizational" umbrella'. In this book I do not interrogate the concept of civilization any further; I treat civilization as a cultural area of distinctive shared values and practices that transcends individual cities and need not equate to states. Much of the chapter will be about Sumer in the fourth and third centuries BC, a clear case of a civilization. What I am interested in is the processes of city-ness and state-ness that unfolded in Sumer.

Since research on the earliest cities is in the field of archaeology, this means that I will be drawing on archaeological and ancient history litera-tures to furnish my empirical needs. Archaeology did not feature in my discussion of formal knowledges in Chapter 1 and therefore I begin this chapter with a brief interpretation of archaeology in the light of my previ-ous arguments. Despite a subject matter dealing with human activities, mainstream archaeology appears not to have seen itself as necessarily part of social science, but this does not mean it is not in thrall to nineteenth-century thinking.

Archaeology *sans* Cities

Gordon Childe is one of the founding fathers of archaeology as a discipline. His classic paper (1950) located the first cities in fourth-millennium-BC Mesopotamia and this remains the consensus within the discipline. There have been other suggestions, as I will relate later in this chapter, but these have been largely dismissed as not providing credible evidence for the existence of earlier cities. But, curiously, this question appears to be of peripheral concern in contemporary archaeology. I use as my evidence the latest edition of the best-selling introductory textbook on archaeology, Renfrew and Bahn's (2008) *Archaeology: Theories, Methods and Practice*. Textbooks are the bedrocks of disciplines; they define what knowledge is necessary for the socialization of the next generation into the fold. The fifth edition of Renfrew and Bahn's book, billed as 'complete' and 'wide-ranging' on its cover, finds no room for discussion of city origins within its massive 656 pages. Why might this be?

Archaeology's obvious academic locale would seem to be as a 'time discipline' alongside history with 'ancient history'. However its formal location in universities is mostly with anthropology. This makes some sense to the degree that anthropology largely deals with contemporary hunter–gatherer and simple agricultural societies and such societal types dominate the prehistory that archaeology investigates. This is to locate archaeology in the outer reaches of comparative anthropology with an inevitable neglect of concern for cities. Thus the index to Renfrew and

Bahn's (2008) book includes no reference for 'city' or 'cities'. However, there are nine references to 'city states'; it would seem that understanding early cities is subsumed into the study of early states.

This appears to be another instance of state-centric thinking relegating concern for cities. Traditionally, cities and states are seen as evolving together as a single institution, hence 'city-state'. But from my perspective they are two very different processes emanating from commercial and guardian practices. There is no reason to assume that these processes run exactly in parallel. Just simply identifying cities as city-states in early civilizations is, from my perspective, and Soja's (2010, p. 364), to conflate two processes in a most unhelpful way. There are several archaeologists who agree with this argument and their work is used below when I deal with this matter in some detail. Therefore it is not necessarily the case that archaeology has missed out on the 'city discoveries' described in Chapter 1, but such ideas seem not to have (yet?) percolated into the archaeological mainstream as represented by Renfrew and Bahn's (2008) textbook.

What does feature prominently in Renfrew and Bahn's (2008) text is 'evolution' indicating a strong theoretical tendency within the discipline. Such a 'social theory', deriving from nineteenth-century obsession with progress, survives more in archaeology that elsewhere in social science: Darwin has his own box feature in Renfrew and Bahn (2008, p. 27) entitled 'Evolution: Darwin's great idea'. Basically, simple evolutionary models have been used to understand the increasing complexity of society but without any recognition of the exceptional complexity of cities.

Very much in the spirit of Wallerstein's (1991) limits of nineteenth-century paradigms, some archaeologists have provided very powerful critiques of traditional evolutionary models of social change (Yoffee 2005, pp. 8–15; Gamble 2007, pp. 10–32). Yoffee (2005, p. 34), in particular, is a trenchant critic of what he calls the current 'neo-evolutionary' approach in archaeology:

> What neo-evolutionalism never was was a theory of social change. Rather, it was a theory of classification, of identification of ideal types in the material record. . . . In a vague sort of way, mainly by talking about different adaptations as if they were somehow like genetic differences, neo-evolutionists drew on the prestige of Darwin's theory and often proclaimed they had created a new science of social evolution. However, neo-evolutionists could not explain change other than in holistic terms and were content to identify as evolutionary mechanisms . . . climatic change or/and population growth. (pp. 31–2)

For Gamble (2007, p. 23) 'change takes the form of future-creep', so that 'differences are expected to happen eventually and can be explained simply by the passage of enough time, a commodity with which human prehistory is abundantly blessed'. For neither scholar is there enough emphasis on process: who are the agents and why do their activities generate social change? Answers to such questions lead to social science. But such scholarship does not appear to be important in mainstream archaeology.

Renfrew and Bahn (2008, pp. 12–13) introduce archaeology by relating it to other disciplines: they identify only three: anthropology, history and science (for techniques). There is no specified relation to the social science trilogy and this is reflected in subsequent substantive chapters. Chapter 5, 'How were societies organized?', makes no reference to sociology literature; there appears to be little or no change since Mann (1986, p. 76) referred to archaeologists only embracing 'rather tired sociological theory'. However geography does feature here in the guise of central place theory (pp. 182–4), albeit somewhat haphazardly: the settlement at the top of the hierarchy is variously called 'regional center' (p. 182), 'large town' (p. 183) and 'city' (p. 184). Chapter 9, 'What contact did they have?', is about 'trade and exchange' and makes no reference to economics literature; Wallerstein's world-systems analysis is briefly described (p. 358), but there is no reference to cities except as 'ceremonial centers' (p. 387). I think this clearly indicates specifically no appreciation of the extraordinariness of cities, and more generally, this is part of a broader distain for social science. Finally, Renfrew and Bahn (2008, pp. 46–7) do have a two-page box feature on Çatalhöyük, the key settlement in the city origins debate that I discuss below, but they use it to illustrate changing approaches to archaeology, with no mention of the controversies over interpreting the urban nature of the settlement. There can be no clearer example of denial of the city origins question in contemporary archaeology.

Towards a Post-Childe Understanding of Early Cities

For most people, both experts and the interested public, the answer to the question 'where were the first cities?' is straightforward: Mesopotamia in the fourth and third centuries BC. Thus is Gwendolyn Leick's (2001) book on Mesopotamia subtitled *The Invention of the City*. She is part of an almost unanimous archaeological tradition that goes back many decades.

The most famous statement of this tradition is that of the Marxist Gordon Childe (1950) – the article previously mentioned for its inclusion in a twenty-first-century reader collection – who coined the term 'urban revolution' to describe the rise of cities in the alluvial civilizations of the Nile, Indus and Tigris–Euphrates, the latter being the earliest. His ideas have been so influential that they deserve quoting at length:

About 5000 years ago irrigation cultivation (combined with stockbreeding and fishing) in the valleys of the Nile, the Tigris-Euphrates and the Indus had begun to yield a social surplus, large enough to support a number of resident specialists who were themselves released from food-production. Water-transport, supplemented in Mesopotamia and the Indus valley by wheeled vehicles, and even in Egypt by pack animals, made it easy to gather food stuffs at a few centres. At the same time dependence on river water for the irrigation of the crops restricted the cultivatable areas while the necessity of canalizing the waters and protecting habitations against annual floods encouraged the aggregation of population. Thus arose the first cities – units of settlement ten times as great as any known Neolithic village.

Despite the massive increase in our knowledge of the subject matter since then, his ideas are assumed to still have contemporary relevance – see Crawford's (2004, p. 17) brief summary of an 'enormous amount ... written over the past 50 years about the causes of the so-called urban revolution'. Terminology may change – the non-Marxist Mumford (1961) prefers 'urban transformation' – but the message is the same: this beginning of cities marks a new stage in an evolutionary social theory.

From the perspective deployed in this book, Childe's argument is intriguing because it posits a place-based explanation for the first cities. Cities arose in special places where food surpluses released people to congregate in new large settlements – cities – that were not sustainable under ordinary (non-irrigated) agriculture. Childe also provides ten 'traits' that identify a city, and this list confirms his thinking of the city as place. The penultimate trait is 'long-distance trade' which defines flows, but this is not an important feature as witnessed by its omission in the above key quote. In any case, the first trait is 'size', which Childe uses above as a fundamental distinction of cities from other settlements. Of course, in the theoretical framework deployed here cities are not simply 'large towns', but more on this below. In any case, this is one area where more recent knowledge compromises Childe's assertion of no prior large settlements before the cities of bronze-age civilization.

In the counter argument to this traditional received wisdom, Childe's position has been described as 'the ideological wall ... that has been placed at 5000 years ago to represent the beginning of history, civilisation and writing' (Rudgley 1998, p. 209). This statement is part of a reaction to under-estimation of the skills and achievements of 'pre-civilization' peoples. In particular, there remains a strong reluctance to admit to the possibility that Neolithic or earlier peoples could have produced cities. The critical empirical challenge to this thinking came with the excavations at Çatalhöyük in the 1950s and 1960s by James Mellaart; he claimed to have found a new civilization with Çatalhöyük as a new 'first city' (Mellaart 1965b). But he failed to fully convince fellow archaeologists:

wrong time, wrong stage; wrong place, wrong settlement type. And this is where the argument may have ended if it had not been for the intervention of Jane Jacobs (1969); she went further and even suggested that agriculture was invented in these early cities. This outrageous intrusion into archaeological thinking will be described in some detail in the next section.

I will attempt to ground Jacobs' position that Çatalhöyük is an early city by developing a wider theoretical and empirical base, one that is both appropriate and available for charting early 'city-ness'. As described in the last chapter, recent literature on the relational natures of cities, more or less deriving from Jacobs' oeuvre, has focused on internal links (clusters/agglomeration) and external links (networks/connectivity) of contemporary cities (Figure 2.3). However Jacobs was very historical in her personal remit and there are important studies that have continued historical applications of these and related ideas. The key examples are Hall (1998) with his description of leading cities as centres of creativity, Soja's (2000; 2010) concepts of synekism and regionality of cityspace in urban revolutions, McNeill and McNeill (2003) with their references to cities in the 'human web' of world history, Algaze's (2005a; 2005b) work on internal and external relations in Sumerian cities, LaBianca and Scham's (2006) applications of Castells' (1996) space of flows to 'antiquity', and Tilly (2010) starting with Uruk to explore city/state relations. These all use specific parts of my conceptual toolboxes in their different ways; their discursive harnessing of evidence to support the critical importance of cities in geohistorical social change are drawn upon below. But I will begin from a different starting point. In the study of cities, both contemporary and historical, there is one common measure that enables comprehensive city comparisons: population size. From modern censuses to the population estimates of historical demographers, this is a basic common denominator that, moreover, is directly implicated in the various relational concepts that assert the importance of cities. In other words I can start with a quantitative grounding to illustrate and confirm the qualitative difference a city makes. I use this general availability of city population estimates to suggest a most basic of city theories, derived from my city toolkit but adapted to delve back to the early origins of extraordinary cities and their effects on geohistory.

City-ness as Communication Potential

Direct measurements that are available for comparison of early settlements are perforce relatively limited. But one common feature that is known is the areal extent of sites. These physical measures have been used to generate indirect measures (estimates) of the populations of early settlements by Tertius Chandler (1987) and George Modelski (2003). In this way I can use demographic size to infer the type of social world past settlements would have encompassed. From population figures it is possible to produce broad relative estimates of the potential quantity of communication that is generated within and through a settlement. These empirical derivations are of theoretical interest because communication is central to both the cluster/agglomeration activities (as classically argued in Meier (1962)), and the network/connectivity activities that define cities as process. In other words the uniqueness of cities as special creative locales should be discernible in terms of measures of potential communications.

This argument can be summarized and operationalized as four basic ways to measure settlement size (Table 3.1):

Table 3.1   *The communicative potential of early cities*

Examples	Measured geographical size of urban site (hectares)*	Estimated demographic size (200 persons per hectare)**	Potential sociological size (square of population)***	Effective Jacobsean size (double sociological size)****
Hunter–gatherer band	–	150	22 500	–
Çatalhöyük (7000 BC)	15.5	5500	30 250 000	60 500 000
Eridu (Early Uruk)	40	8000	64 000 000	128 000 000
Ur (Ur Dynasty III)	50	10 000	100 000 000	200 000 000
Mohenjo-daro (2000 BC)	100	20 000	400 000 000	800 000 000
Uruk (3000 BC)	250	50 000	2 500 000 000	5 000 000 000
Uruk (Early Dynastic I)	400	80 000	6 400 000 000	12 800 000 000

Notes:
*   Taken from data in Modelski (2003: 8, Table 1) except for Çatalhöyük, which is from Hodder (2006: 7).
**   This is the site-density multiplier used by Modelski (2003); for Çatalhöyük I use the midpoint of the range of estimates given by Hodder (2006: 7).
***   This is the total number of potential contacts.
****   This is a new measure that tries to incorporate additional external contacts through networks using the assumption that internal and external linkages are equally weighted.

- *Geographical size* is the direct measurement of area of a site.
- *Demographic size* is derived by assuming a given population density of persons per hectare.
- *Sociological size* represents potential contacts between people; it relates to economic opportunity and innovation potentials of population concentration. This is what Urry (2003, p. 52) means when he relates size to complexity. It is also a network measure known as 'Metcalf's law', in which size is computed by the square of the number of members: this defines the total potential number of connections (Algaze 2005b, p. 21).
- *Jacobsean size* is how settlements are understood from a full communication perspective. This is an attempt to combine internal links with cosmopolitan connections to other cities in a city's network. Obviously this generates many more and richer contacts than sociological size alone. There is no straightforward way to estimate this addition. Assuming external contacts are as equally important as internal ones, I simply double sociological size to generate this new measure (in network theory terms: a 'double Metcalf').

The purpose of this exercise is to show how this basic communication approach of city-ness produces such massively large quantitative sizes in communication potentials that early cities can be reasonably represented as completely new social worlds of human experience.

But before proceeding with interpretation I should critically assess each of the city size measures. They should all be viewed as problematic as the literature tells us. When measuring the area of a settlement site, a decision has to be made on where to draw the boundary. This may be easy if we are dealing with just a walled settlement, but what about suburbs on or near the wall? This is particularly problematic with African cities, where separate mounds various distances apart are being considered as a single ancient city. Obviously the population density assumption is vital for the demographic estimates and will be culture-sensitive. This is well discussed by the producers of such estimates – see Modelski (2003, pp. 7–12) and Chandler (1987, pp. 6–7), the two most comprehensive sources. I will draw on the work of both below. However, their results should never be treated as exact measures; despite the massive amount of work involved in producing estimates for hundreds of cities, Modelski (2003) remains modest in his description of the outcome: 'estimates are necessarily speculative, and basically belong to the category of educated guesses' (p. 9). With the emphasis on the 'educated', I go along with this assessment and forgo any sophisticated analysis: I present estimates only as tables. The sociological size measures are merely potentials and no more. They reflect 'a multiplication of interactions' consequent upon increasing urbanization (Algaze 2005b, p. 21). Arguments can be made to both lower or raise the figures. Obviously divisions in a city (segregation, ghettoes) will lessen contact but on the other hand cultural variety will enhance the value of contacts. However, because sociological size does not take into account the all-important contacts with visitors, foreign outsiders with very different knowledge networks, the final Jacobsean size measure is required. These cosmopolitan interactions are integral to our definition of cities in networks and therefore have to be taken into account; although overall external connections will likely be smaller than internal city contacts, they are especially crucial for Jacobs' (1969) key process of economic expansion via import replacement. Therefore, combining potential internal and external linkages as equal components of this measure is reasonable given the lack of any other guide in this area. Thus are geographic and demographic measures of size of place transmuted into communication potentials to infer that the rise of cities creates a completely different world of social and economic relations.

To make this point in Table 3.1, I have added a 'hunter–gatherer group' that has a population of 150 persons; such groups constituted the common human experience for the vast majority of the modern human species' existence. The full communication boost that city-ness generates can be found in the fourth column of Table 3.1. For the smallest settlement in the table, Çatalhöyük, its effective Jacobsean size makes it 5688 times larger than our ubiquitous passing band. This huge differential illustrates the new economic and innovative power that comes with even the earliest cities, what Soja (2010, p. 365) calls 'an explosive leap in societal scale and complexity'. For the later Uruk, the enhanced communication potential is really staggering: 568 889 times more potential communication than a hunter–gatherer band. This can be contrasted with Childe's (1950) place-based interpretation of his 'first cities' being 'units of settlement ten times as great as any known Neolithic village'; clearly his reading of cities in terms of a large demographic difference bears no comparison with the major divergences suggested by communication potential. For reasons given above, the exact numbers listed in Table 3.1 are to be treated as more indicative than definitive. This is why precise numerical comparison is not the key point – what I am showing is evidence to support the notion that cities are a distinctive *qualitative* change from life in a small relatively isolated band. The numbers in Table 3.1 give a sense of this world-changing difference of human experience, so that from this communication perspective, I can argue that innovations as fundamental as inventing agriculture or states would, in all probability, have occurred and diffused as part of a city-ness process.

One last point, these size measures are only to be used for broad comparative, illustrative purposes. In fact, although I have argued that the sociological size and Jacobsean size are most important to city-ness, I will normally just provide the demographic size measures in the text. This is what readers are used to in comparing cities. And it avoids lots and lots of zeros in communication potential numbers that may be difficult to comprehend. But throughout all the text that follows, when demographic sizes are presented, please remember Table 3.1 and the explosive relations, internal and external, that they entail.

The remainder of this chapter consists of two main sections. The first section considers Jacob's controversial theses on early cities and agricultural development. I focus on the debates surrounding interpretations of Çatalhöyük in Anatolia as a very early (pre-Mesopotamian) city, and outline a city-based mechanism for the 'invention of agriculture'. The second section then moves on to interpretations of the great cities of Mesopotamia in the third and fourth millennia BC. Separating the concepts of city and state, I trace how the former generated the conditions for 'invention of the states', initially as city-states. Both these substantive sections each deal in detail with just one large case study. However, the basic argument of the essay is that the city-ness process is generic, and has developed in several different places at different times. Thus this chapter has a role of developing and substantiating ideas in two Western Asian case studies that will then be further evaluated more broadly as multiple 'creative interludes' across the world in the next chapter. The bottom line of my argument in Part II is that something as world-changing as agriculture and state formation requires *qualitatively* new social worlds – extraordinary cities – for their inventions.

THE ÇATALHÖYÜK STORY: CITIES AND AGRICULTURE AS TWO REVOLUTIONS OR ONE?

General statements about specific phenomenon are always vulnerable to simple empirical refutation. 'All swans are white' seemed to be a statement of fact until black swans were found in Western Australia. Such problems are particularly acute for claims of origins; somebody will invariably be able to find something earlier. This is especially problematic for archaeology with its endemic, limited knowledge of its universe of phenomena. And so it is with claims for Mesopotamia housing the very first cities. Jericho was the first black swan: very soon after Childe's (1950) celebrated identification of the 'urban revolution' in Mesopotamia,

Kenyon's (1960) excavations at Jericho revealed what seemed like a city. Writing a decade after Childe, Mumford (1961, p. 33) treated Jericho as an exception but within a few years Jericho's black swan had a mate: Mellaart's (1965a) excavations at Çatalhöyük indicated another settlement that appeared to be a city. This led to Jacobs' intervention referred to earlier. She has subsequently been strongly supported by Soja (2000) who has described a veritable 'flock' of such findings (pp. 28–9). The question asked is whether the conceptual toolkits employed in this book can help clarify the issues.

By restricting cities to just the last five or six thousand years, conventional wisdom precludes cities from having role to play in the invention of agriculture because its origins can be traced to many millennia earlier. This means that there have to be two 'revolutions': first an 'agricultural' one and then, much later, an 'urban' one. The only possible link between them is that the former had developed to such a degree that it generated the food surpluses that enabled cities to be invented. This is a supply theory of city origins: when the food becomes available, cities arise. As previously indicated, Jacobs' turns this around and implicates cities in the invention of agriculture. Pushing back the beginnings of cities several millennia before 5000 years makes Jacobs' heresy possible. Jacobs provides a demand theory of agricultural beginnings: when food supply for cities becomes inadequate, agriculture is invented to solve this early urban problem. Therefore there is just one 'revolution': the 'urban' one that precipitates a dependent innovation that is agriculture. I will compare and contrast these two positions using simple schematic diagrams that strip out the details except for consequent settlements.

In Figure 3.1(a) I have described the conventional position as basic evolutionary thinking in terms of a standard settlement sequence of increasing size. The key transformation is the invention of agriculture by hunter–gatherers that leads to agricultural villages. Evolution is indicated by the increasing size of settlements consequent upon agricultural improvements (adding to the food supply) leading first to market towns when production exceeds subsistence needs, and finally to Childe's cities where surpluses are much greater due to irrigated agriculture. But as Soja (2010, p. 365) has pointed out, 'there is no clear evidence of early agricultural villages that somehow grew into cities'. With its emphasis on generating surpluses, the question arises – why produce more food than you need? Why not just work less? In other words, it is not obvious where the demand comes from to provide the initial stimulus for surplus generation. It is for this reason that in this argument I stay with Jacobs' 'cities first' position rather than modifying it to Soja's (2010, p. 366) 'mutually stimulating development of cities and agriculture'.

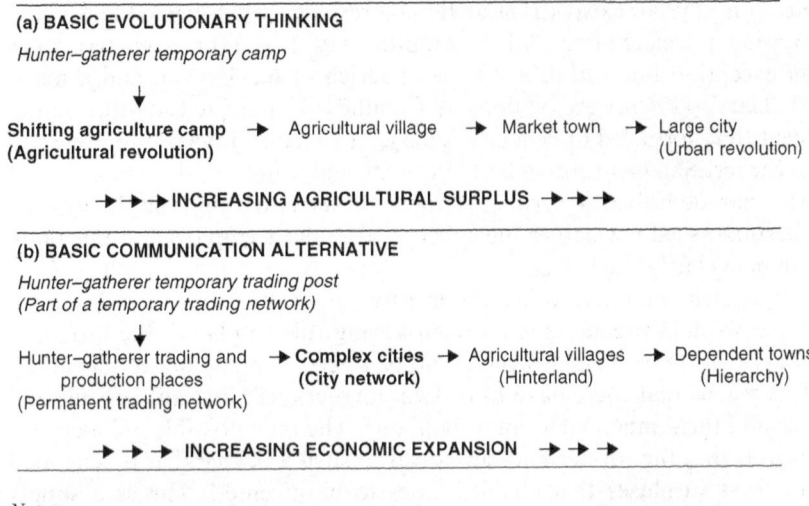

Notes:
Starting point in italics.
Pivotal stage/step in bold.

Figure 3.1   Origins: two settlement development sequences

Mellaart's Çatalhöyük and Jacobs' Alternative Thesis

For Jacobs (1969; 1984), cities are the crucibles of fundamental economic change and this includes agriculture. In Figure 3.1(b) I provide another schematic based on her ideas: this is a communication alternative sequence that is demand-led. Following Soja's (2010, p. 365) argument that trade is 'the primary urbanizing force', in this figure it is trading networks of hunter–gatherers that are emphasized. These may lead to economic specialization at trading posts and, in relatively rare circumstances, large increases in trade and production may create unprecedented population concentrations of several times more than the 150 norm of hunter–gatherer bands. If several such posts generate a strong and permanent trading network, these populations can gain a communication potential that qualifies them as small cities. Such cities are the critical step: they usher in Jacobs' (1969) 'explosive' economic expansion. The point of the two diagrams in Figure 3.1 is to contrast the two 'pivotal' steps: complex cities seem much more likely locales for agricultural invention than conventional evolution's emphasis on the invention of small hunter–gathererer bands.

However, it is this link to agriculture that remains the really controversial step in Jacobs' argument. Her specific thesis is that within the trading networks, the posts (that are to become cities) originally imported their food from hunter–gatherers in exchange for their trading goods, but with population growth the demand for food begins to outstrip what hunter–gathering can provide. Thus is agriculture invented in city hinterlands as an import replacement, opening up more growth through new import shifts (allowing extra commodities to be traded into the settlement) as described in the last chapter. The result is that with growth of agriculture (and herding) keeping up with the consequent new population growth, the amount of food production will necessitate workers being located outside the city: villages are created. If the food-producing hinterland grows further there may be the need for some urban functions to be transferred to the hinterland to service the villages: market towns are created. Thus the initial 'common-sense' evolutionary sequence of increasing size – village to town to city – is replaced by a communication-derived sequence – city to village to town.

This is all very well in theory but where is the evidence for cities existing as early as agriculture? For Jacobs (1969) the answer is Çatalhöyük. This site, a large mound of some 32 acres in Anatolia, was excavated by James Mellaart in the 1950s and 1960s. He estimated the population of the settlement possibly as high as 10 000. And he dated it at 7000 BC, four millennia before the Mesopotamian cities. Jacobs calls it 'a city of crafts, of artists, manufacturers and merchants' (p. 32) and the evidence does seem to show strong city-ness characteristics. Specifically, Mellaart (1964; 1965a) provides descriptions of how Çatalhöyük functioned both internally and externally. In terms of the internal relations of cities, Jacobs famously quotes Mellaart as follows:

> ... the weavers and basketmakers; the matmakers; the carpenters and joiners; the men who made the polished stone tools (axes and adzes, polishers and grinders, chisets, maceheads and palettes); the beadmakers who drilled in stone beads holes that no modern steel needle can penetrate and who carved pendants and used stone inlays; the makers of shell beads from dentalium, cowrie and fossil oyster; the flint and obsidian knappers who produced the pressure-flaked daggers, spearheads, lanceheads, arrowheads, knives, sickle blades, scrapers and borers; the merchants of skin, leather and fur; the workers in bone who made the awls, punches, knives, scrapers, ladles, spoons, bows, scoops, spatulas, bodkins, belt hooks, antler toggles, pins and cosmetic sticks; the carvers of wooden bowls and boxes; the mirrormakers, the bowmakers; the men who hammered native copper into sheets and worked it into beads, pendants, rings and other trinkets; the builders; the merchants and traders who obtained all the raw materials; and finally the artists – the carvers of statuettes, the modelers and the painters. (pp. 32–3 and Soja (2000, pp. 39–40), both from Mellaart (1964))

I have quoted this at full length to show the detail of the complex division of labour from Mellaart that so impressed Jacobs and Soja. But elsewhere, in terms of fuller exposition of the external relations of Çatalhöyük,

Mellaart considered that trade might be 'the most important source of income' because the city held 'the monopoly of obsidian trade with the west of Anatolia, Cyprus and the Levant' (Mellaart 1965b, p. 84). He describes a classic case of entwining trade with production:

> In exchange for obsidian, the fine tabular flint of Syria was obtained and widely used for manufacture of daggers and other tools. Sea shells, especially dentalia, were imported in great quantities from the Mediterranean for the manufacture of beads and stones of great variety were brought to the city for manufacture of stone luxury vessels, beads and pendants, polishers, grinding stones, pounders, mortars and querns, or to be used (like alabaster and marble, black and brown limestone) for the manufacture of small cult statues. Greenstone occurs on a ridge in the plain and it was used for fully polished adzes and axes, and for jewellery. Ochres and other paints came from the hills around the plain together with fossil shells, lignite, copper and iron ores, native copper, cinnabar and galena. (pp. 84–5)

For Mellaart this makes Çatalhöyük 'worthy of a metropolis' (p. 134) but Jacobs (1969) and Soja (2000) are more theoretically specific: Jacobs (1969, p. 35) spies a settlement exhibiting that most 'valuable' and 'wondrous' resource: 'a creative local economy', and Soja (2000, pp. 41–2) finds 'extraordinary creativity and innovation . . . in an "urban Neolithic"'. For this to have emerged, Jacobs (1969, p. 35) conjectures a city network: 'several little cities were simultaneously serving as expanding markets for one another' (p. 35). Thus, she concludes, 'it was the fact of sustained, interdependent, creative city economies that made possible many kinds of new work, agriculture among them' (p. 36).

On reading Mellaart (1964; 1965a; 1965b) his findings at Çatalhöyük appear to fit Jacobs' ideas on city as process almost to the letter. It is very tempting to reverse the relation: her ideas about city economies in *The Economy of Cities* (Jacobs 1969) are so far advanced from those initially developed in *The Death and Life of Great American Cities* (Jacobs 1960) that I would wager Çatalhöyük had a prime role in developing her theory of cities. This may explain why, in the later book on economics (Jacobs 1969), she took the surprising decision to begin with ancient history in a first chapter entitled 'Cities first – rural development later'. It is here that she presented her outlandish idea that agriculture was invented in cities in order to produce the food such new large settlements required (as sketched out in Figure 3.1(b)). Thus was Mellaart's empirical challenge to archaeological orthodoxy supplemented by a new and original urban theory that is a key part of my conceptual toolkit in Chapter 2. But Jacobs' undermining of the sequence of 'two revolutions' in archaeology's evolutionary thinking appears to have been a step too far in historical studies (Soja 2000, p. 42). In this area of research Hansen (2000b, p. 11) makes the assessment that her ideas have 'been rejected almost unanimously'. For instance, in a typical dismissal, Balter (2005, p. 112) describes Mellaart's claim of finding the first city as being 'a notion popularized by Jane Jacobs', seemingly unaware of her social science status as an important urban theorist.

And so two parts of academia – social science/urban studies and archaeology/ancient history – have parted company when it comes to appreciating the work of Jane Jacobs. For my part I do think a communications approach to the rise of cities, and a concomitant view on the invention of agriculture, remains far more compelling than the archaeologists' basic model (Figure 3.1(a)). As a social scientist, I look for credible mechanisms of social change; this is what Jacobs provides but they appear conspicuous by their absence in evolutionary thinking. This is indicated in the spatial framework they use: instead of central flow theory their interpretations remain wedded to traditional central place theory.

The Downgrading of Çatalhöyük Using Central Place Theory

One very obvious indication that archaeologists have a problem dealing with Çatalhöyük is they don't know what to call it (Soja 2000, p. 29). Here are some descriptions of Çatalhöyük that indicate the conceptual confusion that has been endemic to the study of this site. Mellaart (1965a) uses both city and town in his initial descriptions – thus indicating 'urban' – but later on, it appears that, under the pressure of archaeological orthodoxy, he preferred the non-committal term 'settlement' (Balter 2005, p. 296). Renfrew (1975, p 7) refers to Çatalhöyük as an 'early farming village . . . almost urban size'. Bairoch (1988, p. 9) coins the strange term 'preurban town', and even 'pre-urban city' can be found (Tellier 2009). Both Nissen (1988) and Hodder (2006) consistently call it a 'town' but with the quotes emphasizing its problematic nature. The 'official biographer' of the current evacuations translates Hodder's 'town' into 'an enormous village' (Balter 2005, p. 3). Yet when the new excavations began at the site, two publications introducing the work trumpeted the 'first city' claim in their titles (Balter 1988; Shane and Küçük 1998)! These equivocal positions are well represented in *The Times Atlas of Archaeology*: the section on Çatalhöyük uses the phrase 'a farming village' for its title (Scarre 1988, p. 82) but quickly finds 'many features . . . puzzling', resulting in later reference to a 'highly sophisticated early town' (p. 83). For all these writers Çatalhöyük is in the wrong place at the wrong time. And it is literally so in Haywood's (2005) historical atlas: in the traditional manner he has a section entitled 'The first farmers' (p. 22), preceding a section entitled 'The first towns' (p. 24), and yet on the 'first farmers map' (p. 23) he has a symbol for 'other important site', which is Çatalhöyük. The intriguing thing is that this is labelled 'an early town' that is somehow before 'the first towns' introduced on the next page. I think this conceptual confusion can be traced back to using an inappropriate inter-urban theory: archaeologists have been searching for town-ness using central place theory rather than city-ness based on central flow theory.

The use of central place theory in archaeology can be traced back to the work of the very influential archaeologist, Colin Renfrew (1975); using quantitative methods 'inspired by geography' (p. 3), he has argued that 'a permanently functioning central place is a feature of every civilization' (p. 12). This implies a system of related settlements in contrast to a landscape of isolated settlements, which is 'the very antithesis of civilization' (p. 7). Such an argument has been developed in full by Nissen (1988) in his early history of ancient Western Asia. For the period 9000 to 6000 BC he traces the development of permanent settlement but notes the lack of 'systematic mutual connections' (p. 33). He calls the next period, 6000 to 3200 BC 'from isolated settlement to town' (p. 39), in which he traces the evolution of settlement systems (p. 41) through three tiers of central places to four. The latter first appears in Sumer with 'Uruk at its head' (p. 66), indicating the emergence of 'early high civilization' (p. 65) and therefore cities (Crawford 2004, p. 16). It is from this perspective of a central place system history that Nissen (1988) engages with the problem of how to interpret the 'type of settlement, sometimes called a "town"' (p. 36) represented by Çatalhöyük and the other inconveniently early large settlement, Jericho (Kenyon 1960; Soja 2000, pp. 27–35).

Basically the argument is that these large Neolithic settlements differ from towns 'in one decisive criterion': they are 'not the center of a settled countryside' (Nissen 1988, p. 36). Thus Jericho, for example, 'was not part of a settlement system' (pp. 36–7); it exhibited no 'real centrality' (p. 37). Hence he is able to comfortably conclude:

> The special development of Jericho and, to a limited extent, also of Çatalhöyük, in no way therefore changes anything in our general characterization of the period as one of separate open settlements. (pp. 37–8)

This is also why Emberling (2003, p. 258) rejects Jericho and Çatalhöyük's city credentials: neither developed 'a differentiated rural hinterland'. In other words, applying central place theory rules out Jericho and Çatalhöyük as cities.

Notice that in the quotation from Nissen above, the 'isolated settlements' he identifies for the time of Jericho and Çatalhöyük are characterized as 'separate open settlements' and it is the openness (trade) that I have previously emphasized. From the perspective of central flow theory,

Çatalhöyük, Jericho and their ilk represent the beginnings of city-ness. They are unusual for our understanding of contemporary cities in that, in these relatively small urban settlements, city-ness appears to dominate town-ness. This is consistent with the communication model where city precedes hinterland and the creation of 'lower order' towns (Figure 3.1(b)). But there is now a fascinating new episode to this debate. Since Mellaart's work reported above there have been new excavations that focus on reinterpreting the internal relations within the settlement.

Hodder's Çatalhöyük: Domestic Mode of Production or City-ness?

The second excavation of Çatalhöyük has been described as 'the greatest concentration of scientific fire power ever focused on an archaeological dig' (Balter 2005, p. 4). What has all this new research revealed? Hodder (2006) provides a fascinating report on the work that focuses on 'the mysteries of the elaborate symbolism at Çatalhöyük' and 'how people were living' (p. 18). He reports new estimates of the population size of the settlement – varying over time between 3500 and 8000 – and then states his key argument against Çatalhöyük being a city or town:

> So in terms of size, we might call this settlement a 'town'. But it has few of the other characteristics that we might mean by that term. Despite careful sampling of the surface of the mound, we have found no public spaces, administrative buildings, elite quarters, or really any specialized functional spaces. . . . Indeed in 2004 we undertook excavation specifically to explore the idea that there might be some centralized functions at the site. . . . What we found was more prosaic. . . . all there is at Çatalhöyük are houses and middens and pens. There is none of the functional differentiation that we normally associate with the term 'town'. Çatalhöyük is just a very large village – it pushed the idea of an egalitarian village to its extreme. Most production, even where there is some specialization of production, is carried out at the house level. And indeed, this is perhaps the greatest enigma of Çatalhöyük – that given the domestic scale of production and much social and economic life, why did people aggregate into such a major centre? (pp. 95, 98–9)

Within this critical argument, the crucial reference is to the nature of production; this goes to the heart of Jacobs and Soja's division of labour interpretations drawn from results of the earlier excavations by Mellaart.

Hodder (2006) describes 'an internal organization of the "town"' that is 'so atomised and small-scale' (p. 107). The houses were all largely separate – with few 'party walls' – and each was largely self-sufficient in function. Thus the production processes described in detail by Mellaart appear to occur in every house. For instance, there are no general builders of houses; each has bricks of 'different composition or shape' (p. 94). Thus, 'it is as if, despite the dense packing, each house retains its autonomy' (p. 95). Since Jacobs and Soja's division of labour argument requires specialization this is a powerful argument against. However, once again I must emphasize city-ness as an ongoing process. Here skills are being honed and, in fact, Hodder presents evidence for supporting Jacobs. As well as house-based activity there are also 'plenty of evidence of collective behaviour' (p. 107). For instance, 'there is much evidence for long-distance trade and exchange' (p. 80), which would have been done collectively like planting and herding (p. 94). Obsidian was an important traded good and there is evidence of possible value-added production in this case:

> It seems clear that obsidian came as pre-forms from the sources in Cappadocia 170 km (105 miles) away, and was taken into the house where it was buried. People then dug up and excavated pieces when they needed them and worked them nearby inside the house. (p. 173)

There appears to be some tension in Hodder's argument between 'town-wide' and house-based activities:

> Undoubtedly, some specialization of production does occur, but in most such cases, such as bead or bone tool production, or obsidian mirror manufacture, the specialization seems at best part-time, and fully embedded within a domestic mode. (p. 179)

In fact, Hodder identifies two important trends: 'specialization of production may have increased through time' (p. 182), and there may have been 'a shift away from the centrality of the house to the importance of exchange between houses' (p. 177). Thus with more specialization, particularly skilled people may have supplied neighbours with bone tools and obsidian mirrors (p. 182). Here there are traces of a possible transition from a domestic mode of production to a city-ness division of labour.

Thus I concur with Soja's (2010, p. 366) reassertion that 'what happened in Çatalhöyük was extraordinary': I think there remains enough evidence to warrant keeping to Jacobs' sophisticated process of city-ness, with its emphasis on process. But the more radical part of her argument – cities inventing agriculture – appears to be more difficult to sustain. To begin with there is a straightforward empirical issue to confront. Hodder (2006) does not deal with the Çatalhöyük–agricultural revolution link for the simple reason that the settlement is only 9000 years old, which still dates it much later than the domestication of animals and plants (Hodder 2006, p. 18). Where does this leave Jacobs' controversial thesis? As she foresaw, there has been subsequent evidence for even earlier urban settlements in Anatolia (Özdoğan and Başgelen 1999), and therefore Jacobs did not tie her theory down to this one particular settlement as the originator of agriculture. She refers to 'cities such as Çatalhöyük' (p. 37) in her discussion, carefully noting that this is only the 'earliest city yet found' (p. 31). To find the putative 'first city' (but it would be in a network of cities), Jacobs invents a fictitious city 'New Obsidian', and it is here that she describes how hunter–gatherer city dwellers invent agriculture. But, as common in archaeological disputes, the actual process of change is unknown, perhaps unknowable; thus one critic of Jacobs, Bairoch (1988, p. 17), concedes: 'while her arguments do not prove that agriculture was invented in the city, the margin of uncertainty around that period is such that the hypothesis cannot be rejected outright' (p. 17).

But I cannot just leave it there. In such situations of knowledge uncertainty, it is the plausibility of theoretical positions that matter. Hodder (2006, p. 250) briefly refers to Sahlins' (2004) concept of domestic mode of production as the structure of Çatalhöyük's house-based organization. And this seems to be appropriate for Hodder's interpretation: Sahlins describes this mode of production as 'a kind of *petite* economy' (p. 78) that was 'atomized and small scale' (p. 79). I will use and elaborate on Sahlins' ideas on 'stone age economics' to explore further Hodder's (2006, p. 99; Balter 1998) very basic question of why people aggregated into places like Çatalhöyük. There are two steps in the argument, one casting doubt on the conventional idea of the agricultural origins of cities, and the other introducing trade as a better candidate for stimulating aggregation.

Sahlins' 'Stone Age Economics' and Developing a Commercial Moral Syndrome

Sahlins (2004, p. 1) has famously described hunter–gatherer societies as the 'original affluent society'. By this he means that their 'wants are finite and few' and therefore their simple means for attending to these wants is generally adequate: 'a people can enjoy unparalleled material plenty – with a low standard of living' (p. 2). This interpretation is the opposite of our usual Hobbsian views of 'primitive peoples' living 'brutish lives'. But anthropological studies of work in hunter–gatherer societies show that rather than struggling for subsistence, these peoples spend only two or three days a week satisfying their needs (pp. 14–26). They have much leisure time; they appear to be lazy (p. 26). The question is, therefore, why should such affluent leisure societies want to domesticate plants and animals? As Sahlins says of a contemporary group of hunter–gatherers, 'tutored by life and not by anthropology (they) reject the Neolithic revolution in order to *keep* their leisure' (p. 27). Given that Palaeolithic hunter–gatherers, unlike their contemporary representatives, were not reduced to living in marginal lands, it follows that their 'pristine affluence' (p. 29) would likely make them even more sceptical of the benefits of farming. Thus Sahlins concludes:

> The Neolithic saw no particular improvement over the Palaeolithic in the amount of time required per capita for the production of subsistence; probably with the advent of agriculture, people had to work harder. (p. 35)

Why and how the Neolithic agricultural revolution therefore? Why bother?

Another common denigration of hunter–gatherers is that they live isolated lives: Sahlins (2004) also disputes this. There was no 'domestic autarky', the households were not self-sufficient and therefore there was swapping of goods (p. 83). But the key point for the domestic mode of production is that production remained for use and not exchange (pp. 83–4). This is because this mode of production 'is intrinsically an anti-surplus system' (p. 82). The result is that Sahlins develops a 'theory of value in nonexchange' (p. 277). Thus although there are examples of long-distance trade, trade networks, and even supply-and-demand effects (p. 280), it is 'social relations, not prices, (that) connect "buyers" and "sellers"' (p. 298). He interprets this as being 'the diplomacy of exchange' (p. 303): guardian arrangements in the valuing of exchanged goods. Thus there exists just one moral syndrome, the guardian; the question now arises as to how and when production for exchange emerged with consequent commercial practices, and the development of a new moral syndrome.

The obvious place to search for the invention of new commercial practices such as commercial diasporas or networks (Curtin 1984) is in the complexities of different spatial forms of trading as portrayed by Renfrew (1975, pp. 41–5). As previously argued (Figure 3.1(b)), the most likely source of change would seem to come from the rise of large aggregations of people, perhaps trading posts adding production to their activities, wherein the enhanced Jacobsean size facilitates the fundamental rethinking required to overcome cultural resistances to creating surpluses for gain. This is such an immense turnaround in making a living that it requires an immense level of social contact to have a reasonable probability of emerging as a new way of doing production. And this is what cities are about; this is where the 'finite and few' wants of the old world could be ditched and spiralling new needs and wants generated, and acted upon, to create a new social world. High, new levels of communication potential are needed to create the social revolution to a commercial way of life. It is the latter that would then enable the innovation for farming to happen alongside hunter–gathering as the latter failed to keep up with city food demands. In other words, Jacobs' (1969) conjecture of 'cities first; agriculture follows' is not all that implausible after all. In fact the story can be developed further.

The evidence presented so far for this process has been limited to just two well-known examples, mainly Çatalhöyük, plus some references to Jericho. What is needed for city-ness is a completely new social context: cities in city networks. The critical size can be debated but I suggest that settlements of 2000 to 5000 people in a network of five to ten such places might be appropriate. In fact Soja (2000) has harnessed evidence for numerous small cities in Western Asia during the millennia before Mesopotamia. Here are his additional cases of potential cities:

> During these four millennia (of Jericho's occupation, 9000 to 5000 BC), a number of other urban centers developed in a broad T-shaped region and became linked together in an expansive trading network of cities: Abu Hureyra (even larger in size than Jericho), Bouqras, and Mureyra along the upper reaches of the Eyphrates and Ras Shamra on the coast of present-day Syria; Ain Ghazal, Abu Gosh, and Beidha in the southern Levant; Zawi Chemi, Jarmo, and Ali Kosh in the borderlands of Iraq and Iran drained by the Tigris; and, from east to west in Anatolia, Çayönü, Asikli Hüyük, Çatalhöyük (probably the largest . . . of the first cities), and Haçilar. (pp. 28–9)

This is a new world of city networks (Düring 2007) originating in Soja's T-shaped region (Anatolia, Levant and northern Mesopotamia) where Asikli Hüyük (Esin and Harmankaya 1999), Cayonu (Özdoğan 1999), and Göbeki Tepe (Schmidt 2008), are the new, best known nodes. This is a totally different world from that described by Nissen (1988); it is not a stagnant world of isolated settlements, it is a new, creative world of economic expansion through city networks that existed millennia before the rise of cities in Mesopotamia.

MESOPOTAMIAN CITIES AND STATES: TWO ERAS OF DEVELOPMENT

Moving on to Mesopotamia, there is, of course, no dispute concerning the existence of cities. Table 3.2 shows the roster of cities in Sumer (southern Mesopotamia) that we will be largely concerned with in this section: 19 cities from 3700 to 2000 BC. The population estimates are drawn from Modelski's (2003) work. His results are used here because Chandler's (1987) 'historical census' only goes back to 2250 BC. In addition Chandler uses a 20 000 threshold for inclusion compared to Modelski's 10 000, thus missing many of the cities we will be interested in. I have emboldened the largest city for each data year in Table 3.2 and these can be used to steer

Table 3.2 *Estimates of Mesopotamian city populations, third and fourth millennia* BC *(in 000s)*

City	3700	3500	3300	3000	**2800**	2500	2400	2300	2200	**2100**	2000
Adab					10	20	10	10	30	10	10
Akkad									30		
Akshak						10	20				
Eridu	**6–10**	10	10	10							
Girsu							40	**80**	**50**	80	**40**
Isin											**40**
Kesh						40	10	10	10		
Kish						30	20				
Lagash						**60**	30				
Larak		10	10	10							
Larsa					16	10					**40**
Nina										10	10
Nippur				10	10	20	20	30	30	30	30
Shuruppak					30	30	10				
Suheri				10	10	10	10		10	10	10
Umma					20	40	**40**	40	10	20	25
Ur					12	10	10	20	40	**100**	20
Uruk		**14**	**40**	**40**	**80**	40	30	30		30	30
Zabalam					10	10	10	10	10	10	10

Note: Emboldened figures and city name indicate the largest at a given time.

Source: Modelski 2003: 22 (Table 2(a)); 28 (Table 2(b)).

an outline story of what happened in the period under discussion, serving as backcloth to more detailed discussions that follow.

Eridu is the only city to (just) make Modelski's threshold in 3700 BC: it is interpreted as Sumer's first city and remained important as a religious site. Uruk appears as the largest of three cities in 3500 BC and maintains its position until 2800 BC. With a population estimate of 80 000 at its peak, it is the first great city in the world. However, shortly afterwards the course of the Euphrates changes from Uruk to Umma, leading to a realignment of city development. This centres on rivalry between first, Umma and Lagash and then Umma and Girsu, the latter replacing Lagash as the main city of its kingdom. These changes and the final victory of Girsu are reflected in the movement in the leading cities from 2500 BC through to 2200 BC. Girsu is declining at the latter date, which corresponds to the rise of the Akkad empire. This first territorial state created its own capital city at Akkad but note that the latter political creation never became the leading city in population terms. However this empire was soon replaced by the empire of the Third Dynasty of Ur. This is based on a long-established city that blossomed to become the first city in the world to reach 100 000 in 2100 BC. This second territorial state is again short-lived and in the final year in Table 3.2, there are three much smaller cities with the highest populations, one of them appearing in the table for only the first time. It is the Isin dynasty that claim Ur's inheritance but they never were able to recreate Ur's territorial state. Instead, another era is beginning that culminates in the rise of the Assyrian and Babylonian empires that will feature in Part III.

My position is that this story encompasses the invention of the earliest-known states. This is conventional in timing but I will be more unconventional in terms of process. That is to say, it is generally understood that Mesopotamia is the locus of the first states, which were city-states. But, as previously signalled, therein lies a problem. Traditionally, cities and states are seen as evolving together as a single institution, hence 'city-state'. But I am treating them as two different processes that do not necessarily develop in parallel. Thus I identify first cities without states to be followed by cities in states, initially one city per state or city-state. Just simply identifying cities as city-states in the rise of Mesopotamian civilization is to conflate two processes in a most unhelpful way (Soja 2010, p. 364). However, compared to the cities-agriculture position, my argument on cities and states does have some support within the archaeology and ancient history literature.

States From Cities, Not Chiefdoms

My position mirrors that of Monica Smith (2003b), who is explicit on the importance of recognizing that 'cities do not require a state level of authority to exist and thrive' (p. 12). Therefore:

> it is . . . time for the understanding of cities to be uncoupled from the necessary presence of states. By breaking this pairing of cities and states, we allow cities to be understood on their own terms as centers of political, economic, and social organization that may be considerably more complex than the territories and regions in which they are located. (p. 13)

She traces this conflation back to Childe (1950, p. 12), who created a framework in which 'theorizing about urbanism has often really been about states rather than cities'. This key point had been made much earlier by Price (1978, p. 175):

> The relation between urbanism and the state, however, has been the cause of profound confusion for a variety of reasons, both scholarly and ideological. Childe's Mesopotamian data combined urbanism and the state in a single sequence and permitted the uncritical evaluation of this particular association.

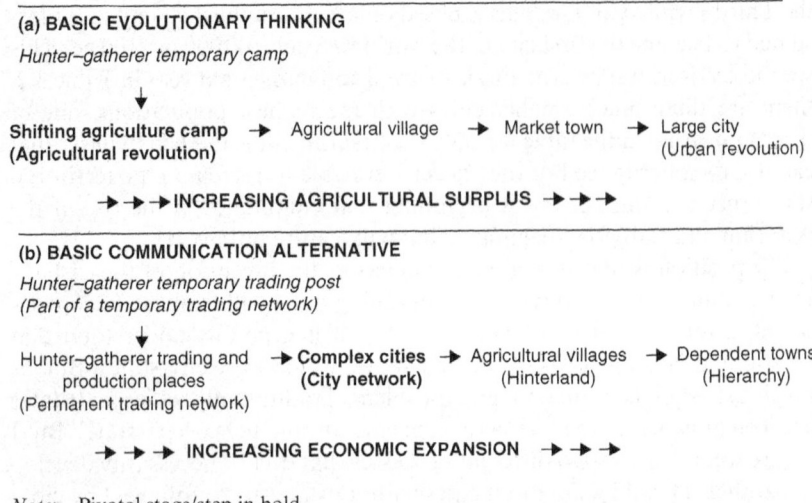

Note: Pivotal stage/step in bold.

Figure 3.2   Alternative origins of states

Smith (2003b) indicts Robert McAdams, the great chronicler of Mesopotamian urbanism; she points out that, paradoxically, in his classic *The Evolution of Urban Society* (Adams 1966) he states that, despite the book's title, his 'central concern is the growth of the state' (p. 90; quoted in Smith (2003b, p. 12)). Conversely Smith's argues that 'cities in the premodern world did not require a state level of organization' (p. 15).

It is only after unravelling the city/state conflation that it is possible to see cities as sites for the invention of states (Figure 3.2(a)). For Yoffee (2005, p. 45) 'cities were the transformative social environments in which states themselves were created', which he explains using the generic sociological concepts of differentiation and integration (pp. 32–3). The communication potential of cities creates new, ongoing differentiation to produce the complex city and city network. This creates a political demand for integration that invention of the state satisfies: new governance, first at the local city-state scale, and then at the non-local, city-empire scale. Thus, as with the invention of agriculture, it is the creation of complex city-ness that is the pivotal step in the invention of the state (Figure 3.2(a)).

Although conflation of city and state is common in the archaeological literature, there is another, more influential, tradition that provides an evolutionary sequencing for the creation of states, and where cities are by no means pivotal. In this approach, states are interpreted as the culmination of a sequence beginning with simple bands that evolve into increasingly more complex 'chiefdoms' (for a recent review see Abrutyn and Lawrence (2010)). In one example, the idea that states derive from chiefdoms is linked to settlements through a rather simplistic application of central place theory: settlement hierarchies are used to define the emergence of states (Figure 3.2(b)). Flannery (1998, p. 16) states this position succinctly

> chiefdoms tend to have only two or three levels (or tiers) of settlements, whereas states tended to have a hierarchy of at least four levels: cities, towns, large villages, and small villages.

Although he qualifies this by calling it a useful 'rule of thumb' rather than a 'law', such an approach invites thinking about states simplistically as a set of attributes. However, the evolutionary sequence in Figure 3.2(b) does not lead on to city-states as four-tier urban systems, as might be expected with cities occupying the top tier. Following Marcus (1998, p. 92), in this diagram I specify chiefdoms evolving into larger 'territorial states'. In her argument the mechanism for city-state creation is a subsequent spatial disintegration of larger territorial states (Figure 3.2(b)). The latter result from the process of 'competing chiefdoms' (p. 62, see also Marcus and Fienman (1998)). In other words, in this argument territorial states come before city-states.

Yoffee (2005, p. 34), a trenchant critic of this 'neo-evolutionary' approach as previously noted, suggests a more process-orientated argument:

> In the process of city-state formation, leaders of various co-resident social groups compete for power. And new arenas for competition are created to channel this struggle. Since these arenas are themselves products of urban interactions (which include new relations with a concomitantly ruralised countryside, (therefore) the city state can be considered an 'invention in itself'. (Yoffee 1997, p. 261)

He argues that states are not the next stage after chiefs; rather he treats states as *qualitatively* different from chiefdoms. From our communications perspective, although both sequences pivot on stages invoking 'complexity' in Figure 3.2(a) and (b), it should be noted that the commercial complexity of cities and city networks is at a completely different level above the political complexity of even the most 'advanced' chiefdoms. Note that I do not dispute that the fragmentation of territorial states can have occurred historically to produce city 'statelets' but I do not accept this to be a primal process: there had to have been earlier city-states to have generated the territorial state before its dissolution.

I broadly follow Yoffee's position below but with more emphasis on external relations as indicated by the need to build city walls. I harness evidence from Mesopotamian studies to put detail on to the abstraction that is Figure 3.2(a). This is done in three parts. First, I specify key elements in identifying two distinctive eras of development. Second, I look in more detail at the city-ness of the initial era in which commercial practice appears specifically important and, third, I look at the state-making process of the second era when guardian practice comes to dominate.

Dividing Mesopotamian Development into Two Eras

In this argument the two eras are separated at about 3000–2800 BC; the earlier period is interpreted as featuring city-ness strongly, the later one as particularly featuring state formation. As such they represent different balances between commercial and guardian practices.

The first period is pre-literate but can be reconstructed from later texts. I draw heavily on the reconstruction by Jacobsen (1970). I have found his interpretations particularly meaningful in relation to the conceptual toolkits I am deploying. His key insight is the division of ancient literature into myths and epics (p. 140). Myths are societal in nature through their treatment of origins with cities as gods; epics deal with later times and are concerned with the deeds of human individuals as heroes. It is this distinction between two 'historical records' that provides the basis for defining and understanding the two eras of development.

In the myths, the Sumerian 'Eden' is not a garden but a city: Eridu is the oldest city, 'a holy place, the very site of creation' (Leick 2001, pp. 2, 29). When Heaven located the city on Earth, a countryside was then created to feed the people. Thus it can be noted that these Sumerian Gods agree with Jacobs' 'cities first, agriculture second' thesis! Current archaeological findings confirm Eridu to be the oldest of Sumerian cities going back to the early fourth millennium BC period but it never grew large. However it remained important symbolically as a small cult centre in mutual relations with other cities. In the myths, Eridu is one of five initial Sumerian cities, the others being Larak, Shuruppak, Sippar and Badtibira. These are on the southern branch of the Euphates and Eridu is the most southern city of all. The key point is that the myths identify five cities, enough to build a small but vibrant network of cities.

But what evidence is there that there was a network of cities and not just separate cities? Back to Jacobsen (1970): he describes a 'regional' pattern of politics in the myths based upon 'the quite unique position held by the city of Nippur and its chief god, Enlil, in Sumerian politics' (p. 139). From earliest times this city was considered the source of Sumer-wide governance but there is no evidence that this was the result of Nippur conquering other cities. Rather it was the locale of an all-Sumer assembly convened to deal with emergencies. This was the transient meeting place for conducting trans-city business. Jacobsen concludes: 'since its temporary and loose character precludes terms like "state" or even "nation" ... (I) ... choose the relatively noncommittal term "Kengir League"'. Jacobsen times this league of cities to coincide with our first era (p. 141). What he describes is a non-state guardian process that deals with crises in an ad hoc manner providing for administrative or military leadership on a temporary basis.

This political network developed parallel to a commercial network of the early cities. Jacobsen (1970) mentions jar seals inscribed with the names of major cities:

> Since such collective seals imply collective responsibility for the goods sent under the seal ... [this is] a feature most easily understandable in terms of a league of cities such as the Kengir League. (p. 141)

In fact when the pre-literate archaeological content of the period is explored in terms of tokens, tablets and seals, it is found that it is economic transactions that are overwhelmingly dominant (Nissen et al. 1993). This is a form of governance primarily concerned for 'control over economic activity' (p. 14): in our first era dominated by the city of Uruk 'the proto-cuneiform script was almost exclusively restricted to bookkeeping; it was an "accountants script"' (p. 30). Even in early written documents there is no religious narrative or historical topics (i.e. myths or epics) (p. 21), since it is only in the third millennium BC that writing achieves 'a degree of complexity to become a universal means of communications' (i.e. representing the human language) (p. 30). In other words, the guardian process developing here is city/city network governance largely for facilitating and regulating commercial practice.

Overall, there is an ongoing economic administration operating alongside transient organization, including military operations. Returning to our key question: do the sum of such organizational processes constitute a state, a city-state? Certainly they are early governance processes, but they have yet to take on a state form in this first era. Emberling (2003, p. 261) defines the position well:

> Our analytical category 'the state' ... had little direct reflection in the practices of early Mesopotamians, and in fact homogenizes a series of disparate political and administrative institutions.

This is an era of dynamic cities that were to *become* the crucible of state-making, but no more.

It is all change during the Early Dynastic I period (after 3000 BC) in a new world described by the epics:

> In the myths life was on the whole peaceful, with only an occasional serious threat of war; in the epics war is the rule, the cities are ringed with huge defensive walls, their rulers think of war and conquest only, danger of sudden attack is ever present. The risks involved in such attacks, furthermore, are real and serious. Large prosperous cities may be looted and burned and even completely destroyed; if a city yields to the attacker it may see the canal system on which it depends readjusted to favor the city of the victor and may have to send its inhabitants off year after year to do forced labor in the victor's fields or on its building projects to the detriment of its own economy. How real and constant these dangers were can be gauged from the prevalence of city walls in the epics, for no community would have accepted the enormous burden of constructing such walls were the need for them not both patent and pressing. (Jacobsen 1970, p. 143)

This quote vividly presents the intensification of guardian practices as zero-sum games; I take the building of city walls to be a signal for the changing balance between commercial and guardian practices that suggests formal state-making. Several features indicate such an interpretation of this change. First, in terms of political leadership *en* meaning 'chief administrator' is replaced by *lugal* the military leader, now translated as 'king' to indicate permanence (p. 144). Second, politics changes with decisions in the city assemblies moving away from voting to be replaced by divine favour (i.e. kings representing the relevant city-god's will) (p. 145). Third, even the gods that had been relatively egalitarian in organization become increasingly hierarchical (Leick 2001, pp. 147–8). This is state-making whereby new concerns for security are concentrated through coercion into a new institutional framework. This is dated by Jacobsen for completion in Early Dynastic II (2800 BC), as indicated by both archaeological evidence of 'the widespread appearance of city walls' and traditional sources of epics such as the Sumerian Kings List (p. 147).

The most famous hero in the Sumerian Kings List is Gilgamesh the king of Uruk in Early Dynastic I. Nissen (1988) uses this example to describe the change to state formation. At the beginning of the epic poem 'we are told how Gilgamesh had to suppress the people of Uruk in order to be able to erect the city wall' (p. 95). And what a wall it was: over nine kilometres long, seven metres high and with some 900 semicircular towers set regularly in the ramparts (Nissen 1988, p. 95; Leick 2001, p. 56). In this new era of inter-city warfare Gilgamesh is able to overrule the city assembly and defeat the aggression of Kish (Leick 2001, p. 81). Uruk is no longer simply a city; it is a city-state.

In the next two sections I consider city-ness and state formation separately. Although the former will be weighted towards the earlier era and the latter to the later era, it is important to note that I do not use a city/ city-state boundary to completely separate the discussion. My argument above is based upon the balance between commercial and guardian practices; commercial practices continue in city-states and governance practices were necessary before the growth of city-states.

Mesopotamian City-ness

In searching out the making of new social spaces that are city-ness and town-ness, I am looking for local commerce and non-local commerce. These coincide with what Yoffce (2005, p. 35) identifies as two sources of economic power in early civilizations: subsistence and storage of surpluses, and mercantile activity. The first derives from the countryside, from a city's hinterland. Yoffee describes this in a very Jacobsean manner: 'the urban implosion was accompanied by an equally important creation of the countryside' (p. 60). This entailed 'first depopulation of the rural and then its reconstruction: new villages, towns and hamlets arose in the backdraft of urbanization' (p. 60). This is clearly an example of the creation of town-ness. At the same time 'long-distance, regular networks of exchange' are important not just because of the direct acquisition of wealth thus obtained, but also because this new wealth is separate from the moral economy of the local (p. 35). This is clearly the making of the process of city-ness. To understand this city-ness in Mesopotamia, I turn to the seminal work of Guillermo Algaze (2005a; 2005b).

Algaze (2005b) draws explicitly on Jacobs (1969) to understand what he terms 'the Sumerian take-off'. Although he does not use the term city-ness, a key feature of his work is that he treats production and exchange together and thereby links the internal complexity of cities to their external connectedness. Thus he incorporates the environmental advantages of southern Mesopotamia (irrigation agriculture) with transport advantages of the vast dendritic network for movement of commodities and information, as well as for hinterland canals.

The 'urban take-off' (p. 12) is described as a process of cumulative multiplier effects drawing on Myrdal (1957), Pred (1966), Jacobs (1969) and Krugman (1995). The most important process derives from the latter two: import replacement. This requires a size of settlement that can sustain economic expansion; this can certainly be placed below the 10 000 entry qualification for Table 3.2. Thus Algaze is able to push back the beginning of a dynamic urban network even to the late fifth and early fourth millennia BC. Here he identifies 'by far the most important case of import substitution processes': the adoption of wool-bearing sheep from the surrounding highlands' (p. 14). Initially imported from the latter regions, by the second half of the fourth millennium BC a new wool textiles industry using local wool was central to the urban economy. With access to a wide range of dyes and with larger pools of labour, the growth of this industry provided for new forward and backward linkages. Algaze describes this as a 'textbook case' of multiplier effects (p. 15); it is worth quoting this process in full:

> [Forward linkages] are provided by the fulling of semi-finished woven textiles with oils and alkali and the dyeing of fulled cloth. Both these practices . . . require a substantial input of value-added labor and new resources . . . Examples of backward linkages, in turn, are provided by a variety of labor-intensive activities that contributed necessary inputs to the weaving establishments but largely took place away from them. Minimally, these included pasturing the sheep, washing, plucking and/or shearing, combing, and spinning the wool, separating the wool by quality, and delivering it . . . No less important . . . this would have required scores of bureaucrats to record, store, and redistribute the output, and also to supervise the housing of the laborers and the distribution of subsistence rations. (p. 15)

In Jacobs' terms this is economic expansion in action in early Sumerian cities.

Dynamic cities encompass multiple economic expansion processes and this was the case in Sumer. Although originally cities were differentiated by different economic niches relating to the resource base they exploited, with success came 'competitive emulation' (Algaze 2005b, p. 13). This replacement of imports from nearby places reduced regional specialization in Sumer but in the process set up a growth spurt due to new productive capacities being developed. It was at this stage, in the Late Uruk period, that longer-distance trade came to prominence as exchanges between Sumer cities decreased. This 'foreign' trade exploited the immense water transport advantages of Sumer and, in addition, coincided with the domestication of the donkey facilitating overland trade (p. 13). The resulting input replacement was now metal-based: from buying fully finished products from metal producing areas like Iran and Anatolia, Sumer cities created new metal-processing industries that relied 'on imports of only lightly processed ores and of semi-processed ingots of smelted copper' (p. 13). This is a network world of cities with people, commodities, ideas and knowledge circulating within and between cities with ever-increasing demands for, and development of, innovations.

By far the greatest innovation of Sumer cities was the invention of writing. I have previously noted how pre-literate accountancy practices were developed through the Uruk period and writing 'appeared for the first time in the Late Uruk period' (Nissen et al. 1993, p. 19). Also previously noted, the new writing was largely about economic administration and therefore supplemented earlier accountancy practices rather than supplanting or transcending them (p. 21). The important point from a city perspective is that this development consolidated a large category of new work – scribes – in a new archetypal urban profession. This was the first 'knowledge industry', what Algaze (2005b, p. 23) calls 'technologies of the intellect'. Nissen and his colleagues find it 'difficult to conceive how the application and maintenance of administrative structures were possible without an orderly transmission of expertise and experience' (p. 105). In other words scribes must have obtained 'training' within a community of scribes. This is the context for 'experiments . . . to achieve more efficient methods of control': writing itself will likely have been a result of such experimentation (p.105). Thus literacy derives from what it is cities do so well, in the first known long-term sustainable network of cities.

The scribes were not the only new addition in the making of an increasingly complex division of labour, and their work records this. Among the few non-economic texts there are 'lexical lists' that order items logically. The most famous is the 'Titles and Professions List' that mixes status positions with economic roles: 'an orderly progression (of) titles, professional names and functional designations'. The best-preserved tablet is from the middle of the third millennium BC, but this is copy of a well-known text that goes back to the late Uruk period (Nissen et al. 1993, p. 110). Since it was copied over a period of 800 years, the assumption is that it was used as scribal training (pp. 106, 111). It is noteworthy that the first rank, although subsequently translated in later languages as 'king', the original Sumerian designates the leading administrator; the Sumerian word for king, *lugal*, is not used (p. 111). At the second level there are functional leaders with responsibilities for administrative areas such as justice/law, the city, the troops, the plough and barley (pp. 106, 111; Nissen 1986, p. 329). Next come other high ranks: high priests, 'chairman of the assembly', advisors ('wise men'), ambassadors, and other court and assembly officials. The remainder consist of lower-ranking priests, gardeners, cooks and craftsmen such as coppersmiths, jewellers, potters and bakers (Nissen 1986, p. 329; Nissen et al. 1993, p. 111). One interpretation is that the text describes an initial Uruk complex division of labour. But it is very hierarchical, putting all work practices in their ranked place. As such it is a simplification, a classic political state document (Scott 1998) that is still deemed to have some relevance in the later world of city-states. The fact that it has lasted so long does indicate that it is used by state officials to simplify, and make sense of, what were highly complex social entities: the cities. However, if the text were still an accurate description of the division of labour in the mid-third millennium this would indicate a sclerotic stagnation, which is known not to be the case (Table 3.2).

Finally, what of the development of relations between these Sumerian cities and other regions? In an earlier work, Algaze (2005a) has interpreted Uruk's non-Sumer relations as a 'Uruk world-system' with Sumer as the 'core'. This leaves the other regions as 'periphery'; indicated by the presence of Uruk trading posts and enclaves in non-Sumerian cities in upper Mesopotamia, Anatolia and Iran. As a world-economy, this terminology seems appropriate; it is a spatial organization in which commercial agents took advantage of the dendritic transport potential of Sumer to link northwards, up the rivers and further into the highland sources of raw materials. Thus a key point of this research is that it is not describing a 'Uruk empire'; these were only dense trading links. Algaze refers to the Uruk expansion as an 'informal empire' in the 'Uruk world-system' (pp. 110–15), a process whereby regions are brought into an economic sphere of influence without the costs of military conquest. (For a contrary position that does not contradict the non-military nature of the relations, see Stein (1999).) And, of course, this is how it must have been, given the 'two eras' argument developed above. Economic power was strongly harnessed in the Uruk period, but governance processes were not yet developed to support non-local warfare and conquest. For this, states were necessary.

Mesopotamian State Formation

The city-ness process in Mesopotamia was immensely successful from an economic perspective and culminated in Uruk reaching a demographic size of some 80 000 people (Table 3.2). But this commercial success was running ahead of guardian capacities. The result is a development of governance that leads to state formation as city-states that Mann (1986, p. 82) calls 'social caging'. I have previously suggested that the building of defensive city walls is a local indicator that state-ness has been achieved – the 'state' has arrived on the historical scene. This idea can be, indeed must be, linked to how we define the state. In his discussion of city-states, Yoffee (2005, p. 45) notes that definitions in the literature are not clear on whether or not they were independent political entities. In the argument developed here I treat city-states as first having internal autonomy, with some also having independence from external political control. And it is this relation to the outside world that the building of walls signifies. It is a basic simplification of urban space into an inside and an outside to augment defence capabilities.

The basic assumption of this simple division of space is that the inside is peaceful and the outside is the source of danger. But the inside – the city – is not in any way an oasis of calm; it has had to be pacified before the building of walls can be contemplated. In fact the bringing together of large numbers of people in a dense space is not only a generator of innovation, it is also a recipe for social conflict as previously noted. The guardian processes that developed with the rise of cities are primarily about solving the inevitable problems consequent upon expanding social relations in a confined space. The graduation of these processes to state-ness implies a degree of success in these spiritual and administrative mechanisms to produce an 'us and them' political frame with just 'us' inside, or brought inside, the wall when militarily necessary. In Yoffee's (2005, p. 61) words: 'the identities of people as citizens and their participation in local networks of . . . political interactions were redefined in cities'. Thus are Sumerian cities transformed into city-states.

Jacobsen (1970, pp. 143–4) uses epic texts to suggest how this change from city to city-state may have come about. As previously described, the separate administrative and military leaderships of Sumerian cities were appointed initially for dealing with specific emergencies. Jacobsen argues that there would have been 'inherent tendencies' for office-holders to try and extend their authority beyond the duration of an emergency (p. 143). When in the epics sporadic war converts to a permanent condition then 'the officer who was dealing with it could not but become permanent with it' (p. 144). Thus arises a 'king' whose personal military followers become a regular standing army; his household locale becomes a 'palace'. In this way cities become garrisoned and walled; hence 'the close connection between Gilgamesh and the building of the city wall of Uruk in the Gilgamesh Epic' (p. 144). This interpretation equates with Webb's (1975) notion of a 'conditional state' (p. 164), wherein the conditionality of leadership has to be overcome to create a state attained through 'reliance on force' (p. 165). Although I do not like the concept of 'conditional state' because of its automatic evolutionary implication, the outcome, with its association between state and coercion, is of course classically Weberian in nature (Weber 1978). Webb (1975) defines very well the process I am describing.

Webb (1975, pp. 184–94) also considers the reason for the increased conflict that enables state formation. He is sympathetic to Carneiro's (1970; 1978) non-urban 'circumscription hypothesis', which evokes an environmental causation: limited agricultural land (e.g. contained in a valley or lake basin) creates a situation where warfare cannot be resolved by movement of the defeated group to new land. The losers have nowhere to retreat to and therefore become slaves in an enhanced social stratification that culminates in a state. Webb (1975, p. 190) considers this argument to be lacking in consideration of trade and its contribution to creating more complex societies. This brings cities into the equation; cities consist of massive investment in social capital (flows/networks) and physical capital (place/territory) that are developed as very 'constricted spaces'. City dwellers have nowhere to retreat except behind their walls: the building of walls says that 'we are not leaving'. This is a city circumscription hypothesis of state-making.

In contrast, other early spatial arguments on state formation are more difficult to incorporate into our argument. In particular, Colin Renfrew's (1975) widely used concept of 'early state modules' suggests the obverse of what I am arguing on cities and states. As well as its evolutionary overtones, he develops his argument from central place theory. This means, from my perspective, that he is building on town-ness (hinterlands) rather than on city-ness (networks). Curiously Renfrew seems to be attracted to central place theory because it does not involve 'analysis of "cities"' (p. 12) – central places can be just places of exchange with little or even no permanent population. If not cities what is Renfrew's focus? His concern is for 'the administrative module in early civilizations', and this leads him to 'the genesis of . . . spatial organization', as specified in central place theory. He identifies 'early state modules' as 'autonomous territorial units, with their central places'. Thus he creates spaces of places for early civilizations by drawing Thiessen polygons around selected settlements (pp. 13–17). However, 'the city with its full complexity' (p. 30) can arise from his spatial organization through exogenous growth involving local exchange and population agglomeration. In this argument, exogenous change such as 'external trade' can be important, but is not a necessary factor (pp. 31–2). Be that as it may, although Renfrew emphasizes the hierarchical outcome of central place theory (pp. 20, 24), the 'intermediate trade' he specifies between central places at the centre of his modules does represent mutual, non-local relations and therefore implies a city network. He uses Mesopotamian cities as examples of his approach (p. 14) and, with specific reference to his implicit network level, we can accommodate his ideas to the argument developed here. But it leads straight to the organization of multi-city-states, without reference to the formation of competitive city-states; it misses out part of the story.

In city-states guardian practices are in the ascendancy above commercial practices. The question arises as to how such a guardian/commercial relation developed and how sustainable it became. When expansion of commercial practices grows the city, it thereby becomes an inviting target, a place of rich pickings for outside or inside military predators. Thus the city network phase without states is ultimately unsustainable: success creates the conditions requiring governance change in order to survive. Enter the city-state. New success in this sphere, expansion of guardian practices, growing the city's territory (hinterland), threatens other cities and their territories. Thus the city-state as a political structure also creates new conditions leading to another round of necessary change to survive. Enter the territorial state or city-empire, a successful city-state that has conquered other city-states and relegated them to provincial status. It is the story of city-empire that is the stuff of the epics.

But let's start with the initial competitive phase of multiple city-states. Nissen (1988, pp. 131–3) provides an interesting example of the competition between city-states in third millennium Mesopotamia. Drawing 'spheres of influence' around the main cities he shows that initially they were far enough apart not to encroach on each other's territory. However, in the early third century BC, when the route of the Euphrates changed to the advantage of the small settlement of Umma, this grew into a new city. It reached a point where it encroached on a neighbouring city-state of Lagash and its major city Girsu. This produced a conflict zone between the cities over water usage and canals (p. 135). This conflict, which became seemingly perennial, is only known because it features prominently in texts of the Early Dynasty III (p. 135; Jacobsen 1970, p. 151), but Nissen (1988, p. 135) argues that it represents a new norm for what he calls 'the period of rival states' from 2800 to 2350 BC (see Table 3.2).

From the epics there are records of rulers, conflicts and successions. Interpretations of these show fluctuating fortunes with different Sumer city-states rising to regional leadership followed by a return to squabbling city-states until another hero-king raises his city to overlordship. Although lacking continuity, the common title taken by those achieving the latter is 'King of Kish', irrespective of their own home city. This is a curious title because the city of Kish is not in Sumer but is located on the Euphrates to the north. Nissen (1988, pp. 144–5) suggests that the city of Kish held a strategic riverine position relative to all Sumer and therefore its kingship meant countrywide control. However, it is not known whether the title merely represented 'power to raid and to exact tribute unopposed', or whether it was a more solid political structure (Jacobsen 1970, p. 153). Jacobsen notes that one such 'king' adjudicated in the long running dispute between Umma and Lagash/Girsa (p. 153) suggesting real jurisdiction.

However the 'kings of Kish' are interesting because their conquests revealed the need for new political mechanisms that were required for the establishment of a multi-city territorial state. This was the conversion of defeated city-states into new imperial provinces:

As soon as a polity was enlarged beyond the boundaries of one city-state, 'branch offices' were needed. Each previous independent state constituted a convenient province, which could be accurately delimitated territorially, on the basis of the previous boundaries of the separate city-states. (Postgate 1992, p. 151)

But this process was fraught with difficulties as the fragile Kish kingships were merely local city-state rulers confronted by the pitfalls of non-local governance. The result of conquest was a centre/non-centre dichotomy. The king represented the centre's rule across the territory but he was opposed by the particularities of other cities and their special gods. And the latter had to be respected. The solution of treating the non-centre as 'provinces' is a new administrative invention. According to Nissen (1988) this political innovation was not made until the end of the third millennium BC in what he calls the 'period of the first territorial states', from 2350 to 2000 BC.

In fact, the new administrative mechanisms were developed twice to produce city-empires that had dynastic reproduction of several generations. Sargon of Akkad, 'the first personality of history' (Mann 1986, p. 133), is generally credited with producing the first 'world empire'. His origins are obscure but he signalled a break from the past by centring his rule on a new city, Akkad. This city became the base of a 'centralized administration and communication system' (Nissen 1988, p. 167). His new rule used 'governors' from Akkad to rule conquered cities that were garrisoned by Akkad soldiers and whose walls were destroyed indicating not just removal of defence but also elimination of their separate statehood (p. 168; Jacobsen 1970, p. 154). The Akkad dynasty lasted five rulers, covering nearly 200 years before succumbing to outside invasion. Sumer was not then unified again until the 'Third Dynasty of Ur', which had five rulers lasting for 109 years. Jacobsen (1970, p. 155) argues that it was this empire that solved the problem of continual non-local rebellion by instituting a senior administrative elite, answerable to the king, who could be moved from post to post to reduce growth of local ties (Nissen 1988, p. 194). A key feature was that military affairs were kept separate from the civil administration (Postgate 1992, p. 152). This is a state bureaucracy treating the former city-states of Sumer as simple provinces. Thus was born what Nissen calls the 'territorial state', which is a city-empire where rival cities are reduced to provinces.

Once this territorial state formation was completed Sumer's relations with other regions changed dramatically. In the cities era of Uruk, it was previously shown that trading led to an 'informal empire' of enclaves and trading posts as the means of projecting the economic power of Sumer's great cities (Algaze 2005a). But states project political power through coercion or the threat thereof to create formal empires, lands of conquest. Sargon attempted to extend his empire far beyond Sumer north into today's Syria and Anatolia but outer areas were not always meant to be permanent possessions, they could represent just a buffer zone (Nissen 1988, p. 168). The Third Dynasty of Ur empire was at least as large as the Akkadian empire and in this case appeared to be more strategic by including regions to the east to protect the eastern flank from threats of peoples of the northeastern mountains (p. 196). Further, the northwest frontier was protected by the erection of the 'Martu wall' as a sort of city-state protection mechanism writ large. It was the over-running of this wall that marks the end of the great empire of Ur.

In summary: I have interpreted this state-ness process as consequent upon an earlier city-ness process. This is entirely consistent with Yoffee's (2005, p. 45) position that 'cities were the transformative social environments in which states themselves were created'. And Yoffee (pp. 32–3) provides a basic rationale for this sequence using the generic sociological concepts of differentiation and integration. First, the commercial practices create new, ongoing differentiation to produce the complex city and city network. The guardian practices respond to this through mechanisms of integration that incorporate through simplifying roles and legitimating new rule, first at the local city-state scale and then at the non-local city-empire scale. This is state power simplifying commercial power by substituting territory for network.

CONCLUSION: A FIRST CREATIVE INTERLUDE

This conclusion will combine the two case studies to provide an overview of the unfolding of Western Asia's 'creative interlude'. I will begin by using what we have learned from the very successful Mesopotamian urban network to reconsider the less successful urban networks of Soja's T-shaped region.

The two eras of the Sumer case study is based upon the sequence cities => city-states (walls) => territorial states (conquests), based upon a changing balance between commercial and guardian processes. Hence when looking at earlier claims for the existence of cities we are searching out large settlements in which there appears to be clear evidence of urban development before the erection of walls. And this is exactly what Kenyon (1960) finds at Jericho. The Pre-Pottery Neolithic A level of the site (c. 8000 BC) shows a large settlement estimated at 2000 people – Mellaart (1965a, p. 32) thinks this to be an under-estimate – that was 'not fortified from the beginning' (Mellaart 1965a, p. 32). In fact there are three or more phases of housing before the building of the walls. The latter were quite spectacular – over five metres high (p. 33). The site was abandoned after about 1000 years and then the same sequence is found for the next settlement in the Pre-Pottery Neolithic B period. These new residents of the site built a larger settlement from just after 7000 BC, and it 'was only provided with defences in the form of walls built of enormous blocks of stone, towards the middle of the period' (p. 38). Thus in both cases, a millennium apart, a city appears to have existed before the need for organizing the huge investment in city walls: 'as the wealth of the settlement grew and powerful neighbours established themselves, city walls became a necessity to protect the town' (p. 33).

Mellaart's (1965a) surmising where the wealth came from is also very consistent with the argument developed above. As an oasis Jericho did not have the material base for an agricultural economy, instead:

> Some other source of revenue must have existed and this was probably trade. Jericho was well situated for commercial enterprise; it commanded the resources of the Dead Sea, salt, bitumen and sulphur, all useful products in early societies. Obsidian, nephrite and other greenstones from Anatolia, turquoise matrix from Sinai and cowries from the Red Sea have been found in the remains of the town. (p. 36)

In addition in the Pre-Pottery B period there are other trading partners identified with similar trading/production functions (p. 43). Mithen (2003, p. 61) also refers to extensive trade networks and reminds us that 'Jericho was not alone in this new Neolithic world'. Thus a preliminary conclusion would be that Jericho was part of a city network, a place where city-ness processes flourished before outside threats necessitated the raising of walls.

That Jericho's 'two eras' appear to match those for the first half of the Sumer sequence is fascinatingly suggestive but nonetheless problematic. Mithen (2003, p. 59) points out that the walls are more likely to have been for defence against floods rather than against military threat (Emberling 2003, p. 257). In the Sumer case the building of walls was only part of the evidence for state-making, textual materials were more important. But for early Jericho we have no such textual evidence. The walls do indicate a society able to harness collective labour for new architecture but this appears to be more of a city-process than state-making given the absence of a military dimension to mark the coercive heart of state-ness. Thus with no evidence of guardian processes consolidating the new enclosed space into a city-state, we appear to be able to show just full development of the first part of the Sumer sequence. In other words, Jericho signals city and city network development but without consequent powerful state formation.

Turning to evidence for Çatalhöyük, it is not possible to determine the first part of the Sumer sequence because of the nature of the city structure. This settlement consisted of a large cluster of houses with no streets and entry to the houses was through the roofs. Therefore it displayed only house walls to the outside, effectively a city wall. Thus in this case it is not possible to ascertain whether defences were needed after a period of city wealth generation, but Mellaart (1965a, p. 84) does note that he found no traces of battles, which we might expect for states.

Nissen (1988, p. 37) dismisses Jericho, and by implication the other large settlements, as a 'dead end'. This is plausible only because these settlements appear to be relatively ephemeral due to their failure to leave a direct place legacy for us to latch on to in historical (in the textual sense) times as is the situation with the Sumerian case study. There is no record of continuity from Soja's T-shaped region to Sumer but this might well be because of the dearth of information on the intervening period (p. 52). The problem, as always, is the incomplete nature of archaeological evidence that is inevitably more fragmentary the further back we look. What we can say about Sumer is that it is characterized by a jump in population sizes of cities. Intensification of trading and production, including agricultural production following invention of large-scale irrigation and how to manage it, created much new work. The resulting unprecedented economic expansion is reflected directly in the city populations in Table 3.2. One basic question is: where did the people attracted to Uruk cities come from? The usual answer posits in-migration from surrounding regions, an early rural–urban migration stream. But the contribution of longer-distance migration along trade routes should not be discounted: Rice (1994) suggests fresh inputs of people from Dilmun in coastal northern Arabia.

The additional potential creativity consequent upon the new scale of Uruk cities is reflected in both commercial and guardian activities. Much more than trading places, Uruk cities become great new production centres. Much more than religious shrine places, Uruk cities invent new means of economic regulation. This resulted in a vibrant city network that generates new unprecedented economic expansion that is sustained for many centuries. There is geographical expansion in the form of an informal (economic) imperialism. The difference with the earlier T-shaped region's city network is more than just the scale of activities. As wealth grows there is more to protect and the guardian processes develop into state formation. This is the key difference from the earlier city network. In this case the building of city walls and inter-city warfare led to eventual creation of a multi-city-state controlled from one militarily successful city, the original 'capital cities'. First Akkad and then Ur created such states that then proceeded to expand by formal imperialism (political). This new political scale required new secularized administrative mechanisms to rule conquered cities without incessant rebellion. The result was the invention of a centralized bureaucracy converting former city-states to provinces governed by agents of the centre. This territorial state was the key legacy of Sumer's precocious city-making processes; the culmination of Western Asia's great 'creative interlude'.

The list of urban innovations that are attributed to Sumer is so impressive it is usually used to define what we call 'civilization'. However, the fact that the guardian side of the process led to the invention of states is hugely significant. State formation is rather different from all the other inventions. Other creations enhanced the city and its power to mould spaces – both places and flows – to its urban needs. But state-ness involves a different spatial organization, a world of territories. In particular the morphing of city-states into larger state realms of multiple cities changed the outlook for cities fundamentally. Guardians with their various forms of coercion came to dominate cities either directly through conquest and government or by threat of the latter. Without their former autonomy, cities and their commercial classes were demoted to below guardians as agents of societal change. City creativity did not cease of course, but it was curtailed by larger states where guardian imperatives over-rode commercial interests. It is imperial cities – capitals of large empires – that now become the largest cities. There is not another rush of massive commercial creativity through cities until the rise of the modern world-system in Western Europe in the long sixteenth century. I will describe this system as the modern creative interlude in Chapter 6. The long period between the Western Asian beginnings creative interlude and the modern creative interlude I will call Normal History, the times of general guardian dominance.

But in order to progress the story from early Western Asia to recent Western Europe I need to take cognisance of the rest of the world. The first creative interlude is based upon interpretation of the empirical evidence from one world region. On the basis of my conceptual toolkits, I conjecture that similar city-based processes should occur elsewhere in the world. Of course I have described only one path of change – hunter–gatherer => city => agriculture => city-state => territorial state => Normal History – and there may be other routes towards invention of state-ness and its consequences, but the logic of my city conjecture does appear powerful. I posit that Western Asia's great creative interlude is the first but is not unique: this thesis is explored in the next chapter.

4. Geographies of beginning creative interludes

INTRODUCTION: GEOHISTORICAL EXTENSIONS

The purpose of this chapter is to extend discussion of Western Asia's great creative interlude in both space and time. Thus I deploy the ideas and interpretations from the two case studies of the previous chapter to new empirical contexts. The logic is straightforward: if my conceptual toolbox is generic, then my interpretations of Uruk and Çatalhöyük should be replicable in other times and places.

The first two sections of the chapter deal with creative interludes in a range of times and places. First, I propose a global conjecture about 'first cities' as 'first city networks'. This is a search for other examples of those large Neolithic (or otherwise early) settlements that orthodox thinking insists are merely 'enormous villages'. I will interpret them as critical transitions from trading networks to city networks. I consider it unnecessary for this search to be exhaustive, since the great majority of large Neolithic settlements will likely never be discovered. Certainly outside semi-arid regions they are unlikely to survive recognizably through the long-term ravages of time and, in addition, many sites will have been subsequently built over making such early traces inaccessible. My aim is merely to show that the precocious city-dwellers of Western Asia are by no means unique among early peoples across the world. This is the final discussion that insists Jacobs' contrarian city–agriculture thesis should be entertained as a credible patterning of these little known times and places.

Second, I consider the states and cities of the other 'early civilizations' beyond Mesopotamia. As mentioned previously, I eschew using the 'civilization' concept in this study since its cultural and hierarchical conceptual baggage potentially obscures my materialist investigation into city/state relations. However, it is in this comparative section that my geography overlaps closely with a long tradition of writings on 'civilizations'. To pinpoint my specific concerns, in the discussion below these cultures will continue to be equated with city networks, as suggested earlier for Mesopotamia. As such I will refer to these important historical areas as regional creative arenas. I focus on eight well-known ancient arenas, including Western Asia where I take the story on from the last chapter. The other arenas are Egypt, the Mediterranean, India, China, West Africa, Mesoamerica and Greater Peru. In each case I am searching out evidence for creative interludes involving cities and states in the manner described in the last chapter. I provide less detail than given for the Mesopotamian case but in each example I try and find a specific relevant theme that enhances and develops the argument presented previously.

In a concluding section I do two things. For a conclusion to this chapter I draw out three themes from across the numerous case studies that support my generic argument. In addition I provide a conclusion to Part II in the form of a final brief discussion of Jacob's ideas on city development. Her work has dominated these two chapters, and after such intensive use of this toolbox I think I can begin to understand how and why she produced ideas that diverge so much from conventional wisdom.

A GLOBAL CONJECTURE ON EARLY CITY NETWORKS

In the previous chapter, the timing of city beginnings was challenged – breaking through the '5000-year wall' – but the geographical focus on Western Asia remained quite conventional. It is important to challenge this regional bias because it is entwined with the 5000-year temporal division to define the time-space path of universal civilization beginning in ancient Mesopotamia moving through the classical Mediterranean (Greece and Rome) and alighting in modern Europe (Britain) to culminate in globalization (US). The section after this one deals with known city/ state relations in a manner similar to 'comparative civilization' studies so that other world regions are drawn into the argument as an addition to the Sumer case study. But what of Jericho and Çatalhöyük and the other Western Asian, large, Neolithic settlements? Are there possible cities that existed before the 'rise' of accepted 'civilizations' elsewhere in the world? My global conjecture is that early signs of city-ness can be found in many regions across the world.

Methodology for Studying Cities at the Wrong Time and Sometimes in the Wrong Place

The conjecture will be supported both conceptually and with some scattered empirical evidence. The use of tools and evidence is somewhat unbalanced for reasons outside my control. However I will continue my efforts to combine and produce plausible and interesting results.

The question of evidence
As far as evidence is concerned there is relatively little to say; obviously material is scarce because I am looking for relatively small urban settlements in periods earlier than most mainstream excavations. I have used a scavenger searching approach with some success but with no claim to be even approaching comprehensiveness. But this is not important. I am not trying to create a census of early urban settlements, rather I just need to find enough evidence to show that Western Asia is not unique in its early cities at wrong times and sometimes wrong places also. To be analogous to Soja's T-shaped region, 'wrong times' is quite straightforward as earlier than commonly expected for a world region; 'wrong places' is simply interpreted as outside the regions of known prime 'civilizations' discussed later, that is to say the case is not just prior manifestation of a 'civilization'. However some examples of the latter are included as simple 'wrong time' examples. And in addition, I need the cases to be worldwide.

In these difficult circumstances, I can point out that serendipity has played an important role. For instance, if a new baseball stadium had not been planned in Aomori City (Japan) in 1992, the surveying work that led to finding the site of Sannai-maruyama would not have happened. And with this very large settlement remaining unknown, the 'dramatic reappraisal of Jomon culture' that it necessitated would not have occurred (Rudgley 1998, p. 30). We will discuss this case below but the point is that we do not, and will never, know the full extent of other lost 'Sannai-maruyamas' across the world. Thus Mithen (2003) bemoans the general lack of knowledge of early African settlements (p. 503) and, for another region, he goes as far as saying: 'While substantial settlements most likely existed in the New Guinea lowlands at 6000 BC, archaeologists have yet to find them' (p. 339). Similarly, in his brief discussion of 'astonishingly early settlements' (Çatalhöyük and Jericho), Southall (1998, p. 23) alludes to numerous other equivalent settlements 'few of which may ever be known to us'. These observations are interesting but ultimately of no use for my evidence collection exercise.

In such a research context, conceptualizing inputs into our understanding takes on an enhanced role in the deductive–inductive nexus that is interpretation and understanding. In this case I suggest an early bifurcation to look out for in the evidence for early city development.

Conceptual contribution: initial bifurcations
The purpose of the conceptual contribution is to suggest what to look for in the early settlement case studies that are unearthed. The reader will not be surprised to learn that the thrust of the argument will be to discount the simple evolutionary assumption that the adoption of agriculture created villages that were largely self-sufficient and subsequently 'grew into towns'

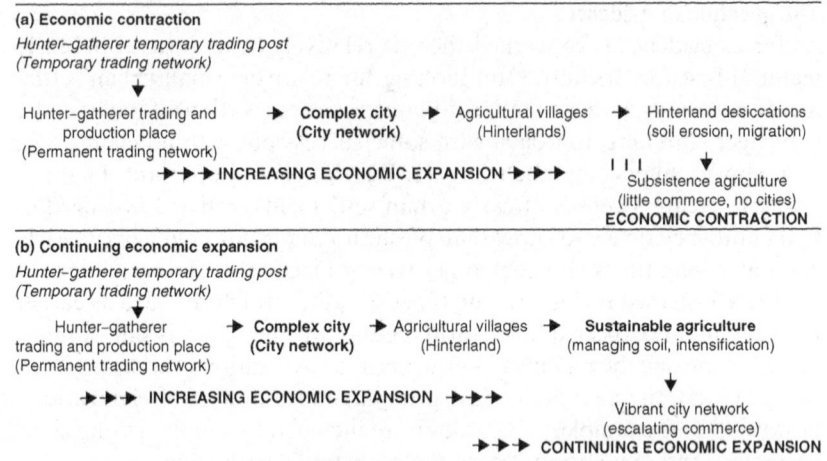

*Figure 4.1   Bifurcation: economic contraction or continuing economic
            expansion*

under particularly bountiful environmental circumstances. Rather I will
be looking for cities possibly before farming, or perhaps evidence of
uncertainty represented by cities existing very early at about the time when
agriculture was to be first found (Figure 3.1(b)).

The additional contribution is a schema for thinking about what came
next. I use a bifurcation model because it is simple; we can know so
little of the cases under consideration that I do not want lean towards
over-interpretation. Bifurcation is seen as defining options at a time of
crisis – I will use this method in the final chapter to characterize twenty-
first-century conjectures. We can envisage the initial crisis as shown in
Figure 4.1(a): a situation where the demand for food in early cities creates
new agricultural practices with little or no knowledge of how to maintain
soil fertility, or of techniques essential for sustainability. With land desiccated around the city, agriculture has to move further and further away.
At some point this process will make food provision impractical and therefore will eventually cause the demise of the city. With the city gone, most
people will migrate to other sites and the new farmers are likely to create
'subsistence villages or hamlets' largely separate from urban worlds. This
is what we suggested for the demise of Çatalhöyük and its city network
in the last chapter, and there is no reason to suppose that such a rise and
fall of an urban world has not occurred in other places and times. The
second option prevents city network disintegration: additional innovation
leading to sustainable agriculture will generate environmentally resilient

city networks (Figure 4.1(b)), leading to urban continuity that generates the known civilizations of the next section. Perhaps the irony of this conceptual contribution is that it confounds an already challenging empirical task: I am about to embark on finding references to 'urban failures', by definition encompassing very limited evidence.

This difficulty has been compounded by evolutionary assumptions traditionally embedded in urban origins discourses. As detailed in the last chapter, the debate about the status of Çatalhöyük has been plagued conceptually for being the wrong place at the wrong time revealing evolutionary thinking linked to the concept of 'civilization'. Such meta-historical assumptions reappear in other cities in wrong times and places identified below. The classic case is the city network of the Mississippian culture that declined more than two centuries before the coming of the Europeans to North America. Finding city remains in the form of deserted mounds at Cahokia, Europeans had difficulty in believing indigenous 'Indians' could ever have been great city builders and dwellers. According to Kennedy (1994, p. 244), 'oscillations of civilization' baffled believers in 'progress', which had no place for failure. There had been 'a cyclical history of the Great Valley before the advent of the Europeans' – a 'flowering' followed by a 'period of exhaustion' – but urban denial has dominated interpretation of the evidence. This was not only a case of wrong place and wrong time; it was also 'wrong people', with its not so covert racist overtones (Pauketat 2004, p. 3). But our TimeSpace toolkit tells us that if trading is ubiquitous to human behaviour before the invention of states, then we can expect that the very early rise and demise of city networks (Figure 3.1(b) and 4.1(a)) is much more common than is generally conceded.

A successful trading post that attracts first specialized storage (warehousing) and then some specialized craft production (workshops), attracting migrants and thereby creating a demand for food production, is where we should be looking for converting domestic modes of production into new, more collective city economies and networks. This is what I think happened in Western Asia as described in the last chapter and I have no reason to believe that it could not have happened many times across the world. I will call this process an incipient creative interlude, indicating the potential Jacobsean size that is created by the development of such city networks but also respecting the possibility that the full potential may not be fulfilled. The new city networks may be the predecessors of later 'civilizations' (Figure 4.1(b)) but they may also stagnate and fail, leaving minimal impact on subsequent history (Figure 4.1(a)). Of course, the archaeological record will not represent these two outcomes equally: it is likely that where the creative places generate an agriculture that regresses into subsistence mode, the initial cities will have become forgotten, unknown places. We come back to serendipity, chance findings such as that which revealed Sannai-maruyama.

Incipient Creative Interludes: a World Tour of 'Hidden Cities'

I will now embark on a world tour of 'large settlements' that are candidates for early city status. They are all to be found at times and/or places when and where cities are widely supposed not to have existed. I will travel from east to west, starting in Sannai-maruyama and ending at Cahokia. Despite the difficulties enumerated above, it has been relatively easy to identify a dozen cases where there is support in the literature for what Kennedy (1994) refers to as 'hidden cities': they can be hidden physically, ideologically, or both. I will present vignettes of the cases in a conventional mode, continent by continent.

Asia: Sannai-Maruyama, Middle Yangtze Valley and Indus Plains

These three cases, separated by thousands of miles, each indicate definite existence of very early cities, with the latter two also indicating developed networks. All three show the expected contention over interpretation.

- *Jomon's Sannai-Maruyama*. The Jomon culture of Japan is famous for being the earliest pottery-making society dating from 11 000 to 500 BC. Unlike other societies with pottery it seems to have been a hunter–gatherer society for almost all its existence (Keally 2005). It is in this example of a 'first affluent society' that Sannai-Maruyama existed between 3500 and 2000 BC (Hudson 1996). Its size has made it famous: it covers some 35 hectares. I have found no population estimates for the settlement but with the total number of buildings over 1000 (Rudgley 1998, p. 31), it surely qualifies as an early city candidate. No other known Jomon sites approach its 'scale and complexity' (Hudson 2006) and this has been interpreted, as might be expected, in two contrasting ways. For Keally (2005) the site 'is unique and not one that can be generalized to the whole of Jomon culture'; for Hudson, the site 'is the largest Jomon site so far discovered'. The latter leaves open the possibility of further large sites, something we would expect if Sannai-Maruyama were part of a city network. In fact, there is craft specialization using exotic minerals such as obsidian and amber indicating 'clear evidence of long distance trading networks' (Rudgley 1998, p. 32).
- *A large early city network in the Middle Yangtze Valley*. Before the reported rise of Chinese dynasties, Neolithic settlements with walled

structures are to be found in this part of China (Shen 2003, p. 291). Dated between 4000 and 2000 BC, I can find no individual city population estimates for these settlements. However, they included within their walls 'many large scale structures' including 'gates, platform foundations [and] public facilities', which distinguishes them from other late Neolithic sites (p. 291). Inevitably, there has been a debate about whether these settlements do constitute 'cities' (p. 291). From the perspective adopted here, the fact that nearly 50 such sites have been found does suggest a possible city-ness process with a large-scale city network.

- *Mehrgarh and an early city network on the Indus Plains.* Mehrgarh, from 7000 BC, is site of the 'earliest known' 'agricultural village' to the east of Western Asia. It only became revealed through a river realignment in the 1970s (Mithen 2003, pp. 407–8). The settlement lasted about 4000 years; it is interpreted as the product of migrant Neolithic farmers from the west. However, excavations have found evidence from animal bones of initial reliance on only wild animals; it is only later that both cattle and sheep bones indicate domestication (p. 410). This new 'economy of the town' as Mithen (2003) calls it, implies a Jacobsean city innovation. In addition, evidence of the earliest known use of cotton has been found at the site; cotton was possibly being cultivated from 5500 BC (pp. 411–12). Further, by 3500 BC, stamp seals 'attest to the growing importance of trade' which 'may have been the stimulus for developing copper work'. With similar 'farming towns' found throughout western Pakistan and eastern Iran by this time, it would seem that this all represents the development of city networks as predecessors to the Indus civilization of Harappa and Mohenjo-daro (of which more in the next section).

These three cases are very different but each provides strong evidence for early cities networks in their own ways.

Europe: South Bug–Dnepr Region, 'Celtic' Oppida, Irish 'Monastic Towns'

Without any 'primal civilizations', Europe is perhaps not a good hunting ground for early city networks but there are interesting cases that warrant consideration.

- *South Bug–Dnepr region of Ukraine.* In Maria Gimbutas' 'Old Europe', the Tripilya culture developed 'proto-cities' in the fourth millennium BC (Modelski 2003, p. 24). Three possible cities are identified between 3800 and 3500 BC: Dobrovody, Maydanets and Tallyanky. Modelski notes that excavations have found 'certain public works such as large buildings and fortified gates', and he estimates that the settlements could each have housed up to 10000 people (p. 25). However, with 'no clear links with the outside world' in a mobile nomadic society, Modelski doubts whether these settlements qualify as 'cities': without developing 'writing or other innovations, [they] soon basically dropped out of sight' (p. 25). Nevertheless, I remain impressed by the population sizes, and therefore will keep this culture as a possible incipient creative interlude, but one that did not lead on directly to further creativity.

- *'Celtic' oppida.* Similar, or even stronger, doubts can be attached to the *oppida* found inland from the Mediterranean in western and central Europe before the defeat of 'tribal states' by the Romans (Collis 2000, p. 230). They were large fortified sites that appear not to have been densely occupied, and they had no public buildings. However, they were places of industrial activity with specialist groups likened to medieval guilds (p. 235). Intriguingly Collis tells us that '*oppida* tend not to be located to best exploit the richest agricultural soils . . . The implications are that trade was considered more important than food supply, and *oppida* relied on importing much of their food' (pp. 235–6). Further he reports that Italian merchants controlled considerable trade in luxury goods with 'merchants resident on some *oppida* . . . representing the interests of major Roman families' (p. 236). This certainly has the ingredients of a city-ness process in operation.

- *'Monastic towns' of the Irish 'golden age'.* There is a surprise inclusion in David Wilkinson's (1987, p. 32) roster of 'civilizations': Irish c. AD 450 to 1050, commonly referred to as the 'Irish golden age'. This is of interest because Wilkinson uses 'connectedness' as his defining criterion for civilizations, including intensely interacting cities. However this golden age is associated with a flowering of Irish Christianity, but it is not usually thought to include city networks. The traditional, 'imported urbanism only' thesis only recognizes urban settlements with the establishment of Viking trading communities (for example, Dublin) and the later Norman invasion (Butlin 1977, p. 25). However, this position has been gradually revised and an 'indigenous urbanism' has been discovered in large monastic settlements with their 'quasi-urban forms' (p. 22). Spiritually flowering about AD 600, monasteries prospered economically so that by AD 800 'they had become towns' (Corráin 2005, p. 599), taking on specialized urban roles (Edwards 2005, p. 295) to become 'centres of population, markets, schools, prisons' (Hughes 2005, p. 316). With populations not exceeding 2000 these were not large cities by any criteria but there does appear to be an unusual city-ness process beginning to operate here. For debate on the 'urban interpretation' see Doherty (1985) and Valente (1998).

Perhaps we should use these European examples to remind ourselves that city-ness is a process and need not always be associated with places that are typically urban. There is another unusual example that could be explored as a further incipient creative interlude: 'Durrington Walls' next to Stonehenge, 'the largest (Neolithic) village known in northwest Europe' (Pearson 2009, p. 2), which appears to put large concentrations of people back into the Stonehenge story.

Africa: Great Zimbabwe and Middle Niger Urban Complexes

Just two examples for Africa but they are both very convincing and instructive:

- *Great Zimbabwe.* The largest centre of some 150 stone ruins between the Zambezi and Limpopo, Great Zimbabwe flourished from AD 1250 to 1450 with an estimated population ranging from 11 000 to 18 000 (Coquery-Vidrovitch 2005, p. 61; Freund 2007, p. 6). It was an industrial and trading centre linked to Indian Ocean trading networks: Indian beads, a Persian bowl and Chinese porcelain have been found at the site (Coquery-Vidrovitch 2005, p. 60; Freund 2007, p. 7). These appear to have been exchanged for gold, for which Zimbabwe controlled the trade route; this came after 'control of over commercial livestock, which stimulated outside trade' upon which the city's origin was based (Coquery-Vidrovitch 2005, p. 60). Freund (2007, p. 7) suggests that 'Great Zimbabwe was perhaps a kind of urban experiment that failed rather than evolving along a path of greater complexity', in other words an incipient creative interlude that led nowhere. Coquery-Vidrovitch (2005, pp. 61–2) suggests a reason that we have encountered before: the city became too large 'for the means available to the society', the trigger probably resulting from depleted soils.
- *Middle Niger urban complexes.* In the first millennium AD 'and perhaps earlier', McIntoch and McIntoch (2003) report on early 'clustered cities'. Eschewing the usual focus on the visible monumental definition of ancient cities, they describe population

aggregations that 'characteristically comprise a large, central settlement mound of up to 10 meters in height and 20 to 80 hectares in area, surrounded by intermediate and smaller mounds at distances of 200 meters or less' (pp. 103–104). Predating the trans-Saharan trade and the spread of Islam (Freund 2007, p. 13), this was a native African urbanism that Europeans 'failed to recognize because it did not conform to concepts of urbanism derived from Western experiences' (p. 106): wrong place, wrong time again. We will return to this example to discuss further in the next section.

My guess is that for reasons indicated in the last case, sub-Saharan Africa is the region with most 'lost cities' that may come to light as archaeology expands in a relatively neglected research arena.

Americas: The Casma Valley, Early Mayan cities, Early Cities in Central Mexico, and Mississippian Cahokia

In contrast to Africa, the Americas is a very active research arena, and therefore early city networks are easily found in four places:

- *The Casma Valley on the north coast of Peru.* The Pampa de las Llamas-Moxeque site dates from 1800 to 900 BC, which Wilson (1997, p. 239) tells us 'is surprisingly early for a center in the Americas with such an "urban" appearance'. In fact it has been publicized as the first city of the Americas (p. 239). When excavated it was interpreted as a 'bustling center that housed about 2500 people' (p. 240), subsequently reduced by Wilson to 2000 (p. 241). This leads him to 'prefer not to see Pampa de las Llamas as a "city"' (p. 241), but his view is also based on an unnecessary central place form of assessment; there is no discussion of trade or other linkages beyond the valley. However, von Hagen and Morris (1998, p. 56) do suggest inter-valley linkages including exchange networks. Thus I think the jury is still out on this case and I keep it as a creative interlude candidate.
- *Early Mayan cities.* Although Mayan cities have been traditionally associated with the Classic Period of the culture starting about AD 250, 'a host of new investigations . . . have now caused major revisions of this view' (Sabloff 1989, p. 76). In the first millennium BC Mayan population growth culminated in 'the beginnings of urban growth in the Maya Lowlands . . . placed at around 300 BC, at least 600 years earlier than had previously been supposed' (p. 77). Grube

(2000, p. 547) refers to 'enormous cities with monumental architecture' dating from early sixth century BC. He complains of a dearth of evidence about these cities (p. 547) but it seems that, according to Sabloff (1989, pp. 77–8), 'experiments with intensive agriculture were initiated, and extensive long-distance trade networks were developed'. This certainly appears to be a little known incipient creative interlude, one that led on to a fully developed Mayan creative interlude.

- *Early cities in central Mexico.* According to Sabloff (1989, p. 34) the Olmecs (from 1250 BC) are considered the '"mother culture" of Mexican civilization'. Their major sites were on the Gulf coast and had populations of less than a thousand but they are said to have laid 'the foundations for the rise of cities' (p. 46). They had trade links into the Highlands and it was here, by 500 BC, that, according to Sabloff, 'the first true city in ancient Mexico' emerged: Monte Alban in the Valley of Oaxaca (p. 46). But this evolutionary story is now being challenged. Charlton and Nichols (1997b, p. 172) point to an earlier possible urban beginning in the Basin of Mexico between 1150 and 900 BC. There are three sites that are deemed to be 'quite large' – Tlatilco, Coapexco and Tlapacoya – and therefore possible candidates for very early creative interludes. Grave goods at Tlatilco indicate 'strategic site location as related to efficient participation in . . . resource exploitation and trade with other regions' (p. 172), which is supportive of this view.
- *The rise and fall of Cahokia.* This case appears to be a perfect replication of Jacobs' (1969) urban process. According to Pauketat (2004: 79), there was a 'historical disjuncture' (p. 67) when the population of Cahokia, near the junctions of the Mississippi, Missouri and Ohio rivers, 'more than quadrupled over a fifty year period' to about 10 200/15 300 by AD 1050. Coincidently, there was a 'transformation of the rural countryside that accompanied the AD 1050 flashpoint' (p. 99). This 'resettlement of farmers that accompanied the Cahokia-centric restructuring of the regional landscape' (p. 97) resulted in them being 'tethered in some way' to Cahokia and other settlements (p. 97). The city, 'throughout this early period . . . existed without palisade walls' (p. 147) but around AD 1150 'a 20 000-log palisade wall complete with bastions spaced at regular intervals was set into a wall trench 3km long around downtown Cahokia' (pp. 148–9). This appears to match the idea developed in the last chapter of commercial processes first dominating city development followed by the rise of guardian elites in state-making. Pauketat (2004) emphasizes guardian processes from the outset but with Cahokia

being at the centre of a huge natural water transport system, there are plenty of examples of both large-scale, non-local patterns of both raw material procurement and production distribution (p. 121 and Figure 6.1, p. 122). Dincauze and Hasenstaub (1989), Kelley (1991) and Peregrine (1992) interpret Cahokia as a mercantile centre controlling large riverine commercial networks. Cahokia declined as quick as it rose: it was abandoned by AD 1300 and 'a huge fourteenth-to-sixteenth century "Vacant Quarter" opened up across the middle-river regions' (Pauketat 2004, p. 41), possibly caused by soil erosion or political unrest (p. 158).

As suggested, this continent provides some of the best evidence for early city networks as both incipient and continuing creative interludes. In addition, the long tradition of searching for pre-Columbian Amazon cities may finally be coming to fruition (Roach 2008).

The 12 vignettes of possible early cities, and those in the initial western Asian case from the last chapter, are very different in very many ways but they all indicate the pushing back of city beginnings for their particular regions. The point is made: cities at the wrong time, and often also in the wrong place, are by no means a rare phenomenon. Therefore, the simple fact that I have been able to find a worldwide range of a dozen examples so easily does suggest that city-ness as a process predates many conventional positions on when cities first appeared across the world. These empirical sketches, together with the initial conceptual prodding, constitute encouraging support for my global conjecture.

A WORLD SURVEY OF KNOWN CREATIVE INTERLUDES

I have treated early city-ness as indicating incipient creative interludes; most, some not all, led to fully blown creative interludes, the subject of this section. This means that we can move onto the more solid empirical ground of known creative arenas. They are 'known' through a mixture of historical sources and archaeological site surveys and excavations: we are back at the evidential level of Uruk and its Mesopotamian consequences dealt with in the last chapter.

What I am looking for in this section is evidence to support my conclusions for the Mesopotamian case study. That is to say, I will be exploring guardian and commercial processes that lead to the creation of cities and states in selected other creative arenas. Once again I will find myself unravelling confusing use of the city-state concept and disputing the assumption that cities and states can be simply equated or just happen to arrive on the historical stage together. I will be scouring the literature for particular information on complex divisions of labour, changing patterns of authority, network processes linking cities, and changing scales of governance. All these empirical findings and interpretations will feed into my overarching concern for commercial/guardian relations and their concrete spatial manifestations as city/state relations. As with the Uruk and Mesopotamian case study I consider the pristine development of city/state relations and their aftermath in terms of the growth of guardian domination relative to commercial activities. This is the tendency towards spatial expansion from city-states to territorial empires as represented in Mesopotamia by Akkad and Ur Third Dynasty states. This rebalancing of the commercial/guardian relation will typify subsequent history for millennia in some creative arenas and for centuries in others in the Normal History that I outline in Part III.

This section is termed a 'world survey' because I wish to cover the leading creative arenas on all major continents (including post-Ur in Western Asia). This leads to obvious logistical problems and practical limits. Clearly with multiple cases to be considered within the confines of this section, I cannot replicate the relative intensive treatment given to the Uruk and Mesopotamian case study previously. Here I will be more extensive in my approach as I sacrifice detail for breadth. In the first part below I describe briefly my practical solution to these logistic and practical problems. This will explain how I have come to select the eight distinctive regional creative arenas. The remaining parts deal with each of these arenas in turn.

Methodology for Identifying Creative Regional Arenas

How to study a range of regional creative arenas and which areas to select are questions answered via a straightforward pragmatic approach to the literature. In the 1990s there were a series of intellectual initiatives that involved different sets of scholars taking stock of our knowledge of early cities and states. Organizing conferences, symposia and workshops, between them they produced four important books that considered the state of the art in this field of research from quite distinctive starting points. Each book consists of numerous chapters by different authors reviewing and comparing evidence about early cities and states around the world. I treat this quartet of books as constituting a unique opportunity to generate my world survey from varied and knowledgeable secondary sources.

The books I have used are as follows:

- Feinman and Marcus' (1997) *Archaic States,* a collection of essays deriving from a School of American Research meeting dedicated to comparing ancient states in the Old and New Worlds;
- Nichols and Charlton's (1997) *The Archaeology of City-States,* with studies drawn from a symposium at an American Anthropological Association meeting;
- Hansen's (2000a) *A Comparative Study of Thirty City-State Cultures* (and its supplement (2002) *A Comparative Study of Six City-State Cultures*) collects together international studies from a symposium at the Copenhagen Polis Centre; and
- Smith's (2003a) *The Social Construction of Ancient Cities,* brings together scholars to compare early cities across continents.

There are two important things to note about these books. First, there is a neat balance of perspective: one book on states, one book on cities and two books on both, i.e. city-states. Second, they all provide a worldwide range of studies but with different emphases; this means that in aggregate the coverage is particularly good for my purposes. This is illustrated in Table 4.1, which also indicates the eight regional creative arenas I will deal with: my choice derives from the regions focused upon in the quartet of books. The 68 cases arrayed in the table constitute the bulk of evidence I use in the remainder of this section.

I supplement these sketches for each region with a table showing population estimates of the cities for times covered in the text. This provides a general context within which the particular regional themes are to be understood. In addition, the figures provide comparisons between regions in terms of numbers and sizes of cities. Initial comparison may be made with Table 4.2 showing city populations during Western Asia's consolidation of its creative interlude. For the latter, results from Modelski (2003) were used but this source's advantage over the standard source, Chandler (1987), ends at 1000 BC. At this point Modelski's threshold for inclusion rises to 100000 whereas Chandler includes cities from 20000. Thus, in order to maximize the number of cities included, the tables below are derived from both sources depending on the time period covered.

Developments in the Western Asian Creative Arena

Discussion of this arena will be different from subsequent sections since we are focusing just on the aftermath of the creative interlude described in the last chapter. After 2000 BC the two guardian inventions of city-state and territorial state continued to be deployed in what is often described as a cyclical pattern of centralization/decentralization (Thuesen 2000;

Table 4.1 World regional distribution of 68 case studies from four secondary sources

Secondary sources	Western Asia	Egypt	India	Mediterranean	China	Mesoamerica	Greater Peru	West Africa
Nichols and Charlton (1997)	1	1	1	2	2	4	2	0
Feinman and Marcus (1998)*	3	1	1	1	1	4	2	0
Hansen (2000a, 2002)**	10	0	2	4	5	4	0	6
Smith (2003a)	3	0	1	0	1	3	2	1
TOTAL	17	2	5	7	9	15	6	7

Notes:
*   Includes comparative regional chapters, each region is counted one half; Polynesian case not included.
** 'Celtic' Oppida not included; Swahili city-states not included; seven medieval and early modern European cases not included.

Table 4.2   *Population estimates for Western Asian cities, 1900–1000* BC *(in 000s)*

City	1900	1800	1700	1600	1500	1400	1300	1200	1100	1000
Isin	**40**	20						40		
Larsa	**40**	40								
Mari	30	**60**								
Uruk	30					**30**	30			
Nippur	20	20				20	20	20		
Ur	10									
Adab	10	10								
Masham-Sha	10	15								
Zabalam	10	10								
Nina	10									
Assur	10	15	10	10	**10**	10	15	20	12	12
Ebla	10	10	10							
Dilmun	10									
Mundigak	10	10								
Girsu	(10?)									
Umma		40								
Qatna		20	20	20	(10?)	(10?)	(10?)			
Hazor		16	(10?)	20						
Badtibira		10								
Eshnunna		10								
Shabat-Enlil		10								
Susa		10	10	10	**10**	10	10	20		
Anshan		10								
Alep		10	10							
Babylon			60	60		(10?)	(10?)	**75**	**75**	**100**
Carchemish			10	20	**10**	10	10	(10?)		
Hattusah				30	(10?)	(10?)	60	60		
Niniveh				10	**10**	10	10	10	10	10
Ugarit					(10?)	10	10	10		
Washukhani						20				
Jarkutan						20	20			
Sapinuwa							**75**	60		
Dur-Kurig							40	20		
Troy							10			
Dur Untash								10		
Tyre										10
Aram										(10?)

Notes:
(10?) indicates no specific estimate but the city probably reaches or exceeds the 10 000 threshold.
Emboldened figures and city name indicate the largest at a given time.

Source: Derived from Modelski (2003: 33 (Table 2(c)).

Strange 2000a). This is clearly shown by the city population estimates in Table 4.2 with the dearth of cities between 1700 and 1500 BC. This shows an initial concentration on Babylon, in which all Sumer cities drop out of the table. An even greater region-wide concentration on Babylon occurs again in the final two centuries in the table. But it should not be assumed that centralization automatically eliminated city-states; quite often internal autonomy survived and just external affairs became controlled from outside. For instance, the Philistine states lasted 550 years from 1100 BC as 'a confederation of five cities, each with a king as a ruler' through three phases: initially under Egyptian overlordship, then as independent states, and finally under Assyrian overlordship (Strange 2000b, pp. 135, 137). In general, city-states pursued a mixture of policies such as alliances, merges (dual kingdoms) and submission to 'friendly domination', but sometimes, military circumstances meant outright subjection was unavoidable (Larsen 2000b). The situation was somewhat different away from the central parts of Western Asia where city-states were located on key trade routes beyond the reach of expanding territorial empires; this was the case with Dilmun on the Gulf (Rice 1994), and much later for Mecca and Medina in western Arabia (Simonsen 2000).

Whatever the changing guardian situations, cities continued as vibrant commercial centres. Keith (2003) describes 'Old Babylonian neighbourhoods' as places buzzing with activities centred on workshops for goldsmiths, reedworkers, carpenters, copper smiths, basket makers, net makers, merchants and potters (pp. 66–8). Other larger-scale commercial practices centred on bakeries (pp. 69–70), flourmills (p. 70), oil-pressing facilities (p. 71) and fullers' works (p. 72). And, of course, there were taverns (p. 71) and shops (p. 72). As Zeder (2003, p. 177) reminds us in very Jacobsean terms, there is much more than just craft production in these old cities:

> ... studies of ancient urban economies must recognize the great diversity of operational alternatives around which these economies might be organized. In any given urban system, many levels of specialization may be operating at once, even within single economic spheres.

But what of the external commercial relations: were cities 'interlocked' by commercial agents in the manner described in Chapter 2?

Larsen (2000a) provides detailed evidence for a large-scale commercial space of flows operating through an interlocking city network centred on Assur from 1920 to 1800 BC. In fact the evidence comes from Kanesh, an Anatolian city far from Assur, where archives of some 20 000 texts have been found. These archives were 'kept by private commercial firms that had offices at ancient Kanesh, but whose main headquarters were in Assur' (p. 79). The size of transactions is impressive: over a 40–50 year period, it is estimated that 20–25 tons of silver, 100000 textiles, and 100 tons of tin were traded (p. 81). The latter, added to Anatolian copper, would have been enough to manufacture as many as one-and-a-half million bronze swords (p. 81). The mechanism for operating this economy was as follows:

> This commerce was in the hands of private family firms whose main offices naturally were in Assur itself. . . . the distant markets in Anatolia, some 1000–1200 km away, were monitored by agents who spent most of their time in one of the branch offices that had been established in the vicinity of, or in some cases within the major towns of Anatolia. These agents were sons, brothers, nephews etc. of the head of the family and firm . . . Kanesh Port was also the administrative and commercial centre for the merchants operating throughout the Anatolian and north Syrian region. (p. 81)

There can be no clearer example of the interlocking process in making a commercial space of flows. And, interestingly, Postgate (1992, p. 211) considers this 'network of complexity and sophistication' to be the result of 'emergence from the restraints of the Ur III empire'; in other words, commercial practices taking advantage of an interlude in guardian dominance.

The governance of Assur at this time is instructive being described as 'a commercial city-state whose entire government structure was pervaded by the power and interests of the great merchant dynasties' (p. 86). There was a king and a city-assembly but the latter dominated (p. 83) and there was also an assembly of merchants in Kanesh (p. 84). A key institution was that of *limmum* who was the main economic administrator, an annual appointment chosen by lot (pp. 84–5). This is an invention that attempts to solve the perennial problem of preventing self-interest from corrupting the economic management of the city; we will come across similar institutions in other times and places that reproduce the commercial moral syndrome.

And, of course, Assur was not alone, it just happens to be evidentially rich:

> It is becoming clear with the publication of new texts that Assur was only one of several commercial centres during this period, and it operated a highly specialised trading network centred on northern Syria and Anatolia. In between Assur and the first 'port' in the system they called 'abroad' was a stretch of several hundred kilometres in northern Iraq and Syria, an area where we find other cities that operated networks of the same kind, for instance the important *entrepôt* on the Euphrates River at ancient Emar. In northern Babylonia we find the city of Sippar, which was in close contact with Assur, but which also controlled a different commercial circuit, one that probably reached along the Euphrates into the Habur area in Syria. (p. 85)

And on the regional scale:

> The wider international system of commercial exchange cannot be described in detail yet, but its main features are relatively clear: it was based on cities which specialised in a certain section of the overall network, and all these individual sections overlapped and fed into each other. For unknown reasons the Assyrians had managed to build up a kind of monopoly on the Anatolian trade, but it was also clear that they were entirely dependent on other similar circuits functioning in such a way that the market at Assur was always well supplied with tin and textiles. Cities close to the Persian Gulf conducted trade overseas with Bahrain and Oman; others had close contacts with Susa, the capital of the state of Elam in southwestern Iran, through which a great deal of the tin from the east was channelled; and Sippar seems to have had a particularly intense exchange with Assur itself. (pp. 85–6)

Although it is the great empires that dominate traditional histories, not least the later Assyrian empire, it is this commercial world of complementary networked cities that is the most important legacy of Western Asia's great creative interlude. Cities not only invented the institutions of states, they made states sustainable by their economic expansion.

The Egyptian Creative Arena

Along with Mesopotamia, Egypt is the oldest of 'civilizations'. However, whereas the former can be reasonably interpreted in terms of guardian and commercial work, this is much less the case for Egypt. In fact, according to Wenke (1997, p. 27), it has become a cliché to refer to Egypt as a 'civilization without cities'. But see the sizeable cities identified by Chandler (1987) in Table 4.3. This contradiction is explored in this section: Egypt would seem to constitute one of the severest challenges to the framework developed in this book.

Egypt is most definitely exceptional – 'cankering exceptional' in Yoffee's (1997, p. 256) terms – in its guardian and commercial developments, but it is not necessarily uninterpretable in terms of city/state relations. The origins of this creative arena can be found shortly after 3800 BC in Upper Egypt, where 'Hierakonpolis, Abydos and other southern communities are known to have had large populations and productive economies' (Wenke 1997, p. 34). It is perhaps surprising that the beginnings are found in the south away from neighbouring Western Asia but there may have been trade links through Red Sea ports (p. 34). However, by 3200 BC Uruk-style local cones are found in Buto, a port in the northern Delta, providing evidence of interactions with Sumer. About this time a 'proto-kingdom' formed in the Hierakonpolis/Nagada/Abydos area which has been called an 'incipient city-state' (p. 32). Thereafter there is a 'cultural

Table 4.3 Population estimates for Egyptian cities, 2500–1000 BC (in 000s)

	2500	2400	2300	2200	2100	2000	1900	1800	1700	1600	1500	1400	1300	1200	1100	1000
Memphis	**30**	**30**	**30**	**30**			**(10?)**	**30**	(10?)	(10?)	**(10?)**	(10?)	(10?)	75	100	**100**
Heliopolis		10	10				(10?)	(10?)				**30**	**30**	30	20	20
Avaris								20	**20**	**50–100**						
Pi-Ramses											(10?)	(10?)	(10?)	**160**	**120**	
Tanis																35
Bubastis																(10?)

Notes:
(10?) indicates no specific estimate but the city probably reaches or exceeds the 10000 threshold.
Emboldened figures and city name indicate the largest at a given time.

Source: Derived from Modelski 2003: 28 (Table 2(b)); 33–4 (Table 2(c)).

explosion' that includes the beginning of writing and 'the foundation of the state' (p. 36). Thus by 3100 BC Wenke is able to list six features of the region that were to typify the Egyptian state for next 3000 years (pp. 33–4). Although these included 'a written language already in use for commodity control [e.g. inscribed mud-sealings on wine jars]', 'craft production of a wide variety of artefacts' and 'exchange networks' there is no mention of urbanization. This omission by Wenke is no accident.

After discussing the general importance of cities as creative places in economic development, Wenke (1997, p. 45) argues that Egypt was able to develop without such processes:

> In sum, urbanism, in the sense that I have discussed it, is simply one way of achieving a goal that early Egyptians reached in a different way: the early Egyptian state was able to do everything necessary for an advanced preindustrial civilization without large, functionally differentiated communities, simply by linking, via the Nile and an elaborate bureaucracy, the many functional elements one might find in a single Mesopotamian city-state. In Egypt these elements were distributed throughout the Nile Valley and Delta.

In other words, economic development was by the state rather than by commercial elites (p. 44). Yoffee (1997, p. 256) initially agrees with this assessment: 'in Egypt the establishment of the unified and centralized polity was characterized more by its territorial extent than by the process of urbanization.' Further, 'government policy appears not to have favored cities, notably by relying on an estate-based system of redistribution' (p. 256). And yet, to repeat myself, Egyptian cities do feature in Modelski's demographic survey of ancient cities – see Table 4.3. Not as plentiful as in Mesopotamia but also not insignificant; in fact in 1600 BC Egypt is recorded as having the largest city in the world (Modelski 2003, p. 34)! How do we square this circle? It could be that Modelski's estimates are simply wrong: certainly Wenke (1997) emphasizes on all his maps that 'The relative sizes of these individual communities are difficult to estimate because most are either destroyed or buried under alluvium and later occupations' (pp. 39, 40, 41). Without accepting Modelski's exact population estimates, I still find it unlikely that this creative arena was able to develop without cities of the size Modelski suggests.

In evolving differences of opinion I take the later position of Yoffee (2005, pp. 46–8). The relationship between cities and states in this creative arena appears to be as follows. First, there is reasonable evidence for early cities as described above, wherein first city-states and then the larger territorial state were invented; as Yoffee describes it: 'the earliest phase of the Egyptian state was marked by rivalries among the growing cities of Hierakonpolis, Naqada, and Abydos' (p. 47). Thus he changes his position by now inserting urbanization into Egyptian state formation: 'the establishment of the unified and centralized polity in Egypt can be characterized by its territorial extent *as well as by* the process of urbanization' (p. 47, italics added). The difference with other creative arenas is not the lack of cities but the fact that they did not play a part in governance sequences of centralization–decentralization. The large 'linear' territorial framework of the state 'made urbanism a part of the trends towards territorial unification rather than a factor opposing such trends, as was the case elsewhere' (p. 48).

But what work was done in Egyptian cities? They were creatures of the state – there is no semblance of continuing city-state autonomy in this case. Cities 'played special roles' in administrating resources, especially ideological resources: 'administration in cities was primarily concerned with managing these displays [of royal power] and the labor needed to build and maintain the edifices of royal and ritual power' (p. 48). Whatever creativity was allowed could only be harnessed to state needs, and with little or no autonomous commercial processes this particular creative arena will have economically ossified: it had cities but surprisingly few at any one time (Table 4.3) suggesting that the potential of a dynamic network of cities along the Nile was severely constrained.

Mediterranean Creative Arenas

Before the late modern era, differential transaction costs were dominated by the economic superiority of water transport over land transport. It is no surprise therefore that creative arenas are commonly associated with waterways; for instance, in Mesopotamia and Egypt above and, as we shall see, in India, China and West Africa below. The great inland sea that is the Mediterranean, therefore, would seem to have the potential of becoming the setting for an exceptionally large creative arena. And this indeed appears to be the case based upon city networks created by Phoenicians and Greeks. Table 4.4 presents population estimates for the end point of the development of what Braudel (1984, p. 25) identifies as an early Mediterranean 'world-economy'. These figures show leadership of the world-economy consecutively by Athens, Alexandria and Rome but before them the groundwork was set by the Phoenicians. Although they are represented in 430 BC only by Sidon and Tyre, they were crucial to the transformation of this sea into a vibrant economic space of flows (Gottman 1984).

Neimeyer (2000, p. 90) refers to the Phoenicians as the 'forgotten people'; sources for understanding their contributions are both meagre and distorted (i.e. the Bible and classical writing) (p. 89). We know from

Table 4.4 *Population estimates for Mediterranean cities, 430 BC to AD 100 (in 000s)*

City	430 BC	200 BC	AD 100
Athens	**155**	75	75
Syracuse	125	100	51–60
Corinth	70	70	50
Carthage	50	150	100
Sparta	40	30	
Agrigentum	40		
Argos	40		
Tarentum	40		
Messina	38	35	
Sidon	36		
Sardis	35		
Rome	35	150	**450**
Croton	35		
Tyre	35		
Cyrene	35	30	
Corcyra	35		
Gela	35		
Alexandria		**300**	250
Antioch		120	150
Rhodes		42	
Ephesus		40	51
Cirta		38–40	
Pergamum		35	40
Olbia		30	
Nisibis			65–70
Cadiz			65
Nimes			44
Seville			37–40
Capua			36
Byzantium			36
Thessalonica			35
Milan			30
Ostia			30

Note: Emboldened figures and city name indicate the largest at a given time.

Source: Derived from Chandler (1987: 461–3).

the two cities of Ugarit and Byblos in the early first millennium that city-states existed with kings and a warrior aristocracy converted into land-owners existing alongside a 'distinct caste' of traders organized into 'partly autonomous organizations' (pp. 90–91). However, it is difficult to unravel these guardian and commercial processes to inform initial city/state relations. What we can learn from the Phoenicians is how a Mediterranean-wide city network was developed.

The Phoenicians embarked on two Mediterranean expansions from their Levant bases: as traders and as settlers. Initially they were responsible for reviving the old Bronze Age trade routes that brought metal ores from east to west in the great sea. The earliest settlements date from c. 1100 BC beyond the Straights of Gibraltar into Atlantic Iberia and Morocco, but major settlements date from the eighth century (p. 97). These settlements developed into city-states in their own right with Gadir (Cadiz) being 'the most important foundation in the West' (p. 100). The key point, therefore, is that this was 'an expansion of a different kind, not one based on power-politics or territorial control' (p. 102). Rather, 'the basic principle behind the foundation of these settlements was . . . the fact that they lay on the main trans-Mediterranean sea routes' (p. 100). Initially this was only a city-ness process since hinterlands were not developed; food had to be imported.

One traditional explanation for this expansion has highlighted competition between cities in the Levantine home area. Certainly, although there are known to be about 50 'city-states' in the area, 'most of them belonged to a small number of more or less powerful city-states, among which four stand out: Arvad, Byblos, Sidon and Tyre' (p. 102). But Neimeyer (2000, p. 103) does not think such competition to be the main stimulus for the massive trading that was developed. He argues: 'Phoenician expansion and settlement in the Mediterranean should be understood as the outcome of Assyrian oppression, initiated and unleashed simply to serve Assyria's ever-growing demand'. The amounts involved were huge: for instance in one year, 732 BC, Tyre paid the Assyrian king a total of 4300 kg of gold (p. 103)! Neimeyer interprets this as follows:

> But over a long period these tributes were apparently paid in a climate of economic and political symbiosis, which on the one hand gave a certain independence from the great military power of Mesopotamia to the small and comparatively weak border states of the coast, and on the other hand granted Mesopotamia a more or less regular supply of luxury goods, vital raw materials (iron is mentioned explicitly as well) and finally financial means in the form of gold and silver. In other words, the agreement was of mutual benefit, and it is out of well-planned political opportunism and the desire to survive as political communities that the Phoenician city-states had developed into a kind of service society for Assyria.

This might seem a strange mutuality, certainly rather one-sided, but it represents the city/state relation that came to be very common in what

I am calling Normal History. Cities remain creative and networked, but are constrained by payments to states as the lesser of two evils: the much greater evil would be a military sacking and economic oblivion (p. 103).

Just as a footnote to this story, the greater evil came about when the Assyrians, the Phoenician's state protectors, were replaced by a new Mesopotamian empire: the Babylonians conquered Tyre in 573/2 BC leaving Carthage, on the north Africa coast, as the leading Phoenician city (p. 105). Carthage was 'fundamentally different' (p. 104); it developed its own agricultural hinterland and eventually became a territorial state: the Carthaginian empire that later competed with Rome (see Table 4.4).

The Phoenicians' major Mediterranean rivals were the Greeks – their 'polis' became a chief historical source of the city-state concept (Hansen 2000b). The Greek expansion differed from that of the Phoenicians by being more settlement-based and created a hinterland to attain relative food self-sufficiency. Hansen (2000c, p. 141) estimates that there were about 1500 poleis, with only just over half in Greece itself. They varied greatly in size and lasted some 1200 years between 750 BC and AD 550. Over this period most poleis were 'dependent poleis', initially in inter-city alliances (federations or leagues), later under imperial rule (Persian, Macedonian, Roman). But the big contrast with the Phoenicians is in the multitude of sources, archaeological and especially textual, that provide the basis for a much more detailed and deeper understanding of guardian and commercial processes.

Against the theoretical position argued in Chapter 3, Hansen (2000c, p. 161) notes that traditionally the literatures on city formation and state formation place the latter about two centuries (c. 700 BC) before the former (c. 500 BC). However, he updates this position by quoting recent excavations that push back the origin of the cities at least 200 years allowing him to conclude that 'the two processes seem to be contemporaneous and go hand in hand' (p. 161). As a result we are presented with 'city-states' occurring in the seventh century by Morris (1997, p. 95). Thus according to Cartledge (2009), the leading early Greek city, Miletus in Asia Minor, has each of: multiple colonies and trade (p. 53), an intellectual flowering (p. 54), and a 'tyrant ruler' (p. 55) by the sixth century BC. But, if we unscramble these outcomes and treat the processes as separate changes in guardian and commercial behaviours – city network formation and state territorial formation – we find that a rather different picture emerges.

In the literature on the Phoenicians the concept of a 'trading aristocracy' is to be found (Neimeyer 2000, p. 102). From the theoretical perspective argued here, this appears to be an oxymoron: aristocrats should be guardians! But in cities and their networks things are not always as simple as we would wish. The Greek case can shed light on this. The Greeks developed

an 'elite economy' that combined ownership of landed estates with an
inter-state monopoly on the grain trade (Small 1997, p. 108). Thus David
Small (1997) argues there were two political economies: this elite economy
was 'distinct' from the city-state's local hinterland economy (p. 107). The
elite economy was a patron–client relation where the client was the polis:

> city-states looked to elites to furnish extra grain from outside the state in times
> of agricultural crisis. The polis never developed a merchant fleet and relied
> instead on elite shipping. (p. 110)

The result was that:

> with few exceptions, the economic goals of the city-states and those of its
> wealthy citizens were not coincident. Although members of the economic elite
> were interested in profiting from interstate commerce, the city-states did little
> to favor them in the conduct of this trade. (p. 111)

And it follows that city-state expansion was of no benefit to this economic
elite (p. 111). City network formation and state territory formation are
clearly different processes. The key point is Small's (1997, p. 112) idea that
on the balance of evidence 'the regional elite economic network . . . existed
prior to the development of states in ancient Greece', and therefore 'since
the polis as a state began to develop in the eighth century, it developed
within the pre-existing network of elite economic power'.

This example is intriguing because it describes a different form of interlocking network from that involving branch networks. Here inter-city
trust underpinning the space of flows is generated in a quite different way.
The key social institution is a ritualized friendship between elites that is
termed *xenia*. Small (1997, p. 110) defined this as:

> [a] fictive kinship that established a reciprocal bond of obligation between elite
> households in different Greek communities . . . The power of an elite [house]
> increased with the growth in numbers of its *xenia*, so houses were constantly
> attempting to form more ties with houses in other poleis. (p. 110)

This is actually a classic multiplicative network growth process as
described in Chapter 2. Thus despite the intense interactions between
poleis there are no permanent envoys because they are not needed, rather
xenia as 'a guest-friendship institution' provides the necessary ongoing
contacts (Hansen 2000c, p. 170). In addition, the inter-state festival circuit
(such as the Olympic Games) supported the 'underlying ideology of elite
economics' by emphasizing 'the institutions of *xenia* rather than the individual states' (Small 1997, p. 112). In this world of perennial wars between

Table 4.5   Population estimates for Indian cities, 2500–2000 BC (in 000s)

City	2500	2400	2300	2200	2100	2000
Mohenjo-daro	**20**	**40**	**40**	**40**	**20**	10
Harappa	15	20	20	20	15	10
Dholavira			15	15	10	10
Ganweriwala			10	10	10	10
Rakhigarhi			10	10	10	10

Note: Emboldened figures and city name indicate the largest at a given time.

Source: Derived from Modelski (2003: 28, Table 2(b)).

poleis, the 'state sanctuaries' of these events favoured 'a more panhellenic character' connected through the 'aristocratic noble house' rather than poleis (p. 112). The Greek city-state only 'developed parallel to this elite network' (p. 112) and therefore 'evolved without elite management of its political economy' (p. 114). In short, this seemingly unusual case supports the general dictum: cities (city-ness) interlock worlds; states (state-ness), even city-states, divide worlds.

Indian Creative Arenas

The Indus Valley 'civilization' is the third of the great, early, riverine 'civilizations'. It lasted from 2600 to 1900 BC and was initially identified by two large cities, Mohenjo-daro and Harappa. More recent excavations have identified two further 'extremely large cities, Ganweriwala and Rakhigarhi, comparable in size' to the earlier revealed cities. These two later cities are located by the dry bed of the former river Ghaggar-Hakra (Kenoyer 1997, p. 52). In addition a fifth large port city, Dholavira, has been discovered. All five centres are over 50 hectares in area and Kenoyer estimates their populations individually as between 30 000 and 40 000 (p. 54). Modelski's population estimates from 2500 to 2000 BC are given in Table 4.5; his lower estimates may reflect lack of access to later site information. Each city is located on key trade routes: Mohenjo-daro 'dominated trade routes leading to the passes in the Bolan Valley to the west and the north–south trade from the coast near modern Karachi' (p. 54); 'Harappa would have dominated north–south movement along the river flood plains leading from Mohenjo-daro to the northwestern passes and east–west trade towards the resource areas of modern Rajasthan' (p. 55); Rakhigarhi and Ganweriwala 'would have controlled the movement of resources from the eastern desert regions and funnelled goods up river from Rann of Kutch' (p. 55); and for Dholavira the 'major support of the population probably derived from trade with Kutch, Saurashtra, and the core areas of the Indus Valley to the north . . . (and) could have monitored shipping of raw materials and subsistence items between these regions, and it may also have had a role in external trade to the Arabian Gulf' (p. 55). The existence of distinctive seals, a writing system and common weights and measures (p. 55; Possehl 1998 p. 288) confirm the 'Harappan civilization' of the Indus Valley to be a large city network similar to Mesopotamia.

Since there is little or no doubt about the urban credentials of this society, Possehl (1998) asks the question 'was the Harappan civilization a state?' (p. 279). Chakrabarti (2000, p. 375) also enters this debate and suggests three possibilities: a single state, which is deemed to be 'generally accepted'; four city-states centred on the largest four cities; and multiple city-states, which he favours. After a thorough review of the evidence, Possehl suggests a more subtle answer: envisaging a process where 'trade and commerce act as stimulants to the growth of more complex management and governmental institutions' (p. 267), he argues that the political structure is neither a state nor even a pre-state, rather he posits a complex 'non-state' (p. 286). This is a 'different sort of polity' (p. 286) based upon 'strong decentralized institutions' (p. 288). It is the result of an 'experiment' in the 'sociocultural complexity' of the cities that creates temporary alliances between cities through decentralized councils (pp. 288–9). This may be similar to Jacobsen's (1970) Kengir League for governance of early Sumerian cities as described in the last chapter. Clearly Possehl is asking us to respect the variability in possible guardian structures based upon cities, and in his argument he clearly makes the case for city formation preceding state formation, if indeed the latter occurred.

In trying to understand more fully the processes operating in this early city network, scholars have looked at later networks and states with written records to use as models or analogies (Kenoyer 1997, p. 62). In particular, use is made of the Early Historic period (600 BC to AD 300), which was a similarly successful economic era:

> The Early Historic period was a time of social and economic growth. By the first century BC, the Indian subcontinent was part of an elaborate trade network that touched the entire littoral of the Indian Ocean and included links to the Roman Mediterranean and to Han China. In addition to participating in long-distance exchange, the subcontinent sustained thriving networks of local and regional exchange. (Smith 2003c, pp. 274–5)

This city network included the Ganges plain and parts of peninsular India as well as the Indus Valley. Temporally, Kenoyer (1997, pp. 62–3) focuses on the early city-state phase (600 to 300 BC) in which he sees continuities – craft technologies, economic structures, weight systems – with the earlier Harappan period. Settlement locations were also similar: 'The most important settlements and the capitals of each *mahajanapada* were situated strategically along trade routes or controlled important resource areas' (p. 65). Because of these many 'linkages', Kenoyer argues that the extensive literature (Verdic and Epic texts) of the Early Historic period can be used to develop 'working hypotheses' about Harappan economic and political processes (p. 62).

The *mahajanapada* were the 'great principalities' of Buddhist literature that were too large to be city-states but there is evidence that they may have been federations of such states (Chakrabarti 2003, pp. 389–90). This is supported by the definition of 'state' in this literature that includes 'allies', which confirms the point that 'a city-state does not evolve in isolation' (Kenoyer 1997, p. 65). Political organization came in two forms: *raja dhina* (kingdom) and *gana dhina* (republic). These are related to an early occupational hierarchy of just four castes: the *kshatriya* (warrior aristocracy), the *brahmana* (ritual specialists), the *vaisya* (merchant classes) and *shudra* (labourers) (p. 66). In the kingdoms the *brahmana* are ranked higher than the *kshatriya* whereas in the republics the positions are reversed. In the latter, although all freemen (including *shudra*) could be members of the ruling assembly, *kshatriya* were likely to form oligarchies (with merchants?). This relates to the fact that 'trade and commerce were important for the wellbeing of the city and were controlled by the military aristocracy and the merchants . . . (although) these two forms of political structure can only be adduced from written documents: they are not visible archaeologically' (p. 67). However, Kenoyer does note that 'the textual evidence . . . identifies most of the oligarchies in the northwestern regions (northern Indus Valley)', which 'has great import for our investigation of political organization during the Harappan phase' (p. 68). Thus this geographical congruence over time enables him to go on and propose a politics of Harappan cities in which the basic castes compete for power. He concludes that 'even though we cannot identify the specific mechanisms for the political control, the current evidence suggests that these larger cities can be identified as city-states', and that 'the integration of this vast geographical area into a single cultural system was probably the result of economic strategies defined by ideology and social relations rather than covert military coercion' (p. 70).

By focusing on processes rather than outcomes, Kenoyer's working hypothesis need not contradict Possehl's (1998) decentralized 'non-state model'. Clearly the Harappan world was a continous world of cities; states probably came later.

Chinese Creative Arenas

There is no doubt that China has been one of the great creative arenas in the history of humanity (Needham 1954; Frank 1998). But cities or city-states appear not to be given an important role in the historical success story that is China, except as imperial capitals. Thus although 'the Spring-and-Autumn period (711 to 481 BC) was the age of the city-state in China' (Lewis 2000, p. 359), 'it left surprisingly little trace in later history' (p. 372). In this case, subsequent political centralization created an imperial tradition wherein, as well as the city-states themselves being 'swept away', so also was 'almost all memory of their historical reality' (p. 372). There is a cruel irony in this process because it was in the cities that 'the institutional innovations to strengthen . . . armies and armed factions . . . led to the rise of great states forged through conquest, and brought an end to the city-state as a political form in China' (p. 359).

Robin Yates (1997) takes a different position on the neglect of cities and city-states in Chinese history. He makes a historiographical critique of the scholarship on ancient China. Basically he argues that both Marxists and traditional Chinese scholars were searching for suitable imperial antecedents in the pre-empire period (before 221 BC) and, for both searches, neither cities nor city-states were of any relevance or interest. The traditional scholars 'read back into the past the conditions and practices of their own day' to identify three initial dynasties (the Xia, Shang and Zhou) (p. 75), whereas the 'official' Marxist and other scholars desired 'to demonstrate that China had not been as backward' as Western imperialists had assumed and indeed 'had actually passed through the same evolutionary sequence as the West, but even earlier' (p. 75). Only recently have new hypotheses based upon contemporary debates, such as state/chiefdom differences, been evaluated using Chinese data (p. 76).

Thus we are on unsure ground in our assessment of early city/state relations in this arena. There were most definitely important cities and city-states before the dominance of the great dynastic empires, but it seems to me that interpretation continues to be very state-centric in nature. Let me illustrate.

We have previously indicated the importance of Neolithic Chinese walled structures in the section on my global conjecture above. According to Shen (2003, p. 291) these settlements became larger in the Xia, Shang and Zhou dynasties and are 'the first that can clearly be called "cities"' (p. 291): population estimates for these early Chinese cities are given in Table 4.6. Shen describes the process as follows: 'Urbanization gave rise to full-scale commercially-based production and market places within royal *centers*, which transformed them into *cities*' (p. 290). This culmi-

Table 4.6 *Population estimates for Chinese cities, 1700–1000 BC (in 000s)*

City	1700	1600	1500	1400	1300	1200	1100	1000
Erlitou	**40**	(10?)						
Bo (Yanshi)		24	(10?)					
Shang			(10?)	(10?)	(10?)	60	(10?)	(10?)
Sanxingdui			(10?)	(10?)	(10?)	35		
Ao				**32**	(10?)	(10?)		
Yin				(10?)	**120**	**120**		
Xiang				(10?)				
Qiyi							(10?)	(10?)
Haoqing								**100**
Zhengzhou								(10?)

Notes:
(10?) indicates no specific estimate but the city probably reaches or exceeds the 10 000 threshold.
Emboldened figures and city name indicate the largest at a given time.

Source: Derived from Modelski (2003: 34, Table 2(c)).

nated in the Eastern Zhou period when 'the number of cities dramatically increased, and urban population grew rapidly', which was related to economic development but still 'royal': 'the "King's City" was transformed into a truly commercially-based urban city aggregating a large number of residents with a wide variety of skills' (p. 292). This is explicitly an interpretation of 'states first, cities second', the reverse of what I have been arguing. To confirm:

> Production and commerce clearly became a very important part of the urban economy during the Eastern Zhou. Political centers, such as capitals of states, quickly turned into commercial cities that attracted a large number of migrants. (p. 295)

And Shen is not alone in this position.

Yates (1997) eschews recent work that locates China in state/chiefdom debates as being too 'western' (p. 81) and for underplaying cities (p. 82). This leads him towards a careful study of city-states but his starting point is unfortunate. He uses a definition of city-state whose economic dimension is 'economic self-sufficiency provided by exploitation of a hinterland' (p. 77). There is no mention of trade: in other words he searches out town-ness but not city-ness. From this position he comes to the following conclusion:

First of all, the states were based on self-sufficient agriculture. In the early period, control of long-distance trade does not seem to have played a significant role in their development, although, of course, there was some circulation of, and trade in, prestige goods, such as cowry shells, jade, and turtle plastrons. ... Trade, the regional specialization in products, metal currency, and an independent merchant class only appeared very late, after 700 B.C., when the conquest of smaller states by the larger and the weaker by the stronger created larger and larger hierarchies, together with an increasing complexity of nested systems – in other words regional city state . . . systems. (p. 87)

There can be no clearer statement that state formation preceded city formation in ancient China.

There are two basic positions that can be taken from the above interpretations. First, if we accept them at face value, they suggest an alternative Chinese path to the making of a creative arena. This is a state-centred process in keeping with the later power of dynastic empires. Without attempting to trace how a state process might generate a complex creative outcome, it can be pointed out that the three early Chinese dynasties are not ideal candidates for generating extraordinary social change. For instance, Lewis (2000, p. 360) describes the Shang state as:

actually a thin network of pathways and encampments along which the king moved or sent his commands, surrounded by regions that never saw the king or his messengers . . . It was not a continuous, territorial state, but a city-state kingdom, a league of towns allied by kinship or shared religious practice, towns which were dispersed amidst alien and hostile settlements.

This most certainly does not sound much like a regional incubator for social innovations!

The second position is that state-centric biases of past scholarship have yet to be fully eroded. The starting point for assessing such an argument is to look at the population estimates for ancient Chinese cities. For the spring and autumn period (711 to 481 BC), Lewis (2000, p. 362) suggests quite sizeable cities: 'a large city would have numbered in the tens of thousands, and the small ones would have had a few thousand people'. Modelski's (2003) estimates support this statement and pushes large cities even back into the possible first dynasty of the Xia (Erlitou culture c. 2000–1750 BC). Table 4.6 shows 700 years of Chinese cities to 1000 BC, and cities in 1400, 1300, 1200 and 1000 BC at least would all be capable of contributing to the making of a regional creative arena as vibrant city networks in the 'Shang empire' (c. 1750–1045 BC). For the spring and autumn period Modelski (2003, p. 42) records large cities (over 100 000) increasing from two (700 BC) to eight (500 BC), peaking at 12 in 400 BC. Modelski does not record cities of less than 100 000 for this period but Lewis (2000,

p. 363) tells us that there were about 200 city-states at this time. This is all in the pre-empire period (before 221 BC), which appears to be relatively neglected as worlds of cities in the literature.

But what of trade in a city-making process? Xiatu, capital of Yan state, which is the largest city recorded in the pre-empire period, housing an estimated, massive 320 000 people in 400 BC (as we move into the Warring States period), has been excavated and found to be a major production centre encompassing both state and private foundries and workshops (Shen 2003, p. 301). The many iron tools found at the site 'must have been acquired through market exchange' (p. 303) and, in addition:

> The more than 30 000 coins recovered from the Yan-Xiadu site are also direct evidence of the extensive trading activities that took place in the marketplaces of the Yan capital city. . . . The fact that many coins belonged to neighbouring states were also found suggests that the Yan state markets attracted people from distant locations. (p. 304)

Of course, 'the Yan state markets' are city markets; city-ness was alive and well, at least in this part of ancient China. Further, we can argue that the largest cities identified in Table 4.6 were, by and large, created by city-ness network processes: most are simply too big to result from local hinterland self-sufficiency.

West African Creative Arenas

West Africa is the least recognized of our regions as a creative arena. Certainly early European traders understood this place as a region of great cities: for instance, Oliver and Fage (1988, p. 89) quote a Dutch author in 1602 comparing Benin with Amsterdam and finding the latter wanting. But later, when Africa became labelled the 'Dark Continent', it was deemed to be a place deficient of 'civilization', and thus without proper cities. Certainly, although sub-Saharan Africa settlements feature in the global conjecture section earlier in this chapter, it is the case that cities came to this arena later than other regions in the 'Old World'. Nevertheless, as Table 4.7 clearly shows, cities there were before European imperialism, plenty of them, and some quite sizeable. This list of 47 cities uses Chandler's (1987) population estimates for West African cities comprising two groups: Guinea cities (coastal/forest) and Sahel cities (largely riverine). Cities are traced over 1100 years to 1800, after which the region becomes gradually dominated by European colonization reflected in a reduction of cities from 19 in 1800 to only ten in 1850 (Chandler 1987, p. 59): this is modern imperialism dismantling creative arenas.

Table 4.7 *Population estimates for West African cities, AD 800–1800 (in 000s)*

City	800	1000	1200	1300	1400	1500	1600	1700	1800
Awdaghost	(20?)								
Gao	(20?)		(20?)	25	40	**60**			
Ghana		**30**	**25**						
Tademekka		(20?)							
Manan		(20?)							
Kano			**25**	30	30	50	40	35	30
Zagha			20						
Kilwa			20	20	30	30			
Njimye			(20?)	(20?)					
Walata			(20?)	(20?)					
Bussa			(20?)	(20?)					
Ngala			(20?)	(20?)		(20?)			
Mali				**40**	**50**	40			
Jenné				20	20	50			
Turunku				(20?)					
Ife				(20?)	(20?)	(20?)			
Nufi				(20?)					
Oyo					**50**	**60**	**60**	**50**	**80**
Timbuktu					20	25			
Durbi					(20?)				
Rao					(20?)	(20?)			
Nupé					(20?)	(20?)			
Krenik					(20?)				
Benin					(20?)	(20?)	50	25	
Ouagadougou					(20?)	(20?)			
Kazargamu						40	**60**	50	50
Gobir						28	35		
Agades						(20?)	30	45	
Katsina						(20?)	**60**	**60**	70
Ijebu						(20?)			
Zaria							40	50	40
Suramé							40		
Gbara							33		24
Masenya							20	30	30
Kikiwhary						(20?)			
Jima								35	
Allada								30	
Naya								30	
Kebbi								(20?)	30
Zamfara								(20?)	
Puje									

Table 4.7 (continued)

City	800	1000	1200	1300	1400	1500	1600	1700	1800
Alkalawa								(20?)	50
Kumasi									40
Kiama									30
Abomey									24
Kiawa									(20?)
Sangha									(20?)

Notes:
(20?) indicates no specific estimate but the city probably reaches or exceeds the 20 000
threshold.
Emboldened figures and city name indicate the largest at a given time.

Source: Derived from Chandler (1987: 55–9).

The Middle Niger region is a riverine region of early urbanization.
McIntoch and McIntoch (2003, p. 104) argue that in the first millennium
AD cities were created as risk adaption to an unpredictable environment and as resistance to political centralization. They are very clear on
this: 'These clustered cities not only existed in the absence of the state
but were organized largely without a centralized hierarchy of any kind'
(p. 105); rather, they 'exhibited specialization and functional interdepend-
ence' (p. 106). Referring specifically to the Jenné-jeno 'urban complex',
McIntoch and McIntoch provide a good description of combining town-
ness and city-ness:

> Jenné's merchants could exploit the maze of streams and major rivers (Niger
> and Bani) giving access to towns and villages within the traditional hinterland
> as well as to distant commercial partners, such as Dia and Timbuktu. . . . the
> clustered towns . . . functioned within the extensive commercial network of the
> first millennium A.D. that predated trans-Saharan trade. (pp. 108, 110)

This relates to one of the smaller settlements in Table 4.7 but illustrates
well city formation without state formation; the guardian processes
involved sacred specialists, not chiefs or kings (p. 115).

Far to the east of Jenné in the Sahel belt a more substantial urbanization
developed in Hausaland. Griffeth (2000, p. 483) writes of the 'great age of
city-state dominance' from 1450 until 1804 when the Fulani jihad created
an empire in which the city-states were converted to emirates (provinces of
a new Caliphate). Traditionally consisting of seven original cities – Kano,
Katsina, Zaria, Biram, Daura, Rano and Gobir – they developed far from

threatening empires in relative isolation (p. 492). However, in the fifteenth century the isolation was abruptly ended by incursions from the Songhay empire centred on Gao and Timbuktu (p. 488). The result was that 'a great period of wall-building all over Hausaland occurred during the late fifteenth and early sixteenth centuries' (p. 490). This is a similar sequence to that found in Uruk over three millennium earlier: 'The walls reflect the beginnings of the city-state system since they were clearly designed as defensive fortifications' (p. 489), although walls did exist before this date. The longer process of state formation is described thus:

> As the city-state grew larger and more complex, as competition and warfare between them increased, and as commerce steadily expanded, the more elaborate instruments of government were required than could be managed by recruitment from the aristocratic lineage alone. Thus, the *masusarauta* came to form a substantial class of bureaucrats and state officials. (p. 494)

This ruling class of aristocrats and sub-officials oversaw and administered a vibrant city of artisan guilds (ironworkers, dyers, artificers, leather workers, musicians, story tellers, prostitutes) plus commercial elites including merchants, bankers, brokers, commission agents, clerks and many foreign merchants. These were dynamic cities in which the evidence suggests that state-making developed. Griffeth (2000, p. 491) considers this guardian development of city-states to be similar to 'other West African grassland societies', but 'only Hausaland evolved and nurtured the city-state society to a high level, whereas its neighbors early found themselves subjects of imperial overlords' (p. 491).

To the south similar city-state cultures developed notably by the Yoruba, located in a 'widespread commercial network' linking the coast and forest to Hausaland via north–south long-distance trade routes (Peel 2000, p. 507). Further south still, a city-state federation based on migrants is reported by Kea (2000, p. 519) in the fifteenth century (it is not at all certain that the original 'migrant city' was a state). This movement spreads out to develop into the Fante city-state federation of the seventeenth and eighteenth centuries. These are interesting specifically because they operate very much in a Jacobsean manner: 'The early and later history of Fante was very much tied up with the history of long-distance trading networks', first the gold trade in the fifteenth to seventeenth centuries and then the slave trade from the seventeenth to eighteenth centuries (p. 519). According to Kea:

> The various Fante towns were the locus of an articulation between two forms of social wealth accumulation and distribution: (1) revenues ('political wealth'), based on systems of surplus extraction and mechanisms of appropriation, and

(2) trading and money-lending capital ('merchant wealth'), based upon marketing networks and the operation of brokers and merchants. (pp. 519–20)

And we know how city formation through interlocking networking
operated. The Fante trading coast has been called 'the most intensely
developed sector of the Euro-African trading system' (p. 525) that operated through Akani 'captaincies'. These were mercantile corporations,
'a varying number (from ten to 100) of traders and brokers . . . under the
authority of a "captain"' (p. 525). This person was usually of noble status
and all nobles belonged to a 'brotherhood of nobles', conferring commercial rights including 'the right to trade anywhere' (p. 525). In other words
here we have another institution invented to facilitate trade and thereby
interlock cities. Note that, as in the Greek case, it is the aristocracy leading
the process; given the longevity of the arrangement, this commercial/
guardian relation may be deemed sustainably balanced.

Mesoamerican Creative Arenas

There are two sub-regional developments of city/state relations in this
creative arena: the Maya 'civilization' in the largely lowland, middle
section of Central America, and the 'civilizations' to the north centred
on the Basin of Mexico culminating in the Aztec empire. Pre-Columbian
population estimates for 33 cities identified by Chandler (1987) are given
in Table 4.8. The sheer number of cities is impressive.

Grube (2000, p. 547) suggests that 'enormous cities with monumental
architecture go back to 6th century BC', but there is limited knowledge of
this period. This means we can know little about the city/state precedence
question. Most studies focus on 'classic Maya culture', which flourished
from AD 250 to 900 through 'a multitude of cities with monumental
architecture, hieroglyphic writing and a complex hierarchy of settlement'
(p. 547). Here there appears to be a straightforward case of a vibrant economic process:

> The economy of the Maya city-states was a complex, multi-layered fabric of
> production and exchange. It combined agrarian production for subsistence
> with craft production on the intrapolity level, with long-distance trade and
> tribute collection on the interpolity level. (p. 558)

But the complexity Grube describes is not without its doubters.

Anne Pyburn (2000, pp. 155–6) points out that 'Western scholars traditionally argue that the Maya did not have either cities or states'. This
relates to genuine problems relating to the nature of the large Maya
settlements: are they 'real cities' or 'vacant ceremonial centers'? (Grube

Table 4.8 Estimates of Mesoamerican city populations, 430 BC–AD 1500

City	430 BC	200 BC	AD 100	361	500	622	800	1000	1200	1300	1400	1500
Cuicuilco	**30–35**	**35–38**										
Izapa		35										
Tres Zapotes		30										
Teotihuacán			**45**	**90**	**125**	**60**						
Tikal*					40–50		40					
Tajín						40	40	**50**				
Copán*							60–70					
Monte Albán							30					
Tilantongo							(20+)	(20+)				
Tollan (Tula)							(20+)	(20+)				
Cholula							(20+)	(20+)	(20+)	(20+)		36
Piedras Negras*							(20+)					
Chichen-Itzá*								(20+)				
Uxmal*								(20+)	(20+)			
Xochicalco*								(20+)				
Tenayuca									**50**			
Mayapán*									25	25	25	
Azcapotzalco										**(20+)**	**66–70**	
Texcoco										**50**	60	60

City			
	(20+)		
Mitla	(20+)		
Utatlán		30	40
Tenochtitlán		(201)	**80**
Tzintzuntzán		(20+)	
Pátzcuaro		(20+)	(20+)
Zaachila		(20+)	
Tiho*		(20+)	25
Chakanputun*		(20+)	20
Tlaxcala			40
Zampoala			30
Iximche			30
Mani*			22

Notes:

Figures refer to populations in thousands.

Thresholds for inclusion vary by column – for 430 BC, 200 BC and AD 400 the threshold is 30000 (20+), for 361, 500 and 622 the threshold is 40000, for the remainder the threshold is 20000.

(20+) indicates no specific estimate but the city probably reaches or exceeds the 20000 threshold; emboldened figures and city name indicate the largest at a given time.

* Mayan cities.

Source: Derived from Chandler (1987: 39–41 and 461–6).

2000, pp. 553–4). Lower population densities lead to problems in estimating population size (pp. 554–6; Webster 1997, pp. 140, 144–5). Further, Webster suggests some capital cities were merely where the ruler had his residence and were not necessarily 'urban' (p. 137). He also doubts whether the Maya had 'state-type institutions, as we think of them' (p. 135). But Pyburn treats this negative thinking as an example of treating the Maya as 'an exoticized other' (2000, p. 156). She challenges a set of unexamined assumptions 'head on', including one that we are familiar with from other creative arenas: 'Most reconstructions of ancient Maya civilization begin with the assumption that individual communities were economically self-sufficient' (p. 156).

The 'othering' negates the complexity of Maya political economy but Pyburn notes with approval that 'the possibility of complex intersite relations of both an economic and political nature has begun to be suggested by some authors for some ancient Maya cities.' She argues explicitly that 'local subsistence patterns and population densities are a product of intersite political economy as much as local resource availability' (pp. 156–7). She is dismissive of the idea of the Maya as a simple two-class society of endogenous elites and endogenous peasants without any middle strata: 'This sounds unlikely, since elites do not go on long trips to get the obsidian they redistribute . . . neither do they . . . train their own slaves . . . nor make their own polychromes' (p. 157). On the question of 'vacant ceremonial centres', she notes that 'there is a growing body of evidence to suggest that the way we have traditionally calculated Maya population density is wrong' (p. 158). Quite simply, whereas the monumental architecture has survived the ravages of the tropics, this would not be the case for the wattle-and-daub structures housing the people.

The key point is that Pyburn (1997) asks the right questions but the research does not currently provide the answers. For instance:

> Uaxactún may be smaller than Tikal because it was a politically and economically independent community with a restricted resource base or it may be smaller because of the nature of its relationship to Tikal. Archaeologists are not in a strong enough position to be sure whether any Maya community was self-sufficient at any given time, since almost no regional synthesis has been done.

But the evidence does locate the Maya as part of a regional creative arena.

For central Mexico there is no debate about the existence of cities and states. Charlton and Nichols (1997b, p. 197) describe three cycles before the Spanish conquest in 1521. Each cycle culminates in a 'city-state': the city-state of Teotihuacán in cycle I (1700 BC to AD 650/750); the city-state of Tula in cycle II (650/750 to 1150/1200); and the city-state of Tenochtitlán in cycle III (1150/1220 to 1521). Both the first and third cycles are associated with the growth of very large cities. Teotihuacán's population is estimated at over 100000 in AD 200 (Cowgill 2003, p.37), from 200000 to 250000 by Hodge (1997, p.210), and Chandler (1987, p.465) ranks it as the fifth largest city in the world in AD 500. Tenochtitlán reaches an estimated population of 212500 (Smith 2000, p.586); Chandler's (1987, pp.477–8) estimates are somewhat lower but he still ranks the city twenty-fourth in the world in 1500. I give these world rankings just to show that, although starting later, this New World urbanization was of a scale comparable to the Old World. It goes without saying that such large cities are associated with a 'flourishing commercial economy' (Tenochtitlán) (Smith 2000, p.588) and this is reflected for Teotihuacán by its growth depopulating the rest of the Basin of Mexico (Cowgill 2003, p.38), a sure sign of a city remaking its economic world.

There are two features of these two sub-regional cases that are held in common. First, there is frequent mention of rapid, and sudden population growth that must involve economic expansion in Jacobs' sense (1969): for instance, 'an explosion of population' (Houston et al. 2003, p.225) and 'extremely rapid rate of growth' (Webster 1997, p.149) for the Maya; and 'population explosion' (Smith 2000, p.585) and 'extraordinary dynamic' (Charlton and Nichols 1997b, p.172) for the Basin of Mexico.

The second feature informs the nature of the state. For the Maya, Grube (2000, pp.550–52) argues that successful city-states did not create territorial empires but rather they formed hegemonic federations in the Greek style. This is because political legitimacy was based on the meaning of places and the rights to govern. We have previously seen Mesopotamian political elites struggle with this problem, in their case cities as gods, in Chapter 3. Again in Maya guardian relations, place-based legitimacy appears to have prevented wars of territorial aggrandizement and therefore expansion took the form of vassal-making: 'Expansionist states would strive not to appropriate foreign territory permanently but to extend a client network' (p.552). And the same process inhibited the later Aztecs (Smith 2000, p.585):

> the city-state remained the primary unit of political organization even under the Aztec empire. The empire was of 'hegemonic' form, employing indirect control of its provinces, and local kings and institutions were generally left alone as long as they cooperated by sending tribute payments to Tenochtitlán. Within most of its territory, the Aztec empire can be viewed as an overlay upon a foundation of city-states who retained their self-government in the face of reduced external autonomy.

Referring back to Grube on the Maya, Smith (2000, p.587) suggests that 'perhaps this is an ancient and basic pattern of territory in Mesoamerica',

Extraordinary cities

Table 4.9   Estimates of Greater Peru city populations, 800–1500 (in 000s)

City	800	1000	1200	1300	1400	1500
Tiahuanaco	**20**	**20**				
Huari	(20?)	(20?)				
Quito			(20?)	**30**	(20?)	30
Túmbez*			(20?)	(20?)	(20?)	
Chanchán*			(20?)	(20?)	25	
Cajamarquilla*			(20?)	(20?)	40	
Riobamba				**30**	**50**	
Moche*				(20?)		
Cuzco					20	**50**
Bogotá						20

Notes:
(20?) indicates no specific estimate but the city probably reaches or exceeds the 20 000 threshold.
Emboldened figures and city name indicate the largest at a given time.
* Cities in the coastal valleys.

Source: Derived from Chandler (1987: 39–41).

an invention on how to change the political scale of guardianship no less impressive for having been previously invented in other regional creative arenas.

Greater Peru Creative Arenas

As in the two previous regions, there are two sub-regions to this creative arena: the northern Peruvian coastal area and the Andes mountainous area. The latter is particularly interesting because it possibly represents the end of an urban network and economy; as Table 4.9 shows, by 1500 it had eliminated the coastal cities as relevant economic entities. Jacobs (1984) uses the example of Ethiopia for a region that had had vibrant cities but when its networking collapsed, its cities stagnated and it stopped expanding economically. The Inca 'civilization' may have been approaching this point when the Spanish arrived.

Starting with the coastal region there are cities along the valleys between mountain and coast on trade routes (Wilson 1997, p. 236). Moore (2003) identifies 'urban societies' in the Moche culture (AD 1 to 600) superseded by the Chimú (AD 900–1470). However, Wilson (1997, p. 243) disputes whether there were indeed cities (using largely size criteria) and refers to the Moche state from AD 200 to 650 as a territorial state. But there is certainly evidence of concentrations of people leading to new creativity.

Attarian (2003) studies the pottery at Mocollope from AD 1 to 200 comparing the pre-urban situation of three villages with the later 'early Moche city'. The pre-urban sites show that rural communities had their own particular styles but when migrants came together at Mocollope 'new styles were created'. He uses this finding to suggest that 'urbanization encouraged the formation of new communities and networks' (p. 204). Thus contra Wilson, this is city-ness as a process operating at the very beginning of the 'civilization'. But all such coastal creativity was threatened by the conquest of the Inca in 1470.

The Inca are fascinating because although they appear to have numerous cities they can be viewed as 'nonurban, perhaps even antiurban' (Kolata 1997, p. 253). Although the capital Cuzco is considered a large city with an estimated population of 50 000 by Chandler (1987, p. 41), its prominence appears to issue solely from its role as a political capital. One of the key 'distinguishing characteristics' of this Andean society is that it had no markets (Kolata 1997, p. 246). So what went on in the cities, what work was done?

> Andean cities were centers for elite cultural definition and self-expression; a large resident population of commoners was inimical to their purpose and function. Apart from commoners incorporated into the cities in a retainer capacity, the masses rarely participated in urban culture, except on ritual occasions. ... The *raison d'être* of the Andean city was not fundamentally economic but political and ideological. (p. 247)

Thus, 'there was no intent to encourage migration to the cities. Indeed there were few economic incentives for rural populations to migrate to the city' (p. 250) – without merchants and guilds of commercial craftsmen, the only work available 'was servicing aristocratic lineages and their entourages' (p. 253). Thus is Kolata able to conclude that 'Andean capitals were essentially "company towns" catering for the interpenetrating businesses of state religion and elite politics' (p. 254). Of course, Jacobs (1984) has a lot to say about 'company towns'. As one-product centres, there is an absence of economic complexity in this form of urbanism: a type of town-ness process dominates. In this case, constrained by simple power relations, unable to develop complex economies, such urban places are doomed to stagnate. Without the diversity of a city, in hard times these towns are the first to decline. The Inca were successful in territorial expansion but this simple guardian strategy alone cannot be sustained indefinitely. Thus from Jacobs' perspective, they perfected 'taking' while neglecting 'making': even if the Spanish had not arrived to collapse the empire militarily, the Inca empire, by banishing creative economic creativity, was not long for this world.

CONCLUDING POINTS ON BEGINNING CREATIVE INTERLUDES

I conclude from this whirlwind tour of beginning creative interludes that the evidence is there to keep the 'cities first, state later' thesis credibly in play. Having made this fundamental point there are three further points I need to briefly bring attention to. These can count as a short concluding discussion for this chapter. Finally, I make one further argument about Jacobs' ideas on cities; what are the origins of her thinking? I suggest a modern 'frontier' source for them. Since her work has dominated the last two chapters, this counts as a concluding argument for Part II.

There are three important points to make in relation to the multiple cases discussed in this chapter.

I do not want to leave the impression that the above list of creative arenas constitutes a final, and therefore, closed roster. Such exclusivity dogged the traditional civilization paradigm and this is unnecessary here. My choice of regional arenas was explicitly pragmatic in nature and it is relatively easy to extend the list. For instance, the two trade routes west from China, by land and by sea, stimulated city-ness processes in both central Asia and southeast Asia. In the former case, Cosmo (2000) describes strings of oasis cities in Tarim Basin, which by the second century BC 'comprised a tight network of communities whose political structure was centred in fortified settlements based on an oasis economy' (p. 405). This is the beginning of the 'Silk Road'. Even earlier, Manguin (2000) identifies coastal urban sites appearing from the Gulf of Thailand to Java and Bali between 500 and 300 BC, which he describes as having 'burgeoned as a consequence of the economic boom of the late first millennium BC, thriving on metal production and trade' (p. 415). Other trade routes had similar city-ness outcomes in Africa such as Axum (at the southern end of the Red Sea) in the first century AD (Coquery-Vidrovitch 2005, pp. 36–8) and the Indian Ocean ports from the Horn of Africa to Mozambique in the fourth century AD (pp. 38–41), but our information on these cases remains sparse.

There are two features relating to our framework that keep reappearing: cities come in groups and cities come before agriculture. The former is found in origin myths similar to that reported for Sumer in the last chapter; for instance, the Philistines had five cities (Strange 2000b, p. 130), the Hausa had seven original cities (Griffeth 2000, p. 487), and the Kotoko had ten (Hansen 2000c, p. 531). The emerging nature of many cities is reflected in a need for food imports: agricultural development only comes later; for example in South East Asia (Manguin 2000, p. 415; Reid 2000, p. 420), the Philistines (Strange 2000b, p. 133); and Mecca and Medina

(Simonsen 2000, p. 242). These examples are all very consistent with Jacobs' ideas.

There are numerous references to social change as cycles. This is the subject matter of Marcus' (1998) comparison of ancient states but it is found, also, in several case studies; for example, ancient western Syria (Thuesen 2000), Palestine (Strange 2000a), central Mexico (Charlton and Nichols (1997b), and the Aztecs 'empire' in particular (Smith 2000). The reason why this is noteworthy is that temporal patterns of social change become one of the Normal History issues discussed in the next chapter.

The basic argument of this chapter has been that, as well as in Western Asia as described previously, and at various times and places across the world, dynamic city networks have emerged to generate great creative interludes culminating in the invention of states. The latter ushers in Normal History, where the guardian practices of world-empires dominate the commercial practices of world-economies until the arrival of modernity. This is the subject of Part III.

Finally to round off Part II, I return to consideration of the work of Jane Jacobs that has dominated these two chapters. In particular her controversial and outrageous thesis of 'cities first, agriculture second' as accepted here can be briefly reassessed in the context of its generation. The thesis is controversial because it goes against conventional archaeological wisdom but, more importantly, it has been seen as outrageous for the simple reason of being empirically wrong. This relates directly to archaeology's general acceptance of the first cities appearing in Mesopotamia about 5000 years ago. Holding this constant, research over the years has been continually pushing back the origins of agriculture so that Jacobs' thesis becomes ever more empirically untenable. My arguments in Part II have tried to address this empirical position but the question remains as to why and how Jacobs came to develop such a contrarian thesis. Clearly her indisciplinarity has something to do with it but her bold departure from what was viewed as plain common sense must have had a more particular stimulus.

I suggest a 'frontier' explanation. A frontier should not be confused with a boundary; the latter is a line, a frontier is an area or zone. Further it is a particular zone that is at the 'front' of a civilization, the place where it is expanding by impinging on others. In Part I, I emphasized the nineteenth-century progressive context in which modern theories of macro-social change have been generated; at the end of Part II I am in a position to add an effect of the geographical context of this knowledge: generation was in Western Europe (Wallerstein et al. 1996), places of relatively long-term settlement in which the memory of city origins had been long lost. But this period also encompassed the world's last great frontiers; the dynamic edges of modernity in the Americas, southern Africa, Siberian Russia and Australasia. Led by commerce (trading posts), with guardian support (forts) to varying degrees, these new settlement areas typically had cities first, with food having to be imported initially until local agriculture developed to provide for local needs. This is broadly the message of James Belich's (2009) magisterial *Replenishing the Earth* that tells a city-led story of the 'settler revolution' in these frontiers.

Direct evidence for the frontier conjecture is difficult to find but I think the fact that Jacobs (1969) begins her treatment of 'how cities start growing' with Detroit (pp. 123–4) 'a city-to-be . . . carved into the wilderness north of Lake Erie' (p. 123) is evocative of Western Asian wildernesses. Further, Detroit is later mentioned alongside Çatalhöyük (p. 127) and Mohenjo-daro and Harappa (p. 130). More generally, new frontier settlement is much more analogous to primary beginnings of cities than experience of long-term settled areas; for the participants in the city network that included Çatalhöyük 9000 years ago, the world they were developing was also a geohistorical frontier zone and revolutionary period between contrasting social worlds, perhaps with a dynamism little inhibited by guardian processes, not so unlike the 'American wild west'.

PART III

Narrative II: world-systems

5. Normal history

This chapter is an intermission; its purpose is the aid the reader in making the imaginative leap from many beginning creative interludes to the singular modern creative interlude. These creative interludes are the chief subjects of this book: exceptional times of change over-supplied with extraordinary cities. Through contrasting Normal History with the creative interludes, the unusual character of the interludes should be brought into sharper relief. And describing Normal History provides the added bonus of providing a link in the narrative, a bridge between the creative interludes.

There are four sections to this textual intermission. First, I focus on defining Normal History and propose a Jacobsean way of specifying it. Second, I describe some key practices and trace them across the bounds of Normal History. Third, I briefly consider more generally the content of Normal History and suggest its basic temporal and spatial properties. Finally I foreground the Normal History of Western Europe as the region in which the modern world-system was created.

WHAT IS 'NORMAL HISTORY'?

By the phrase 'Normal History' I wish to indicate a common pattern of social change that has dominated the historical eras of all major world regions. My thesis is that in each of these regions there was an initial successful creative interlude that set the social parameters for subsequent centuries or millennia of Normal History. All of these situations have been interrupted by the advent of a second creative interlude, Western Europe's invention of modernity that spread across the world in the second half of the second millennium AD to eliminate particular Normal Histories worldwide.

Therefore Normal History is a period of time, which varies by world region. Variation in length is from when a region's beginning creative interlude invented states until the coming of modernity to disrupt the region's Normal History. It follows that in world-regions that did not experience successful beginning creative interludes, such as Australia,

there was no Normal History created, and 'prehistory' succumbed directly
to the expansion of modernity.

   Normal History is a social time; it is identified by its content, the dominant process that it encapsulates. Every region's Normal History has its
particularities, and these are important, but there is a basic similarity that
provides coherence to the concept. This is the macro-process consequent
upon the invention of states: curbing the autonomy of cities enabled guardian work to generally prevail over commercial work. Thus Normal History
describes guardian worlds; what Wallerstein calls world-empires. At this
level of generalization there are numerous analyses of pre-modern societies
related to the world-empire concept that share a characterization of them
as essentially rural. My first task, therefore, is to get out other parts of my
toolkit to counter this neglect of cities; the latter may be typically dominated
by states but they remain important. To write cities out the story at this
level of generalization, that is to say relegating cities to the particulars, is to
remove the chief momentum to macro-social change. My Normal History
is about the relations between cities and states in pre-modern societies.

The Limitations of 'Rural' Specifications of Pre-modern Social Structures

Wallerstein (1979, pp.156–9) describes world-empires as having a
'redistributive-tributary mode of production' (p.157) firmly based upon
agricultural production. He argues that although with 'many variations
in terms of political superstructure' (p.156), there is a common structure
of surplus production from the land channelled upwards by forced appropriation called 'tribute'. Although using different terminology indicating
alternative theoretical positions, this pre-modern social structure is widely
recognized. Sanderson (1995, p.261) gives four common descriptors:
agrarian state, traditional aristocratic empires, agrarian coercive societies and tributary mode of production; to which we can add the Marxist's
feudal mode of production and Asiatic mode of production. As Sanderson
points out, they all share a basic argument pivoting on a nobility–peasant
structure of material inequality. This is a coercive guardian process that
clearly omits commercial activities. I have already countered this in my
world-systems toolkit in Chapter 2 by employing Braudel's framework to
supplement Wallerstein's analysis: this recognizes that every world-empire
co-exists with a world-economy thus enabling consideration of guardian/
commercial relations and thereby state/city relations. The crucial difference is that Wallerstein's initial concept of world-empire continues in the
tradition of viewing pre-modern societies as essentially agricultural. I have
coined the concept of Normal History as a neutral term that does not
emphasize one economic sector over any other.

The argument for this 'rural bias' in describing the pre-modern appears to be obvious: something like 90 per cent of the population of these societies were rural. Thus the vast majority of production was rural, the basis for the economic surplus that was distributed upwards. Furthermore, there was a fundamental difference of power between rural elites (aristocracy) and urban elites (merchants). Thus Normal History is undoubtedly a rural world demographically, economically and politically. And yet, Normal History is more than the rise and fall of empires. As commonly noted (for example, Chase-Dunn and Hall 1997), rise and fall does not operate around a steady state of empire and city sizes; rather, the sizes of empires and cities have tended to increase over time. This is an important finding from my perspective: the economic expansion enabling such system growth is to be found in the city networks of Normal History. This is supported by Rennstich's (2006, p. 208) argument that it is 'systems of cities' (I would prefer networks) that grow societies through overcoming '"blockages" brought about by military and political "choke-holds on world-trade"'; 'active innovation agents . . . adapt in the form of circumvention and the development of new connections' to create extensions of city networks. Rennstich's historical examples are about overcoming blockages in the 'Silk Road'. Thus his argument is about the external relations of cities being identified as crucial to commercial expansion against guardian constraints. What all this means is that unless we wish to have an image of world-empire sequences as largely static over time – 'stagnant civilizations' in past parlance – we really do need to find room for city networks in our conceptualization of pre-modern societies.

There is a keen debate on how to do this. It begins with a severe challenge to the aristocracy–peasant fulcrum of pre-modern societies: the Frank and Gills (1993) thesis of a 5000-year world-system. They identify 'an overarching and interpenetrating world-system process of capital accumulation' that transcends the long sixteenth century so as to unify Wallerstein's world-system – modern world-systems and world-empires – into a single narrative, thereby also eliminating my distinction between modern creative interlude and Normal History (Gills and Frank 1993a, p. 105). In considering this refutation of Wallerstein's systems, I am going to follow Sanderson's (1995, p. 263) position; he praises Frank and Gills for showing the limitations in neglecting commercial processes in world-empires while arguing that what Frank and Gills' work reveals is pre-modern 'commercialization rather than capital accumulation'. His key point is that 'expanding world commercialization is a historical process of tremendous significance' that is related to 'growth in the size and density of trade networks' relating to increasing urbanization (pp. 267–8). Thus Sanderson's revision of Frank and Gills' thesis counters the agrarian 'lethargy and stagnation' argument, which he associates with Weber and Wallerstein.

However, by only partially accepting the Frank and Gills thesis, Sanderson (1995) avoids their elimination of the 'pre-modern' and brings cities back into the argument. Frank and Gills' (1993) emphasis on the continuity of economic process across the 'long sixteenth century' becomes disingenuous. Sanderson does recognize a break in the historical process because, he argues, capital accumulation did not dominate society before 1500 AD (p. 263). Thus, overall Normal History experienced 'considerable social growth' (involving their cities) but not 'social evolution' in the sense of structural change (p. 269): there were changes of guardians but not changes in the nature of society. Commercialization is generic as represented by Jacobs' (1992) commercial moral syndrome in all creative interludes and Normal History; capitalism is specific to the intensification of commercial processes in the modern world-system. That is the really crucial point.

Braudel, Jacobs and *Modus Vivendi*

Sanderson (1995) is somewhat equivocal in his criticism of Wallerstein's 'rural bias': 'it is not entirely erroneous', he writes, 'but it is one-sided and misleading' (p. 268). What I think this is implying is that just because we are correcting the rural bias, this does not mean that the importance of the rural component to our Normal History should be neglected. An appropriate balance can be achieved by drawing on Braudel (1984), and linking his ideas to Jacobs' moral syndromes.

To further specify Normal History, I will reprise Braudel's treatment of world-economy from Chapter 2. He differs crucially from Wallerstein by defining world-economies as complementing world-empires: concomitant with the archetypal world-empire of Rome, there was a Roman world-economy (Braudel 1984, p. 25). This is in keeping with the spirit of Chase-Dunn and Hall's (1997, pp. 52–4) introduction of variable boundaries for world-systems depending on the relations studied: they suggest four networks of exchange: bulk goods, prestige goods, political/military and information. Staying with Wallerstein's two structures, world-economy and world-empire, I interpret them in Braudel's way. It follows that throughout Normal History there were both world-empires and world-economies co-existing with varying degrees of co-spatiality and co-temporality. In this way both agrarian–guardian processes and trading–commercial processes are equally incorporated into the analysis.

Once we admit these two processes operating together in this way we can define Normal History in more sophisticated Jacobsean terms. In

Chapter 2, in introducing the two moral syndromes, the dangers of their ethics being violated through mixing were described. To avoid creating such 'monstrous hybrids', social arrangements need to be in place that allow each to operate without their integrity being violated by the other. Jacobs (1992) identifies two methods for achieving this end. The most straightforward is the imposition of strict caste/class distinctions to separate different types of work (pp. 179–89). I argue that such separation is the *modus vivendi* that defines Normal History. Guardian tasks and commercial activities are deemed to be socially distinctive and there can be no justifiable reassignment. Both rulers and traders are born into their positions; for rulers to trade is unthinkable, for traders to rule is illegitimate. Of course, there will be varying degrees to which this separation actually operates but the basic principle of occupational castes/classes will dominate relations between economics and politics, and therefore between cities and states, in Normal History. And, of course, this arrangement is hierarchical: as Sanderson (1995, p. 261) points out 'merchants sometimes enjoyed great wealth, but their social status was almost invariably low'. We can expect this social arrangement to be most under challenge in cities but even the most autonomous cities would usually be under the nominal rule of an absent territorial guardian. The role of the state in this process is summed up by Robert Dodgshon (1998, p. 84):

> Despite the changes that have helped transform them . . . states have experienced powerful inertias or rigidities that have acted to retard, deflect or refract these changes.

It is this process that dominates Normal History.

Basic Premises of Normal History

My Normal History concept postulates a sandwich structure whereby 'traditional' city/state relations are encompassed by city-dominated 'creative intervals', respectively 'beginnings' and 'modern'. It is important to note that I am not alone in identifying such a temporal structure. A very similar pattern has been discerned in historical studies of gender relations. Drawing on the work of Gerda Lerner (1986), David Graeber (2011, p. 178) describes the process as follows:

> In the very earliest Sumerian texts, particularly those from roughly 3000 to 2500 BC, women are everywhere. Early histories not only record names of numerous female rulers, but make it clear that women were well represented among the ranks of doctors, merchants, scribes, and public officials, and generally free to take part in all aspects of public life. One cannot speak of full gender equality:

men still outnumbered women in all these areas. Still one gets the sense of a
society not so different than that which prevails in much of the developed world
today. Over the course of the next thousand years or so, all this changes. The
place of women in civic life erodes; gradually the more familiar patriarchal
pattern takes shape . . . By the end of the Bronze Age, around 1200 BC, we begin
to see large numbers of women sequestered away in harems and (in some places
at least), subjected to obligatory veiling.

This is interpreted as reflecting 'a much broader worldwide pattern'
(including India and China) consequent upon war and state centralization:
'the more militaristic the state, the harsher the laws tended to be toward
women' (p. 179). The latter is represented by the Assyrian law code (1400–
1100 BC) that is 'the first known reference to veiling in the Middle East' in
'the most notoriously militaristic state' (p. 184) of the region.

    More generally, Graeber (2011, p. 182) argues:

'Patriarchy' originated, first and foremost, in a rejection of the great urban
civilizations in the name of a kind of purity, a reassertion of paternal control
against the great cities like Uruk, Lagash, and Babylon, seen as places of
bureaucrats, traders and whores.

It is in such 'patriarchal hatred of the city' (p. 183) that this process intersects with my account of Normal History and the issue of 'rural bias'.
Clearly this gender history could be couched in terms of Jacobs' guardian
and commercial syndromes as city/state relations but I do not broach this
here. Quite simply, this is a different massive narrative that entwines with
mine but which I choose not to add to my already large subject matter:
hence my mere deploying of this fascinating argument to support and
bolster my sandwich specification of Normal History.

    To clarify and take stock, the narratives of this chapter are based on
four basic premises.

- The economic and political innovations of the beginning creative
  interludes produce a social matrix of relations that encompasses all
  the key institutions of subsequent Normal History. This means that
  these creative interludes are 'new world-making', the worlds they
  bequeath to Normal Histories are patterns of social change that are
  not altered in their basic structures until modernity. In other words,
  macro-social change in creative interludes is a change in the nature
  of the social system; macro-social change in Normal History is only
  a changing of the guards.
- But guardians do not simply dominate. There is a social hierarchical
  division of guardian and commercial work and this has an important

purpose. It is the *modus vivendi* solution to maintaining syndrome integrity, thereby enabling the reproduction of world-empires.

- The *modus vivendi* leaves commercial agents with some autonomy to continue their work. Therefore within Normal History, cities do not cease to be centres of creativity and change. The reproduction of world-systems continues to incorporate new innovations that emanate out of cities but they are no longer world-changing. Rather they embellish, improve and adapt existing technologies and institutions, carrying out old functions in new and improved ways but without challenging the existing social structure.
- Finally, it is important to note that there is not a 'normal geography' to complement Normal History. There will be variations in the degree of political centralization and this will affect the *modus vivendi*. This will vary over time in the rise and fall of empire but it will also vary across world regions. This variation in guardian geography is central to Wallerstein's (1974) interpretation of transition to modernity in Europe, of which much more later in this chapter.

The corollary of these premises is that to transcend Normal History, cities have to escape their political shackles and convert to being world-makers again. That is precisely what modernity represents.

THE BOUNDS OF NORMAL HISTORY: KEY COMMERCIAL AND GUARDIAN PRACTICES

To illustrate change but not fundamental change in Normal History, I am going to consider one archetypal guardian process – walls and fortifications – and one archetypal commercial process – accountancy. Both have been identified as important in earlier discussions – they featured especially prominently in the case of the Western Asian creative interlude. Both can be considered in general terms to represent solutions to distinctive security problems: walls are a guardian solution to political insecurity and accountancy is a commercial solution to economic insecurity. These security problems were ubiquitous to emerging societies of cities and states and therefore specific solutions will have been generated in different initial creative interludes. Subsequently these solutions proved to be essential throughout Normal Histories; they were only superseded in Europe in the 'long sixteenth century', and with the growth of the modern world-system in the rest of the world. Due to the bias in the literature, and my more detailed creative arena focus in Chapter 3, I will concentrate on what Mesopotamia bequeathed to its subsequent Normal History, which included Europe: there will be only limited reference to equivalent security solutions in other beginning creative interludes.

In both cases of security enhancement I describe two steps in the transformations from Normal History to the modern world-system. Following the initial creative interlude there is innovation in improving existing accountancy and military technology within Normal History but, crucially, the process transmutes into a fundamental shift in Western Europe to practices that have come to be understood as part of the transition to the modern world-system.

City Walls: Inventing Technologies of Defence and Attack

As previously noted, the association of walls as fortifications and cities goes way back to pre-biblical Jericho. As cities create wealth they attract the attention of those who would use coercion to steal the wealth. Hence, historically, city walls are, as Tracy (2000, p. 2) shows, 'global in scope'. In China, the symbol for city is the same as for wall, in other words it is its wall that defines a city. This very guardian attitude towards cities is even reflected in the Chinese entry to my tour of incipient creative interludes in Chapter 4, where it is walled settlements that have been found to be the very earliest cities. But I have argued that there has to be a commercial centre created to be worth defending (i.e. a city) before walls are needed. And whereas the commercial centre is a multiple private endeavour, the subsequent walls required a large-scale mobilization of labour that can only be a public project, an indication of state-making. This dual process is lost in the Chinese case, perhaps for ideological reasons as argued previously, but was clearly illustrated in the Mesopotamian case. Here, once the state is invented, creativity focuses upon defence and attack. Kern (1999, p. 21) describes it thus:

> By the end of the second millennium B.C., then, siege warfare, already at least five thousand years old, had reached a high degree of development. A variety of tactical methods, including the use of siege machinery, had prompted the development of astonishingly large and elaborate fortifications. Ancient engineers showed great ingenuity in constructing sophisticated, integrated defense systems that were effective against both escalade and early battering rams. More powerful rams would be developed, and the introduction of the catapult would add a powerful weapon to siege warfare; but in its essential elements, siege warfare would change little until the introduction of gunpowder in modern times revolutionized the ancient arts of fortification and siege.

Tracy (2000, p. 15) concurs; after describing the interplay between technologies of defence and attack in 'a single grand tradition tracing back to the ancient Near East' (p. 7), he concludes:

the recorded history of town wall building begins with the kings of ancient Sumer and ends with the rulers who disposed over the huge siege armies of seventeenth and eighteenth-century Europe.

And he adds, 'the most striking common theme to emerge . . . is the association between royal power or sovereignty and the enclosure of towns' (p.6). This process is grist to the mill that is Normal History. In these guardian-dominated times, zero-sum is the name of the game: 'Siege warfare was total war. When a city chose to resist a siege, it risked annihilation' (Kern 1999, p. 25).

In brief, the European 'long sixteenth century' route out of this predicament for cities can be charted as follows. The French success in siege technologies in the fifteenth century generated a defence response that began 'the age of transition to the fortress architecture *alla moderna*, inaugurated by Italian military engineers of the late fifteenth century' (Tracy 2000, p. 12). This culminated in huge new walls of buttresses and ramparts to protect cities; the most famous being the new Venetian city of Palma Nuova of 1593, whose geometric design epitomized the new Rennaissance science of town planning (Johnson 1967, pp. 31–2). More practically, at Leiden, a reinforced wall, including 50 million new bricks, enabled the city to withstand a Spanish siege for almost a year in 1573–4 (Tracy 2000, pp. 12–13). But by the seventeenth century, such huge investments in defence were becoming problematic for two reasons. First, concentration of political power in Europe created resources to overcome city defences, however large – Vauben, the French military architect, calculated that he could take a city if he commanded a force ten times greater than that of the defenders; his prince Louis IV could afford it (p. 14). Second, in any case, expenditure on defence was getting out of hand:

> a fully built bastioned trace could take up as much ground as the area occupied by the city itself. The city as a form of human society was apparently not well adapted to enclosure within such a massive girdle. (p. 14)

Vibrant cities could not sustain such an unbalanced existence; there certainly could not be another round in the defence/attack spiral of technologies at the city scale. There was a need for a new political invention: the rise of the sovereign territorial state as classically described by Herz (1957). This resulted in a different structure of guardian action at a new defensive scale in early modern Europe, consolidated at the Treaty of Westphalia (1648) that brought the demographically disastrous Thirty Years War to a close. The key point about the new territorial sovereignty was its mutuality; international law emerged wherein state boundaries proved better than city walls for providing a peaceful context for commercial practice.

As described in Chapter 2, this is the inter-state system, integral to the modern world-system, and critical to both system survival and reproduction (Wallerstein 1984).

Accountancy: Inventing Technologies of Profit and Loss

I have discussed how business accounting led to writing in Mesopotamia in Chapter 3. Here I rehearse this argument from the perspective of accounting history with particular reference to the work of Mattessich (2000). He describes two main innovation chains in the ancient development of accountancy that broadly coincide with the city-making and state-making sequence I have proposed. In each chain he has several steps within which he identifies one key innovation.

In the city-making chain there are four steps. First, there is the use of tokens of different shapes to represent commodities from about 8000 BC. Second, these are refined into complex tokens with specific markings to incorporate more information. Third, the tokens are collected and encased in clay envelopes ('bullae') to represent an aggregation of goods in a transaction. Fourth, which Mattessich (2000, p. 121) calls 'the most decisive of these innovations', the hard tokens are pressed on to the outside of the soft envelope before being hardened (fired) and sealed to leave a record of the contents. Mattessich regards this as 'a particular kind of double entry' (p. 121) because it gives two separate records of a transaction (on the inside and the outside). This latter breakthrough in accountancy is dated at 3200 BC, which is the height of city development in the Uruk period. This is the technology for commerce: accountancy has 'a major role in coordinating and facilitating many private activities, including . . . for barter and semi-barter exchange', with time and place recorded, and through the establishment of 'a system of equivalence between the goods given and received from another party' (Carmona and Ezzamel 2009, p. 91).

In the state-making chain, the first step is the substitution of clay envelopes by flat clay tablets and the move from impressions to specific incised marks – proto-cuneiform writing; Mattessich (2000, p. 121) identifies this as the 'decisive step' in this chain. Second, this leads on to 'a series of important accounting innovations' (p. 24), including from the beginning of the third millennium BC having debit and credit information on opposite sides of the tablet. Third, from the middle of the third millennium BC 'relatively sophisticated budgeting procedures' are developed reflecting 'the bureaucratization of economic life' (p. 122): that is to say, the invention of the state. It is in this context, 'in times of centralized and bureaucratic governments . . . the recording of a "surplus" or "deficit", the transfer of balances to the subsequent period, and their ultimate settlement became a pivotal feature' (p. 122). This is a technology for guardians: ensuring 'the regular monitoring of state projects', tax levies could be assessed, collected and transferred to state coffers', with 'accounting-based targets' including 'determining precise rations or wages' to be paid on projects (Carmona and Ezzamel 2009, p. 90).

Mattessich (2000, p. 123) concludes that the 'Sumerian token-envelope accounting of the 4th millennium BC is linked to the very different proto-cuneiform and cuneiform bookkeeping of the subsequent 3rd millennium BC', and between them that provide basic tools that were to last through-out Normal History. In conjunction with early banking (Renger 2003, p. 220) and early insurance related to trade (Pearson 2003, p. 83) including maritime insurance (Thowsen 2003, p. 87), the technologies for commerce, and its relations to the state, were in place by 2000 BC. But this initial innovative flowering notwithstanding, in the *modus vivendi* of Normal History the guardians, both spiritual and secular, dominated the customs and rules of society in such a way as to diminish and denigrate commercial work.

In brief, the European 'long sixteenth century' route out of this predica-ment for merchants in their cities can be charted as follows. Double-entry bookkeeping was a key innovation. Although generally thought to have originated in fourteenth-century Genoa, it was only with its codification in printed books that it qualified as a 'system of knowledge' that could be 'an apologist for mercantile honesty' (Poovey 1998, p. 37). This arrived in 1494 with Luca Pacioli's *Summa de Arithmetica, Geometria, Proportioni, et Proportionalita* at the very beginning of the modernity creative inter-lude (Previts and Murwanto 2003, p. 3). Printing diffused it to northern Europe as partnership gave way to corporate forms of business, with publication in Antwerp in 1543, in Leyden in 1607, and in London in 1632. In its written form it became part of the university field of rheto-ric, thus enhancing the status of commercial work (Poovey 1998, p. 38). With every item recorded twice, as debit and credit, a classic balance was created in the symmetry of facing papers, which was a classic sign of virtue (pp. 54–5). Thus was profit making legitimated. But there is a second step in Poovey's argument. Double-entry bookkeeping contributed to the entry of merchants into state policy-making. Poovey calls this 'from rhetoric to reason of state' (p. 66) whereby the specialist knowledge of commerce was recognized as separate from the monarch's duties derived from God. If the 'system of trade' were to strengthen the state then mercantilist poli-cies were necessary. Thus it was that 'the seventeenth century witnessed a realignment of the relations among politics, religion, economic activity, and the production of knowledge' (p. 71) due to:

> mercantile writing – both double-entry booking and mercantile accommoda-
> tion more generally – [playing a major] role in the transition from the old status
> hierarchy to modern, functionally differentiated domains. (p. 91)

For 'old status hierarchy', read Normal History's *modus vivendi*; for
'modern, functionally differentiated domains', read the modern world-
system's *modus operandi*.

THE TIMES AND SPACES OF NORMAL HISTORY

It is not my intention to even begin to describe the general content of the
Normal Histories that have developed out of beginning creative interludes.
A new school of 'world history' has burgeoned in the last few decades and
within this work world-systems studies are very strong. There are numerous examples that seriously apply world-systems concepts and ideas –
cycles, hegemonies, and core/peripheries abound – to the period before
Wallerstein's modern world-system. There have been two basic tendencies
in this new work. Some scholars are developing a 'comparative world-
systems' approach, which takes Wallerstein's (1979) simple identification
of world-empires and mini-systems preceding the modern world-system
to more complex and sophisticated levels by bringing in anthropological categories and concepts. As noted previously, the key publication
is Chase-Dunn and Hall's (1997) *Rise and Demise: Comparing World-
Systems*. In addition, Marcus (1998), whom we have met before in the
last chapter, has embarked on a similar 'comparative cycles' exercise. The
second development we encountered in defining Normal History above.
This is the argument that focuses upon continuity in world-system processes and disputes Wallerstein's basic notion of a modern world-system.
The key publication presenting this argument, and debates surrounding
it, is Frank and Gills' (1993) *The World System: Five Hundred Years or
Five Thousand?* Subsequent discussion and debate can be found in a series
of edited volumes: Sanderson (1995), Kardulias (1999), Denemark et al.
(2000), Friedman and Chase-Dunn (2005), Gills and Thompson (2006)
and Thompson (2009). An invaluable feature of these researches is that
there is a strong empirical dimension: a wonderful harnessing of evidence,
both quantitative and qualitative, worldwide over thousands of years.

It is also not my intention to attempt a systematic critique this material;
for my purposes here I let it stand as a dynamic body of knowledge that is
providing new insights into the content of Normal History. For instance,
in Table 5.1 I reproduce a summary of the original argument of Gills and
Frank (1993b) for simultaneity in Afro-Eurasian social change from 2000

Table 5.1   *Gills and Frank's expansions and contractions, 2000 BC–AD 1450*

Phase	Dates (approximate)	Main Afro-Eurasian changes
A	2000–1700 BC	*Non-synchronized change* Ur Third Dynasty/Amorite Babylon Middle Kingdom Egypt
B	1700–1500/1400 BC	*Simultaneous disintegration* Hittites and Kassites – Anatolia/ Mesopotamia Hurrians and Hyksos – Levant/Egypt Aryans – Indus Shang – north China
A	1400–1200 BC	*Interlinking empires* Hittite empire New Kingdom Egypt Babylon; Mittani Assyria Mycenaean Greece
B	1200–1000 BC	*Collapse of Bronze Age empires* Sea people – Egypt/Hittite empire Dorians – Greece Chaldean and Aramaeans – Babylon Zhou – Shang
A	1000–800 BC	*Iron Age integration* Phoenicians Assyrian empire
B	800–550 BC	*Age of rivalries* Scythians – Medes – Asyrian empire Babylonia/Medes/Persian rivalry Zhou disintegrate into independent states
A	550–450 BC	*Shift in logistical interlinkage* Aegina/Corinth/Lydia/ Athens Achaemenid Persian empire
B	450–350 BC	*Revolts and wars* Disintegration of the Persian empire (Egypt, Indus) Greek wars Celts – Italy
A	350–250/200 BC	*Hellenistic expansion* Macedonian empire Qin dynasty in China Mauryans in India

Table 5.1 (continued)

Phase	Dates (approximate)	Main Afro-Eurasian changes
B	250/200–100/50 BC	*Non-synchronized change* Bactria, Han dynasty in China consolidation Conflict in Greece and Italy Decline of Egypt

A	100/50 BC–AD 150/200	*Unbroken interlinked empires*:
		Rome – Parthia (Mesopotamia/Persia) –
		  Kushan (central Asia) – Han China (plus
		  India, South East Asia and Armenia)

B	AD 150/200–500	*Pan-Eurasian systematic crisis* Disintegration of Roman, Parthian, Kushan and Han empires Germans – western Roman empire

A	AD 500–750/800	*To the Islamic caliphate*
		Sassanid empire Anatolia, Levant, Egypt;
		  Byzantium
		Sri Harsha India and China reunification
		  (Siu dynasty/Tang)
		Turkish central Asia
		Abbasid Arab/Muslim empire (Baghdad)

B	AD 750/800–1000/1050	*Chain of repercussions* Rebellions and end of Tang China Turkish expansion Division of Muslim Caliphate Tang China
A	AD 1000/1050–1250/1300	*Eurasian expansion* Rise of Western Europe Egypt (Cairo) Turkish Ottoman empire Sung China; Indian and South East Asian coasts
B	AD 1250/1300–1450	*The great Mongol disruption* Mongol conquests from Russia to China Later Tamerlane in central Asia and India

Source: Derived from Gills and Frank (1993b).

Table 5.2   Economic fluctuations in Afro-Eurasia, 4000 BC–BC 200

Economic change	Phase dates
Contraction	4000?–3800
Expansion	3800–3200
Contraction	3200–?
Expansion	2700–2300
Contraction	2300–2050
Expansion	2050–?
Contraction	1750–1700/1600
Expansion	1600–1250
Contraction	1200–750
Expansion	750–550/500
Contraction	500–300/350
Expansion	300–150
Contraction?	150–50 insufficient evidence
Expansion	50–AD 200

Source: Derived from Frank and Thompson (2005; 2006).

BC to AD 1450. This is part of their 5000-year-old world-system proposition; the post-1450 'modern world-system' is not included in Table 5.1 since I deal with this specifically in the next chapter. Gills and Frank identify eight cycles each with an A and B phase of expansion and contraction.

There are two things to note at this stage. First, the cycles are quite irregular in length ranging from 200 to 600 years. Second, their descriptions of the cycles and phases are mostly about political changes. Subsequently, Frank and Thompson (2005; 2006) have produced a different sequence of phases based upon a thorough examination of economic evidence; this is presented in Table 5.2. This table starts much earlier; it covers the creative interlude previously described for Mesopotamia, and finishes much earlier at the end of the 'classic era'. But in the 2000-year overlap between the tables, in my 'Normal History', there are important differences. Three phases in Table 5.1 'Interlinking empires', 'Collapse of Bronze Age empires' and 'Iron Age integration' are conflated into one long economic cycle from 1600 to 750 BC in Table 5.2, and this is repeated for the next three phases in Table 5.1 conflated into the economic cycle from 750 to 300 BC in Table 5.2. The point about these differences is that they are important but not surprising since the criterion for identifying phases has been altered. Frank and Thompson (2006, p. 141) justify the new concentration on just economic evidence, avoiding 'mixing in alternative types of information (such as urban expansion, wars and migration)', so that 'subsequent analyses can examine the relationships, if any, among economic growth, war, migrations, and urban expansion'. In other words, they are unpicking the earlier social change sequences in order to understand better the processes generating the change.

This glimpse at the content of a Normal History provides a flavour of this social change but no more. Without taking these empirics any further I wish to make a modest conceptual contribution to this dynamic, pluralist research mix. Although sharing many concepts and ideas with these 'world-systems historians', I am working with additional concepts drawn from Jacobs' oeuvre. My purpose is to suggest how a more city-centric approach plus the moral syndromes might inform their research. I am offering a new way of thinking to embellish the rich evidential interpretations and debates that already exist. I will do this by considering time and space constructs in turn.

Constructing Times: Events and Cycles

I will start by referring to my conceptual toolkit to support Frank and Thompson's (2006) empirical justification for separating out economic process. In my approach, Tables 5.1 and 5.2 represent temporal outcomes of guardian and commercial processes respectively. Given that the agents creating these times are operating through quite distinctive moral syndromes, it follows that the processes should be measured and assessed separately. But I can take the argument beyond this basic position. Further, moral syndromes imply agents not only creating different times; they create different types of time. From Chapter 2 we know that guardians are implicated in contingent times and commercial agents in cyclical times.

In the literature of world-systems history time is described in several different ways. While 'cycles' is the most common term, there are also references to rhythms, pulsations, fluctuations and traditional historical periods. The order in which I have listed these time-forms is from regular to more irregular: we might expect cycles with their expansions and contractions to be more regular in pattern than historical periods where irregular length is not an issue. To reprise my TimeSpace toolkit I will treat just these two types here as limiting cases that are associated with Jacobs' two syndromes. Since these syndromes are generic, it can be argued that, left to unfold on their own, commercial agents should create reasonable regular, long economic cycles in Normal History. In contrast guardian zero-sum games can only create irregular periods – contingency is a critical determinant for their success or failure. Although it is possible to construct a cyclical model of consolidation and breakdown of states/empires using an over-stretching territorial process (e.g. Marcus 1998), such patterns of centralization and decentralization are ultimately subject to contingent events rather than structured cycles. Thus, although all world regions have periods of centralization and decentralization, that is precisely what they are, just periods. For instance, in the Chinese case, periods of unification and partition can range in size from a few decades to many centuries. In Marcus' (1998) work, where she extends a model derived from Mayan states to Mexican and Peruvian cases and then further to Mesopotamia, Egypt and the Aegean, the results are referred to as cycles but the diagrams show very irregular time sequences: I would call them periods, not cycles.

Left alone therefore, guardians produce periods and commercial agents produce cycles. But, of course, neither is ever alone. Actual historical sequences will merge periods and cycles in ways that reflect their guardian–commercial interactions. And these are never straightforward. On the one hand, commercial work can be facilitated by guardian unification though providing a peaceful context for trade and production; on the other hand, unification provides the few 'winning' guardians with exceptional power that they may use to raise additional revenues for even bigger armies. If taxes are large, arbitrary and unpredictable, trade and production will suffer. The obverse pertains during decentralized times: Frank and Thompson (2006, p. 141) point out that 'intense conflict and economic growth' can co-exist, giving the example of the Chinese Warring States period. Possibly, commercial agents can play off rival states against one another for provision of capital and warfare commodities. Therefore, when looking at 'general' historical sequences we have no expectation for regularity: Table 5.1 illustrates irregular periods dominated by guardian processes. In contrast, we should expect commercially created sequences to show regularity tendencies while also remembering that a particular example of the process might be curtailed or extended because of guardian actions. In Table 5.2, the cycles with stated beginnings and ends are 650 years, 450 years, 850 years and 450 years. We can note that the 850-year cycle is longer than the others because of its extended contraction period; this is a candidate for investigating whether a guardian period was instrumental in delaying an economic upturn. Otherwise, long cycles of about half a millennium seem to be created by commercial processes in this Normal History.

Constructing Spaces: Empires and Networks

The approach to understanding the construction of spaces that I outlined in Chapter 2 suggests further revisionist ideas for the historical world-systems literature. Here is a quick reprise – there are two basic types of spaces: guardians are orientated towards territory and produce spaces of places as states or empires; commercial elites are orientated towards networks and produce spaces of flows as city networks. And, of course, these spaces are never constructed alone; they are created simultaneously as intertwining places and flows. This is most clearly illustrated in the role of selected cities as political centres. As well as cities becoming important because of the commercial process, some also gain immensely by being the capital city of successful states or empires. The spoils of war are 'repatriated' to the great city that displays the empire's military prowess: Tamerlane's imperial capital Samarkand is an extreme case for its rapid rise and fall (Marozzi 2004, pp. 210–16). In the creation of his great empire in the fourteenth century, Tamerlane conquered all the great cities of western Asia – Baghdad, Damascus, Cairo, Shiraz and Sultaniya – and degraded them by renaming mere suburbs of Samarkand after them; on approaching his imperial capital visitors passed through 'Baghdad', 'Damascus', etc. (p. 211). This guardian process can be found to different degrees in any state where governance is no longer mobile, but is centralized into a capital city. Obviously this complicates any analysis of cities and their population sizes: large capital cities will continue to be important production centres but they may be more important as consumption centres resulting from hugely ostentatious guardian behaviour.

Given that Normal History is a guardian-dominated world, it makes sense to study cities initially from a territorial perspective. This is in keeping with traditional urban geography analyses of population sizes of cities that assume hierarchical arrangements, as discussed in Part I. The technique of choice in such studies is rank-size analysis based upon cities ranked by their populations. The analysis involves relating city sizes to city ranks. There is a 'rank-size rule' that describes an 'ideal' hierarchy: the first ranked is twice the size of the second ranked city, three times the size of the third ranked city, and so on. This was originally devised to illustrate the nature of the urban hierarchy in modern complex 'national economies'. This economic process is contrasted with a political process – the 'Law of the primate city' – where the largest city, usually the capital city, dominates a national urban hierarchy. Brian Berry (1961) uses this contrast to indicate different levels of economic development. Christopher Chase-Dunn and his colleagues have employed this method to describe inter-city relations across a wide range of world regions from 2000 BC (Chase-Dunn and Willard 1993; Chase-Dunn and Hall 1995). He analyses the largest five cities in these regions at different times using a 'standardized primacy index', in which the rank-size rule scores zero and positive values represent increasing primacy. When applied to pre-modern cases the expectation is

Table 5.3 *Tendencies towards city networks in Normal History, 2000 BC–AD 1400*

Standard primacy index	Frequency	Inter-city pattern
1.51 to 2.0	1	
1.01 to 1.5	0	Tendency towards primacy
0.51 to 1.0	1	
0.01 to 0.5	13	
Exactly zero	Rank-size rule	Regular hierarchy
−0.01 to −0.5	22	
−0.51 to −1.0	7	
−1.01 to −1.5	3	
−1.51 to −2.0	6	Tendency towards network
−2.01 to −2.5	3	
−2.51 to −3.0	3	
−3.01 to −3.5	0	
−3.51 to −4.0	1	

Source: Derived from Chase-Dunn and Willard (1993).

that the rank-size rule is 'normal' (i.e. a neat hierarchical arrangement of cities), but centralizing political/military processes will tend to create more primate settlement hierarchies (Chase-Dunn and Hall 1995, p. 122). Thus inter-city relations in Normal History should vary from rank-size rule to primacy depending on the degree of guardian centralization. But their results produce a major surprise.

Most regions at most times have negative index scores. This points towards a 'flatter distribution' of cities than the rank-size rule, the opposite of primate hierarchies. Such outcomes are not part of the rank-size rule versus primate city discourse, but the empirics force this possibility on to the research agenda. I interpret negative indices as indicating tendencies towards more networked inter-city relations. In Table 5.3 I have taken the 60 index scores that represent Normal History (that is, up to 1400 AD) and have arrayed them about the rank-size ideal. The asymmetry is clearly displayed, indicating that even in Normal History when guardian processes prevail, economic city network outcomes are far commoner than tendencies towards primacy. This suggests the *modus vivendi* between guardian and commercial work is genuinely reflected in inter-city relations, thus allowing cities to prosper beyond imperial capitals. However, to take these findings further, secondary text materials have to be considered to ascertain the varying importance of guardian and commercial processes in contributing to a city's population as an indication of its importance. An initial attempt to systematically separate out guardian and commercial process in cities is deferred to Chapter 6.

The different spaces generated by commercial and guardian processes may also have implications for the core–periphery model. This is the basic spatial structure that Wallerstein (1979) describes for the modern world-system, and it has been transferred wholesale into spatial analyses of pre-modern situations. As described in Chapter 2, core–periphery is shorthand for processes of domination and exploitation that explain uneven economic development within the modern world-system. In such explanations guardian processes have a role to play, but the imperialism is essentially economic in nature; it is commercial processes that maintain the inequalities in the routine operation of the capitalist world-economy. It is doubtful, to say the least, whether this mix of processes can be transferred to Normal History. Certainly there will be differences in political and economic power in pre-modern situations but the processes reproducing them must surely be different in nature to the modern world-system. In fact with the *modus vivendi* of guardian and commercial processes, we might expect two different spatial organizations. Guardian processes generate centralization of power, and therefore we might be conceptualizing the spatial structure as centre–edge, or more specifically centre–frontier, and leave the core–periphery terminology to commercial processes.

One of the main innovations of Wallerstein's world-systems analysis, the semi-peripheral category, has also been carried over into pre-modern analyses with mixed results. In the modern world-system it is the dynamic shift category through which states move up and down in the inter-state system (Wallerstein 1979). In transferring the concept to pre-modern situations Chase-Dunn et al. (2006, p. 16), do not assume all world-systems have a semi-periphery: this is treated as 'a research question to be determined in each case'. Chase-Dunn and Hall (1997) identify two key cases: semi-peripheral marcher states (pp. 84–9) and autonomous capitalist city-states (pp. 90–93). These two cases are obviously very different and it can be argued that to lump them together converts the semi-periphery into a chaotic conception. Clearly, from the perspective adopted here, they are products of guardian and commercial processes respectively. Given the previous discussion we might term the former category semi-frontier, those polities on the outside forcing their way into the centre through military means. Hence just as semi-periphery is about the possibility of functionally moving from periphery to core, semi-frontier is about the possibility of functionally moving from frontier to centre.

The second category is described as 'capitalist city-states in the semi-peripheral interstices of empires dominated by a tributary mode of production', where capitalist here means 'the notion of degrees of com-modification' (p. 90). Chase-Dunn and his colleagues (2009, pp. 270–71) link their concept to the older literature on ports of trade and this brings the argument closer to how their form of semi-periphery might be interpreted here as 'semi-edge'. Instead of the emphasis on city-states, semi-edge in Normal History is identified by a network of cities, relatively autonomous from adjacent territorial states. It is in these regions that much economic expansion in Normal History is achieved to fuel the guardian processes behind 'upward sweeps', through which empires and their imperial capi-tals get larger and larger throughout Normal History, culminating in the Umayyads and Abbissids Islamic empire with its capital in Baghdad in the ninth and tenth centuries AD (pp. 262–6). This identification of semi-periphery as city network is important for subsequent arguments, because medieval Europe is sometimes categorized as a 'semi-periphery' that meta-morphosed to create the modern world-system (Chase-Dunn and Hall 1997, pp. 93–4, 189–92). I will develop this notion of 'semi-edge' Europe turning around its economic fortune in the next chapter.

HISTORICAL WORLD CITY NETWORKS

Before we leave Normal Histories I will make a short empirical excursion to describe the leading world city networks that were created in these times. There are many studies that celebrate the great cities of the past, and two recent volumes are especially enlightening. Peter Hall, in his *Cities in Civilization* (1998), is concerned for the 'unique creativity of great cities' (p. 7); 27 chapters describe cities as the primary sites of creativity and inno-vation starting with Athens in 500–400 BC and concluding with London in 1979–1993. Although breathtaking in its substantive coverage of social change through cities, it is limited due to a focus on 'Western Civilization'. In contrast John Julius Norwich (2009) has edited a volume *The Great Cities in History* that includes cities from the beginnings of urbaniza-tion in all parts of the world. It consists of 70 vignettes of cities that have made their mark on history in politics, commerce or culture, starting with Mesopotamian Uruk as the 'world's first city' and concluding with Shanghai today as 'China's super city'. These are wonderful books but, as previously noted, they do not represent the way I approach world cities of the past.

Devoting study to great cities one at a time risks losing the geohis-torical context through which the cities became great in the first place. Parallel to the now discredited political 'great men history' we are in danger of creating an urban 'great cities history'. Rather my toolkits insist that cities are at all times connected in spaces of flows. It is through networks, orbits, circuits and chains of commodities that information, people, knowledge and all manner of cultural ideas are transmitted within and between cities. Thus a city never occurs on its own, von Thunen-like, with just its hinterland for company. As argued in detail in Chapter 2, cities come in groups because they need each other to be successful, that is the prime premise of this book. Thus the world cities of Normal History constitute city networks that feature a number of major cities. I identify eight such major city networks that precede the modern world-system. In addition I identify a European 'early modern' major city network at the time of its beginnings and before the onset of industrialization in the late eighteenth century. Hence the substance of this section is to define and describe these nine major city networks prior to the rise of great modern industrial cities.

There is one recent scholar who takes a similar view to me in the roles that cities take historically. George Modelski (2003) in his book *World Cities: −3000 to 2000*, which I have previously used for its demographic data, introduces the contemporary concept of world city in his own analysis of his data. He defines world cities as complex centres of organization that are part of wider networks of cities:

> World cities are bases of institutions capable or organizing vast regions of the world into an integrated world system. They might be mighty capitals and centers of wide-ranging international political responsibilities. They might serve world-wide religious institutions. Or else they might function as global centers of learning and stores of knowledge (as in the library of Alexandria). They obviously provide the infrastructure of world trade. (p. 4)

Because of the lack of historical data for this range of functions he operationalizes this city 'importance' as demographic size, the assumption being that large urban populations are associated with the complex division of labour necessary for world city functions.

To illustrate his definition he uses the example of Uruk 5000 years ago:

> . . . why should Uruk be called a world city? Well, for one, it was in its time the world's largest city; secondly, it was the center of a nucleus of cities that would expand world-wide, and third, it was also the cradle of writing; in all three respects, a city of worldly import. (p. 4)

Thus although Uruk reaches a maximum population of only 80000, not particularly large today, it qualifies, for Modelski, as the very first world city because of its contemporary impact and world-changing legacy. I will use this case prominently in my later analyses.

Defining Historical World City Networks

There are two ways I diverge a little from Modelski's (2003) work. First, there is always a danger when using a place-based measure, such as population size, as a surrogate for the complexity of world cities, that the space of flows – the essence of the complexity – is neglected. This is, I fear, what has happened to a degree in Modelski's text. Second, and to rectify this, I employ Braudel's (1984) concept of world-economy as a framework for cities in spaces of flows with world-economies existing in tandem with world-empires. I will argue it is city networks that provide the basic organization frame for such 'worlds' as world-economies. Hence for these specific worlds, their cities constitute a world city network just as contemporary cities define the world city network of our globalizing world. I realize this emphasis on economy dilutes Modelski's more comprehensive definition of world city, but this can be justified as follows. I am interested in city networks that are reasonably longlasting, at least 200 years. Such sustainability requires complex commercial transactions across many cities for their mutual benefit. There will be important imperial capitals that depend on simpler patterns of tribute but ultimately city dynamism will be tested through integration into the network rather than just being a site for stacking up imperial capital. However, there will never be a purely commercial network of cities; the degree of political influence will be manifest in different levels of hierarchical tendency within world city networks.

World city networks consist of groupings of leading cities. Two thresholds have to be set for membership: (1) the population size to qualify as a leading city, and (2) the number of such cities that make a network. The threshold I use to define a leading city is 80 000, the population of Uruk in 2800 BC. As noted previously, Modelski used this case to clarify his world city concept: it is truly the world's first great city. Just think of the economic and political logistics for the everyday reproduction of a city of this size some five thousand years ago. Table 5.4 shows Uruk's precociousness in terms of sheer size. The cities in this table are all those with populations of 80 000 or more from 2800 to 600 BC. Notice for over a millennium after Uruk, only one other city reached this threshold: Ur, the first major imperial capital and the first city of 100 000. In later years there is a mixture of Egyptian and Chinese cities that join the list but, even with these additional regions, cities of such a size remain rare. And most are not far above the threshold; only one city in Table 5.4 has a population over twice the size of Uruk: Luoyang was the first 200 000 city in the final century recorded in Table 5.4. Uruk sets the threshold for what is a leading city in Normal History.

Table 5.4   Cities with populations of 80 000 or more, 2800–600 BC

Date (all BC)	Cities with estimated populations of 80 000 or more
2800	Uruk
2700	–
2600	–
2500	–
2400	–
2300	–
2200	–
2100	Ur
2000	–
1900	–
1800	–
1700	–
1600	Avaris
1500	–
1400	Thebes
1300	Thebes, Yin
1200	Pi-Ramses, Thebes, Yin
1100	Memphis, Pi-Ramses, Thebes
1000	Babylon, Haoqing, Memphis, Thebes
900	Haoqing, Memphis, Thebes
800	Haoqing, Memphis, Thebes
700	Linzi, Luoyang, Memphis, Thebes
600	Carthage, Gelonus, Linzi, Luoyang, Xiatu

Source: Modelski (2003).

How many of these cities are required to indicate a fully flourishing world city network? Such a threshold is obviously arbitrary and can be manipulated to ensure a number that is manageable for purpose. In this case I have set a high threshold of ten leading cities within a common cultural area ('civilization') to constitute a world city network. Such a grouping of cities provides the network structure of flows that reproduces the world that is a 'civilization'. I search out such places with ten or more 'Uruks' over a two-century period to reflect sustained reproduction. Operationalizing this methodology generates nine world city networks.

Of course, the original Sumerian cities of which Uruk is the head do not qualify as a world city network by the criteria applied here. But this does not mean it was not an important city network. In fact Modelski (2003, p. 28) identifies 12 cities including Uruk in 2800 BC with populations over 10 000 (Table 3.2). Clearly not great cities, the second highest population was only 40 000, but nevertheless they constituted a vibrant city network, possibly the very first (Algaze 2005a). The point I am making is that the world city networks I identify are only the major networks amongst myriad such organization that were created in Normal History. But they are the most impressive, ten-plus Uruks' worth of spatial organization, and they begin to appear in the final half-millennium BC.

The results of this exercise show successive world city networks from two world regions. First, the majority are found in East Asia, China and surrounding countries. Starting in 400 BC and only ending as the Chinese Empire is beginning to be absorbed into the modern world-system in AD 1800, most great city networks of the world have been Sino-centric. Second, there are Middle East/European world city networks that can ultimately be traced back to the earliest known city network in Mesopotamia. This includes the pre-industrial European world city network of the early modern period. In what follows I introduce these networks briefly in each region in turn. For each world city network I have produced a table of qualifying cities with their highest estimated populations over the two centuries of the network's existence. Discussion of each world city network focuses on these tables.

There is one hypothesis to keep in mind when considering these world city networks. In numerous forays into historical city analyses, Christopher Case-Dunn has suggested that cities flourish when political structures are weak (e.g. Chase-Dunn and Hall 1997, p. 90). Thus the impressive world city networks I have identified might be expected to occur in periods where there is little or no political centralization by world-empires.

Sino-centric Leading World City Networks

The very first major world city network in history is the *first East Asian world city network straddling 400 to 300 BC*. With 14 leading cities, five with a population over 200 000, it is clearly a well-established network (Table 5.5).

This world city network developed in the Eastern Zhou period before the first Chinese unification in 221 BC, and therefore seems to reflect the commercial advantages of decentralized politics. According to Shen (2003, p. 290) this was a period when 'the number of cities dramatically increased, and urban population grew rapidly'. He captures the process as follows:

> Production and commerce clearly became a very important part of the urban economy during the Eastern Zhou. Political centers, such as capitals of states, quickly turned into commercial cities that attracted a large number of migrants. (p. 295)

Table 5.5   The first East Asian world city network, 400–300 BC

Leading cities	Population estimates (in 000s)
Linzi	350
Xiatu	320
Luoyang	250
Daliang	200
Yiyang	200
Qufu/Lu	180
Yenhsiatu	180
Shangqiu	130
Xinzheng	120
Handan	100
Suzhou	100
Anyi	100
Yong	100
Yianyang	100

Source: Modelski (2003: 42) supplemented by Chandler (1987: 461).

We may interpret this as the network of China's creative interlude: as 'evidence of the extensive trading activities' (p. 304), I have previously noted that he refers to one city site where over 30 000 coins have been found, many originating from other city-states. This appears to be a very worthy first major world city network in world history.

The *second East Asian world city network straddling AD 700 to 800* occurs during the disintegration phase of the Tang Dynasty (618–907). Strong centralizers, they created their great new capital at Changan as a forward base for growing their empire westwards. However, military defeat and internal rebellion changed the situation dramatically after 755. This is how Barraclough (1979, p. 126) describes it:

> The imperial authority was much reduced, and the uniform centralised policies of the 7th century were abandoned. Power passed to the provinces, and many provincial capitals grew into large and wealthy metropolises. There was a massive movement of population into the fertile Yangtze valley, where new methods of farming produced large surpluses of grain. Trade boomed, and a network of small market towns grew up everywhere.

But our data, Table 5.6, shows much more than 'small market towns', Barraclough appears to have missed the boom in great cities that Table 5.6 illustrates. Thus this seems to be another case where political weakness has allowed the blooming of a Chinese world city network.

Table 5.6   The second East Asian world city network, AD 700–800

Leading cities	Population estimates (in 000s)
Changan	1000
Luoyang	500
Guangzhou	200
Suzhou	100
Chengdu	100
Xin Jang	100
Youzhou	100
Kaifeng	100
Nara	100
Kyoto	100
Lsasa	100
Wuchang	84

Source: Modelski (2000: 44) supplemented by Chandler (1987: 467–8).

The *third East Asian world city network straddling AD 1300 to 1400* is shown in Table 5.7. This depicts a complete change from the previous East Asian network (Table 5.6). Two features stand out: first, the retreat from the west in terms of the largest cities, and second, a much flatter distribution of cities is indicated. This is a network that flourished in the period of transfer from the Mongol Yuan dynasty to the domestic Ming dynasty. In this period of political uncertainty there is no one capital city that dominates before the Ming dynasty moved back to Peking in 1421.

The *fourth East Asian world city network straddling AD 1500 to 1600* (Table 5.8) and the *fifth East Asian world city network straddling AD 1700 to 1800 AD* (Table 5.9) are particularly interesting because they coincide with the rise of the modern world-system. The first thing to note is that these two world city networks are quite similar and might be interpreted as a single large network that grew to full fruition in 1800. At this point Peking was still the largest city in the world, at the head of what was by far the largest world city network developed before industrial modernity. The reasons why this 'pre-modern' network remained the prime world city network in the early centuries of the modern world-system have been described in detail by Frank (1998, pp. 231–7). The point being made here is that it is Chinese Normal History that produced the greatest sequence of world city networks right up to the world-empire's incorporation into the capitalist world-economy.

Table 5.7   The third East Asian world city network, AD 1300–1400

Leading cities	Population estimates (in 000s)
Nanking	487
Hangchow	432
Peking	401
Kamakura	200
Canton	150
Kyoto	150
Soochow	129
Sian	118
Seoul	100
Kaifeng	90
Wuchang	90
Yangchow	85
Fuchow	81
Chuanchow	80

Source: Chandler (1987: 73–4).

Table 5.8   The fourth East Asian world city network, AD 1500–1600

Leading cities	Population estimates (in 000s)
Peking	706
Osaka	360
Kyoto	300
Hangchow	270
Nanking	194
Canton	180
Sian	138
Soochow	134
Seoul	125
Chengdu	100
Sumpu	100
Changchun	85
Fuchow	83
Kaifeng	80
Yamagushi	80

Source: Chandler (1987: 75–6).

Table 5.9   The fifth East Asian world city network, AD 1700–1800

Leading cities	Population estimates (in 000s)
Peking	1100
Canton	800
Yedo	688
Hangchow	387
Osaka	383
Kyoto	377
Soochow	243
Sian	224
Seoul	194
Kingtehchen	164
Tientsin	130
Fuchow	130
Foshan	124
Chengdu	97
Nagoya	92
Lanchow	90
Shanghai	90
Ninghsia	90
Changsha	85
Ningpo	80
Kaifeng	80

Source: Chandler (1987: 77, 79).

The Mesopotamian Legacy of Leading World City Networks in the West

In the Mesopotamian legacy the initial focus of leading city networks incorporated the Mediterranean. As described in Chapter 4, there had been important Mediterranean city networks developed first by the Phoenicians and latterly by the Greeks (Gottman 1984) but neither grew large enough to become major world city networks by my definition. But this changed with the *first Mediterranean world city network straddling 200 to 100 BC* coinciding with the rise of Rome, dominant in the eastern Mediterranean from 188 BC, at the period when some Alexandrian city development remained (Table 5.10). This is reflected in there being more hierarchical tendencies in this network: the city of Alexandria is identified by Modelski as the first 'millionaire city', and Rome is also recorded as very large. This is the world city network of Republican Rome: it consisted largely of cities to the east often in alliance with Rome, incorporated into the Roman world by conquest and trade (Grimal 1983, p. 6).

Table 5.10   The first Mediterranean world city network, 200–100 BC

Leading cities	Population estimates (in 000s)
Alexandria	1000
Rome	400
Carthage	200
Pergamum	200
Antioch	125
Jerusalem	100
Ephesus	100
Apamea	100
Cibyra	100
Syracuse	100

Source: Modelski (2003: 49) supplemented by Chandler (1987: 462).

The *second Mediterranean world city network straddling AD 200 to 300* is the world city network of Imperial Rome. However this should not be interpreted as simply extreme political centralization because, as Grimal (1983, p. 109) has pointed out: 'the Roman Empire was, legally and in practice, a federation of city-states', so that 'until the late third century AD, the Roman Empire consisted essentially of cities, each of which had a territory attached to it' (p. 329).

According to Grimal (1983, p. 7), 'the apogee of the Roman cities [occurred] in the first and second centuries of our era'. The leading cities listed in Table 5.11 reflect the subsequent outcome as a network with relatively high hierarchical tendencies featuring Rome at the apex easily topping over one million according to Modelski (2003, p. 49). One-and-a-half times larger than the Republican network, the Imperial network also had a larger geographical spread. Although still biased towards the eastern Mediterranean, there are now large cities to the west, two extra in Italy (Capua and Milan), one in Spain (Emerita), and one in Gaul (Trier). However this imperial urban development to the west was soon made problematic by the movement of the capital from Rome to Constantinople in 330.

The *Moslem world city network straddling AD 900 to 1000* is the most impressive world city network to have been developed outside East Asia before modern industrialization. In Table 5.12 there are 16 cities listed with a geographical spread from Iberia to central Asia. And at the centre there is Baghdad, capital of the Caliphate, the largest city in the world at its peak.

The rise of Islam produced what Hourani (1991, p. 110) calls 'a chain of

Table 5.11   The second Mediterranean world city network, AD 200–300

Leading cities	Population estimates (in 000s)
Rome	1200
Alexandria	600
Antioch	400
Carthage	300
Capua	240
Ephesus	200
Pergamum	170
Apamea	120
Caesarea	110
Smyrna	100
Caesarea Mazaca	100
Trier	100
Milan	100
Emerita	100
Nicomedia	100

Source: Modelski (2003: 49) supplemented by Chandler (1987: 464).

Table 5.12   The Moslem world city network, AD 900–1000

Leading cities	Population estimates (in 000s)
Baghdad	1200
Cordova	450
Fustat/Cairo	200
Samarkand	200
Alexandria	175
Nishapur	130
Basrah	100
Samarra	100
Kairouan	100
Bokhara	100
Mopsuetia	100
Al Ahsa	100
Seville	100
Isfahan	100
Tinnis	100
Ravy	100

Source: Modelski (2003: 55) supplemented by Chandler (1987: 468–9).

Table 5.13   The European world city network, AD 1500–1600

Leading cities	Population estimates (in 000s)
Paris	245
Naples	224
London	187
Venice	151
Seville	126
Prague	110
Milan	107
Potosí	105
Palermo	105
Rome	102
Lisbon	100
Ghent	80
Madrid	80

Source: Chandler (1987: 19–20, 42).

great cities running from one end of the world of Islam to the other' thereby 'linking the world of the Indian Ocean with that of the Mediterranean'. Here is his description of the network processes that ensued:

> The canons of correct behaviour and thought . . . linked cities with each other. A network of routes ran through the world of Islam and beyond it. Along them moved not only caravans of camels or donkeys carrying silks, spices, glass and precious metals, but ideas, news, fashions, patterns of thought and behaviour . . . Merchants from one city settled in others and kept a close and permanent link between them.

In other words this was a classic case of a vast world city network inter-locked by teachers and merchants.

The *European world city network straddling AD 1500 to 1600* describes the initial inter-city relations within the modern world-system before the consolidation of the system through Dutch hegemony in the early seventeenth century (Wallerstein 1984). Table 5.13 shows that it appears to have very little coordinating structure – ranging from a major capital city (Paris) to a key trading city (Venice), an American silver production centre (Potosí) and a precocious manufacturing city (Ghent) – and did not survive into the seventeenth century. Clearly this is a very poor relation to its East Asian contemporary network. Nevertheless it does show that this region did contain the economic potential to create a major world city network, no mean feat and therefore portends what was to come. This certainly warrants further investigation.

FOREGROUNDING EUROPEAN HISTORICAL CHANGE

As has been clearly established, China was the most successful world region of Normal History. Thus it might seem natural to focus on China in any further detailed consideration of Normal History process. But I conclude this chapter by foregrounding Europe, a region with a much less salubrious Normal History. However, the criterion for selection is simply hindsight: we move on to Europe because this is where modernity was born. Focusing on this region is sometimes seen as privileging Europe and Europeans over other peoples in world history. But the choice here is not a case of unreflexive, casual Eurocentrism, it is about historical process, or to be more specific, change of process. Wallerstein (1993, p. 295) has best stated the case that justifies this position: 'Far from being Eurocentric, my analysis "exoticizes" Europe. Europe is historically aberrant.' In my terminology, Europe is the region that escaped from the processes of Normal History to create a new matrix of social processes we call modernity. Relatively speaking, our history, modern history, is hugely abnormal: it represents another great creative interval. Thus understanding the particular Normal History that precedes the modern world-system is specifically pertinent for my purposes.

European historical narrative usually begins where the Roman Empire (in the West) ends: the starting point, in the title of Wickham's (2009) seminal text, is to understand *The Inheritance of Rome*. One of the greatest world-empires of Normal History, the significance of its being named after a city is not always appreciated. The name derives from the empire's origin in the city of Rome of course, but cities were also central to expansion and subsequent administration. For Wickham there was:

> [a] lasting Roman commitment to city life. The whole world of culture was bound up in city-ness, *civilitas* in Latin, from which come our words 'civilized' and 'civilization', and which precisely implied city dwelling to the Romans. The empire was in one sense a union of all its cities (some thousand in number), each of which had its own city council . . . that was traditionally autonomous. (p. 24)

Thus, he argues that '(i)t is possible to see the network of cities as the major element of Roman society, more important even than the central government.' (p. 26). But there was always an uneven geography to this 'city-ness', as previously noted. According to Grimal (1983, p. 109) there were two distinctive processes: 'making treaties with "allied cities"', and 'founding colonies and *municipia*'. This was the basis of an East–West contrast in which existing cities were incorporated into the state in the

Table 5.14   Major cities of the late Roman Empire, AD 361

City	Population (000s)
Constantinople	300
Rome	150
Antioch	150
Alexandria	125
Edessa	75
Carthage	66
Trier	60
Athens	50–60
Nisibis	50–60
Caesarea	50–60
Jerusalem	50
Leptis	50
Syracuse	45–50
Smyrna	45–50
Vienna	45
Thessalonica	42
Damascus	40
Milan	40
Arles	40
Hippo	40

Source: Abstracted from Chandler (1987: 464).

East, whereas cities had to be 'planted' in the West (beyond Italy) literally to 'civilize' (i.e. 'Romanize') conquered territories (p. 4).

This uneven geography of cities was discussed within the imperial Roman world city network (Table 5.11) and is further reflected in Table 5.14 showing the population estimates for Roman cities just before the state's demise in the west. The source (Chandler 1987) lists only cities with populations of at least 40 000 resulting in just 20 cities despite this lower population threshold.

However, only three of these cities are west of Italy – Trier in northern Gaul, and Vienne and Arles in southern Gaul. Trier is identified as the largest of the three and this reflects its new found political status in 361; from 324 the state had two capitals, and Trier replaced Rome as the capital of the western empire before the administration moved finally to Ravenna in 402 (Wickham 2009, p. 23). Not surprisingly this geography of cities was reflected in economic contrasts with northern Gaul, in particular, being different. Wickham refers to 'large-scale distribution networks' and complex economies based on 'a dense network of inter-city and city-country exchange' to be found around the Mediterranean littoral. He bases this interpretation in part on the distribution of distinctive tableware pottery and continues:

> In northern Gaul and Britain and in inland Spain [this pottery] was not available in more than tiny quantities, but large-scale local production is found instead; for this reason above all we can say that those areas, although active, were separate from the main Mediterranean economic network. (p. 40)

The main stimulus for economic activity in northern Gaul was based on supplying commodities for the army defending the German frontier. This relative separation of the region of the northern Gaul economy from the Mediterranean core of the Roman world-economy continues after the fall of the empire in the west and is central to what has come to be known as the Pirenne thesis.

Reviewing and Renewing the Pirenne Thesis

Henri Pirenne was a rare historian of the first half of the twentieth century who put cities and trade to the fore in understanding European history. His ideas contributed crucially to the work of both Jacobs (1969, pp. 131–2) and Braudel (1984, pp. 92–3); for our purposes here his key text is *Medieval Cities: Their Origins and the Revival of Trade* (Pirenne 1969), first published in 1925. Pirenne's historical narrative broadly adheres to the penultimate three phases of Gills and Frank's expansions and contractions in Table 5.1. He argues that the deposing of the last Roman Emperor in the West in 476 was not decisive (Pirenne 1969, p. 10), the Mediterranean 'commonwealth of civilization' survived under new Germanic guardianship so that there was 'a clear-cut, direct continuation of the economy of the Roman Empire' (p. 12). His key point was that 'the world-order which survived the Germanic invasions was not able to survive the invasion of Islam' (p. 23). The Islamic invasion from the south and into Spain cut the Franks off from the Mediterranean links to the East (p. 26). Hence Charlemagne and his Carolingian state – by 800 it had become the largest empire in Europe between Rome and Napoleon – represents regression, not revival (p. 40): it was 'a closed state; a state without foreign markets, living in a condition of almost complete isolation' (p. 29). He argued that the Carolingian Franks had only small towns and no cities: Aachen, Charlemagne's 'capital' was ridiculed for its small size, perhaps 3000 (Barraclough 1989), and dismissed as merely the Emperor's favourite residence, which became a 'real city only four centuries later' (Pirenne 1969, p. 62). It was only in the tenth century that there was 'real commercial revival': 'just as the trade of the west disappeared with the shutting off of its foreign markets, just so it was renewed when these markets were reopened' (p. 82).

This, in a nutshell, is the 'Pirenne thesis' that, according to McCormick (2001, p. 2), has dominated scholarly interpretation of early medieval Europe for nearly a century. The debates were brought together in a single text, *The Pirenne Thesis: Analysis, Criticism, and Revision*, in 1958 and expanded in 1976 (Havighurst 1976). For McCormick (2001, p. 2), 'Carolingian commerce ranks among the most controversial issues in medieval history' and he thinks that, allowing for important changes reflecting more recent research, Pirenne's thesis still 'predominates today'. Such longevity is impressive, albeit conditional.

This is a fascinating debate about Normal History episodes in a small regional context. I will attempt to contribute in two specific ways. First, I consider the latest text on the subject and interpret its findings within the theoretical framework of this book. Second and more specifically, I consider the nature of the space that was being constructed as a means of renewing the Pirenne thesis.

My source for the latest historical take on Pirenne's subject matter is Wickham (2009). He argues that his account represents 'a break from Pirenne-based scholarship' for two reasons (p. 223). First, since Pirenne there is much new evidence, notably archaeological, which requires important changes. The most fundamental relates to the role of the Islamic invasion: 'well before the Arabs arrived, the western part of the (Mediterranean) sea already had dramatically less shipping' (p. 224). This breaks the demise of Europe/rise of Islam link necessitating important revision – the conditional referred to just above. Second, he criticizes Pirenne for his focus on luxuries and long-distance trade, which he argues were marginal to economic complexity. I will deal with this as the new narrative unfolds.

For Wickham (2009), the expansion phase after 500 (see Table 5.1) is emphatically recognized but the expansion this represents does not extend to the post-Roman West:

> One thing archaeology makes clear . . . is the dramatic economic simplification of most of the West: this is visible north of the Loire in the early fifth century, and in the northern Mediterranean lands during the sixth. (p. 95)

Thus 'there is a steady simplification of economic structure in most of the West by 550 or so', reflected in reduced trade and towns (p. 104), which contrasts with the East where both empire and economic complexity survived: 'This correlation is exact: economic complexity depended on

Table 5.15   Cities of Western Christendom, AD 800

City	Population (000s)
Rome	50
Naples	30
Verona	30
Metz	25
Paris	25
Milan	25
Pavia	22
Tours	20
Reims	20
Benevento	15–30
Cologne	15
Trier	15

imperial unity, in both the eastern and western empire' (p. 105). For the latter, the result was that from 550 to 750 'exchange became much more localized' (p. 218), with predictable effects:

> Marseille, the traditional entrepôt at the mouth of the Rhone for all traffic going from the Mediterranean north into what was by now the Frankish heartland, went into an eclipse at the beginning of the eighth century, and not even the luxury trade had much effect on it after that for some time. Localized production systems do not need such entrepôts, and it is this localization, even if at a decent quality of product, which marks the seventh, and even more, the eighth century in the western Mediterranean as a whole. (p. 220)

This timing is wholly counter to Pirenne, of course, but so too is the resulting spatial economic process. Wickham further argues that 'the largest-scale economy in the early medieval West was the Frankish heartland' between the Loire and the Rhine (previously northern Gaul) (p. 220). In an embellishment of this claim he makes an interesting comparison to Italy; his evidence showed that:

> northern Francia had a much more complex and active exchange system than anywhere else in the West before 800, [and] that the Mediterranean lands were more fragmented, with pockets of greater complexity and greater simplicity. (pp. 221–2)

This pattern is perhaps confirmed for city population estimates at this time (Table 5.15). With a lower threshold of 15000, Chandler (1987) identifies 12 cities that qualify, evenly divided between Italy and 'northern Francia'.

The largest cities tend to be in Italy (pockets of greater complexity?) but the northern cities may have had more coherent economic linkages within Frankland. Mainz, Dorestad, Cologne and Paris are identified by Wickham as 'major artisanal and mercantile centres' (p. 546) with 'trade routes . . . linking the great river basins' (p. 546). This gets to the crux of interpreting the Carolingian commercial economy.

A key point that Wickham (2009, p. 226) makes with respect to the Pirenne thesis is that 'exchange . . . was overwhelmingly focused on buying and selling inside regions'. Outside links are described as being to peripheral neighbours rather than to the rich world of the Caliphate to the south and east.

> In the seventh century, at least two Frankish channel ports appeared, Quentovic south of Boulogne and Dorestad in the Rhine delta. Both, particularly Dorestad . . . expanded considerably in the eighth century, and they began in the decades around 700 to have equivalents on the other side of the channel, at Hamwic (now Southampton) in Wessex. London in Mercia, Ipswich in East Anglia, York in Norhumbria – as well as Ribe in Denmark and Birka in Sweden. These *emporia*, as archaeologists call them . . . were interconnected, and buying and selling across the English Channel and North Sea developed consistently in the eighth century and early ninth, when other such ports came onstream as well, such as Domburg in the Rhine delta and Hedeby of the Baltic coast of Denmark . . . The North Sea in the eighth century almost certainly had more shipping than the Mediterranean . . . there were no equivalents to the nodal ports of the North in the Mediterranean between the decline of Marseille around 700 and the rise of Venice after around 780. (pp. 229–30)

But what does this all mean? Clearly, the Carolingian economy was not as static as Pirenne sometimes implies, but is it dynamic enough to refute the conclusion of Pirenne's thesis that Western Europe's economic revival did not occur until the tenth century? Here opinions continue to diverge. Wickham concludes that 'there was thus some exchange vitality in Western Europe at the end of our period, but not exchange take-off' (p. 550). This is because the motor of exchange in the Carolingian economy was not city growth but still aristocratic wealth based upon value extraction from the peasantry. In contrast McCormack's (2001, p. 791) primary conclusion is that:

> The rise of the European commercial economy, indeed the rise of the European economy, period, did not begin in the tenth or eleventh centuries. It began, decisively, in the concluding decades of the eighth century.

Clearly, the evidence he marshals to support this confident assertion needs to be evaluated and interpreted carefully.

McCormack's (2001, p. 3) argues that 'the volume of scholarly discussion' on the Pirenne thesis 'far outweighs the evidence to which it is devoted'. He sets about confronting this evidential challenge with a prosopographical research exercise that puts together what evidence is available in one large data collection exercise in order to create a geography of communications for this period. Although there is little information on commerce there is a lot of evidence for the movements of travellers, information and various artefacts. He creates data sets based upon nearly 700 journeys between 700 and 900, over 400 letters and over 800 movements culled from documentary sources from 600 to 970, plus other evidence such as coin hoards. The result is an immense amount of information and his book, *Origins of the European Economy: Communication and Commerce AD 300–900*, describes an historical space of flows not equalled for any other Normal History period or region to my knowledge.

McCormack (2001, p. 573) accuses Pirenne of imagining the Carolingian economy in terms of a nineteenth-century modern economy with professional merchants operating foreign trade through cities. He disagrees with the statement that 'trade cannot be important in a world without cities' (p. 575) because 'the fact that an economy was primarily agrarian ... does not negate the importance of commerce' (p. 578). This is where the confusion lies. Obviously there has been commerce without cities – I have argued that cities derive from trade. What is important is the nature of the commerce and its role in the wider economy. McCormack describes a 'world of trading' consisting of two main elements. First, there is 'a growth of small rural markets' (p. 661), which Pirenne (1969, pp. 65–6) does not dispute; he also describes weekly markets in towns that are not cities. Second, there is additional demand generated by the Carolingian state itself: 'general assemblies should have functioned ... as great, fair-like markets catering to the rich and offering an additional if sporadic stimulus to the commercial structures developing in the regions where they occurred' (McCormack 2001, p. 666). He also mentions Jewish merchants maintaining 'permanent residences at Aachen' (p. 667) but, again and as noted earlier, Pirenne (1969) dealt with this by emphasizing the smallness of Aachen. What McCormack (2001, p. 676, Map 23.1) presents is a space of flows in which networks are clearly discernible in the West and across the Mediterranean, but proactive nodes (i.e. cities) are conspicuous by their absence in his discussion. However, the commercial networks he finds are important for interpreting the nature of this post-Roman world, because they link to the Caliphate, the richest state in the world at this time.

In countering Pirenne's notion of Carolingian economic isolation, McCormack asks the rhetorical question:

> The Carolingian empire was surrounded by a series of distinct trading worlds
> which were now beginning to intersect and interweave. Are we to believe that it
> alone went unwashed by the currents of trade? (p. 613)

Interestingly McCormack's results differ from the trading picture
described above drawn from Wickham (2009). Archaeological evidence
might point to links across the North Sea but McCormack's (2001, p. 676)
textual evidence on communications most definitely privileges the Moslem
south from Cordova to Baghdad. And what did the Europeans trade?
From the little evidence there is, McCormack identifies four commodities:
lumber, furs, swords and slaves (p. 730). Note that, with the exception of
swords, these are not manufactured goods, there is very little 'value-added'
by the Europeans. Furthermore by far the main trade from Europe was
Europeans: it is sales of slaves that linked Europe to other trading worlds.

McCormack (2001, p. 738) observes that 'the slave trade seems strangely
disconnected from slave labor inside the Frankish empire.' The nature of
this new business is revealed by the change in language; those in bondage
are for the first time called 'slaves', derived from Slav. An enhanced
market in human labour was initially created through the matching of
two events. First there was the expansion of the Caliphate, and a rise in
demand due to the catastrophic bubonic plagues of 745 to 752 (p. 753).
Second, the was a coincidental rise in supply: 'the last five decades of the
eighth century were also the era when the Carolingian conquests could
well have flooded the market through the capture of large numbers of war
slaves' (p. 776). As McCormack tells it: 'the demand was great, the money
good, and the doing easy'. And who were these 'doers'? Venice, it seems,
was crucial.

In what McCormack (2001, Chapter 18) refers to as 'Venetian breakthrough', there is a rise in Adriatic trade around 750 with Venice the indisputable 'dynamic center of gravity' (p. 526). And the centrality derives
from the slave market: the first record of Venice selling slaves to the
Moslem world is in 748:

> The Venetians ... seized a very specific opportunity, created by a spike in
> demand for labor that arose out of heavy mortality in the Caliphate. The con-
> figuration was new. That mortality had not much affected western Europe,
> which was then 'unplugged' from the Mediterranean shipping world that con-
> veyed the contagion. (pp. 753–4)

This new configuration of 'the export of Europeans to the richer countries of the south' (p. 775) continued and expanded into the ninth century
(p. 775). And 'agreements governing relations between Venice and the
Carolingian empire confirm the importance of the slave trade' (p. 763); the

earliest treaty in 840 (based upon earlier pacts) 'makes perfectly clear that Venice was a major center for the slave trade' (p. 764). And McCormack interprets this as the birth of 'the European commercial economy in the Mediterranean' (p. 776).

How to interpret this particular Normal History? The key question is what type of European economy has McCormack described? He is keen to be modest about the size of the economic processes he has uncovered: 'In the flush of new findings, it is essential not to exaggerate the scale of these commercial beginnings' (p. 794), because 'the power and production of these new economic networks were only nascent' (p. 793). But scale is not the important point, what matters is the nature of the economy. Two features stand out: the simplicity of the rural-based economy with its lack of major cities in the Carolingian political heartland, and the simplicity of the external trading with Venice's centrality in slave trading not constituting a complex city function. What we have is a semi-frontier state, the Carolingian Empire, economically focused on internal commerce but with its 'disconnected' external slave trade premised upon political expansion into Slavic marginal areas, enabling it to buy luxury goods – 'eastern silks, new Arab drugs, and old eastern spices' (p. 776) – in a wider world-economy. But the motors of this world-economy are to be found in the Caliphate; it is the great Moslem cities that are creating new demands leading to economic expansion upon which Frankish involvement is dependent. In contrast to the populations in Table 5.6, Chandler's population estimates for other cities in this world-economy in 800 are of a completely different order: as noted previously Baghdad stands out with 700 000, but Cordova with 140 000, Fostat (Cairo) with 100 000 and Alexandria with 95 000 are great metropolises. It is demand for labour in the Moslem city network that is the main force linking Europe to this world-economy. In world-systems terms Western Europe, along with other labour suppliers – sub-Saharan Africa and Turkish central Asia – are impoverished 'dependent frontiers' of the Caliphate economic centre.

How does Venice fit into this pattern? It might be thought that the city represents a critical new dynamic locale in the European economy but this would be incorrect. An entrepôt focused upon slaving does not constitute a creative city. Certainly the very high profit margins of this trade (McCormick 2001, p. 758) would have generated a lot of capital, but for this to be locally productive required local investment opportunities. These were not available because Venice's economy remained essentially simple. Therefore it is also part of the margins of the Caliphate's world-economy. In hindsight we know that an important Venetian economy was to emerge in the tenth century but whether 'dependent frontier' gateway represents a 'nascent' step in this direction is a moot point. McCormack claims that 'it is now undeniable that, right from the outset, Venice followed a different course, and that this course marked an important new departure for the future' (p. 547) but this is best interpreted politically. Although located in northern Italy, Venice was part of the Byzantium Empire and therefore when Charlemagne conquered Lombardy, Venice was vulnerable to incorporation into the Carolingian Empire. This was a real possibility (Norwich 1982, pp. 15–26), but in 806–807:

> the main imperial war fleet (of Byzantium) . . . came to fight the Franks over control of Venice .. In equally eloquent testimony to the Veneto's new found value, the Byzantine government accepted the unthinkable and recognized the Frankish king's imperial title in exchange for uncontested sovereignty over Venice. (p. 527)

The latter was agreed in 811. Norwich (1982, p. 24) properly identifies the winner of this agreement between two empires:

> The Franks obtained recognition of their imperial status while, for the Byzantines, Charlemagne's renunciation of all his claims over the province of Venetia meant . . . the continuation of their own suzerainty . . . The gain on each side, however, involved a corresponding concession by the other; only for Venice herself were the benefits unmitigated. Henceforth she was to enjoy all the advantages . . . of being a Byzantine province, without any real diminution of her independence.

This mix of local (commercial) autonomy and distant guardian lordship can be a recipe for city success; it certainly was for a medieval Venice politically separate from Italy and the rest of Western Europe.

And finally, whither the Pirenne thesis? Our main sources, McCormack (2001) and Wickham (2009), have sometimes diverged in their narratives, which is to be expected for a period and region with a dearth of definitive evidence, but they are in agreement that Pirenne's initial historical narrative has been undermined. Islam remains important but not for isolating the Carolingian Empire and the West but for marginalizing it. Not unlike the African Atlantic coast zone in the early modern world-system, Europe responded to a demand for slave labour in a more intensive production zone, the Islamic world-economy, to become a marginal appendage of the Islamic world-system. Isolation and marginalization are very different processes but the outcome in how we understand Europe in the Mediterranean world-economy is not so different. Pirenne's key point, and contra McCormack (2001), is that the 'revival' of Europe as an expanding economy did not arise until the tenth century. Ultimately, McCormack's evidence does not refute this. To be sure there were economic processes operating in Europe before the tenth century, even 'a dramatic surge between about 775 and 825' (p. 788), but this was not a creative dynamic growth, in Pirenne's (1969, p. 82) sense of 'real commercial revival'. In other words McCormack's European economy generated no complex city economies upon which to build a growing economy. Instead, in the eighth and ninth centuries its leading trading settlement, Venice, was aiding in building a distant world-economy core through supplying it with the necessary labour for the growing the Caliphate economy. A self-propelling European economy would only appear when a more complex Venice city-region would diffuse economic growth in Europe in the tenth century *à la* Pirenne.

Cities in the European Late Medieval Cycle

In Table 5.1 the final two phases indicate the arrival of Western Europe as a region in Eurasian trade and commerce. In the expansion from 1000/1050, the rise of Western Europe is part of the larger Eurasian expansion to 1250/1300. In the B-phase Western Europe is affected by the 'great Mongol disruption' indicating stagnation lasting until 1450. In this section I look at this European late medieval cycle in some detail as the precursor of the modern world-system. Given that the latter is interpreted as a city-led creative interlude, the focus again will be a comparative city analysis in time and space.

In terms of time, it should be mentioned that the literature on this cycle differs slightly from the timing in Table 5.1. In his summary of the situation for Europe, Braudel (1984, p. 77) delineates a rather later cycle starting in 1250, peaking in 1350 and ending in 1510. He is keen to emphasize that these dates are 'somewhat approximate' and 'uncertain' and also suggests 1200 rather than 1250 for the start of the cycle (p. 78). This is more in line with recent scholarship that identifies the medieval 'commercial revolution' generally with the thirteenth century (Spufford 2002, p. 16). But such a revolution will not appear out of nothing: Pirenne (1969, p. 82) identifies 'a real commercial revival' from the eleventh century and Braudel (1984: 92) agrees with this. This brings Europe back in line with the timing of Table 5.1. I will explore the thesis that the origins of Western Europe should be sought at this earlier time.

In this 'long gestation process', Braudel (1984, p. 92) argues that 'the cities naturally played a leading part'. In terms of space, Pirenne (1969, p. 82), locates the early commercial revival in 'two centers of activity, one located in the south and the other in the north: Venice on the one side and the Flemish coast on the other'. Braudel (1984, p. 97) follows Pirenne and emphasizes the new commercial geography:

For the true beginning of the new Europe, we have to look at the growth of
these two complexes, the North and the South, the Low Countries and Italy,
the North Sea-Baltic and the Mediterranean. There was not one pole of attraction in the West but two, and this bipolarity, pulling the continent in two direc-
tions, would last in some form for several centuries. This was to be one of the
major features of European history – possibly the most important of all.

But these two poles should not be seen as strictly equivalent: the northern Italian cities were consistently more important throughout the long
cycle: Spufford (2002, p. 380) estimates that northern Italian trade in the
Mediterranean to be about ten times greater in value than that taking
place in the Baltic.

Initially the two poles were relatively independent of each other but
in the thirteenth century they were connected by the Champagne fairs
to the southeast of Paris. On the overland route between the two poles,
these were six continuous fairs of two months each starting the year in
Lagny-sur-Marne, then on to Bar-sur-Aybe, before alternating between
Provins and Troyes. At each fair the first month was given over to commodity trading, the second to settling accounts. The latter was dominated
by Italian financial houses, indicating the commercial superiority of
the southern pole: as Braudel (1984, p. 112) tells it, 'Italian credit would
be able . . . to exploit to its own advantage the huge market of western
Europe'. Each of these small urban places was temporarily the economic
centre of Europe, an incipient city-ness that never transpired. They represent the rise of a European-wide market but with the coming of the economic slowdown the fairs did not survive. Contributory factors were the
incorporation of Champagne into the expanding French state in the late
thirteenth century and ships from Genoa bypassing the fairs in 1277 by
sailing through the Straits of Gibraltar to Bruges. Note again the decisive
action is Italian; Genoa seeks out Bruges not vice versa. Braudel (1984,
p. 99) calls it 'a decisive invasion by the southerners'. This direct linking of
the two poles is a symbolic change in European commerce from an extensive market centred on fairs to a Europe-wide network of cities. And it is
the latter that is the precursor to a modern Europe in a process described
in more detail in the next chapter, where the economic power gradually
transfers to the northern pole.

In Table 5.16 I have used Chandler's (1987) population estimates for
European cities through the late medieval cycle at century intervals from
1000. For comparative purposes I have supplemented the estimates by
world ranking in terms of size. Because Chandler's worldwide data only
treats cities with populations of 40 000 and above, this is the threshold I
have had to use here. How is the story told above reflected in these statistics? Does the data suggest any need for revisions?

Table 5.16   The rise of city-rich medieval Europe, AD 1000–1500

City	Population (000s)	World rank	Interpretation of cities as new entrants
1000			
Venice	45	51	The starting point for a new 'Europe of cities'
1100			
Venice	55	38	
Milan	42	58	Expansion to start Braudel's 'southern pole'
1200			
Paris	110	13	First major 'political city'
Venice	70	28	
Milan	60	35	
Cologne	50	42	Start of 'northern pole'
Leon	40	68	First Spanish political centre
London	40	68	Anglo-Norman political centre
Rouen	40	68	Anglo-Norman political centre
1300			
Paris	228	4	
Venice	110	10	
Seville	90	18	Former Islamic Spain
Genoa	85	23	Rise of Venice's great rival
Florence	60	33	Expansion of 'southern pole'
Milan	60	33	
Cologne	54	39	
Bruges	50	40	Expansion of 'northern pole'
Rouen	50	40	
London	45	57	
Ghent	42	58	Expansion of 'northern pole'
Bologne	40	59	Expansion of 'southern pole'
Caffa	40	59	Expansion of 'southern pole'
Cordova	40	59	Former Islamic Spain
Naples	40	59	Political centre of South Italy
Prague	40	59	Imperial political centre
1400			
Paris	280	4	
Venice	110	14	
Prague	95	16	
Milan	80	24	
Rouen	80	24	
Caffa	75	27	Expansion of 'southern pole'
Ghent	70	33	

Table 5.16   (continued)

City	Population (000s)	World rank	Interpretation of cities as new entrants
1400			
Genoa	66	38	
Florence	61	40	
Bruges	60	41	
Seville	60	41	
Lisbon	55	51	
London	50	53	
Troki	50	53	Expansion to Baltic region
Valencia	45	73	Former Islamic Spain
Bologna	43	77	
Cologne	40	78	
Naples	40	78	
1500			
Paris	185	8	
Venice	115	18	
Naples	114	19	
Milan	89	21	
Ghent	80	24	
Florence	70	29	
Granada	70	29	Former Islamic Spain
Prague	70	29	
Genoa	62	37	
Bruges	60	39	
Bologna	55	52	
Lisbon	55	52	
London	50	55	
Rouen	50	55	
Smolensk	50	55	Expansion to Baltic region
Seville	46	72	
Brescia	40	79	Expansion of 'southern pole'
Cremona	40	79	Expansion of 'southern pole'
Lyons	40	79	Rise of French trading centre
Valencia	40	79	
Valladolid	40	79	Old Castile political centre
Vienna	40	79	Rival imperial centre

Note: Populations and rankings include all European cities with populations estimated at 40 000 and above. The choice of this threshold is forced upon me by the data but nevertheless seems to be a reasonable size to define major cities at these times. European cities are from 'western Christendom', i.e. omitting Islamic Iberia and orthodox Eastern Europe.

Source: Populations and rankings are derived from Chandler (1987).

In the year 1000 only one Western European city reaches Chandler's threshold: Venice. Although only ranked a lowly fifty-first in the world, this is, in fact, the commercial breakthrough. For Pirenne (1969, p. 83) Venice's 'influence was felt from the very start', giving her a 'singular place in the economic history of Europe'. Following Pirenne, Jacobs (1969, pp. 173–4) interprets the change as follows:

> ... in the tenth and eleventh centuries Venice had become an explosively growing city with an expanding market for raw materials from the west and north of Europe. It was this market that made possible the relatively swift economic growth of Europe that followed. ... behind all this (trade) lay an import-shifting, explosively expanding market of Venice.

By 1000 the Caliphate was in decline (Baghdad's population fell from 900 000 in 900 to only 125 000 in 1000) but Constantinople remained a constant large market of 300 000 people, plus the ostentatious capital functions of its empire. And it was other northern Italian cities that first benefitted from Venice's new economic expansion as reflected in the appearance of Milan in Table 5.16 in 1100. By 1200 there are seven cities listed including two new features. First, the northern pole comes into view with the arrival of Cologne (before Flemish cities). Second, there is the rise of political cities, notably Paris, capital of a centralizing French state, the first European city to rise to over 100 000, and ranked a very high thirteenth in the world. The other new cities are also political centres. But note for these first three century years, it is the economic spark that comes first, and then, in other parts of the world region, there is enough wealth generated to support some initial state centralization. This is the familiar city first thesis, in this case stimulating the economy to enable state formation.

It is only in 1300 that leading Flemish cities – Bruges and Ghent – appear in Table 5.16. They are part of an explosion of European cities in the thirteenth century – Spufford's (2002) 'commercial revolution' – with 16 making the threshold and two, Paris and Venice, actually to be found in the world top ten. In her classic cross-sectional analysis of world trade between cities at this time entitled *Before European Hegemony*, Janet Abu-Lughod (1989, p. 13) considers Europe to be 'still very much part of the periphery'. Perhaps this needs to be rethought: since Chandler lists only 75 cities worldwide at this date, Europe's 16 entries constitute 21 per cent of the world's top cities. This is hardly what is expected for a peripheral region; rather, at the beginning of a European network of cities, this is reasonably balanced between important consumption places (guardian-dominated cities) and production places (commercial cities), epitomized respectively by Paris and Venice.

The final pair of century lists should reflect the fact of the downside of the medieval economic cycle, but this does not appear to be the case. In 1400 the number of cities increases to 18 and it rises to 22 in 1500. Overall the pattern remains fairly stable, Paris and Venice remain the top two and are still relatively important in worldwide comparison. In these more troubled times it might be expected that political centres would tend to prosper, but economic centres are by no means quiescent. Ghent, in particular, rises as a great Flemish textile production centre reaching a population of 80 000 in 1500. Thus European cities, at least as represented by Chandler's population estimates, present something of a conundrum here: they were not doing as badly as we might have thought for an economic downturn. Since this is occurring just as the transition to the modern world-system was being set in train, the potentially far-reaching finding is further investigated in the next chapter.

CONCLUSION: MEDIEVAL EUROPE WITH AND WITHOUT HINDSIGHT

Fernand Braudel (1972a) has argued that the historian has one crucial advantage over the social scientist: hindsight. By this he means that in studying the past we know what comes next and therefore can see what features of a past society had an effect on the future. But hindsight also sets challenges for my narratives at this time: knowing what comes next creates serious teleological dangers. People in the past were not striving to make our world: they were making their own worlds, therefore there was nothing inevitable about the rise of a modern world-system in Europe. We should not impose our present on interpreting their past, but neither should we ignore the benefit of hindsight. One benefit of the TimeSpace toolkit is that it lessens the tendency to misuse hindsight.

Although Table 5.16 has given some food for thought with European cities seemingly holding up well in the late medieval downturn, we would still not choose Europe as the site of the next great creative interlude without the benefit of hindsight. This is because this world region's Normal History did not mark it out as a very successful region in comparison to Normal Histories in other regions. Certainly the region seemed to be 'catching up', but it still had some way to go. In 1450, the date usually used for when the modern world-system was beginning to stir, the Muslim Spanish city Granada was still the largest city in the area of today's Europe. China had four cities larger than Paris, the largest city in western Christendom, which ranked only ninth in the world. The leading Chinese city (Peking) was four times bigger than Paris, the largest Indian city three times bigger (Vijayanagar) and the largest Muslim city (Cairo) more than twice as big. In Chapter 2, city size was particularly related to innovation potential so why not a new creative interval in one of these latter regions? The answer is to be found in the nature of Normal History, in the relative dominance of guardians.

In Normal History, the great cities are imperial capitals; they are vital elements in the guardian reproduction of world-empires. Therefore we cannot expect these cities to be party to the despatching of Normal History to history. Simple hindsight has often led to an assumption that the new system should be created out of the old – we search for evidence of success in Normal History (usually China) for signs of the modern world-system. But the latter is not a *growth* out of Normal History; it is a *subverting* of Normal History. Pomeranz and Topik (1999, p. 51) provide a clear sense of this process:

> To make big ships and long voyages worth the investment required ulterior motives, or the desire to monopolize the seas and bypass the competitive markets in all these ports. The Chinese left such ambitious projects to the Europeans, who proved willing to defy market principles, thereby launching a new era and pattern for world trade.

It is all about macro-social change to a capitalist world-economy, which is 'world-making': in Chapter 2 this is identified as inter-systemic change, as opposed to intra-systemic change. The requirement, therefore, is conditions enabling structural change, not success in reproducing current world-empires. There is no reason to think that structural change should emanate from success in Normal History, where cities are constrained in their innovative potential. Rather there will be particular circumstances that enable structural change and this is what we need to search out. The modern world-system developed as a new creative interval in Europe because of the latter's 'Abnormal History'.

6. Making the modern world-system: Western Europe's great creative interlude

INTRODUCTION: ABNORMALITY, CONTINGENCY AND DUALITY

In a thorough review and evaluation of how scholars from different traditions have identified the distinctiveness of capitalist or modern societies, Wallerstein (1992, pp. 566–80) finds among myriad conflicting ideas that:

> The one thing that seems unquestionable, and unquestioned, is the hyperbolic growth curves – in production, population, and the accumulation of capital – that have been a continuing reality from the sixteenth century. (p. 580)

This is an excellent starting point for considering the modern world-system from the perspective of this book because I argue that such growth can *only* be generated by dynamic networks of vibrant cities. Thus I would add the urbanization hyperbolic growth curve to Wallerstein's three curves as the one that links the process together.

In this chapter I deal with two substantive issues. First, Europe is considered as the world region where modernity was created; where Normal History was superseded. What does a focus on cities add to the myriad treatments of Europe as midwife of modernity? Or, as more commonly phrased, what was the role of cities in the transition from feudalism to capitalism? I hope to clarify some key mechanisms of transition through my commercial city/guardian state toolkits. Second, the focus is on modern hegemonic cycles within the modern world-system. Do cities have roles in cyclical generation that indicate anything new about these very well-researched phenomenon? I show that cities are crucial and that their analysis does suggest a revision to ideas about how these cycles are generated and therefore timed. Overall, this chapter is a revisionist statement on the modern world-system and its origins that treats cities as strategic places in social change. Contemporary globalization and the world city network is the culmination of this process, and is discussed in the next chapter.

As in previous chapters, my approach is strongly evidential; I collect empirical evidence and interpret it through my conceptual toolkit. In this introduction I set up the two substantive sections by rehearsing the key arguments behind the transition to the modern world-system, and what constitutes its *differentia specifica*.

Opportunity: Endogenous and Exogenous Guardian Weaknesses

The last chapter ended with Europe being recognized as having an Abnormal History. Normal Histories have varied in very many ways across the world but the important comparative feature is their relative degrees of centralization. Within a world region this will vary over time as world-empires weaken and successor states compete for new dominance producing consecutive periods of imperial peace and warring states. In the case of Western Europe the key feature was a millennium with no centralized imperial control after the fall of Rome. The revival in the second half of the millennium was commercial-led and resulted in state formation, but without generating a single central political entity. Right at the beginning of his world-systems analysis, Wallerstein (1974) saw this as an anomaly – he doubted whether feudal Europe with its parcellized sovereignty really qualified as a world-empire structure (p. 28). And in addition to this endemic guardian frailty, with the downturn of the medieval cycle, there was a catastrophe within this already weak geohistorical system – the crisis of feudalism. This contraction was directly reflected in wars between guardians within and between states as well as peasant revolts indicating further challenges to guardian rule. In addition, the power of the Roman Catholic Church, the institution that provided cultural continuity and ideological glue was losing its moral compass resulting in religious divisions and challenges. Part of the endemic weakness was because of the division between spiritual and secular power; the church claimed a universal sovereignty that was not so much challenged as simply laid aside in guardian conflict. Wallerstein (1992, p. 609) sums up these multiple crises as follows:

> Overall, the period, 1250–1450 was a disastrous period for the ruling classes of western Europe, collectively. Their incomes were squeezed. They were involved in an exceptionally high level of internecine struggle, which negatively affected their wealth, their authority and their lives. They were faced by popular revolt – peasant rebellions, heretical movements. Public disorder was high, as was public intellectual turmoil. What had been solid was melting away. There was a 'crisis' in the historical system.

Notice that this listing is all about guardians; there is no direct reference to the position of commerce although it did not avoid the contraction.

However in the last chapter we noted that European cities seemed not to fare as badly as cities from richer world regions in this turndown. How was this possible?

Of course, periods of warring states are relatively commonplace and if there is no winner to succeed to the imperial state, this normally 'allowed for the possibility of external conquest' (Wallerstein 1992, p. 610), producing a new set of rulers for Normal History to continue unchallenged. But this never happened to this most frail of geohistorical systems. Wallerstein calls it 'this crucial non-event' (p. 610) and relates it to the collapse of Mongol power in the aftermath of the Black Death producing political turmoil: this stopped the Silk Road trading pattern resulting in a severe diminution of Eurasian trading across all regions. Wallerstein tells it thus:

> It caused the various 'subregions' to pull into themselves. None had the strength at that moment to engage in imperial expansion. Western Europe was unthreatened in the critical period 1350–1450, when it would precisely have been most vulnerable because of the triple collapse (of nobility, states and church) it was undergoing. The local west European aristocracy/ruling strata would be neither replaced nor reinvigorated by an outside force.

This left a Normal History in limbo, an opportunity for commercial agents in cities to come into play and lead along a path to a unique disruption of Normal History.

It is still important not to see the outcome, the modern world-system, as in any sense inevitable. I'm not sure if Wallerstein's 'crucial non-event' qualifies as a contingency but in any case we can easily find a real one. The last potential challenge from central Asia came with Tamerlane at the beginning of the fifteenth century. His army defeated the Ottoman Empire in 1402 and reached the Aegean, the very edge of Europe. According to Marozzi (2004, pp. 338–9):

> Christendom now lay prostate before the Lame Conqueror. Its armies were no match for these rough men of the steppes, steeled by years of victory. If the emperor's famous crimson standard, the swinging horse-tail beneath a shining golden crescent, were to appear on the European mainland, the days of Christendom were surely over.

But this did not happen and Marozzi's explanation is intriguing:

> Her poverty was (Europe's) best defence against invasion. From the Aegean to the Atlantic, there was little to tempt Temur (Tamerlane) into launching another holy war. Killing or converting the infidels was a noble aim in itself, of course, but Temur regarded such considerations with a more mercantile eye. Europe's coffers and treasure houses were bare. No jewels, no *jihad*. (pp. 345–6)

Of course, his assessment was relative, Europe's coffers were not literally bare, but they were meagre compared to what Tamerlane was used to in his military procession through Asia, vanquishing cities. Instead Tamerlane turned east for a campaign to capture the biggest prize of all: China. He died before he could launch his invasion but in his decision-making, the choice between Europe and China was what we would today call a 'no-brainer'. Such are the contingencies of Normal History: Europe survived.

Dual Ambiguity: a Nexus of Guardian Work and Commercial Work

Europe did much more than just survive: in Western Europe a new creative interlude emerged as the production of a different type of world-system. Previously I have interpreted this change as an alteration in the relations between guardian and commercial practices in terms of a traditional *modus vivendi* being replaced in Western Europe by a *modus operandi*. In the latter, the two practices are joined together in the social nexus that is modernity. The result is a complex political economy *modus operandi* that has embedded an ambiguity within the meaning of modernity. Considering modernity from a guardian perspective, modern complexity is a problem, something the state needs to tame through planning; but considering modernity from a commercial perspective, this same complexity is an opportunity, something in cities from which to make money. For instance, social change in the modern world has been viewed in two totally different ways: state modernization models portrayed simple stages of ordered conversion from traditional to modern society (Lerner et al. 1968); in contrast Berman (1988, p. 15) famously described modernity as a celebration of complexity, 'a maelstrom of perpetual disintegration and renewal'. This contrast is the widely recognized 'dual ambiguity' (Taylor 1999a, p. 15) inherent in the concept of modernity.

The link to Jacobs' moral syndromes that I have made between what Lash and Friedman (1992, p. 2) call the two 'faces' of modernity is important because it invites us to focus on the relations between guardian and commercial modernities. The generality of the duality as expressions of Jacobs' moral syndromes is illustrated in Table 6.1. Six different authorities on modernity use different terminologies but the natures of the two faces are clear enough: they represent different meanings of modernity produced through guardian and commercial work. In their different ways the sources for Table 6.1 illustrate the new *modus operandi* as a tension between guardian and commercial work at the heart of the condition of modernity.

The paired opposites in Table 6.1 are witness to how Jacobs' moral

Table 6.1   Dual ambiguity: the two faces of modernity

Faces (meanings) derived from Guardian work	Faces (meanings) derived from Commercial work	Source
Order	Chaos	Bauman (1991: 15)
Discipline	Liberty	Wagner (1994: xi)
Regulation	Emancipation	De Sousa Santos (1995: 2)
Orderliness	Ambivalence	Smart (1999: 6)
Security	Danger	Giddens (1990: 7)
Reason and order	Flow, flux and change	Ogborn (1998: 5)

Source: Taylor (2009: 257).

syndromes are entwined in the modern world-system. And each face of modernity has its own space. States are clearly producers and outcomes of modernity as order: planning in its many guises removes complexities to create the simplification of planned spaces. Cities on the other hand are implicated in disorder; they are locales that thrive on complexity consequent upon myriad functions. Thus this is a specific case, modernity, of the generic construction of social spaces described in Chapter 2: while the world of the state is a simple space of places, a mosaic of territorial containers; the world of the city is a multifarious space of flows, a veritable blizzard of innumerable networks, circuits and chains. In the modern world-system they exist as a nexus of relations between the inter-state system and the world-economy. Unlike in world-empires, the modern *modus operandi* means that an accommodation between guardian practices and commercial practices is maintained informally. Whereas guardian centralization/decentralization defines temporal variation in world-empires, it is the changing balance in the guardian/commerce relationship that defines temporal variation in the modern world-system. This is most clearly expressed in the hegemonic cycles that I describe in the second substantive section of this chapter. Unlike Normal History with its only loosely related economic cycles and political periods, within this new political economy, guardian and commercial times are merged to generate reasonably regular long cycles.

Wallerstein has developed and honed this basic world-systems analysis for over three decades to inform our understandings of historical modernities, contemporary dilemmas, and future scenarios for the demise of modernity: the most accessible sources of these ideas can be found in Wallerstein (1983; 2004). However, cities are conspicuous by their critical neglect in Wallerstein's voluminous writings on the modern world-system. Wallerstein has developed a mode of analysis and theoretical framework

wherein cities are mere locales among other places where historical processes such as core-making and cyclical generation occur. In other words,
cities are not proactive clusterings of processes in the way they are portrayed in this book. The purpose of this chapter is to take Wallerstein's
TimeSpace structures and expose them to the city-centric arguments previously deployed to comprehend beginning creative interludes and the consequent Normal History. The aim is to add a new layer of understanding
to the creation of modernity in Western Europe and the consequent 'modernization' of the rest of the world: Wallerstein's (1979) 'rise and future
demise of the modern world-system' becomes translated into Western
Europe's creative interval produced in cities, and which is now reaching its
geohistorical limits in contemporary globalization.

EUROPEAN CITIES IN THE TRANSITION TO MODERNITY

Most of the arguments for the 'rise of Europe/West' or 'transition to
modernity/capitalism' identify an aspect of European superiority that
makes all the difference (Wallerstein 1992): the West was destined to rule
the world. Perhaps the most well known of the Europhilic explanations is
Max Weber's 'Protestant ethic', undergirding the 'capitalist spirit'. This
incorporates a special geography; it is in northern Europe that capitalism is made. However, unlike Wallerstein, Weber does consider cities an
important part of his argument. Thus I begin this section with a simple
critique of Weber's particular brand of Eurocentrism.

Contra-Weber and his 'Occidental Cities' Thesis

In the last chapter I provided a dynamic urban geography of medieval Europe (Table 5.16) based upon Henri Pirenne's (1969) thesis of a
European city revival based upon a commercial revolution in northern
Italy and the Low Countries. Writing roughly contemporaneously with
Pirenne (the 1920s), Weber (1958) attempted to understand European
cities in a more comprehensive manner than Pirenne's focus on commerce,
and this produced a very different urban geography. Locating European
urban development in a wider global context, he creates two concepts of
city forms that he calls 'occidental' and 'oriental'. Their key difference is
that the latter is lacking in 'freedom'. Whereas in Europe 'city air makes
man free' (p. 94), this was not the case for eastern cities. He contrasted
cities that lacked 'autonomy, community organizations, and a privileged
citizen estate' (p. 84) in Asia with 'politically autonomous cities and a

burgher stratum of Occidental type' (p. 85). It is from this archetypal early twentieth-century Eurocentrism that Weber derives his urban geography of Europe. He argued that within medieval Europe, this autonomous citizenry was to be found in its purest form north of the Alps (p. 91), so that 'the southern European city forms a transition stage between Asiatic and North European cities' (p. 95). Obviously he is thinking largely of the German imperial, free and territorial cities with their privileges within the Holy Roman Empire. Thus Weber's more political conceptualization of cities generates a very different European urban geography.

Jim Blaut (2000, pp. 19–30) begins with Weber in his wonderful *Eight Eurocentric Historians* and treats Weber's ideas on cities as replications of his wider concern for Europe's unique role in 'the ascent of human "rationality"' (p. 19): 'modern European society was not only the most rational of all societies but also the product of conscious human choice: voluntarism' (p. 20). Thus 'urban society was able to lead Occidental civilization towards modernity but was unable to do so in the East' (p. 28). Blaut points out that cities, east and west, were not so different before 1500, and in fact my empirical treatment of pre-1500 cities in the previous chapter showed European cities still lagging behind in terms of population throughout the medieval period. I can now take this further and show Weber's European urban geography to be equally problematic. Table 6.2 shows cities with populations over 25000 in northern Italy compared to those in the far vaster German lands in 1300. The contrast is stark: there are more than twice as many leading cities within northern Italy. Ranking all cities in Table 6.2 together, Italian cities appear first, second, third, fourth, sixth, seventh, eighth and ninth in the top ten: a very good performance for a supposed 'transition stage' to freedom! Weber's geography, and thereby his 'freedom' theory, is evidentially unsound. In the rest of this section we stick with Pirenne's urban geography of medieval Europe interpreted through Braudel's 'two poles of development'.

I have made this short detour into things Weberian for three reasons. First, it is useful to present briefly one pertinent example of Eurocentrism as a check against which to compare what I am offering, starting with my 'foregrounding' of European cities in the last chapter. Second, Weber's freedom relates to guardian processes, but what is important is how such institutional freedom is used commercially. It is commercial autonomy that is the really important process, and this waxed and waned across all Normal History; Europe's medieval waxing, especially in northern Italy, was real but not that exceptional. Third, it is important to distance Wallerstein's argument about Europe's lack of strong world-empire structures, in which I locate my narrative, from Weber's use of 'oriental despotism' as a reason for the stagnation of non-European civilizations. At

Table 6.2 Northern Italian and German cities, 1300

Leading northern Italian cities	Population (000s)	Leading German cities	Pop (000s)
Venice	110	Cologne	54
Genoa	85	Metz	32
Milan	60	Erfurt	30
Florence	60	Speyer	30
Bologna	40		
Padua	39		
Cremona	38		
Verona	36		
Pavia	30		
Pisa	25		

Source: Derived from Chandler (1987: 17).

first glance they appear to be simply obverse sides of the same argument; one position emphasizing what is missing from Europe is what the other emphasizes is found elsewhere. But the two positions are ontologically distinct. Wallerstein's argument is a contingent one, it concerns opportunities that we know were taken but that did not have to be. Weber's position treats Europe as fundamentally special, always destined to rise to the top; this inevitability is what Blaut (2000, p. 6) calls 'tunnel history', all progress runs through Europe and its immediate environs (stretching to ancient Mesopotamia). Wallerstein's world-systems analysis, and all parts of my toolkit, are an utter negation of that way of thinking.

Revisiting the Dobb–Sweezy Debate

The usual place to start a consideration of cities in the transition to capitalism is the Dobb–Sweezy debate in which the role of cities is central. In this key debate Wallerstein (1979) comes down on the side of Sweezy because of their common concern for the importance of systemic thinking. However they remain very different in their interpretations of the transition with Sweezy bringing cities to the fore. Here is an opportunity to probe an old debate by juxtapositioning guardian and commercial practices. From my position states and cities must both be considered: for modernity they exist as key processes operating in tandem. The critical point is that it is necessary to treat both in any considered understanding of the transition to the modern world-system.

In the 1950s a debate was initiated between Maurice Dobb and Paul

Sweezy about the nature of the transition from feudalism to capitalism. Although focusing on a dispute within Marxist scholarship, it reverberated more generally within history in subsequent decades (Hilton 1976a). The debate focuses upon 'the problems of the urban element in feudal society' (Hilton 1976b, p. 19), and therefore relates to the discussion in the last chapter about the tendency in studies of Normal History to undervalue the contribution of cities. The problem with the European feudalism case of Normal History is that we know it is followed by a new social system – modernity, capitalism – in which urbanization increases to new, historically unprecedented levels. Therefore if cities are to become so important after the feudalism, it begs the question about the role of cities in the feudal period itself. Were the cities in feudal Europe in some way responsible for the subsequent rise of a very urban modern world-system?

The answer to this question is superficially straightforward – surely there is an urban continuity here that implies medieval European cities being implicated in the development of modern cities. However, as previously noted, this position can become Eurocentric in its application since it spawns a further question: why was it that these European cities are the precursors of modernity and not more important cities in other regions and times of Normal History? In other words, are medieval European cities in some ways special? Merrington (1976, pp. 170–74) shows that the idea of urban origins of capitalism/modernity, going back to Pirenne and before, was the generally accepted position before the Dobb–Sweezy debate opened up the question anew.

In his *Studies in the Development of Capitalism*, Dobb (1946) set forth an orthodox Marxist interpretation of the transition from feudalism in terms of changing modes of production. In this book and subsequent refinements (Hilton 1976a), he defined feudalism as a particular class structure of landowning nobles and dependent serfs, and it was the pressure of the former on the latter to extract more value that precipitated the disintegration of feudalism. Thus feudalism was destroyed by its internal class contradictions and, if cities did contribute to this, it was only in a subordinate way. The debate begins when Sweezy critiques this position in 1950. He argued that feudalism needed an outside pressure to break its self-perpetuating motion and that intervention came from merchants in cities (Hilton 1976b, p. 26). As Sweezy (1976, p. 39) tells it, the flight of the serfs from the land is not so much a push factor from landlords as oppressor, but rather it was a pull factor of cities as 'powerful magnets' (p. 40). Drawing on Pirenne's ideas, he argues that 'trade emerged as a *system* of production' (p. 41, italics in original). This 'creative force' generated 'a *system* of production for exchange alongside the old feudal system of production for use' (p. 42). It is through the juxtaposing and interacting of these two systems that the latter economic process was undermined. And it was 'the rise of towns, which were the centres and breeders of exchange economy'; cities were the destroyer of feudalism.

Overall the debate seems to have swung towards Dobb's orthodox position and against Sweezy (Hilton 1976b). Wallerstein (1979, p. 9) goes against this tendency: he is drawn to this debate by Sweezy's reference to a system of production: 'the substantive issue . . . concerns the appropriate unit of analysis'. Economic change as transition must be understood at a systemic level, not at the level of national class analyses. But Wallerstein avoids endorsing the core of Sweeny's argument relating to trade and cities. This is probably because of the 'dualistic tendency' to separate the urban and rural in Sweezy's position, identified by Merrington (1976, p. 195). Merrington poses the key question that undermines Sweezy's position within the debate: 'How can towns be "internal" and "external" at the same time?', concluding that we must reject 'the dualistic hypothesis' (p. 175).

However the debate cannot be left there as yet another devaluing of the role of cities in understanding social change. The essence of Sweezy's position can be recovered and Merrington's question answered, by bringing Jacobs' (1992) moral syndromes into the argument. The argument is as follows:

1. European feudalism is a case of Normal History and therefore operates through a *modus vivendi*, wherein guardian and commercial work are separated (seemingly dualistic).
2. But both ways of making a living are intrinsically necessary for the reproduction of the system: even in feudalism they require each other.
3. Thus landowner guardians need cities and their production, while commercial elites need guardian markets and protection.
4. However in Normal History such as this, their work spheres are largely separated into rural and urban locales.
5. This spatial separation was based upon a hierarchical relation with guardian work socially superior to commercial work.
6. But the coming of modernity is precisely the undermining of that social ordering of guardian and commerce; cities come to the fore and the modern world-system replaces Normal History.

In other words, the process called the transition from feudalism to capitalism in Western Europe is readily interpretable in Jacobs' (1992) moral syndrome analysis as a reordering of guardian and commercial work in a new spatial organization.

The remainder of this first part of the chapter is all about bringing cities back into the transition. This is done in the systemic spirit of Wallerstein and Sweezy, by going beyond the common territorial focus on England and France in considering the 'feudal' predecessor of capitalism. We will continue to be Europe-wide in our analyses, but with the focus turned towards Braudel's two poles of development, the city-rich regions of northern Italy and the Low Countries.

How Well Were Western European Cities Doing Before the Transition?

In Table 5.16 it was shown that Western European cities were doing reasonably well in comparison with the rest of the world during its late medieval cycle. In this section I move from cross-sections at given points of time to changes over given periods: what were the trajectories of European cities before the transition? I have created two new tables that attempt to indicate the material restructuring that was occurring through the late medieval cycle. Restructuring creates both winners and losers: for instance the blocking of the Silk Road is catastrophic for Eurasian inland trading centres but boosts the port cities used to bypass the blockage. In Figures 6.1 and 6.2 I attempt to identify city winners and losers for 1000–1250 and 1250–1450 respectively using Chandler's estimates for cities with populations over 40 000. The method used is a simple one. For each period there are three categories of city changes: category A, cities that drop out (for instance they appear in the 1000 list but not in 1250); category B, cities that come in (the obverse of the above – they appear only in the 1250 list); and category C, cities that appear in both lists. Cities designated losers are those in category A and those in category C whose population declined. Cities designated winners are those in category B and those in category C whose population increased. Both rosters were then divided into four categories in terms of degree of loss or gain. For instance, in the restructuring from 1000 to 1250 in Figure 6.1, Cordova (a very large loser) was from category A and was the largest city in 1000 that fell below 40 000 in 1250 (and hence dropped out), whereas Fez (a very large winner) from category B is the largest city in 1250 whose population was less than 40 000 in 1000. From category C the biggest gainer of population from 1000 to 1250 was Hangchow, and Kaifeng was the biggest loser of population in this period. These figures are designed to provide a better sense of how well Western European cities were doing in this medieval cycle.

The first point to note about Figure 6.1 is that Western Europe has no losers. This is hardly surprising because only one city qualified in 1000: Venice, which we know was a success. In 1250 nine Western European cities are featured as winners, with Venice joined by Milan as 'large winners'. Above them, however, is Paris as a 'very large winner'. This

Very large losers	Cordova Nishapur Hasa Rayy Tanjore Tsinchow Tinnis Kairwan Kyoto Constantinople Kaifeng	*Very large winners*	Fez Kamakura **Paris** Marrakesh Cuttack Konia Hangchow Cairo Pagan Canton Peking
Large losers	Ani Samarkand Kanauj Manyakheta Chunar Ozkend Mansura Ghazni Jerusalem Songdo Nanning Somnath Shiraz Tollan Baghdad Isfahan Anhilvada Angkor	*Large winners*	Damascus Gaur Delhi Sarai Granada Tunis **Milan** Warangal Nanking Sian **Venice** Chuanchow
		Winners	Kingtehchen Ninghsia Trebizond Acre Alexandria **Bologna** **Genoa** Tenayuca **Cologne** Yangchow Aleppo Chengdu Wuchang
Losers	Basra Loyang Pyongyang Siraf Tajin Benares Prambanan Kiev Seville		
Small losers	Balasaghun Thaneswar Ujjain Amida Caesarea Khajuraho Liaoyang Ochrida Palermo Thessalonica Soochow Bokhara	*Small winners*	Bougie **Pisa** Quilon Trnovo Mosul **Rouen** Cueta Hormuz Madurai **Marseille** Sale Tlemcen Vijaya Kayseri Tali Fuchow Qus Siangyang Kashgar Cambay

Note: Emboldened type indicates West European cities (Christian).

Figure 6.1   Restructuring through cities, 1000–1250

Very large losers	Kamakura Pagan Angkor Baghdad Konia Tali Sarai Hangchow Fez Marrakesh	*Very large winners*	Vijayanagar Tabriz Bursa Seoul Ayutia Jaunpur Peking Granada Cairo Kyoto
Large losers	Palermo Isfahan Warangal Anhilvada Ninghsia Trebizond Acre Alexandria Tenayuca **Cologne**	*Large winners*	Adrianople **Ghent** Karaman Shiraz **Naples** Samarkand Mandu **Prague** Damietta Gaur Soochow Canton
Losers	Bougie Fuchow Kayseri **Pisa** Qus Trnovo Siangyang Kashgar Mosul Seville Wuchang Bokhara Damascus Delhi Constantinople	*Winners*	Ava Bidar **Bruges** **Caffa** **Lisbon** **London** Pegu Riobamba Novgorod **Florence** **Genoa** Kingtehchen Nanking Sian **Milan** Aleppo
Small losers	Cueta Madurai **Marseille** Sale Thessalonica Vijaya Cambay Cuttack Tunis **Bologna** Yangchow Chuanchow Kaifeng **Paris**	*Small winners*	Ahmedabad Chitor Heart Hsuchow Nanchang Ningpo Taiyuan **Troki** Yunnanfu Calicut Chengdu Hormuz Quilon Tlemcen **Venice** **Rouen**

Note: Emboldened type indicates West European cities (Christian).

Figure 6.2   Restructuring through cities, 1250–1450

latter category is constituted of political centres; remember that in Normal History it is guardian processes that are able to create the very largest cities. Paris is Western Europe's only capital city of a territorial state among the winners, the other eight, including Venice and Milan, are primarily commercial centres. Clearly Paris is the exception that proves the rule of Europe's weak political structure.

In Figure 6.2 Western Europe's 18 cities exhibit both losers and winners. However the ratio of only five losers to 13 winners confirms earlier evidence (Table 5.16) that European cities are doing relatively well in the downturn restructuring just before the transition to the modern world-system. The five losers are four smaller commercial centres plus Paris, reflecting the difficulties facing the French state after its earlier centralization. In this period, Western Europe exhibits no 'very large winners', but has three 'large winners' the Flemish textile centre, Ghent, plus two political centres Naples and Prague. There are three other political centres among the Western European winners, Lisbon, London and Troki (Vilnius), but all three also had important trading functions. In other words Western European urban success was heavily weighted towards commercial processes rather than guardian processes. This provides some support to Wallerstein's key argument: Western Europe's weak political structures allowed space for a flowering of commercial functions in cities. This does not confirm that 'occidental cities' are special (Paris, the biggest city was hardly autonomous (Hilton 1976b, p. 19)), but it does confirm the importance of the varying relationship between guardian and commercial practices (Merrington 1976, pp. 179–87).

To illustrate how this relationship has operated in the European medieval cycle I will focus on some particularly interesting cities. I will start exploring guardian–commercial relations in Genoa, and then move on to the northern pole and investigate how Bruges was overtaken by Antwerp as the modern era dawned. These examples are in no sense meant to be typical; rather they are strategic choices of cities that make key contribution to the transition to the modern world-system.

Genoa: *Modus Vivendi* in Extreme

As the title above suggests Genoa has been chosen for examination because it represents an acute expression of the separation of guardian and commercial practices. Genoa had a tradition of 'outside' guardians from the medieval period through to the early modern. In the latter case it illustrates *modus vivendi* extending into the middle of the transition to the modern world-system with its development of a new guardian–commercial *modus operandi*. The Genoese negotiation of outside guardians comes in three phases.

The first two phases of 'outside' governance of Genoa broadly reflect the medieval European economic cycle. Arrighi (1994, p. 88) has shown that in northern Italy, during the growth period, city cooperation was commonplace, whereas with the onset of stagnation competition and rivalry became the norm and this is reflected in the changing form of Genoa's governance. In the first phase Genoa is not untypical of other northern Italian cities, but diverges from other cities in the dangerous second phase.

The norm of governance for many Italian cities in the thirteenth century was the institution of podesteria (Waley 1969). This was an instrument to solve the problem of conflict inherent in the concentration of people into cities. This problem had become endemic and critical in northern Italy reflecting imperial-versus-papal rivalries. A *podestà* was a 'single executive official . . . from another (not neighbouring) commune trained in law and holding his office for six months or a year' (p. 68) who came with a team of lawyers and guards. The key point is in the temporal (short-term, temporary) and spatial (from distant, non-competing city) natures of the guardian position that were deemed to provide government 'above the fray'. Various rules were instituted to reinforce the neutrality through space-of-place making, including prohibition on trading while in office and not leaving the city without permission (pp. 68–9). Genoa decided to suspend its government and change to the *podestà* system in 1190 'because of so much civil discord, conspiracies and divisions wracked the city' (Epstein 1996, p. 88). The first *podestà* in 1191 was from Brescia (p. 88), a second in 1194–5 was from Pavia (p. 89), and the system continued through the next century until the last *podestà* in 1296 (p. 325). Epstein (1996, p. 88) refers to the *podestà* as 'a temporary foreign ruler', but in the next century Genoa turned to foreign rulers that were not so temporary.

After the neutrality of the *podestà* system, foreign guardianship was still sought but without the neutrality: important political figures were offered the government of the city to reflect the current winners in the local empire-versus-papacy conflicts. Thus was Emperor Henry IV made ruler of Genoa in 1310:

> An agreement was made: Genoa agreed to cede itself to Henry for twenty years, and he agreed to end divisions in the city and restore peace. . . . the Genoese renounced their own autonomy, not in the face of external force, for Henry's power and resources were limited, but because self-rule no longer worked. (Epstein 1996, p. 184)

He was followed by Robert of Naples (with Pope John XXII) in 1318 (p. 196); the Archbishop of Milan in 1354 (p. 220); Charles VI of France in 1396 (p. 245); Francesco Viscounti, Lord of Milan in 1421 (p. 265); and Charles VII of France in 1458 (p. 286). This serial love of 'foreign rule' is even more curious when we consider how Charles VI was chosen: 'After public deliberations and backstairs dealings in 1396, the Genoese decided to hand themselves over to the king of France, even though they knew that from time to time he suffered from mental illness' (p. 245). He may not have appeared to be a good candidate but he was not without competition; in the debate the proposal was that:

> the doge and a group of citizens negotiate with the king of France, or England, or the emperor, or another prince, or the Tuscan league, to find a leader. (p. 247)

It seems any guardian would be suitable as long as they are foreign and powerful. Finally, the Genoese finished up making their money under Hapsburg guardianship in the fifteenth century in the commercial world of Seville, while guardian matters were attended to in Madrid (Pike 1966).

Of course, this extreme process of *modus vivendi* is difficult to comprehend from our modern expectations but all we have here is a traditional separation of commercial and guardian work in the specific circumstances of church and state rivalry in medieval Italy. First, the *podestà* system was invented to counter internal conflict and second, powerful foreign rulers were brought in to provide protection also, this time from outside enemies. However neither the *podestà* as a 'hired hand' nor powerful rulers were ever allowed to control the Bank of San Giorgio:

> [Machiavelli writing in the 1480s] astutely observed that even as the Genoese handed over their state several times to various foreign rulers, San Giorgio remained firmly in local hands and carefully secured its privileged status from whatever ruler controlled the state. (Epstein 1996, p. 220)

This defined the boundaries of the *modus vivendi* at the end of the medieval economic cycle.

The political effect of the contraction of trade in the late Middle ages, was incessant war in northern Italy – the 'Italian hundred years war' – that ends with the Treaty of Lodi in 1454: many smaller cities lost their independence and a new balance of power was established with just four major cities, Florence, Genoa, Milan and Venice. In the period of transition to the modern world-system these cities take two different paths to modernity. Three of them, Florence, Milan and Venice, elided their war-making into new state-making. Using Pirenne (1962), Arrighi (1994) argues that the elites of these three cities 'aristocratized', meaning that the leading citizens turned away from commercial towards more guardian imperatives. Their increasing concern was for new territories that they were tending and consolidating. The practical effect was conversion from cities-in-networks to city-states. This might look like a precursor to the modern *modus operandi* but, in fact, it marked the confirmation of the end of these cities as major players on the European scene. When the next large expansion of trade began towards the end of the fifteenth century they were in no position to take full advantage. And as territorial states, they were small and vulnerable compared to larger territorial rivals beyond Italy, as the successful French invasion of northern Italy in 1494 showed.

But Genoa was different; it took a quite dissimilar path to modernity than its erstwhile city rivals. It did not use its surplus capital for state-building; in the war-making it had kept its independence from the other cities but had not increased its hinterland. This provided the option for an alternative way forward: city elites restructured their trading pattern from the eastern to the western Mediterranean and developed a new financial capitalism based upon 'sound money' (Arrighi 1994, p. 113). But there was still a problem of surplus money requiring further new trade routes and a need for protection. Enter the Kingdom of Castile as guardian. With its expansion into the Atlantic and its crusader state credentials, Castile provided Genoa with the perfect partner. And the relationship was of mutual benefit: specializations of Iberian protection/power and Genoese trade/profit, 'complemented one another' (Arrighi 1994, p. 120). They were brought together in the sixteenth century because each needed the other: Genoa harnessed northern Italian surplus capital to provide for Castile's permanent financial crisis, while Castile opened new trading spaces culminating in the *asentos* (contracts for American silver) for Genoa. This created a triangular space of flows in the sixteenth century: silver from America came into Seville, it was transferred to Genoa for conversion into gold and bills of exchange that were sent to Antwerp to pay for Spanish troops fighting the Dutch. Castile/Spain paid with new contracts for silver that were exchanged in Seville and so the process continued (Arrighi 1994, p. 130; Kindleberger 1993, p. 26). This created what Braudel (1984, p. 164) proclaimed the 'age of the Genoese' through their 'discrete rule' of Europe in the late sixteenth and early seventeenth centuries. Consequently, Arrighi (1994, pp. 109–26) identifies Genoa as the first city at the centre-of-the-world economy in an initial cycle of accumulation of the modern world-system.

But note that the process that places Genoa at the economic centre cannot be separated from its outside governance through the Hapsburgs. This success of Genoa as dominant city a century after the demise of its more martial Italian city rivals, was based upon a continuation of the medieval *modus vivendi* between commercial and guardian practices. This 'dichotomous agency' of spatially separated economic and political loci is very alien to our modern sensibilities but was supremely successful for a while in early modern Europe. This is city success as commercial power, with extra-mural guardian agents that lasted into the early seventeenth century.

Bruges, Antwerp and Guardian Power in the North

Meanwhile in the northern pole Bruges, which had dominated from the coming of the Genoese in 1377 into the fifteenth century, was replaced by Antwerp as the leading economic centre of the Low Countries. Further, for the first half of the sixteenth century, Braudel (1984, p. 148) designates Antwerp the dominant city in the European world-economy. Thus Antwerp is the first signal of the ascendancy of northwest Europe but without fully completing the transition to the modern world-economy. Let us see how and why.

According to Braudel (1984, p. 101) Bruges was never a 'world-city'; he terms it merely a 'world market'. But there is no doubt that it was the leading city of the northern European pole for about two centuries. It was where the Hanseatic traders of north Germany and the Baltic met with Italian merchants, Genoese and Venetians after 1314. Although it has been characterized as a large entrepôt, – Braudel's 'world market' implies as such – Brulez (1973, pp. 15–16) has successfully critiqued the common notion that Bruges merchants were 'passive', just local mediators between foreign interests. To be sure much trading was dominated by outside merchants but this is to be expected in an interlocking commercial network of cities; Bruges merchants were part of the network with their factors abroad trading across Europe from Italy to the Baltic (p. 16). This is important because the replacement of Bruges by Antwerp as the leading city of the Low Countries by 1500 has been interpreted as the latter having the 'active merchants' that Bruges lacked. If this was not the case how can we account for the geographical transfer of commercial power? Brulez describes a 'generally accepted position' (pp. 2–6) that focuses on differences between Bruges and Antwerp in terms of types and places of trade. Basically, the argument is that there was a change in trading patterns and content from linking two seas (Baltic and Mediterranean) to one that featured the inland continent (especially south Germany) and Atlantic colonies (from Portugal). Hence:

> Antwerp cannot . . . be considered simply the heir and successor of Bruges. We are confronted with a very different trade, a new trade – new in the sense that it is characteristic of the Modern Age . . . the antithesis between Bruges and Antwerp becomes an antithesis between the Middle Ages and the Modern Age. (p. 5)

But in his critique of this position, Brulez thinks the differences have been over-emphasized: 'we find a shift, but no antithesis' (p. 20). The situation was much more complex than a simple transition from medieval to modern. Further, he rejects the classic notion of city competition imbued in the traditional interpretation of Bruges–Antwerp relations. The shift was a long slow one, with both cities prospering through much of the fifteenth century:

> Perhaps too much attention has been paid to the rivalry between Bruges and Antwerp and the interests of the two towns have been considered to be too exclusively opposed. This rivalry is of course a striking phenomenon and is certainly real enough, but some significant indications point to a kind of symbiosis of the two towns, and to the fact that they played a kind of complementary role. It would seem, therefore, that the two towns could live with each other, and that the prosperity of one did not necessarily imply the death of the other. (Brulez 1973, p. 8)

Brulez's symbiosis can be interpreted as the rise of Antwerp strengthening the northern pole within the European city network and therefore being good for Bruges as a leading city of that pole. Uytven (1995, p. 260) provides an example that explicitly supports this position:

> Throughout the fifteenth century the central market place and the adjacent streets in Antwerp lodged a colony of Bruges merchants during the (Brabant) fairs. They practically dominated the spice trade in Antwerp.

This was, of course, a key part of the colonial trade that made Antwerp seem more modern to later historians.

Uytven (1995, p. 269) replaces the economic competition argument by a series of guardian actions that generated the urban shift:

> Political events in Flanders (in the late 1430s) had broken the inertia and routine that had made them (merchants) bear the drawbacks of their Bruges' seats for so long . . . the political events of the thirties and forties, however, triggered the decline that during the last decades of the century turned into real disaster.

And the 'real disaster' occurred in the 1480s; Uytven describes it thus:

> According to all our parameters and contemporary witnesses the final breakdown of Bruges occurred in the 1480s. The causes are well-known: a continuous state of war with Flanders, successive blockages of Bruges, archduke Maximilian's instructions for the desertion of the town by the foreign merchants (1484 and 1488); the financial exhausting of the town due to military expenses and heavy fines; the intolerable burden of taxes driving people away from Bruges; the neglect of the indispensable dredging and other works to keep the waterways open, due to the insecurity of the times and the lack of financial means. It should be stressed that practically all those causes were more or less political. (p. 267)

Here we see guardian processes directly impinging on inter-city economics (see also Limberger 2001, p. 44). Unlike in northern Italy, the leading cities were not politically independent; the Low Countries were part of the Duchy of Burgundy. The Maximilian referred to above was the Hapsburg prince whose marriage brought Burgundy under Hapsburg rule. In the Low Countries, cities, not least Bruges, were commonly in revolt against the territorial policies of their Duke and therefore the degree of autonomy of cities varied with political conditions and was always subject to guardian coercion. This was a case of the *modus vivendi* continually breaking down. I guess what Uytven is arguing is that Antwerp in Brabant negotiated this political quagmire better than Bruges in Flanders through the fifteenth century. Thus the shift from 'medieval' Bruges to 'modern' Antwerp was by no means a simple case of inter-city competition; the more critical conflict was between commercial processes and guardian processes that were particularly harmful to Bruges.

The end result was that Antwerp entered the sixteenth century as Braudel's first northern city to dominate the European world-economy. But we should be wary of Braudel's 'great city' interpretation. Lesger (2006) directly refutes this way of thinking and offers a complex network approach that is perfectly in keeping with my conceptual toolkits. For the mid-sixteenth century, he argues that despite the 'enormous size' of Antwerp's trade and Pirenne's widely accepted claim that the city's hinterland encompassed all of the Low Countries, 'it is impossible to rank the gateways of the Low Countries unambiguously in a hierarchy of gateway cities' (p. 187). His empirical argument goes as follows:

> For some products, spices among them, the hinterland of the Antwerp market did indeed extend over the whole of the Low Countries and even beyond, but for other goods it certainly did not. For Baltic grain, in fact, it is truer to say that Antwerp itself fell within the hinterland of Amsterdam, and for Rhine wines, within that of Dordrecht. In the 1540s and 1550s, Antwerp was still waging a bitter struggle with Middelburg for the staple of western wines. Thus, even in nearby Middelburg, it was by no means easy to say whether Antwerp was within the hinterland of Middelburg or Middlelburg in that of Antwerp, for this product. In this case, the empirical facts diverge very widely from the theory of a hierarchy of distribution and staple centres. (pp. 187–8)

Lesger calls this a 'gateway system' reflecting his focus on trade, but from a generic (going back to Uruk and Sumer) and broader perspective, we can interpret the Low Countries as constituting a dynamic multi-nodal city-region in which Antwerp is the lead city, no more but also no less. However, its path to commercial success remained dependent on a *modus vivendi*, in which guardian processes were crucial and ultimately determining. The Low Countries were part of the Hapsburgs' realm and, in the early stages the Dutch Revolt against state centralization, Antwerp was sacked by Spanish troops in 1585, leaving it commercially on the wrong side of the new political divide. The construction of the modern *modus operandi* had to await the rise of a different 'northern pole city': Amsterdam in the victorious 'Dutch Republic' of the seventeenth century.

Amsterdam and the Creation of a new *Modus Operandi*

Amsterdam appears twice in this story of modernity; here as the last episode of the transition, and in the second substantive section below as the consolidation and beginning of reproduction of the modern world-system. The latter takes the form of hegemonic cycles that are based upon the creation of a new *modus operandi* between guardian and commercial work. How did this momentous change in city/state relations come about? Certainly in the military, social, political and economic confusion of the Dutch Revolt there was no intention to produce such an outcome but varied political, economic and religious agents operating through a range of self-interests did happen upon a new political economy. The contingency is political, the Dutch Revolt, and it is guardian practices where the transformation occurs to enable a capitalist world-economy. Thus I tell the story as two parallel processes. First there is the 'Dutch economic miracle' that has strong continuities with what went before in Antwerp, and second, there is the political transformation: Amsterdam in the Dutch Republic is in a completely different political world from Antwerp in the Hapsburg Low Countries.

In the still unresolved debates on reasons for the commercial rise of Amsterdam there are two main traditions (Lesger 2006). The exogenous argument argues that the 1585 sacking of Antwerp led to a dispersal of the city's economic elite whose resettlement was concentrated in Amsterdam. It was these migrants who propelled their new city into worldwide prominence. This is criticized as being too simple – too much continuity in handing on the baton – and suggests Amsterdam as part of a backward region requiring outsiders for economic development. In contrast, the endogenous argument is based on the discovery of Holland before the Revolt as being precociously 'modern' in her economic practices. It was the evolution of this proto-advanced region that led to the economic miracle in the seventeenth century. This is criticized because it tends towards inevitability; Holland and Amsterdam were destined to come out on top. But there is common agreement on the economic geography outcome: the economic success results in Amsterdam becoming the leading intermediary in international trade, a staple market in control of the world-economy in Europe.

In his revisionist account, Lesger (2006) reinterprets both arguments in network terms: the endogenous situation is about development of a 'gateway system' *à la* Antwerp; the exogenous addition is one of new networks of contacts and trust. Thus Lesger's (2006, p. 171) account of the influence of migrants on the rise of Amsterdam stresses its importance, but also accepts the necessary inputs of existing structures:

> From their old homes, they brought with them to Amsterdam more or less extensive networks of business relations. Once they had settled in their new home, they involved these contacts in their commercial activities, and this gave the commerce of Amsterdam a new and different character. ... The coming of the migrants gave the direct overseas trade a powerful stimulus. The networks of newcomers and established residents in Amsterdam became interwoven ... Naturally, they profited from the extensive merchant fleet available in Holland, and from existing expertise in Amsterdam, but these were only necessary and not sufficient conditions for the rapid expansion of the city's trade.

In this argument he invokes Schumpeter's view on new economic elites pioneering 'new combinations' (pp. 139–40 and 179–80), which is suggestive of a Jacobs' process of economic growth, but Lesger's focus on trade appears to preclude such an interpretation. In fact, Peter de la Court's (1972) famous seventeenth-century publication provides a 'Schumpeter before Schumpeter' interpretation:

> newcomers leaving their own country upon any accident, and besides their moveable goods, bringing with them the knowledge of what is abounding, or wanting in their native country, and of all sorts of manufacture; they cannot live in Holland upon the interests of their money, nor on their real estates: so that they are compelled to lay out all their skill and estate in devising and forming new fisheries, manufactures, traffic and navigation, with the danger of losing all they have. (p. 57)

I quote this here because it goes beyond trade and markets with specific reference to the generation of new work to replace old work:

> He that ventures may gain, and sometimes find out and meet with a good fishery, manufacture, merchandize or traffic: and then the other inhabitants may come in for a share in that new occupation, which is very needful, because the old handicraft works being beaten down lower and lower in price, yield less profit. (p. 57)

This is also 'Jacobs before Jacobs'! Hence the result is more than a trading success; de la Court provides the following estimates of the population maintained by different economic sectors in the 1660s:

- manufacture and its shipping trade – 650 000
- food drink, clothing (for internal market) – 650 000
- sea fishing industry – 450 000
- navigation, shipping, trade – 250 000
- inland agriculture and fishing – 200 000
- non-productive (gentry, magistrates, estate/money, soldiers, poor, beggars) – 200 000.

This is quite a rounded economy: in terms of our toolkits, de la Court identifies a complex division of labour with commercial work divided between (1) city-ness supporting 1 350 000 people (manufacturing, sea fishing, navigation), and (2) town-ness supporting 850 000 people (food, inland agriculture), plus 200 000 supported by guardian work (non-productive).

Returning to Lesger (2006), his bringing together the two arguments for the rise of Amsterdam/the Dutch Republic leads on to undermining the prior agreement on the economic geography as a simple 'Amsterdam city-region'. For Lesger (2006) the product is a complex network of trading cities in which Amsterdam is embedded as the indisputable leading centre. He provides a deal of evidence showing that the generally accepted position of Amsterdam as a world market staple, with its hierarchical implications, and with which both Braudel and Wallerstein are identified as accepting (p. 198), is false. He describes a spatial economic structure, his 'gateway system', which I generalize to multi-nodal city-region. In this space of flows:

> Every gateway derived its function and significance from the structure of the larger whole of which it formed a part . . . infrastructure included not just docks, warehouses, and other physical assets, but also knowledge and skills of people who carried on commerce[.] (p. 195)

In such a situation, where cities depend on each other, it follows that:

> there was no question of a hierarchy culminating in a permanent central or world staple market. For some goods, the Amsterdam market was at times indeed at the apex of staple or distribution centres, but for other goods, or for the same goods at different times, that was by no means the case. (pp. 211–12)

The continuity with his prior analysis of Antwerp in the Low Countries in the mid-sixteenth century is both marked and intended. Amsterdam may have been the centre of more intense and more worldwide trading practices than Antwerp, but for Lesger they are essentially the same commercial process. If this is accepted then the newness of Amsterdam is to be found in its guardian relations.

The north–south political division of the Low Countries came in 1579 with the defensive alliance of seven northern provinces in the Union of Utrecht, consolidated two years later by deposing Phillip II, the Hapsburg ruler. A subsequent search for a new sovereign was unsuccessful and the 'United Provinces' drifted into a republican form of government that latterly became known as the Dutch Republic. There is a debate on whether this was the last 'city-state' in the tradition of republican Venice (Barbour 1963) or an early, unusual, modern territorial state ('t Hart 1993). Braudel (1984) interprets it as a halfway house between these two state forms; however, by locating the Dutch polity in this way, its contemporary relevance is inevitably neglected. Thus, instead of the Dutch polity being a stop on the evolutionary path to modern statehood, it is better viewed as a particular early capitalist polity, historically superseded by modern states but theoretically still available as a possible political category for future reference. I have previously characterized this polity as a 'domesticated state' (Taylor 1996a, pp. 49–5); I now interpret this as a new *modus operandi* between guardian and commercial practices.

There is a similarity between economic and political interpretations of the United Provinces in that both are commonly seduced by the power that is Amsterdam. In the politics literature this has resulted in the new polity being adjudged 'Amsterdam's city-state', a view that requires a debunking similar to that for a world market staple. Basically there was no such city-state for the fundamental reason that the city of Amsterdam did not rule this new political space either directly or indirectly by some subtle form of subterfuge that is difficult to reveal. It is now generally agreed that the Dutch polity operated through shifting coalitions of cities, provinces and provincial governors known as stadholders. And Amsterdam was not even the political capital: a minor city, The Hague, was chosen 'to avoid all rivalry' ('t Hart 1989, p. 668), because it was not important enough to be represented in the Holland provincial assembly or the (republic-wide) States General. Even more telling, in key foreign policy, for all its economic importance, Amsterdam could be and was outmanoeuvred by counter coalitions. Venice, a true city-state, could never have lost control of Venetian foreign policy!

If not a city-state, what? This is not an easy question to answer. The work of 't Hart (1989, p. 1993) carefully delineates the Dutch polity as a 'state of 58 cities' (1989, p. 666) that emerged in a war *against* centralization. Thus it is to be expected that the resulting polity would be a decentralized state, the opposite to the centralizing states of the times. However because the ideal model of the early modern state has come from the ranks of the latter, France to be precise, it follows that Dutch state credentials are left open to doubt. Her research strives to show the fiscal novelty of the Dutch in an alternative form of modern state-making. It was formally a confederation of provinces that acted like a league of cities (Boogman 1979, p. 389), a sort of 'confederation of Venices' (Pocock 1992). 't Hart's reference to 58 cities indicates the number of cities represented in the provincial assemblies and the States General. To make matters even more unusual, war making was 'subcontracted out' as a 'specialized activity' for the stadholders, prominently selected from the House of Orange-Nassau (Zolberg 1986, p. 88).

We can only conclude that this was in fact a peculiar form of state-making with a unique political outcome. Created from a defensive alliance, it originally had no name – according to Schama (1987) the name 'United Provinces' was coined by a contemporary Englishman, and 'Dutch Republic' is a more recent statist appellation. This was a polycentric city-region state with a very specific spatial structure: a vibrant core of many cities surrounded by a defensive frontier of fortifications (Taylor 1994). Braudel (1984, p. 202) calls the result a 'fortified island' in the middle of which is a 'high-voltage urban economy' (p. 180); in other words, territoriality and networking were combined. Of course there had been polycentric city polities in the past – city leagues as trading networks of cities with political institutions (e.g. the Hanseatic League) and coalitions of city-states (e.g. in northern Italy) but none of these formed a city-regional structure within a defensive shell. The latter operated as a military buffer with fortifications paid for jointly by the seven provinces (Kossmann and Mellick 1974, pp. 167–8). It is the latter's territorial defensive practices that make such an unusual polity, combining guardian cooperation with commercial competition among its constituents. Cooperation is basic to the defensive function as written into the founding treaty but the complex division of labour was a perennial source of competition within the polity. For instance, industry and trade interests differed with respect to war and peace, with Haarlem and Leiden leading the 'war party' that prevented the 'peace party', led by Amsterdam and Rotterdam, from concluding a truce in 1630 (Israel 1990, p. 56). Of course, all polities are a matrix of conflict and compromise but what makes the Dutch polycentric city-region polity so unusual is that it had no institution to act as political umpire to resolve differences: a unanimity rule ruled. In modern states the 'umpire' role is the function of the executive, with varying degrees of constraint by the legislature and judiciary, backed up by the coercive arm of the state. The nearest the Dutch got to an executive with coercive capability was the stadholder position, which was periodically powerful but never attained sovereign status. The Dutch political space was filled by a unique political entity, a polycentric city-region state.

It is this guardian process of resisting centralization while engaging in a form of state-making that enabled the new *modus operandi* to evolve.

Boogman's (1978; 1979) work is the best source for describing how this came about. He argues that the early Dutch polity invented a new *raison d'état*. This idea was itself a modern concept that was originally used to separate the political interest of sovereigns from traditional religious motives (Boogman 1978, p. 55). The effect was to equate the state with the glory of the monarch, thereby legitimating its role as a war-machine. Hence, in typical guardian fashion, resources of the state were to be used for ostentatious display by the king and territorial expansion. But this is exactly what the Dutch avoided: they inverted the state/society relation so that 'in the United Provinces the State was already at an early stage regarded as a function of society' (Boogman 1979, p. 402). This was the new *raison d'état*: the purpose of the state was to maintain, sustain and aid in begetting more wealth. Territoriality remained as necessary defence, but with no policy of expansion. It is this intertwining of guardian and commercial practices that I have called the *modus operandi* of the modern world-system.

This flexible mixing of syndromes is explicitly illustrated in the structure of the Dutch East India Company (commonly known by its Dutch initials VOC), an organizational invention to solve the problem of 'chaotic oscillations in the market' for spices consequent on inter-city competition: by 1599 there were eight different companies involved in the trade, leading to 14 separate Dutch fleets sailing to the East Indies two years later (Israel 1995, pp. 320–21). The merchants asked the Holland and Zeeland assemblies to intervene to create a sustainable trade. They devised:

> a totally new kind of commercial organization, a chartered, joint-stock monopoly strongly backed by the state which was, at the same time, federated into chambers which kept their capital, and commercial operations, and policies, set by a federal board of directors. (p. 321)

Amsterdam provided slightly over half the capital but was not given a majority on the board; the breakdown was Amsterdam eight, Zeeland cities four, Hoorn, Enkhuizen, Delft and Rotterdam one each, with a seventeenth director nominated by the non-Amsterdam cities in rotation (p. 321). However neither Holland nor Zeeland could confer delegated sovereign powers and therefore it was the Estates General that chartered the company giving it rights to 'maintain troops, fit out warships, impose governors upon Asian populations, and conduct diplomacy with eastern potentates, as well as sign treaties and make alliances' (p. 322).

A key point is that while the company 'enjoyed a great deal of freedom of action', the Dutch state still conducted supervision, for instance, by having subsequently to approve treaties and alliances (p. 322) and, above all, by authorizing the monopoly of the spice trade (Brook 2008, p. 15). For summary and consequence Timothy Brook (2008, pp. 15–16) describes the situation admirably:

> What at first sight looked like an unworkable compromise – separate chambers controlled their own capital and operations while adhering to uniform guidelines and policies – turned out to be a brilliant innovation. Only a unique federal state such as the Dutch Republic could have dreamed up a federal company structure. The VOC combined flexibility with strength, giving the Dutch a huge advantage in the competition to dominate maritime trade to Asia. Within a few decades, the VOC proved itself to be the most powerful trading corporation in the seventeenth century world, and the model for large-scale business enterprises that now dominate the global economy.

The latter point is made in detail by Stephen Hymer (1972); from my perspective it represents the origins and continuing salience of the modern *modus operandi*.

I will conclude by returning to the wisdom of the precocious contemporary writer, Pieter de la Court. His classic *The True Interest and Political Maxims of the Republic of Holland* was written to legitimize the new political arrangements and as a guide to the rulers of this unusual state, a typical Advice-to-the-Prince tract, but without the prince. He begins by describing maxims for all countries and argues that basically monarchs' interests diverge from country interests, especially reflected in the treatment of cities. Their need to control means that they 'wait for an opportunity to command such populous cities and strongholds by citadels, and to render them weak and defenceless' (pp. 3–4). Such a process can be traced back as far as Sargon of Akkad. De la Court then draws this contrast:

> the overthrow of great and prosperous cities may be attributed to monarchs and princes of all times but never to republics, unless when they have inconsiderately subdued great cities. (p. 4)

And from this he derives the new *raison d'état*:

> It follows then to be the duty of the governors of republics to seek for great cities, and to make them as populous and strong as possible. (p. 5)

Treating the international realm as a jungle full of wild animals, he develops a powerful metaphor equating monarchs with beasts to be contrasted with 'the commendable example of the Cat' (i.e. Holland):

> For she never converses with strange beasts, but either keeps at home, or accompanies those of her own species, meddling with none, but in order to

defend her own; very vigilant to provide food, and preserve her young ones . . . But if it happens that she can by no means avoid combat, she is more fierce than a Lion, defends herself with tooth and nail . . . A Cat indeed is outwardly like a Lion, yet she is, and will remain but a Cat still: and so we who are naturally merchants, cannot be turned into soldiers. (pp. 212–13)

Obviously this is originally where I got the idea of a 'domesticated state'; now I argue that this is a most clear expression of a new *modus operandi* between guardians and commerce.

Contra-Braudel and his Predisposition for City Hierarchy

In this discussion of cities in the transition to the modern world-system, it has been useful to draw on Braudel's (1984) majestic description of the importance of cities in the rise of capitalism. He provides a framework for understanding early modern cities in systemic terms that have proven to be invaluable to world-systems analysis. Like Jacobs (1969), he draws on Henri Pirenne's pioneering work from which ideas are transferred forward into the seminal works of Wallerstein (1979) and Arrighi (1994). Therefore Braudel's strong influence on my text above is hardly surprising. But I am concluding this section with a contra argument to emphasize a departure from Braudel's ideas in one key respect. This was briefly broached in drawing on Lesger's work on Amsterdam where he supports a network interpretation over a hierarchical one. It is not that Braudel fails to appreciate the significance of cities other than Amsterdam in the rise of the United Provinces; in fact, he provides a sound exposition of the complex spatial division of labour in the United Provinces:

[I]ndustry prospered in Leyden, Haarlem and Delft; shipbuilding in Brill and Rotterdam; Dordrecht made a living from the heavy flow of traffic along the Rhine; Enkhuisen and Rotterdam controlled the fisheries of the North Sea; Rotterdam, again, the most important city after Amsterdam, handled the lion's share of trade with France and England; the Hague, the political capital . . . (Braudel 1984, p. 184)

And there is no disagreement on whether Amsterdam was the 'most important city'; rather it is how this importance is interpreted. In other words I am in a conceptual dispute with Braudel, not an empirical one.

Braudel (1984) provides 'ground rules' on how world-economies operate, 'Rule Two' is described thus:

A world-economy always has an urban centre of gravity, a city, as the logistic heart of its activities. News, merchandise, capital, credit, people, instructions, correspondence all flow into and out of the city. (Braudel 1984, p. 27)

These dominant cities are then implicated in 'Rule Three: there is always a hierarchy of zones within a world-economy' (p. 35). This rule conflates dominant cities with Wallerstein's core–periphery zone model (pp. 39–42) via 'Von Thunen's zones' (pp. 38–9). The latter economic model, of course, features just a single city at the centre of an economy and thus accentuates the idea of dominance by one city as commercial 'centre of gravity'. When arguing that Bruges was never such a dominant city he coins the term 'world-city' to describe such centres as 'undisputed stars at the centre of the galaxy' (p. 101). But this terminology is not developed; in the sequence of dominant cities in early modern Europe he refers to Venice (in the fifteenth century) 'reigning supreme', Antwerp (from 1501 to 1557) as 'world capital', and Genoa (1557 to 1627) as having 'discrete rule'.

This guardian-style language is, of course, appropriate for describing a hierarchical process but leads to a massive devaluation of other cities in the commercial networks that constituted the early modern European world-economy. This was always an interlocking network of cities with banks and merchant houses having branches (factors, agents, and so on) in numerous cities as Kindleberger (1993) has described for financial houses in the fifteenth and sixteenth centuries as previously noted in Chapter 2. Thus Braudel's focus on one dominant city provides a misleading impression of the role of cities in the transition to the modern world-system. His position might be more appropriate for situations with very powerful guardian structures such as the Roman Empire, Ming China and the Caliphate, which housed the huge cities of Rome, Peking and Baghdad respectively at the centre of their world-economies. But since post-Rome Western Europe never experienced such a strong guardian processes, it is commercial networks that have been able to dominate inter-city relations. This is important because early European city networks are a sign of things to come in the modern world-system, and will influence how we conceive of modern inter-city relations.

MODERN HEGEMONIES

Finally we reach the modern world-system. Because it is not a world-empire it will have developed in ways different from Normal History. Thus my concern is how this geohistorical system has reproduced itself over the last half-millennium. Because it is a world-economy, this reproduction is expected to take the form of economic cycles; these are identified across a wide range of time spans (Goldstein 1988) and I focus on the longest, which are termed hegemonic cycles. Three such cycles are identified and these describe the commercial rise and fall of the Dutch, the British and the US consecutively. Gleaning from a variety of sources (including Goldstein (1988) and Chase-Dunn (1989)), the typical timings for these cycles would appear to be 1570 to 1740 for the Dutch cycle, 1740 to 1897 for the British cycle, and 1897 to the present for the US cycle.

But the new *modus operandi* does not eliminate the influence of guardians; they operate largely through a competitive inter-state system that brings contingency into the reproduction process. Thus each hegemonic cycle is associated with a protracted 'world war', so-named because the survival of the modern world-system is at stake. These are the Thirty Years War (1618–1648), in which the Dutch triumph over the Hapsburg 'empire', the Revolutionary and Napoleonic Wars (1792–1815), when the British see off the French Empire, and the twentieth century World Wars I and II (1918–1945), which see the US defeat the German Empire and then curtail the 'thousand-year Reich' to just a decade. In each case the hegemonic state and its allies prevent political conversion to world-empire, which would have terminated the modern world-system. The purpose of this second substantive section of the chapter is to put meat on the bones of this argument using my conceptual toolkit. This means foregrounding cities in the genesis of hegemonies, but before this is carried through, the development of the modern hegemonies thesis will be described to provide the context for my addition of cities.

From Braudel's World-cities to Wallerstein's Hegemonic States

Braudel's (1984, pp. 32, 34) full sequence of dominant cities is Venice, Antwerp, Genoa, Amsterdam, London and New York, as the European world-economy morphs into a global-scale world-economy. Braudel's study finishes in the eighteenth century, and so London makes an appearance but not New York. However Arrighi (1994) does extend Braudel's model to the present and in the process refines and modifies it. He devises a model of systematic cycles of accumulation divided into two phases: first, material expansion based upon expanding commodity capital, and second, financial rebirth through increasing flexible money capital. The emphasis is on the shift to financial expansion, wherein the liquidity marks both the end of one cycle of one fixed specialist commodity investment and the beginning of another. He identifies four such cycles:

> a Genoese cycle, from the fifteenth century to the early seventeenth centuries; a Dutch cycle, from the late sixteenth through most of the eighteenth century; a British cycle, from the latter half of the eighteenth century through the early twentieth century; and a US cycle, which began in the late nineteenth century and has continued into the current phase of financial expansion. (Arrighi 1994, p. 6)

There are several things to note about this model. First, it diverges from Braudel through assimilating both Venice's and Antwerp's periods of dominance into Genoa's cycle. Thus this one cycle covers most of the transition period to the modern world-system. Second, the cycles overlap reflecting both ends and beginnings. Third, although keeping with the sequence of Amsterdam, London and New York as leading financial centres, the cycles are named for states, not cities, after the first cycle.

In this nomenclature for his final three cycles, Arrighi follows Wallerstein's (1984) terminology for modern hegemonies. This derives from Arrighi's (1990) initial study in which 'the three hegemonies (Dutch, British, US) of historical capitalism' are his subject matter in a framework very similar to that of Wallerstein. Subsequently he has characterized this work as a 'first genealogy' of capitalist development; his consequent four cycles model constitutes an alternative 'closely related but distinct' genealogy (Arrighi 1994, p. 84). In fact, nearly all world-system analyses continue to use the Dutch–British–US three hegemonies model. Given my focus on just the modern world-system in this section I will follow this practice here. However, we should note now that the choice of this model has generally involved following Wallerstein (1984) in foregrounding a state-based interpretation of hegemony.

Wallerstein (1984, pp. 38–9) defines hegemony as follows:

> Hegemony in the inter-state system refers to that situation in which the ongoing rivalry between the so-called 'great powers' is so unbalanced that one power is truly *primus inter pares*; that is, one power can largely impose its rules and wishes (at the very least by effective veto power) in the economic, political, military, diplomatic, and cultural arenas. The material base of such power lies in the ability of enterprises domiciled in that power to operate more efficiently in all three major economic arenas – agro-industrial production, commerce and finance.

Note that there are two main dimensions to Wallerstein's model, a materialist argument and a geopolitical argument. Although closely entwined they represent two different processes, one commercial, the other guardian.

In the materialist part of the model there is a specific sequence through which a state achieves its hegemonic position. The state initially achieves efficiencies in production so that it has an economic edge in the world market that may extend into rival states' home markets. From this advantage it is able to build its prowess in commerce, to become the leading trader in the world. The resulting accumulation of capital leads the state to become the financial centre of the world-economy. When the state is economically dominant in all three spheres, it has reached the position of hegemony (Wallerstein 1984, pp. 39–40). For the three instances of hegemony, Wallerstein dates these at 1620–72 for the Dutch, 1815–73 for the British and 1945–67 for the US. After this the hegemonic state loses its prowess in reverse order: other states 'catch up' first in production, then in commerce, and finally in finance (p. 40). The latter is represented by the continuing importance of Amsterdam as a financial centre in the eighteenth century, London in the late nineteenth and early twentieth centuries, and New York in the late twentieth century – this is where the model links to Arrighi's (1994) systematic cycles of accumulation. The whole process from the beginning of outstanding production efficiencies through to the demise of financial leadership constitutes the hegemonic cycle. Thus there is a rise phase before hegemony and a fall phase after hegemony. Given that the whole cycle is referred to as hegemonic, and that the middle phase, when all three relative efficiencies are in place, is also called hegemony, the latter 'special time' is sometimes termed 'high hegemony'.

In the geopolitical part of the model it is not military prowess that is central; rather the hegemonic state operates more by consensus, but with coercive powers latent and sometimes operational. The latter is crucial when the hegemonic state performs its prime geopolitical task: to prevent a powerful militaristic state conquering the modern world-system and converting it into a world-empire. The three 'world wars' all take a similar geopolitical structure: the hegemonic state is a sea or sea/air power combating a largely land-based power. Given this similarity across hegemonic states, a sequence has appeared whereby the erstwhile hegemonic state allies with the new hegemonic state to defeat the land threat: the Dutch ally with Britain against France and the British ally with the US against Germany. The outcome of the world wars has been a restructuring of the inter-state system through the Treaty of Westphalia, the Concert of Europe and the United Nations (with Bretton Woods) respectively, in each case reaffirming the *modus operandi*. But these are all wars of such a scale – lasting about three decades – that the wealth of most warring countries shrinks alarmingly – except for the winner. Only the hegemonic state has a 'good war', emerging stronger than at the start. This political victory cements growing economic prowess, allowing the hegemonic state to invent a new form of modernity in its own image. Thus instead of conversion to world-empire, the modern world-system is renewed in hegemonic world restructuring. With much less need for coercion, the process works through emulation, a general copying of the formula of success that the hegemonic state presents (Taylor 1996b). Thus the reaction to the Dutch 'economic miracle' was for rival states to adopt mercantilism; copying the British is called industrialization; and the Americans promoted consumerism. This combination of guardian and commercial success has meant that hegemonic cycles are generators of new forms of modernity: successively mercantile modernity, industrial modernity, and consumer modernity (Taylor 1996b; 1999a).

From the perspective of this book the key point of the story so far is that states are the units for defining hegemony. To be sure the guardian and commercial processes are closely entwined, with the latter creating the material foundation for the former – a *modus operandi* – but the overall process is firmly placed as a matter of the inter-state system: in both of Wallerstein's (1983; 2004) general texts hegemony is located in their respective 'politics' chapters. But states are territorial units and it was not the whole territories that were the focus of emulations in the restructurings of modernity. Mercantilism was based upon commercial activities in Holland, not the economic backwaters of the eastern and northern provinces; industrialization was based upon northern Britain, not the clearance lands of the Scottish Highlands and Ireland; and consumerism grew out of the US North (plus California) and certainly not from the South. In fact all the counter-regions listed above were distinctively 'non-hegemonic' despite their locations within the United Provinces, the United Kingdom and the United States. This suggests we should prioritize the commercial rather than the guardian side of hegemony.

Identifying Explosive City Growth in the Modern World-system

Focusing on the commercial side of hegemony immediately problematizes the use of states as the prime way of analysing modern hegemony. In my toolbox economic success is the product of city economies and therefore the massive economic growth that hegemonic cycles represent must be related to cities. Elementary geohistorical knowledge tells us that it was the dynamism of city-rich regions – Holland, northern Britain, and US North/California – that generated the commercial edge at the heart of hegemony. These are groups of cities that experienced simultaneous rapid economic spurts. As described in Chapter 2, Jacobs (1969) ascribes immense economic power to cities in the form of 'explosive city growths'. In this section I report on a research project that has attempted to find such city spurts through the life of the modern world-system – for specific details see Taylor et al. (2010a).

Data collection included both quantitative measurement and qualitative assessments as follows.

Supplementing Chandler's data with the de Vries (1984) city population database, populations of cities were collected from 1500 to 1950, at 50-year intervals. Tracing the expansion of the modern world-system, the study included European and European settler cities from the beginning and throughout, Russian and Indian cities were added from 1750, and Chinese and Japanese cities after 1850.

Rosters of cities for each century were selected using a simple formula to produce equivalent lists; cities qualified if they had 10 per cent of the average population of the top three ranked cities. For these city rosters population change was computed for every 50-year period and annualized. One hundred and seventy-five cases of cities with a population growth of over 1 per cent per annum were identified as demographic explosive growths from 1500 to 1950. These were each scrutinized individually, sometimes using secondary sources such as city history texts, to allocate the demographic growth to either political or economic categories in terms of the dominant cause of the explosive demographic growth. Of course, this proved difficult in several cases, and therefore a mixed category was instituted for cities that experienced approximately equal economic and political boosts.

Because the link between demographic growth and economic growth is broken in the mid-twentieth century (Castells 1978), I take this analysis only up to 1950. The question of demographic size of recent and current cities is dealt with in the next chapter.

It is, of course, the economic category that fits Jacobs' explosive city growth process. However since the mixed category includes important economic change this will be added to the list of economic spurts in subsequent discussion: of the 175 demographic bursts there are 150 with important economic content.

A summary of the results of the categorization is shown in Table 6.3. Generally these findings appear credible. Looking at the totals first, the slowdown in the seventeenth century is clearly marked and so is the urban–industrial explosion of the nineteenth century. Concentrating on the smallest list in the table, for 1650 to 1700, this will be used to help clarify the research process. In this half-century there was only one economic case of explosive city growth – the rise of the Dutch port of Rotterdam; one mixed case – Seville, where the Spanish state chose to land its South American silver; and four political cases – Berlin, Copenhagen, Dublin and Vienna, all examples of cities benefitting from new state centralization. Note that it is these political processes that dominate city growth in this economically trying time (Europe's crisis of the seventeenth century); this is the only time the political category is largest in Table 6.3. After 1800 the political category becomes proportionally very small, the economic dominates, but the mixed category also grows substantially. The latter reflects the maturing of the political economy, wherein most capital cities are now also important commercial centres.

The inventory of all 150 economic spurts from Table 6.3 is given in Table 6.4. City spurts by time period are listed in rank order by size of change. The top row of cities, therefore, is the sequence of largest explosive

Table 6.3   Distribution of types of large demographic spurts, 1500–1950

Type	1500–50	1550–1600	1600–50	1650–1700	1700–50	1750–1800	1800–50	1850–1900	1900–50
Economic	9	7	6	1	6	6	17	23	21
Mixed	3	4	2	1	1	0	9	16	18
Political	1	3	2	4	5	5	3	1	1
Total	**13**	**14**	**10**	**6**	**12**	**11**	**29**	**40**	**40**

city growths in the modern world-system: from Lisbon to Los Angeles via London, Amsterdam, Seville, Liverpool, Manchester, New York and Chicago. These are all reasonably predictable, except perhaps for two: Seville in the second half of the seventeenth century, the receiving port for 'Spanish' silver, and 'Shakespeare's London' a century earlier, an important city spurt identified originally by Jacobs (1969, pp.154–6).

The geography of the economic spurts shows two types of city. First, explosive city growths are found in world-regional concentrations initially in Western Europe, then North America. Such concentrations of dynamic cities indicate the existence of core-making processes. Second, beyond this core zone there is a scatter of economic spurts within more isolated cities. These 'islands' of core-making processes within predominantly peripheral regions define where the semi-periphery exists (Taylor 2005). Examples are Moscow/Russia in 1750–1800, New York/US in 1800–1850, Buenos Aires/Argentina in 1850–1900, and Shanghai/China in 1900–1950. The periphery is marked by the absence of economic spurts as typified by sub-Saharan Africa, whose cities do not feature in Tables 6.3 and 6.4.

There is a lot of detail in Table 6.4 and I will initially focus on the first and last time periods in this initial perusal. At the beginning of the modern world-system, we see the remnants of Braudel's (1984) 'two poles' of medieval European economic development. Already the formerly dominant southern pole of northern Italy is in decline, represented by just three cities, whereas the northern pole of the (greater) Low Countries is represented by four cities led by Antwerp. However this pole is rather dispersed within a Hamburg–London–Rouen triangle. The important change, however, are two fresh areas of important growth, two German centres, and Iberia housing the top two explosive city growths based upon new Atlantic trade. This mixture of old and new explosive city growths was to herald in a new world, the modern world-system.

A quick perusal of the other columns in Table 6.4 will reveal the fact that the cities in Wallerstein's hegemonic states are well represented. The

Table 6.4 *Inventory of explosive city growths in the modern world-system, 1500–1950*

1500–1550	1550–1600	1600–1650	1650–1700	1700–1750	1750–1800	1800–1850	1850–1900	1900–1950
Lisbon	London	Amsterdam	Seville	Liverpool	Manchester	New York	Chicago	Los Angeles
Seville	Amsterdam	Leiden	Rotterdam	Birmingham	Liverpool	Baltimore	Buenos Aires	Houston
Augsburg	Haarlem	Rotterdam		Cadiz	Glasgow	Philadelphia	Leipzig	Dallas
Antwerp	Leiden	London		Cork	Birmingham	Boston	Pittsburgh	Hong Kong
Magdeburg	Bordeaux	Paris		Manchester	Barcelona	Liverpool	New York	Detroit
Amsterdam	Cuenca	Lyon		Glasgow	Moscow	Manchester	Berlin	São Paulo
Hamburg	Vicenza	Hamburg		Bristol		Birmingham	Newcastle	Shanghai
London	Milan	Marseille				Glasgow	Dresden	Seoul
Lecce	Torino					Bombay	Boston	Seattle
Rouen	Paris					Rio de Janeiro	Budapest	Buenos Aires
Venice	Jerez					Brussels	Hamburg	Atlanta
Catania						Newcastle	Rio de Janeiro	Toronto
						Budapest	Warsaw	Tokyo
						Madras	Munich	Washington
						London	Birmingham	Moscow
						Kolkata	Prague	San Francisco
						Paris	Vienna	Santiago
						Munich	Tientsin	Nagoya
						Buenos Aires	Manchester	Singapore
						Shanghai	Copenhagen	Montréal
						Leipzig	Shanghai	Rome

Table 6.4 (continued)

1500–1550	1550–1600	1600–1650	1650–1700	1700–1750	1750–1800	1800–1850	1850–1900	1900–1950
						Lyon	Philadelphia	Osaka
						Hamburg	Barcelona	Sydney
						Dresden	Osaka	New York
						Prague	Baltimore	Milan
						Moscow	Moscow	Madrid
							Glasgow	Melbourne
							St Petersburg	Minneapolis
							London	Lisbon
							Milan	Stuttgart
							Brussels	Naples
							Kolkata	Boston
							Paris	Philadelphia
							Lyon	Beijing
							Cairo	Paris
							Amsterdam	Hamburg
							Liverpool	Birmingham
							Tokyo	Munich
							Madras	Manchester

remainder of this analysis of explosive city growths in the modern world-system will be interpreted through the hegemonic cycle framework.

Hegemonic Cycles as Extraordinary City-led Change

In Wallerstein's (1984) world-systems analysis, hegemonic states are a sort of 'core within the core'; it is where the most creative 'high tech, high wage' economic processes emanate to generate such a strong economic situation that cultural and political dominance follows as other countries try to emulate the hegemon's conspicuous success (Taylor 1996b). From the perspective of this book this situation cries out 'CITIES'. Although modern hegemony literature is explicit on defining the times of high hegemony, it is not so sure when it comes to temporal bounding of the cycles themselves. The study of explosive city growths suggests a different patterning of hegemonic cycles. Theoretically hitching the creativity that generates and sustains high hegemony to Jacobs' explosive city growths, this new look at the cycles is grounded in the commercial dimension of hegemony. Even in our cursory examination at Table 6.4, to search out Dutch, British and US cities, suggests there are three cycles of equal length, two centuries each, with the British and American cycles sharing the nineteenth century. The sheer weight of American city spurts in the nineteenth century means that the economic antecedents of US high hegemony need to be rethought and recognized earlier. Thus the three cycles can now be specified as a separate Dutch cycle in the fifteenth and sixteenth centuries, a British cycle in the eighteenth and nineteenth centuries overlapping with an American cycle in the nineteenth and twentieth centuries. Treatment of each double century separately will confirm this new interpretation.

In Table 6.5 part of Table 6.4 is reproduced highlighting Dutch cities in Dutch hegemony. Four Dutch cities are featured that experienced eight examples of explosive city growth between them. Led by Amsterdam with three such spurts, this table confirms that the Dutch Republic was not simply 'Amsterdam's city-state' as has been suggested, but was a multi-nodal city-region of multiple vibrant cities (Taylor 2005). Starting with Amsterdam's first explosive city growth, before the creation of the Dutch Republic, there are three explosive city growths that build up Dutch hegemony (Amsterdam, Haarlem and Leiden), three such spurts that continue during high hegemony (Amsterdam, Leiden and Rotterdam) with only the latter city continuing with a final Dutch city spurt in the downside of the cycle. During this period the Dutch went largely without a serious economic rival; France came the closest with four cities (Bordeaux, Paris, Lyon and Marseille) and five spurts, but all are smaller than the Dutch city growths.

Table 6.5   Dutch cities in the Dutch hegemonic cycle

1500–1550	1550–1600	1600–1650	1650–1700
Lisbon	London	**AMSTERDAM**	Seville
Seville	**AMSTERDAM**	**LEIDEN**	**ROTTERDAM**
Augsburg	**HAARLEM**	**ROTTERDAM**	
Antwerp	**LEIDEN**	London	
Magdeburg	Bordeaux	Paris	
AMSTERDAM	Cuenca	Lyon	
Hamburg	Vicenza	Hamburg	
London	Milan	Marseille	
Lecce	Torino		
Rouen	Paris		
Venice	Jerez		
Catania			

Note: Dutch cities are emphasized.

Source: Taylor et al. (2010a: Table 4).

In Table 6.6 part of Table 6.4 is reproduced, highlighting British cities in British hegemony. In this case seven British cities are featured with 21 explosive city growths between them. The key feature is the dominance of the four great cities of northern Britain: Birmingham, Glasgow, Liverpool and Manchester. These four cities dominate the eighteenth century with eight of the 13 economic spurts recorded plus an additional spurt from Bristol. The big four cities continue with explosive growth in both nineteenth-century periods, although gradually falling down the ranks. Their clustered position just below four US cities in 1800–1850 reflects the fact that the US cities were starting from a lower population base, that is to say, Liverpool, Manchester, Birmingham and Glasgow still dominated the world-economy. In both nineteenth-century lists they are joined by Newcastle and London. London was conspicuous by its absence among eighteenth-century city spurts and, although featuring in the nineteenth century, its economic spurts are lowly ranked. Newcastle is somewhat like Rotterdam in the Dutch cycle: it arrives late and has its largest spurt at the end of the hegemonic cycle. France is usually seen as Britain's main rival during its hegemony but its economic competition was severely weak: in Table 6.6 only two French cities are featured, Paris and Lyon, both with lowly ranked spurts in both nineteenth-century time periods. This suggests the French were less of an economic rival to the British than they were to the Dutch in the previous cycle.

In Table 6.7 part of Table 6.4 is reproduced, highlighting American cities in American hegemony. In this case, 15 US cities are featured with 25

Table 6.6   British cities in the British hegemonic cycle

1700–1750	*1750–1800*	*1800–1850*	*1850–1900*
LIVERPOOL	**MANCHESTER**	New York	Chicago
BIRMINGHAM	**LIVERPOOL**	Baltimore	Buenos Aires
Cadiz	**GLASGOW**	Philadelphia	Leipzig
Cork	**BIRMINGHAM**	Boston	Pittsburgh
MANCHESTER	Barcelona	**LIVERPOOL**	New York
GLASGOW	Moscow	**MANCHESTER**	Berlin
BRISTOL		**BIRMINGHAM**	**NEWCASTLE**
		GLASGOW	Dresden
		Bombay	Boston
		Rio de Janeiro	Budapest
		Brussels	Hamburg
		NEWCASTLE	Rio de Janeiro
		Budapest	Warsaw
		Madras	Munich
		LONDON	**BIRMINGHAM**
		Kolkata	Prague
		Paris	Vienna
		Munich	Tientsin
		Buenos Aires	**MANCHESTER**
		Leipzig	Copenhagen
		Lyon	Shanghai
		Hamburg	Philadelphia
		Dresden	Barcelona
		Prague	Osaka
		Moscow	Baltimore
			Moscow
			GLASGOW
			St Petersburg
			LONDON
			Milan
			Brussels
			Kolkata
			Paris
			Lyon
			Cairo
			Amsterdam
			LIVERPOOL
			Tokyo
			Madras

Note: British cities are emphasized.

Source: Taylor et al. (2010a: Table 5).

Table 6.7   American cities in the American hegemonic cycle

1800–1850	1850–1900	1900–1950	1970–2005
NEW YORK	**CHICAGO**	**LOS ANGELES**	Beijing
BALTIMORE	Buenos Aires	**HOUSTON**	Shanghai
PHILADELPHIA	Leipzig	**DALLAS**	**WASHINGTON**
BOSTON	**PITTSBURGH**	Hong Kong	Osaka
Liverpool	**NEW YORK**	**DETROIT**	Seoul
Manchester	Berlin	São Paulo	Singapore
Birmingham	Newcastle	Shanghai	Budapest
Glasgow	Dresden	Seoul	Madrid
Bombay	**BOSTON**	**SEATTLE**	Vienna
Rio de Janeiro	Budapest	Buenos Aires	Berlin
Brussels	Hamburg	**ATLANTA**	Tokyo
Newcastle	Rio de Janeiro	Toronto	Hamburg
Budapest	Warsaw	Tokyo	Moscow
Madras	Munich	**WASHINGTON**	Stockholm
London	Birmingham	Moscow	**LOS ANGELES**
Kolkata	Prague	**SAN FRANCISCO**	Hong Kong
Paris	Vienna	Santiago	Milan
Munich	Tientsin	Nagoya	Istanbul
Buenos Aires	Manchester	Singapore	Buenos Aires
Shanghai	Copenhagen	Montréal	**MIAMI**
Leipzig	Shanghai	Rome	Santiago
Lyon	**PHILADELPHIA**	Osaka	Munich
Hamburg	Barcelona	Sydney	São Paulo
Dresden	Osaka	**NEW YORK**	Bangkok
Prague	**BALTIMORE**	Milan	Toronto
Moscow	Moscow	Madrid	Frankfurt
	Glasgow	Melbourne	Amsterdam
	St Petersburg	Minneapolis	**CHICAGO**
	London	Lisbon	Zurich
	Milan	Stuttgart	Brussels
	Brussels	Naples	London
	Kolkata	**BOSTON**	Copenhagen
	Paris	**PHILADELPHIA**	Paris
	Lyon	Beijing	Geneva
	Cairo	Paris	Rome
	Amsterdam	Hamburg	
	Liverpool	Birmingham	
	Tokyo	Munich	
	Madras	Manchester	

Note: US cities are emphasized.

Source: Taylor et al. (2010a: Table 6).

explosive city growths between them. The surprise is the top four ranking in 1800–1850 for the leading east coast cities: New York, Baltimore, Philadelphia and Boston. These cities continue to feature in the second half of the nineteenth century, albeit with much lower rankings, but now Chicago, ranked first, and Pittsburgh, ranked fourth, show important inland explosive city growths. US dominance of spurts is greatest in the first half of the twentieth century, with four of the top five places: explosive city growth has now reached the Pacific coast with Los Angeles ranked first, two southern cities ranked second and third, Houston and Dallas, with another inland industrial centre, Detroit, ranked fifth. In addition, San Francisco and Seattle add to the Pacific coast representation and Atlanta to southern representation. Washington, DC also features for the first time and New York, Boston and Philadelphia, but not Baltimore, continue with economic spurts in the new century. In this hegemonic cycle the main rival is very clear: Germany has seven cities with 16 episodes of explosive city growth. The main challenge was in the second half of the nineteenth century, when there were five German cities near the top of the economic spurts: Leipzig (ranked third), Berlin (sixth), Dresden (eighth), Hamburg (eleventh) and Munich (fourteenth).

In comparing these three hegemonies two simple empirical points can be made. First, although the US features most cities in its hegemonic cycle, this is largely a result of the overall growth of the modern world-system; therefore, despite having least explosive city growths, it is Dutch cities that most dominate their hegemonic cycle. This result argues against the notion that the relative strength of economic hegemony is increasing as the world-economy grows. Second, mention must be made again of the nineteenth-century overlap of the British and American cycles; this is a unique feature of this city-centric analysis and needs to be taken seriously by those who prefer neat sequential cycles. This result argues against both the idea of simple sequential cycles and the notion that the cycles are becoming shorter as the world-economy grows.

Much more profound, because of its theoretical importance, is the fact that in all three hegemonic cycles, cases of explosive growth in leading cities are weighted towards the beginning of each cycle and trail off towards the end of the cycle. Broadly stated, there are two theoretical positions that can be held on how the economic growth of cities relates to hegemonic status. For the majority of world-systems analysis that neglects cities and focuses on states, cities merely reflect the hegemonic status of their state so that their economic growth is an outcome of state hegemony. In this case explosive growths should be relatively even in the distribution over the cycle, with perhaps a concentration during high hegemony. From a city-centric view, cities are the engines of economic growth, and therefore they are where hegemony is created. This is the position taken here: not mere outcomes, cities are the makers of hegemony. For this position, explosive economic spurts should be front-loaded on the cycle in order to get the hegemony started. This is exactly what we have found. Hence we have very strong empirical evidence for the crucial importance of dynamic cities for creating hegemony, and therefore for the whole development and mainte-nance of the modern world-system.

Where does the guardian side of hegemony fit into this new concep-tualization of hegemonic cycles? There are three features that suggest Wallerstein's emphasis on the state is seriously mistaken. First, there is the very basic point that for the first hegemonic cycle depicted in Table 6.5, Amsterdam begins her precipitous growth in 1500–1550, decades before the Dutch rebellion began, and the three spurts recorded for 1550–1600 occur when the state has been established only towards the end of the 50-year period. Thus fully half the explosive city spurts that create the Dutch hegemonic cycle actually occur largely before the actual development of the Dutch state. Second, in all three cases, capital cities were not major players in the economic hegemonic processes. For the Dutch Republic, as noted previously, The Hague was specifically chosen as the capital because of its smallness and weakness. In terms of importance, the opposite is the case for London, prior to British hegemony it was a major European city and during the whole cycle it remained by far the largest British city. And yet it was not implicated in the explosive city growths that created British hegemony. And, of course, Washington, DC has been a relatively minor city in the US for most of its history, hence like London it is not at all implicated in its state's rise to economic hegemony. Third, thinking in terms of state territoriality, there were parts of each of Wallerstein's hege-monic states that seem anything but hegemonic in nature. This has been noted earlier but it worth repeating. Living in Deventer in 1650, or Galway in 1850, or Montgomery in 1950, would certainly not be experienced as being at the cutting-edge of the most high-tech high wage economy of the times.

However, there is a guardian role in hegemony-making, but it is not about economic process in any direct sense. States are important in the modern world-system; they facilitate commercial expansion through their legal frameworks and infrastructural support. And, of course, they have the important defence function, protection at a territorial scale. Like all other states, the Dutch, British and US states did these things during their hegemony but they had an additional contribution to the defence func-tion; a special role at a trans-territorial scale. As reported above, under the special circumstances of hegemony, the hegemonic state forges a coalition to prevent a militaristic rival from destroying the world-economy. Success in defeating this powerful political rival is largely down to the accumulated wealth of the state that houses the dynamic cities that created the hegemony. This is the political face of the hegemonic network of cities in relating to the inter-state system. Here we have Wallerstein's (1984) 'world wars' politics of the hegemonic state interwoven with the cities. Thus we can retain the concept of hegemonic state as long as its special nature is focused on inter-state relations. This revision of the hegemonic model can now be seen as the two faces of modernity expressed in the modern world-system's hegemonic cycles as both commercial and guardian successes.

In the remainder of this second section I consider each of the hegemonic cycles in turn. By providing more detail, some of the limitations of the broad system-wide study reported above will be assuaged. For instance, only the largest cities were included for pragmatic, manageable reasons in the system-wide study. The result is that although we have identified 27 cities having 46 explosive city growths within the three hegemonic cycles, this will not constitute the total economic spurts that created and sustained hegemonic positions. The hegemonic process cannot be limited to just a few large cities, as noted previously it occurs in economic regions, and these have many more economically vibrant cities than the 27 included in Tables 6.5, 6.6 and 6.7. Furthermore it should be recognized that important large cities may be missing from these tables because of the methodology employed. Early data sources led to use of specific 50-year intervals for measuring city growth and this approach can lead to some successful cities being overlooked. For instance, a city with rapid growth between, say, 1880 and 1820 may not have its demographic spurt recorded since its population gain is divided between two recording periods.

We will overcome these problems by looking at new data for each hegemonic cycle; we shall look at demographic change in a manner customised for each case. For Dutch hegemony, the focus is on the geographical distribution of city growths through the period of their rebellion (before and including high hegemony). For British hegemony, a very detailed geography of high urban growth patterns at census ten-year intervals is used to illustrate concentrated regional patterns. For US hegemony, the changing geography of cities creating the hegemony is described, again at ten-year census intervals. Each case shows the importance of geography to hegemonic creation.

In addition, the understanding of hegemonic cycles will be taken forward in a new direction. Hegemony denotes massive economic expansion, which creates new demand for movement. This putative denser space of flows requires more and better infrastructure to facilitate the myriad movements being newly generated. And each of our hegemonic cases has responded with original solutions to its transport problems. In a final section innovative infrastructural networks will be described for each hegemonic cycle.

The Cities of Dutch Hegemony

In Table 6.5 the identification of Amsterdam for the period 1500–1550 is a little misleading, to the degree that it implies that Amsterdam dominated the northern Netherlands in the first half of the sixteenth century. In 1500 there were several Dutch cities about the same size as Amsterdam and all were much smaller than the great cities of the southern Netherlands: Antwerp, Brussels, Ghent and Bruges. Israel's (1995, p. 116) interpretation of this is fascinating:

> This absence of a real metropolis before the Revolt, and the evenness of distribution of urban population, especially in Holland, was a circumstance of overriding importance for the subsequent development of Dutch politics and society. For it reflected the wide dispersal of wealth and economic assets inherent in the bulk carrying trade, river traffic, and herring fishery, and the dependence of main centres on a large number of outports and subsidiary depots.

Israel specifically notes the political and social effects but a key point is that this urbanization structure is highly conducive for Jacobs' (1969) economic expansion process as described in Chapter 2. Although at this time wealth was based on bulk trades from the Baltic (grains, lumber, navy stores) rather than the 'rich trades' (textiles, spices, sugar, metals), this did stimulate an early innovative shipping industry from building to ship equipment and stores (p. 117). They produced an immense seafaring shipping fleet of some 1800 ships in Holland by the 1560s – this can be compared to Venice's 300 ships at its peak in 1450 (p. 117). And the Holland fleet was very distinctive:

> Lacking 'rich trades', Dutch shipbuilders constructed cheap vessels designed to carry maximum cargo at low cost, with simple designs, a minimum of rigging, no armaments, and small crews . . . Building for bulk freightage culminated in the famous *fluit*, a design which originated at Hoorn in the 1590s. (Israel 1995, p. 118)

The result was a unique situation at this time of a huge merchant fleet 'owned in numerous shares, thirty-second and sixty-fourth parts' and therefore 'without any significant concentration of capital' (p. 118).

This appears to be a collection of cities ripe for economic expansion. In the meantime the Dutch Revolt against their Hapsburg overlord began in the late 1560s throughout the Low Countries, but after 1579 it became converted into a Spanish south versus a rebel north contest. In the last decade of the century the Dutch cities were able to break into the 'rich trades' in the East Indies leading an 'economic "miracle"'; Israel (1995, p. 328) actually refers to it as 'the explosive growth of the cities of the Dutch maritime zone'. The latter is, of course, 'pure' Jacobs' language. Similarly, Braudel (1984, p. 180) called it 'a high-voltage urban economy', and emphasized the city networking for even though Dutch cities were:

> quarrelsome and jealous, they were nevertheless subject to the law of the beehive, which obliged them to combine their efforts and cooperate in commercial and industrial activity. Together they formed a power bloc. (p. 180)

Thus even though, as we have seen, Braudel's model is extremely hierarchical, when confronted with the empirical evidence of this case study he finds a complex regional division of labour in a city network process. Thus was Dutch hegemony created.

But this vibrant city network did not constitute the whole of the United Provinces. This was noted previously, and now we can show the details covering the whole 80 years of war with Hapsburg Spain that only concluded at Westphalia in 1648. The spatial structure of the new state consisted of the maritime strip that was the hegemonic core area, largely Holland plus Zeeland; enclosed by defensive buffers in the east (Friesland, Groningen, Overijsseland) and south (Utrecht, Gelderland and the Generality lands (captured from the Spanish Netherlands)). The result was that:

> The rapid growth in the maritime provinces . . . turned the Republic into a land with two economies, that of the west expanding, dynamic, and prosperous, and that of the inland provinces largely stagnant and much poorer. (Israel 1995, p. 331)

This is very clearly illustrated in Table 6.8, which shows which cities did well and which did not through the whole period of the war. These dates are specially chosen and do not correspond to the 50-year intervals used earlier, but we can note that, using the rules applied in the system-wide study, the growth in ten of the 21 cities listed would have qualified as demographic spurts, including all but one in Holland and Zeeland. This sizeable number represents the city network that created Dutch hegemony. Clearly the buffer cities fared much worse and five actually lost population through the establishment of the Dutch Republic. This was recognized by contemporaries; guardian rulers in Groningen, Kampen, Utrecht and Zutphen all provided incentives for migrants to settle in their cities, but to no avail (p. 331). What growth did occur was guardian-produced but consisted of 'expansion of fixed garrisons, military construction, and

Table 6.8   *Growth of United Provinces cities during the 80-year rebellion (1570/52–1647)*

City	Propor'l growth	Annual % growth	Province	Region
Amsterdam	3.67	4.76	Holland	Hegemonic core
Rotterdam	3.29	4.27	Holland	Hegemonic core
Leiden	3.00	3.90	Holland	Hegemonic core
The Hague	2.60	3.38	Holland	Hegemonic core
Middelburg	2.00	2.60	Zeeland	Hegemonic core
Haarlem	1.81	2.35	Holland	Hegemonic core
Enkhuizen	1.25	1.62	Holland	Hegemonic core
Dordrecht	1.00	1.30	Holland	Hegemonic core
Hoorn	1.00	1.30	Holland	Hegemonic core
Leeuwarden	0.88	1.17	Friesland	Eastern buffer
Gouda	0.67	0.87	Holland	Hegemonic core
Delft	0.50	0.65	Holland	Hegemonic core
Utrecht	0.20	0.27	Utrecht	Southern buffer
Zutphen	0.17	0.22	Gelderland	Eastern buffer
Groningen	0.00	0.00	Friesland	Eastern buffer
Nijmegen	0.00	0.00	Gelderland	Eastern buffer
Maastricht	−0.06	−0.08	Generality	Southern buffer
s-Hertogenosch	−0.12	−0.16	Generality	Southern buffer
Zwolle	−0.18	−0.24	Overijssel	Eastern buffer
Kampen	−0.30	−0.40	Overijssel	Eastern buffer
Deventer	−0.36	−0.48	Overijssel	Eastern buffer

Source: Derived from Israel (1995: Tables 12 and 14).

provisioning, rather than commerce and industry' (p. 332). In other words the Dutch Republic consisted of two distinctive worlds of work: a commercial dynamic world at the centre and a guardian stagnant world in the state periphery.

The Cities of British Hegemony

The British 'industrial revolution' is one of the most researched topics in historical scholarship. Whatever the debates, there is general acceptance that this provided Britain with a decisive economic advantage based upon new innovation and entrepreneurship. This is the basis of the commercial side of Britain's hegemonic cycle. The geography of this revolution is also well known and researched; the economic expansion occurred in neither the traditional economic core of Britain, London and the southeast, nor in the periphery of Britain in western and southern Ireland, northern Scotland, and central Wales. Instead the new industrialization developed in-between, what I have termed northern Britain (but not too northern!). In Table 6.6 this is represented by the initial four explosive growth cities, Birmingham, Glasgow, Liverpool and Manchester; the land between Birmingham in the south and Glasgow in the north encompasses almost all the major sites of the industrial revolution.

Of course, these four cities are only the tip of the iceberg for the industrial urbanization that occurred in Britain. Missing from Table 6.6 are such important industrial cities as Leeds, Bradford, Sheffield, Nottingham, Stoke, Bolton, Middlesbrough, Dundee, Cardiff, Rochdale, Leicester, Blackburn, Preston, Derby, Barnsley . . . I could go on and on. The point is that this case of hegemonic expansion represents a new and unprecedented level of urbanization. The Dutch had numerous expanding cities; Britain had numerous expanding industrial regions. These were multi-urban industrial districts that Alfred Marshall famously described as having an 'atmosphere' conducive to economic growth. With their dense populations including both the entrepreneurs with the knowledge and the workers with the skills, it is as if critical externalities (free because outside the market) 'are in the air'. Therefore in going beyond the few cities in Table 6.6 I am going to explore briefly Marshall's industrial districts through Jacobs' (1984) concept of city-region.

As described in Chapter 2, Jacobs (1984, p. 45) describes 'cities' own regions' in the following terms: 'In the hinterlands of some cities – beginning just beyond their suburbs – rural, industrial and commercial work places are all mixed up together.' Unlike Marshall she starts with the city, which creates the vibrant economic region. Basically she argues that the economic advantages of cities are diffused to their surrounding area, which can become an industrial district. But she emphasizes market, jobs, capital, transplants, and technology all being available *together* to generate economic expansion beyond the city. Not all cities generate city-regions, however; examples of British cities that she says have not created their own regions are Liverpool and Glasgow (p. 46). But we might think this to be unlikely given the fact both cities are centres of well-attested industrial districts, each with established names, Merseyside and Clydeside respectively. I will attempt to search out such city-regions empirically.

My source is Brian Robson's (1973) statistical analysis of urban growth in nineteenth-century England and Wales. In contrast to emphasizing the largest cities, as I have been prone to, Robson uses administrative areas above a certain population density to ensure their urban character and then produces a roster of urban places above a threshold of just 2500 people for every census from 1801 to 1911. He justifies this threshold as:

being large enough to exclude many of the purely mining communities which
sprang up in counties such as Durham during the later part of the century
and also large enough to exclude most of the small market towns which never
attracted industry to them. (p.47)

In this way he produces rosters of hundreds of urban places, from 256 in
1801 growing to 885 in 1901. Being restricted to census data means these
data cannot inform early parts of Britain's hegemonic cycle, but there
are figures for before high hegemony (1801 and 1811) and the end of the
cycle (1881, 1891 and 1901). He computes the population change of each
urban place between censuses and has produced ten maps showing the
distribution of 'high', 'medium' and 'low' change. These are defined using
standardized growth rates: 'high' change is reported for urban places with
growth more than one standard deviation above the average. I concentrate
on just these high growth rates.

From 1801 to 1901 Robson (1973) identifies 576 high growth places.
Table 6.9 shows the distribution of 435 of these high growth places
across city-regions and/or major industrial districts. The relatively few
high growth places not included were largely coastal resorts and from
smaller industrial districts. Numbers are summed for both the first and
second halves of the century and for the whole century (total). Thus if
we begin with London in Table 6.9 we see there were only four urban
growth places between 1801 and 1851, but there were 56 between 1851 and
1901. Therefore although London's region records by far the most urban
growth places, these are very lop-sided in distribution across the century
as Table 6.6 previously suggested.

The following results can be gleaned from Table 6.9.

As just reported, London generates a large city-region of growth but
only in the final decades of the century. Bristol is included in the analysis
as a control. An important city outside industrializing England, it generates no urban growth places throughout the century.

In the first half of the century the textile and metal-producing regions
predominate in generating high growth places: Manchester, Birmingham
and Leeds are implicated; plus the central Lancashire region not dominated by either of their main cities, Preston and Blackburn. This pattern
can be interpreted as continuity of an economic geography emanating in
the previous century.

In the second half of the century Manchester continues to generate
urban growth but Birmingham generates much less. Liverpool generates
fewer urban growth places over the whole century than other northern
cities; a vindication of Jacobs' assessment above.

In the second half of the century Newcastle is second only to London

Table 6.9 Urban areas with high population growth in city-regions and industrial districts in England and Wales, 1801–1901

City-region/ industrial district	1801– 11	1811– 21	1821– 31	1831– 41	1841– 51	1801– 1851 total	1851– 61	1861– 71	1971– 81	1881– 91	1891– 1901	1851– 1901 total	TOTAL
London	0	0	2	2	0	**4**	2	6	10	18	20	**56**	**60**
North West													
Liverpool	3	0	3	2	1	**9**	3	2	2	1	0	**8**	**17**
Manchester	3	3	5	1	3	**15**	4	6	6	7	5	**28**	**43**
Central Lancashire	3	4	1	3	3	**14**	5	2	5	6	3	**21**	**35**
Midlands													
Birmingham/Black country	4	0	3	5	2	**14**	4	1	1	0	2	**8**	**22**
Nottingham/East Midlands	1	1	2	0	0	**4**	3	3	5	7	3	**21**	**25**
North East													
Newcastle/Tyne/Wear	0	2	1	1	3	**7**	5	2	6	6	11	**30**	**37**
Teesside/South Durham	0	0	2	0	2	**4**	4	8	5	3	1	**21**	**25**
Yorkshire													
Leeds/Bradford/W. Yorkshire	2	3	2	4	4	**15**	5	8	5	3	3	**24**	**39**
Sheffield/South Yorkshire	0	1	0	1	0	**2**	3	5	8	1	4	**21**	**23**
South West/Wales													
Bristol	0	0	0	0	0	**0**	0	0	0	0	0	**0**	**0**
Cardiff/South East Wales	1	1	2	3	3	**10**	2	4	4	9	7	**26**	**36**
TOTAL	**17**	**15**	**23**	**22**	**21**	**98**	**40**	**47**	**57**	**61**	**59**	**264**	**362**

Source: Derived from Robson (1973:100–109 (Figures 4.1 to 4.10)).

in generating growth places, confirming its importance in Table 6.5. Three other regions generate growth places in the second half of the century: Nottingham and the East Midlands, Teesside, and the South Wales coalfield. These results strongly suggest that during the British hegemonic cycle, key cities were generating growth places beyond their bounds to create vibrant city-regions and industrial districts.

One interesting feature of these areas of high urban growths is the difference between clear city-centred regions and multi-centred industrial regions. London, Liverpool, Manchester, Birmingham and Sheffield are centres of their regions; but Leeds shared its centrality of West Yorkshire with Bradford at this time, and Nottingham with Leicester and Derby. There is definitely no one centre in West Lancashire (Preston and Blackburn) or Teeside (Middlesbrough, Stockton), as Cardiff was not central to South Wales (Rhondda) economically or geographically. Jacobs (1984) does not envisage such multi-centred regions, but they are becoming much more common today (Hall and Pain 2006). For the nineteenth century there is more investigation to be done on inter-city relations in regions without a dominant city – but this is not the place.

The Cities of American Hegemony

With our extension of the beginnings of the US hegemonic cycle back to 1800 (Table 6.7) we are effectively including the whole period of the United States' existence. In this case, therefore, there is a large literature precisely on cities of this cycle: the national urban systems school of research was largely developed through researching the US 'urban system' and its history (Berry and Horton 1970). Borchert's (1967) study of the evolution of this 'system' still remains the classic understanding of this history. Starting with mercantile cities, first on the Atlantic coast and subsequently on inland rivers, the US began its industrial transformation, which restructured its economic geography, after about 1850:

> The heartland of the American manufacturing belt developed westward from New York, in the area bounded by the iron ores of Lake Superior, and the Pennsylvanian coalfields, on the one hand, and the capital, entrepreneurial experience, and engineering trades of the northeast on the other. (p. 364)

This core dominated the space-economy and developed new peripheral regions for its own needs. The result was a complex industrial economy in the North East and Mid West serviced by specialized resource regions with their gateway cities. Subsequently with the coming of a more service-orientated economy the US city network has become more evenly spread,

Table 6.10   *Growth rates of large US cities up to high hegemony*

	Over 10%	5–10%	1–5%	0–1%	Loss	**Total**
1790–1800	0	1	0	0	0	**1**
1800–10	0	1	1	0	0	**2**
1810–20	0	0	3	0	0	**3**
1820–30	0	1	3	0	0	**4**
1830–40	1	2	2	0	0	**5**
1840–50	1	2	3	0	0	**6**
1850–60	4	2	6	0	0	**12**
1860–70	3	5	10	0	0	**18**
1870–80	0	6	13	0	0	**19**
1880–90	5	5	14	0	0	**24**
1890–1900	1	4	23	1	0	**29**
1900–10	4	5	19	2	0	**30**
1910–20	1	2	26	1	0	**30**
1920–30	2	1	21	6	0	**30**
1930–40	0	0	5	17	8	**30**
Total	**22**	**37**	**149**	**27**	**8**	**243**

beginning with the rise of cities in California, then Texas, the rest of the West, and finally in the South. Johnston (1982) has elaborated on this history by linking it into wider economic processes.

My contribution to this knowledge will be very modest. I will focus on population changes of cities in the period leading to American high hegemony. By using the US census I can measure growth at ten-year intervals from 1790 to 1940. For my roster of cities I have chosen those with a population of over 300 000 in 1940. This produces the USA's top 30 cities up to high hegemony. Since these are by definition the most successful US cities of the time, they can be said to constitute the main building blocks of US hegemony. For measuring change I include a city into the analysis from the year it reaches 40 000. The 30 cities over 15 time intervals generate 243 city population changes, which are converted to annualized percentage rates for consistency with previous analyses.

The 243 city population changes are shown in Table 6.10 distributed across five growth rates. Note that these rates are not directly comparable to the 50-year analyses since, quite obviously, it is far more likely for a city to sustain high growth rates over ten years than it is over a period five times longer. Nevertheless, these results do seem remarkable. We find 22 cases where cities have an annual growth rate of over 10 per cent. The vast majority of changes are above the 1 per cent per annum threshold used to define demographic spurts in the 50-year data. Most changes below 1

Table 6.11   Regional distribution of city spurts that made US hegemony

North East		Mid West		West		South	
City	*Spurts*	*City*	*Spurts*	*City*	*Spurts*	*City*	*Spurts*
New York	6	Chicago	5	Los Angeles	5	Houston	3
Philadelphia	1	Detroit	5	San Francisco	2	Washington	2
Baltimore	1	Cleveland	3	Seattle	2	New Orleans	1
Boston	1	Milwaukee	3	Portland	2	Louisville	1
		St Louis	2	Denver	1	Atlanta	1
		Pittsburgh	2	Oakland	1		
		Buffalo	2				
		Kansas City	2				
		Indianapolis	2				
		Minneapolis	1				
		Cincinnati	1				
		Columbus	1				

Notes:
Spurts are defined as annualized growth of more than 5% over a decade.
Three cities did not qualify, but came close: their highest growth rates are Jersey City 4.6%, Newark 4.6%, and Rochester 4.3%.
Baltimore was included in the North East because its economy was of this region.

per cent are in the final two decades; all losses are in the last decade. Thus there is an almost continuous large-scale growth in these US cities until the Great Depression of the 1930s. What this shows is that the US has been a country of unprecedented city growth, an accolade befitting its hegemonic status.

Given the relatively short time intervals, I have defined demographic spurts as being above 5 per cent in Table 6.11. Here the cities are listed under their regional locations and in terms of the number of spurts they experienced. This is a sort of roll call of honour for the cities that made US hegemony; New York, Chicago, Detroit and Los Angeles get distinguished honours. Note the importance of the Mid West; this is the region with approximately half (29) of all demographic spurts leading to high hegemony. Using Tables 6.10 and 6.11, I have identified three key periods in the rise towards hegemony.

The first period is the first four decades, the very beginning, not just of the state, but perhaps, also, of the rise to hegemony. Previously I interpreted Table 6.7 as indicating the latter, and here I look at this possibility in more detail. There were four fast-growing US cities in the first column of Table 6.7, and these all feature in the first four decades of the new analysis as shown in Table 6.11. According to Borchert (1967) these are largely mercantile cities but the growth rates, although relatively low

Table 6.12   Northeastern beginning of incipient hegemonic city growth

1790–1800		1800–10		1810–20		1820–30	
City	%	City	%	City	%	City	%
New York	6.0	New York	5.1	Baltimore	3.5	New York	6.4
		Philadelphia	3.3	New York	3.0	Boston	5.2
				Philadelphia	2.9	Baltimore	2.7
						Philadelphia	1.6

compared to later decades, are quite impressive. Only New York appears in 1790–1800 (the only US city with a population above 40000), and its high growth rate might be deemed typical for a primate mercantile city, the gateway between the US and the rest of the world-economy. If the city network remained simply primate then New York and the US might have gone the way of Buenos Aires and Argentina. But New York was not Buenos Aires; it proved to be part of a vibrant US city network. The entry of Philadelphia, Baltimore and then Boston into Table 6.12 so that all four 'mercantile' ports are growing and prospering along the Northeast coast suggests a very different process than a simple mercantile entrepôt economy. US cities are breaking their economic dependence through growth rates, which we know are the highest in the world-economy from Table 6.7, which proclaims mutual complexities, the first stirrings of future hegemony.

The second period I have chosen is from when Borchert (1967) finds the beginning of an industrial economy; there is a burst of seven very high spurts in the decades before and including the Civil War (1850–70). This period is shown in Table 6.13 and the high spurts are dominated by Midwest cities – hence I have called this the Midwest consolidation of the incipient hegemonic growth previously recorded. (The Philadelphia growth aberration based upon annexation is ignored for the purposes of this discussion.) With these results there is no need for benefit of hindsight to see that city growth marks the US as the coming economic power. The Civil War decade's results are quite exceptional: seven Midwest cities have growth rates above 5 per cent per annum, most far above this level. This is a true urban revolution.

The third period I have chosen are the three decades before World War I in which ten excessively large growth spurts are recorded in Table 6.10. Los Angeles leads all three columns in Table 6.14; its sustained growth rate is again historically exceptional.

Although Midwest cities continue to be very important in this table, four Pacific cities come to be top of the list in the first decade of the

Table 6.13 Midwest consolidation of incipient hegemonic city growth

1850–60		1860–70	
City	*%*	*City*	*%*
Philadelphia	36.6*	Chicago	17.4
Chicago	26.5	San Francisco	16.3
Buffalo	11.1	Cleveland	11.4
St Louis	10.6	St Louis	9.3
New York	6.9	Pittsburgh	7.9
Louisville	5.8	Detroit	7.4
Washington	4.5	Milwaukee	5.8
New Orleans	4.5	Washington	5.1
Cincinnati	4.0	Louisville	4.8
Boston	3.0	Newark	4.6
Baltimore	2.6	Boston	4.1
Pittsburgh	1.5	Cincinnati	3.4
		Buffalo	3.2
		Rochester	2.9
		Baltimore	2.6
		New York	2.6
		Philadelphia	1.9
		New Orleans	1.3

Note: * Philadelphia annexed Philadelphia County in 1854.

twentieth century, all with growth rates above 10 per cent per annum – another urban revolution. I have called this phase the Western beginning of rapacious hegemonic city growth, and this requires some explanation. In a previous publication I used the terms incipient, rapacious and resonant to describe 'Americanization' across the US hegemonic cycle, defined conventionally as the twentieth century (Taylor 1999a, Chapter 7). Rapacious Americanization coincided with high hegemony. On the basis of the evidence provided above, I think that in terms of economic change through cities, the rapacious phase of hegemony occurs before high hegemony. Once again we have the commercial as creator preceding the guardian phase of hegemony, which is the hegemonic state wielding the political power consequent upon its cities' economic power (i.e. in this case in the twentieth-century world wars). By 1910 something has already stirred in the US that indicates the beginnings of the commercial phase of 'true' hegemony – Wallerstein's production cutting edge. Obviously we now know that this advantage did not have a simple evolution (with World War I followed by political isolationism, capped by the Great Depression),

Table 6.14   Western beginning of rapacious hegemonic city growth

1880–1890		1890–1900		1900–10	
City	*%*	*City*	*%*	*City*	*%*
Los Angeles	35.1	Los Angeles	10.3	Los Angeles	21.1
Minneapolis	25.1	Portland	9.5	Seattle	19.4
Kansas City	13.8	Seattle	8.8	Portland	12.9
Chicago	18.9	Indianapolis	6.0	Oakland	12.4
Indianapolis	18.9	Chicago	5.4	Houston	7.7
Detroit	7.7	Cleveland	4.6	Atlanta	7.2
Milwaukee	7.7	Columbus	4.2	Detroit	6.3
Columbus	7.1	Milwaukee	4.0	Denver	5.9
Buffalo	6.5	Detroit	3.9	Kansas City	5.2
Cleveland	6.3	Buffalo	3.8	Minneapolis	4.9
Rochester	5.0	Oakland	3.8	Cleveland	4.7
Pittsburgh	4.6	Atlanta	3.7	Columbus	4.5
Jersey City	3.5	New York	3.7	Newark	4.1
Newark	3.3	Newark	3.5	New York	3.9
New York	3.1	Pittsburgh	3.1	Indianapolis	3.8
Baltimore	3.1	St Louis	2.7	Rochester	3.4
Louisville	3.0	Louisville	2.7	Milwaukee	3.1
Washington	3.0	Jersey City	2.7	Jersey City	3.0
St Louis	2.9	Denver	2.7	Chicago	2.9
San Francisco	2.8	Boston	2.5	Buffalo	2.3
Boston	2.4	Philadelphia	2.4	San Francisco	2.2
Philadelphia	2.4	Kansas City	2.3	Philadelphia	2.0
Cincinnati	1.6	Minneapolis	2.3	Boston	2.0
New Orleans	1.2	Rochester	2.1	St Louis	1.9
		Washington	2.1	Washington	1.9
		New Orleans	1.9	Pittsburgh	1.8
		Baltimore	1.7	New Orleans	1.8
		San Francisco	1.5	Cincinnati	1.2
		Cincinnati	1.0	Baltimore	1.0
				Louisville	0.9

but after 1940 the US built an economic superiority in its high hegemony that was exceptional even in hegemonic comparison. The US, the land of extraordinary cities, became an extraordinary hegemonic state.

Hegemonic Transformations of Spaces of Flows

The contrarian tendency in Jacobs' work is no better illustrated than by one chapter in *The Economy of Cities* that is entitled 'The valuable inefficiencies and impracticalities of cities' (Jacobs 1969, pp. 85–111). Here she presents the following paradox:

> Cities are indeed inefficient and impractical compared with towns; and among cities themselves, the largest and most rapidly growing at any given time are apt to be the least efficient. But I propose to argue that these grave and real deficiencies are necessary to economic development . . . I do not mean that cities are economically valuable in spite of their inefficiency and impracticality but rather because they are inefficient and impractical. (p. 86)

One way in which this operates is through a vibrant city economy outgrowing its logistic infrastructure. A long queue of ships waiting to enter a city's harbour is a sure sign of that city's commercial success, with a consequent inefficiency requiring attention. Cities are busy places, always on the edge of capacity to maintain movement, and such problems can be expected to stimulate new work solutions through either innovations or imitations.

In the case of hegemonies in the modern creative interval, their multi-nodal regional centres means that inefficiencies and impracticalities are multiplied and will be specifically acute for the infrastructure handling regional inter-city links. Since these are 'problems of success' of multiple dynamic cities, it follows that we would not expect logistic innovations or imitations to occur with the urban origins of hegemony. Rather the inefficiencies and impracticalities should come to a head with high hegemony, at the height of commercial success. We can postulate that during the rise to hegemony the emphasis will be on improving, developing and adapting existing logistics. As long as this is possible such change will be preferred because of the capital costs of implementing new transport infrastructures. When the latter is no longer practical – the antiquated logistics are severely hindering economic growth – then new solutions are needed and will be forthcoming to maintain hegemonic economic leadership, at least for a while. But such infrastructural solutions require large quantities of capital investment, often involving the state as provider and/ or guarantor, and promoter and/or regulator. The resulting city/state relations are interesting because the guardian role is much more than the physical defence described above; here it is integral to the actual commercial process. This is the modern *modus operandi* at its sharpest. I will present these city/state relations for logistically networking cities in each hegemonic cycle.

The Dutch Trekvaart Network

Cities of the Low Countries had the key natural advantages of being on the Rhine delta thereby linking river and sea connections. This location meant that inter-city connections between cities in the United Provinces were facilitated by what de Vries (1981, p. 17) calls 'a unique capacity for human interaction that profoundly affected both economic and social life.' His wonderful book *Barges and Capitalism* is the source for my discussion below.

The story begins with *beurtveren* (from the Dutch *beurt* meaning a turn). These are a simple organizational method for improving inter-city relations by regularizing travel on the waterways. According to de Vries (1981, p. 17):

> After the worst years of the Dutch Revolt the cities of this very urban region began negotiations with their most important trading partners. They aimed to conclude agreements whereby a regular, regulated transport service could be established between them. . . . A characteristic of these agreements was that the appointees of the two cities took turns in maintaining the scheduled services.

Such schemes go back to the fifteenth century but they only began to become numerous after the 1580s culminating in a situation where 'every important city could boast of a regulated *beurtveer* with most of its important trading partners' (p. 18). Early examples are Leiden–Delft in 1583 and Amsterdam–Haarlem in 1598. These can be interpreted as adapting existing logistics to increasing demand. *Beurtveer* shared the waterways with *marktschip*, market boats that provided a service 'between the cities and the villages of their rural hinterland' (p. 18). Thus were both city-ness and town-ness facilitated in the early decades of the Dutch hegemonic cycle.

This was an advanced water transport system but it did have problems, generally slowness on circuitous routes, and unpredictability due to treacherous waters, variable winds and weather (pp. 19–20). These inefficiencies led directly to the development of the *trekvaart* network, new straighter canals with towpaths for horses to replace sailing vessels. De Vries (1981, p. 24) argues:

> the Dutch *trekvaart* was an organizational innovation that used long-existing component parts to produce a new product – the dependable, convenient, and cheap movement of a large volume of passengers over an extensive, interconnected network of routes. (p. 24)

To make this improvement starts with an *accord* between two cities and a request (*octrooi*) to the provincial assembly for the right to build a new canal. The reasons given in these requests included speed, winter, known timing and commerce. The latter dominated: 'By reducing the time needed to travel to and from Amsterdam, [the chief merchants] argued, Leiden would become a more attractive commercial center' (pp. 21–2). More generally:

> The new demands being placed on the transportation system by a growing and developing economy were such that contemporaries came to regard the development of a *trekvaart* network as crucial to the satisfaction of those requirements. (p. 24)

One very tangible result was inter-city timetables not equalled for business travel until railway timetables in the nineteenth century.

There were two booms in *trekvaart* investment and construction, a small one from the 1630s producing four separate mini-networks by 1650 (de Vries 1981, p. 30), and the major boom from 1656 to 1665 when most of the *trekvaart* were constructed. The end result was:

> 658 kilometres of *trekvaart*, costing over four and a half million guilders [that] endowed the Republic's diliuvial territories with a well-integrated passenger transport network. This achievement is remarkable not only because of its precocity. At least as remarkable is the fact that it was built without any overall plan and without any leadership from central authorities. The provincial *Staten* (assemblies) which granted *octrooi* did so exclusively in response to municipal requests. Initiative rested with the cities, altogether with 30 cities. (pp. 42–3)

Importantly, de Vries concludes that 'While the *beurtveren* served the cities as competing central places, the *trekschuiten* served them as members of an urban system' (p. 53), or city network as I would call it.

The cooperative essence of this multi-city logistic innovation is entirely consistent with the inter-city relations I have called city-ness. Thus de Vries (1981, pp. 74–5) points out:

> Despite Amsterdam's great size and enormous importance, the *trekvaart* network was not entirely focused on that city. The other important cities had access to the whole region directly, and not only via Amsterdam. This fact is of particular importance in a pre-telegraphic age, because it implies not only equalization of physical accessibility, but also the equalization of accessibility to information.

This egalitarian imperative can be seen in the dispersal of mail from England, which was based on 'the principle of equalizing accessibility to information' (p. 76). The mail did not go direct to any favoured city, rather it was relayed through neutral venues: packet boats docked in the little port of Hellevoetsluis, mail was sent unsorted to the village of Waddinxveen in central Holland, and from there distributed to cities.

The importance of this new infrastructure in terms of actual flows is shown in Table 6.15. There are two obvious features that show up. First, the huge quantity of human interaction, unrivalled in its time and not challenged until the railway in the mid-nineteenth century; de Vries (1981,

Table 6.15   Top 10 average annual trekvaart *passenger flows for the 1660s and 1670s*

Rank	City-dyad	Flows (000s)
1	The Hague–Delft	362
2	Amsterdam–Haarlem	298
3	Leiden–The Hague/Delft	220
4	Delft–Rotterdam	193
5	Haarlem–Leiden	132
6	Amsterdam–Monnikendam	82
7	Monnikendam–Edam	58
8	Amsterdam–Purmerend	50
9	Edam–Hoorn	43
10	Leiden–Utrecht	38

Source: de Vries (1981: 162).

p. 9) summarizes it correctly as 'a large-scale, highly organized passenger transport system . . . a unique phenomenon'. Second, this is clearly more network than hierarchical in structure with Amsterdam featuring in only three of the top ten flows. Furthermore there is a suggestion of a movement of economic growth to south Holland (i.e. away from Amsterdam) with three of the top four flows, featuring Delft, Leiden, Rotterdam and The Hague, together constituting the majority of flows in Table 6.15. This may reflect earlier identification of Rotterdam as the United Provinces late rising city (Table 6.5). And one more insight from de Vries: he suggests that such huge networked flows included business travel for face-to-face meetings that fundamentally countered the need for one large city in generating economic growth (p. 89). I will only add that multi-nodal city-regions at the heart of modern hegemony can act as intensely networked creative places powerful enough to generate new forms of modernity.

The British Railway Network

The British transport revolution unfolded in three stages, the first two improving and adding to existing movement. The first was improvement of roads as turnpikes; stretches of roads charging tolls for maintaining and improving roads. By 1770 there was a turnpike network of 15 000 miles increasing to 22 000 miles by the 1830s (Freeman 1986, p. 80). Second, came the canals, initially they were short links for transporting industrial raw materials into an existing 1400 miles of navigable rivers. But the idea of 'trunk canals' to create a national waterway network soon emerged and by the 1790s the five river basins of Humber, Mersey, Severn, Thames and Trent were first linked together. By 1830 there were 2500 miles of canal that constituted a clear inland waterway network (Freeman 1986, p. 86). There was a relatively even spread of the network linking both London to Bristol and Lancashire to Yorkshire but with a higher density of local canals around Birmingham, which made it the centre of the network. Nevertheless, the most impressive part of the network was undoubtedly in the north where the Pennine hills, separating the Lancashire and Yorkshire textile regions, were breached three times (Liverpool–Leeds, Manchester–Wakefield, Macclesfield–Huddersfield). This is a classic case of an infrastructure being built to satisfy the fast-rising demand for connection. And it changed the structure of British space-economy; for instance, with its canal linkage Liverpool could become the main port of export for Yorkshire woollen textiles.

The third stage is the truly innovative stage: the creation of a national railway network. Road travel was expensive and very slow, canal travel was cheaper but still slow; it seemed logistics was falling behind production in Britain's industrial revolution thereby creating critical inefficiencies in inter-city relations. Railway technology was British hegemony's great innovation in logistics. Steam engines and railways were not new to the nineteenth century and nor was their combination but it was the massive economic expansion in Britain in the early part of the century that created a new demand for movement that the new canals could no longer satisfy. It was this potential that attracted the massive levels of capital investment that were needed to create a completely new network out of nothing. Responding to the particular demand of colliery owners in northeast England, this region became 'the Silicon Valley of its day' (Wolmar 2007, p. 13), and the first modern railway, from Stockton to Darlington, was opened in 1825. The 'world's first steam-hauled and twin tracked railway' was opened in 1830 between 'two "world-class cities" of their age', Liverpool and Manchester (p. 21). According to Wolmar this was 'the obvious place to start and the time was ripe for such an investment':

> The Liverpool & Manchester represented the start of the railway age – just as it marked a significant advance in the technology – and was far grander in scale and conception than any of its predecessors. (p. 21)

By 1838 there were 250 miles of railway including connecting Birmingham and London to Liverpool and Manchester; five years later there was the semblance of a network consisting of 1800 miles (p. 75). This is marked by the first publication of Bradshaw's train timetables in 1842, as a now necessary guide to all scheduled rail services (p. 77). From 1844 to 1847 there was the great 'rail mania' of investors (p. 88) so that by 1851 a national railway network was in place consisting of 6100 route miles (p. xvi). Compared to the canal network, the spread is right across Britain but again there is a greater density of network in the Midlands and Lancashire–Yorkshire reflecting the industrial demand.

Finally, there is an interesting geographical note. Not only does this logistic revolution have to 'wait' until high hegemony, its innovative centre in northeast England is outside the original canal network: the region did not feature at all in canal investment. This late hegemonic geography is reproducing a previous result, the identification of Newcastle as Britain's late rising city (Table 6.6). And alongside this finding, Table 6.6 featured the renewal of London's growth, which is also reflected in the coming of the railways: even as early as 1851 there is the beginning of rail network nodality in London, which was to be far greater by the late nineteenth century (Robson 1986, p. 219). To conclude: from high hegemony, Britain finally had a transport infrastructure that met its needs as the fastest growing space-economy of the times.

The US Airline Network and Interstate Highway System

As with Dutch and British hegemony, the rise of the US is initially based on existing logistical solutions to demand for economic flows. In this case Edward Taaffe and his colleagues (1996, p. 76), drawing on Vance (1986), identify 'four eras of US transportation development'. The first, the 'Local Era', featured the Atlantic ports carving out their hinterlands involving the development of both local canals and turnpike roads (Taaffe et al. 1996, pp. 79–81). The Appalachian mountains were a major barrier to hinterland development; overcoming this obstacle resulted in the second 'Trans-Appalachian Era'. The major ports all developed crossings, the most important being the Erie Canal linking New York to the Great Lakes in 1825. This provided an alternative northeast route to trade travelling south down the Mississippi valley to New Orleans (p. 84). But even more important, these new routes east stimulated development of a mix of numerous canals and railways to create, by 1850, an integrated Midwest as a network of new fast-growing cities (p. 89). The third 'Era of Rail Dominance' ushered in transcontinental connections to produce a national transport network (p. 95). Initially, intensifying Midwest connections – between 1850 and 1860 the rail network grew more than three-fold to over 30 000 miles – the first transcontinental connection was made in 1869. This was not a commercial-led process; the

US government promoted and subsidized all the transcontinental routes as a guardian territorial imperative. The state's regulation was equally important – the 1886 declaration of a standard rail gauge consolidated railway connections into a real national network by the end of the nineteenth century (p. 106).

It is the fourth era of transport development, the 'Era of Competition', that is of particular interest here. Taaffe et al. (1996) emphasize, as their terminology suggests, competition between different modes of transport: 'railroad, highway, waterway, and air' (p. 109) but from my perspective the important feature is that the geography of logistic innovation has moved from Britain to the US. Therefore I focus on just two modes, first the rise in air-flights and then the inter-state system of roads. As with railways in the nineteenth century, these two leading transport modes in the twentieth have involved major state involvement reflecting prohibitive commercial costs associated with the sheer size of the US. Thus although air transportation was not competitive before World War II, there was a pattern of air 'trunkline' services across the country by 1940 (pp. 118–19). But 'phenomenal growth of US air transportation' only occurred after World War II (p. 127) to produce by far the largest national network. With jet aircraft becoming available in the early 1960s, air transport formed a national network with hierarchical tendencies, airlines' hub and spoke services in the final decades of the twentieth century. Taaffe et al. (1996, p. 131) identify Dallas, Los Angeles, and New York as the 'three dominant centers'. Notice that two of these three come into the category of late rising city in Table 6.7: Dallas and Los Angeles join Rotterdam and Newcastle in logistic revolutions being associated with regions (south Holland, northeast England and California/Texas) outside initial hegemonic growth.

However, there has been no such pattern with the revival of roads. This transport revolution is based upon commercial innovation – the internal combustion engine enabling individual car transport and heavy truck transport – but required a road network to enable it to function to its potential. The provision of roads was traditionally a local service and improvements were initially made as toll road initiatives through local states. This ensured densely travelled inter-city routes were developed, but was a long way from generating a national network when the federal government intervened in 1956 with its proposed Interstate Highway System. A 41 000-mile road-building programme, largely completed within a decade, this massive political investment produced a nationwide network taking the form of a continental grid of north–south and east–west 'divided, limited-access, freeways' (Taaffe et al. 1996, p. 122). This was guardian territoriality without spatial hierarchy, mildly reminiscent of 1930s German autobahns but much greater in scale and consistent in pattern. It is the classic case of guardian necessity for providing large-scale infrastructure needs to counter inter-city relational inefficiencies.

These three stories of hegemonic innovations to keep the great wheels of commerce moving have generated one of the most conspicuous effects of the modern creative interval; the modern world is experienced as a 'shrinking world'. Famously described by Donald Janelle (1969) as 'time–space convergence' he showed that travel times between cities had reduced at multitudinous levels in progressing from stage coaches to cars and planes across the *longue durée* that is the modern world-system. For David Harvey (1990) this represents 'time–space compression', a direct product of capitalism described by Marx during Britain's railway age as the annihilation of space by time. As well as the world getting smaller, Harvey implies that the pace of life has speeded up. In terms of my conceptual toolkit, this is cities becoming even busier in the modern creative interval as Castells' level one space of flows directly intrudes into level two, social relations, to do much more than simply enable; as hegemonic innovations they are directly implicated in creating new modern worlds.

CONCLUSION: MODERNITY AS AN (ABNORMAL) HISTORICAL INTERLUDE

And so modernity, our world, is an abnormal interval in the general scheme of geohistorical change. This is the result of commercial practice in European cities, after the fall of Rome, escaping the more severe guardian constraints found in other world regions. However, Europe was so far behind economically that it took a millennium for these commercial advantageous to start to become fully realized. The result is the modern world-system as capitalist world-economy encompassing multiple sovereignties in the inter-state system. The enabling contingencies in creation of the modern creative interval and its hegemonic cycles for reproduction are shown schematically in Figure 6.1. Contingencies did not disappear with coming of this new world-system and they became crucial in three 'world wars' in which hegemonic victories ushered in three different forms of modernity – mercantile, industrial and consumer. This brings us to the end of the twentieth century where American-led consumer modernity has morphed into economic globalization in the 'smallest world' yet experienced. But will contingency make a comeback in the twenty-first century?

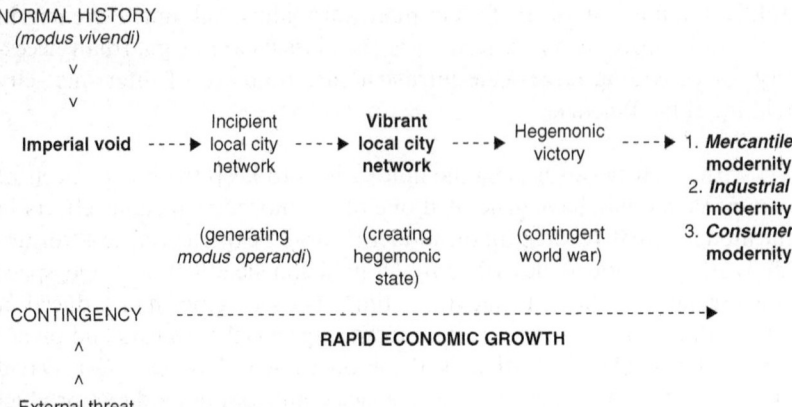

NORMAL HISTORY
(modus vivendi)

v

v

Imperial void ----▶ Incipient ----▶ **Vibrant** ----▶ Hegemonic ----▶ 1. *Mercantile*
              local city   **local city**   victory   *modernity*
              network   **network**   2. *Industrial*
                                                      modernity
            (generating   (creating   (contingent   3. *Consumer*
            modus operandi) hegemonic   world war)   *modernity*
                            state)

CONTINGENCY   ---▶
                            RAPID ECONOMIC GROWTH

^

^

External threat

Figure 6.3   Western Europe's modern creative interlude: generating hegemonic cycles

PART IV

Narrative III: prospective conjectures –
where are we and where are we going?

7.   Working in an urban world

INTRODUCTION: *SANS* HINDSIGHT

This final part of the book is headed 'prospective conjectures': as with Part II, the narrative is described as a 'conjecture' because the discussion cannot be based upon as sound an evidential grounding as we would wish. In the case of beginnings it is impossible to think that we will ever assemble enough surviving evidence to answer definitively the questions asked, and for futures, the subject of the next chapter, empirics is simply impossible: there can be no evidence on an upcoming world, only extrapolation of the present and theoretical arguments about why such extrapolation will not be. But what of the present? Our present world is dominated by globalization, which is richly researched. It may be surprising that the contemporary globalization of the early twenty-first century is included in conjectures. To be sure today's macro-social change can be interpreted as a continuation of the narrative describing the modern historical interlude in the last chapter, for instance as Americanization eliding into globalization, but the present can never be that simple.

Here once again I follow Fernand Braudel (1980) in his comparison between social science research and historical scholarship. Although the former researchers have an array of methods not available to historians through simply being present in their subject matter, social scientists suffer from one crucial disadvantage: contemporary analysis can have no hindsight. Interpretations in history can relate to both before and after. This hindsight was used to foreground Europe in Chapter 5. However, social scientists only have knowledge of before: current things that seem important might turn out to have little future relevance or a different significance than expected. Alternatively something little discussed today might become crucial to future macro-social change. We cannot know: our ignorance of the future impinges on our knowledge of the present. Therefore my descriptions of contemporary globalization cannot be a narrative like the two previous chapters because we do not know where it is going; I treat it as a prospective conjecture that precedes future conjectures.

The most reported 'global fact' of the early twenty-first century has been that the world's population is now more than 50 per cent urban. As we have seen in the last chapter, this is directly the result of the abnormal modern interlude; in Normal History regional levels of urbanization probably never reached beyond 10 per cent. The twenty-first century is therefore humanity's first urban century, increasingly so if the current urbanization trajectory continues as most expect. For me the most interesting take on this new human condition is that of Fred Pearce (2010, p. 146) when he remarks:

> the trend towards feminization of cities is near-universal. Unremarked, it is women who are leading the urbanization of the planet.

By this he means that cities, as social melting pots where new human relations are forged, have generated a new gender relations where children are viewed very differently from within rural peasant contexts:

> City dwellers have few children – the billion squatters like everyone else. Thanks to that by-product of urban growth, the core environmentalist panic about overpopulation is quietly being undermined, but the news hasn't got around. (Brand 2010, p. 55)

The resulting reduction in numbers of children has made old estimates of world population growth – up to 15 billion – very wide of the mark because of not understanding this fundamental behavioural change consequent upon living in an urban world. Whether women work staying at home or work in the labour market or both, fewer children is becoming the norm thereby opening up new opportunities (relative to their peasant ancestors) across a range of commercial and guardian practices. I guess that this will have future meaning for the rest of century in unforeseen ways.

This chapter is divided into three main sections. There are two largely separate literatures on cities in contemporary globalization and the first two sections deal with each in turn. First, I consider world city networks, specifically how they provide the commercial infrastructures for servicing global capital. Contemporary structures of one key network are described and interpreted in a geohistorical context. Second, megacities, defined simply by their demographic size, are mainly to be found in poorer countries. This urban geography is a genuinely new phenomenon, something unique to our late modern times. Interpretations of its meaning are severely contested – we could really do with hindsight here, but will have to make do with evaluating contrasting positions. In the third section I bring states back into the argument. Although some globalization devotees predict a demise of the state, this is hardly borne out in contemporary commercial and guardian activities. The geohistorical tango shows no sign of losing its passion; the roles of states are adjusting, as they have done several times in the modern world-system, and I review the current situation with particular reference to the US and China. My concluding section contrasts looking back (is China continuing hegemonic reproduction of modernity?) with looking forward (is the future something we would not even wish on an enemy, China or otherwise?).

CITIES IN GLOBALIZATION I: WORLD CITY NETWORKS

As indicated briefly in Chapter 2 the whole concept of this book derives ultimately from my studies of the contemporary world city network over the last decade or so. As described in Chapter 2, linking the inter-city relations enhanced by economic globalization to Jane Jacobs' seminal work on cities led me to reassess my modelling of today's world city network as generic, as the current expression of what I called 'central flow theory' (Taylor at al. 2010b). I have now reached my own research efforts in the narrative of my geohistorical tango.

My own research products have themselves been highly networked as I have collaborated with many colleagues in the Globalization and World Cities (GaWC) Research Network (www.lboro.ac.uk/gawc). I summarized the original modelling and early (2000) results in my *World City Network* (Taylor 2004) and more comprehensive detailing of recent results can be found in *Global Urban Analysis* (Taylor et al. 2011). A broader range of studies – 'greater GaWC' – can be found in *International Handbook of Cities and Globalization* (Derudder et al. 2012), which I mention here because my reprise of GaWC research below is, perforce, limited by space constraints. I have used the plural – world city networks – for my section heading in order to emphasize the multiplicity of networks in contemporary global spaces of flows. In the *Handbook* there are chapters on all three of Castells' levels in his space of flows framework: physical and electronic infrastructures, various worldwide work networks, and elite networks. Here I focus on the second level, and within work networks I describe just one example: the collective network of business services. I have been apt to refer to this as 'the' world city network; below I justify this choice in terms of its practical and indicative importance in contemporary globalization. My main purpose is to present the latest GaWC research (2010) as summarizing the current positioning of dynamic cities in the modern world-system.

Contemporary City-ness: World City Hierarchy, Global City and World City Network

From the conceptual toolkits in Chapter 2, I start with Manual Castells' (1996) description of contemporary society as network society premised upon constructing new spaces of flows in the electronic era of communication. He used Saskia Sassen's concept of the 'global city' as a key example of the social construction of what he subsequently referred to as global spaces of flows (Castells 1996). Sassen (1991) argued that contemporary globalization had created a new type of city, a limited number of 'global cities', perhaps 20 or 25, epitomized by New York, London and Tokyo. They were characterized, not just by command and control functions (corporate headquarters), but also by advanced producer service functions, knowledge-based firms specializing in financial, professional and creative work such as investment banking, commercial law and advertising respectively. Sassen's global cities were both the production centres and the corporate markets for these advanced services: they provide the special expertise that has enabled contemporary capitalism to be global.

Cities have always been service centres, including advanced producer services. Major seaports, for instance, have been important innovation centres for the development of insurance services. But mostly, and for most of their history, such services have been offered in cities for local clients. Typically firms became identified by their city-location as in 'London merchant bank', 'Boston law firm' and 'New York advertising agency'. Varying by country and service sector, from the nineteenth century onwards some local client lists grew in size to become national in scope. And in the last quarter of the twentieth century a few national firms globalized their services. There were two important reasons for this upscaling of their servicing. First, many of their clients were globalizing their production, which meant they wanted to be serviced at this scale. In advertising, for instance, if a client planned a global advertising campaign, their existing advertising agency would then have to provide new global services or else lose the business. This 'following strategy' soon became a global strategy in its own right: if you are servicing old local or national clients globally, it makes sense to search for new clients globally. Second, these are knowledge-based services for which reputation is crucial. In the past, if a client had some international business, the service firm would have 'preferred partners' in other countries who would be recommended to undertake the foreign work. This was commonplace in banking, where there were networks of independent 'correspondence banks'. With the massive growth of globalizing, these arrangements have become much less frequent: put simply, global business became too important to service companies for them to risk putting work out to a local firm elsewhere. Outsourcing advanced producer services means losing direct control of the quality of the product, and that is simply unacceptable in an era of branding. To protect the firm's brand required a presence across the world to handle clients personally wherever they might be.

The outcome can be seen in the cityscapes of leading cities across the world with huge office blocks housing numerous major service firms: varieties of banks, insurance companies, managements consultancies, advertising agencies, law partnerships and accountancy firms. Each office of a firm in a given city tower block is but one part of that firm's worldwide office network. Offices work together within firms to provide services for clients: the global spread of their service knowledge is part of their specialist expertise. Inter-jurisdictional law is a clear case of this. For instance, drawing up agreements and contracts for investment in China by a German firm in partnership with an Australian firm requires a legal package that encompasses Chinese, German and Australian law: this would likely be drawn up by a London law firm using English common law as the basic frame, with necessary inputs from their expertise in Shanghai, Frankfurt and Sydney offices. I interpret the contemporary world city network as the aggregation of all these many office networks (Taylor 2001; 2004). Although the office blocks make distinctive local places, their *raison d'être* is non-local; it is their location within networks of work which straddle the globe that matter. Therefore the world city network consists of the myriad flows of information, knowledge, instruction, plans, strategies, direction and personnel that travel between cities in the everyday practice of the service work that supports global capital.

To describe this network requires measurement of these flows. Unfortunately this is realistically impossible, not due the daunting massive quantity of flows, but simply because as intra-firm business they constitute highly sensitive commercial information that will always remain confidential. Therefore we have to fall back on indirect measures of these flows. This requires a model of the process that uses available data to estimate inter-city flows. To this end I developed the interlocking network model for cities that uses data on the office networks of major service firms; specifically for each firm, their city locations and the importance of each city presence to the operations of the firm (Taylor 2001). These office networks are interpreted as the location strategies developed by firms to service their global clients. Estimates of potential work flows are based on the principle that the more important the office, the more flows it will generate to, and attract from, other offices. Thus two cities with important offices will have more potential work flows between them than two cities with less important offices. It is the aggregation of these individual estimated flows within firms that define potential inter-city potential work flows, and from these we can estimate the connectivity of each city within the world city network (Taylor 2001; 2004). This network connectivity measures a city's degree of integration into the world city network; it is the measure I start with to describe the world city network in the early twenty-first century.

Global Urban Analysis, 2010

As part of the Globalization and World Cities (GaWC) Research Network I have been monitoring the world city network since 2000. A glimpse of the latest results for 2010 is shown in Table 7.1. This is a list of the 25 cities with the highest network connectivities of 526 cities in the study. The results are aggregated from the office networks of 175 advanced producer service firms: 75 leading financial services firms and 25 each of the leading accountancy, advertising, law and management consultancy firms. London turns out to be the world city network's most connected city and the connectivities of all cities are given as percentages of London's total of potential work flows. There are two main things to notice about this list. First, the dominance of London and New York: these are outstanding within the network with a large gap between them and the city ranked third, Hong Kong. Second, the spread of these leading cities across world regions: there are eight in Europe, seven in the Americas (four in Anglo America, three in Latin America), seven in Pacific Asia, and one each in Australasia, the Middle East and South Asia. Africa is the only continent missing. (Johannesburg ranks 47th with 40.42 per cent of London's connectivity.) I have presented this top 25 to show the cities that Sassen (1991) was thinking about when she coined the term 'global city'. But the world city network is much larger than a relatively small selection of leading cities. The firms in the study typically have offices in many more than just 25 cities and this has enabled analyses to delve much deeper into the geographies of cities in globalization (Taylor et al. 2011). Here I present two additional analyses relating first to some leading states and second to strategic patterns of globalization.

Table 7.2 shows the top five cities in terms of world city network connectivity for six countries, three core countries and three semi-peripheral countries. The key point I am making is that the globalizing processes that generate the world city network are not independent of the inter-state system: contemporary flows transcend state boundaries but this does not mean that the cities are separated from their states. There has been an early debate on this (Hill and Kim 2000): territorial state-building processes do not simply stop when global city or world city network processes begin; but the latter do add an extra layer of complexity to city/state relations.

Table 7.1   Global network connectivity, 2010: top 25 cities

Rank	City	Connectivity compared with London (%)
1	London	100.00
2	New York	94.35
3	Hong Kong	72.96
4	Paris	68.29
5	Singapore	67.47
6	Tokyo	63.75
7	Shanghai	62.71
8	Chicago	61.61
9	Dubai	61.36
10	Sydney	61.06
11	Milan	58.87
12	Beijing	58.37
13	Toronto	58.27
14	São Paulo	55.74
15	Madrid	55.24
16	Mumbai	55.16
17	Los Angeles	55.11
18	Moscow	54.29
19	Frankfurt	52.62
20	Mexico City	52.51
21	Amsterdam	51.86
22	Buenos Aires	50.15
23	Kuala Lumpur	49.88
24	Seoul	49.78
25	Brussels	49.74

There is a degree of path dependency in how cities are integrated into the world city network and this relates to previous state processes. The 'shape' of rankings within countries very clearly reflects specific ordering of cities prior to contemporary globalization. It is obviously no accident that London ranks top in Table 7.1; this follows prior prowess of London as the capital of the erstwhile hegemon, the UK, in the modern world-system, and especially its legacy in transnational finance. But other British cities have fared much worse: in Table 7.2, from Manchester down they appear to be in London's shadow within contemporary globalization reflecting their relative decline from the late nineteenth century. Today this means that many, perhaps most, of the firms in our study service the needs of their clients in Britain just through their London office. In contrast to Britain's very 'vertical' pattern of cities in globalization, Germany's is much more 'horizontal': Frankfurt is the leading city through its financial

Table 7.2   City connectivities, selected countries

(a) Core countries

World rank	City	Connectivity compared with London (%)
	Core countries	
	USA	
2	New York	94.35
8	Chicago	61.61
17	Los Angeles	55.11
27	San Francisco	48.77
28	Washington	47.51
	Germany	
19	Frankfurt	52.62
34	Munich	43.70
48	Düsseldorf	38.91
53	Hamburg	37.30
56	Berlin	36.83
	UK	
1	London	100.00
76	Manchester	31.43
85	Birmingham	29.52
112	Glasgow	24.94
114	Bristol	24.62

(b) Emerging (semi-peripheral) countries

	China	
3	Hong Kong	72.96
7	Shanghai	62.71
12	Beijing	58.37
43	Taipei	41.65
67	Guangzhou	34.13
	Brazil	
14	São Paulo	55.74
86	Rio De Janeiro	29.48
156	Porto Alegre	19.77
176	Curitiba	18.17
184	Brasília	17.16
	India	
16	Mumbai	55.16
33	New Delhi	44.39
59	Bangalore	36.59
74	Chennai	32.81
89	Kolkata	28.47

services but other German cities are also relatively important within the world city network, all being much more connected than Manchester. The US is somewhat between these two cases in terms of shape, not as vertical as Britain or as horizontal as Germany but as befits the country with the largest 'national economy', its five cities in Table 7.1 are all ranked higher than Germany's second ranked city. The three emerging countries in Table 7.2 show a similar range of shapes in their leading city connectivities, with India similar to Germany, Brazil more like Britain, and China looking like a second US. This is, of course, very much in keeping with what we know about these emerging countries: China now houses the second largest 'national economy' and this is explicitly reflected in the relative importance of Hong Kong, Shanghai and Beijing, all ranked higher than both São Paulo and Mumbai. Overall this table indicates how state-scale processes, both past and present, are implicated within the creation of the contemporary world city network. However, in overall analyses of this world city network, it is world-regions that generally feature as important structures.

Spatial Organization: Home-regions and Global Outreach

Drawing on Taylor et al. (2013), I present a regionalization of the world by focusing on advanced producer service firms as key agents who through their global strategies construct new regional formations. Through their everyday work, these financial, professional and creative firms have created a practical global spatial organization reflected in the way they divide up the world-economy. In the monitoring of the world city network since 2000, one robust feature of the analyses stands out: the results always show strong regional patterns of cities. It is clear that this particular economic globalization process – world city network formation – does not support stories about a blanket effect of global processes; rather than homogenizing the world-economy, results show new regional geographies being created to satisfy different servicing needs.

Obviously the firms being studied are not necessarily bent on devising regional schemes, but they do partake in location decision-making through which regional patterns can be discerned. Leading advanced producer service firms have reacted to, and contributed to, economic globalization through their location decisions on placing offices to service clients in cities across the world. Spatially they are network-makers rather than region-builders, but their creation of a world city network for servicing global capital inevitably reflects uneven market geographies for their services, and firms' world-regional origins. The result is a regional geography customized for contemporary economic globalization.

As a follower of Jacobs my empirical expectation is not for a neat geographical regionalization; instead inherent messiness of our dynamic world in global processes, as in processes at other scales, is hypothesized. In the context of Castells' (1996) social space constructs, this suggests that from a 'spaces of places' perspective boundaries can be expected to be fuzzy, and from a 'spaces of flows' perspective boundaries can be expected to be porous. In practice this means that instead of a usual neat mosaic of regions, there will likely be a deal of overlapping regions in the new region-alization. In fact, it is found that it is not only regional boundaries that are fuzzy and porous, the centres of regions are similarly fuzzy and porous! This requires the invention of a new conceptual framework consisting of two operational working realms: home-region and global-outreach. Advanced producer service firms tend to operate through both a regional concentration of servicing provision relating to their region of origin and headquarter location, and a dispersed worldwide distribution of service provision, which is their globalizing strategy. Taylor et al. (2013) defines this 'home and away' geography as follows:

1. The simplest concept is *home-region*, a geographical concentration of cities through which a common set of services are directed and pro-vided. However it is important not to view this as indicating a territory filled by like-cities forming a homogeneous space. There can be cities in the home-region that are not part of the regional formation because they are relatively weak purveyors of the services otherwise dominant in the region.
2. The *global outreach* is constituted by cities from outside the home-region that form part of the location strategies of the firms responsible for the services defining the home-region. In this context we define 'global' minimally as location strategies having presence in the three dynamic globalization arenas, the US, Europe and Pacific Asia. All the home-regions we identify have such global outreach.

This spatial organization has been revealed through using a principle com-ponents analysis on the 2010 data on 175 firms' office networks. Before the results are described this methodology needs to be briefly introduced.

Principal components analysis (PCA) is a means of data reduction; it reduces a large data matrix into a smaller one by combining like-variables into new common variables called components. In applying this tech-nique, the firms' location strategies are the variables and therefore the components represent common location strategies constituted by groups of firms with similar office network geographies across cities. In large data sets there will always be firms with particular location strategies like no others; these will not feature in any of the common strategies. Thus a PCA interpretation divides the data into two parts: that identified as common (like-strategies), and the part constituted by specific (idiosyncratic) strategies. The idea is to focus on the former in the hope that just a few components account for a sizeable proportion of the variation in the data matrix: PCA is a tool of parsimony that excavates common patterns within multifarious data sets.

Table 7.3 has been designed to illustrate the basic principles of PCA and to help interpret the key outputs from such analysis. This simple made-up data matrix is defined by ten firms' strategies across 12 leading cities (Table 7.3), where the importance of a city office to a service firm's network is rated from 1 to 5; 0 indicates a firm having no office in a city. Statistically, the firms are variables and in a PCA they are standardized to ensure they are weighted equally. This means that the variance (variation) of each firms' strategy is set to 1, and the total variance in Table 7.3(a) is therefore 10 (i.e. the number of variables). Looking at Table 7.3(a), it can be seen that Firm 1 and Firm 5 have identical location strategies. This pattern is also shared with Firm 7. These three firms therefore constitute one common strategy between them, and this strategy accounts for 30 per cent of the overall variance (3 variables out of 10). This is shown in the second column of Table 7.3(b) as the first common strategy. There are two other common strategies in Table 7.3(a), and these are also identified in Table 7.3(b), each constituted by two firms and therefore accounting for 20 per cent of the overall variance. However three firms have strategies specific to only themselves. This means that 30 per cent of the overall variance cannot be accounted for by common strategies; this is the idiosyncratic residual. In this analysis, therefore, ten firms' strategies have been reduced to three common strategies that between them account for 70 per cent of the original variance.

As well as a number of common strategies and accounted-for variance, a PCA provides two further vital results:

- *Relating firms to common strategies.* In Table 7.3 this is very simple; for instance, Firm 1's strategy is exactly the same as the common strategy – their correlation is a perfect 1.0. In actual analyses such perfect results do not occur but correlations are produced – they are called *component loadings* in this context. Just like correlations, loadings range from +1.0 to -1.0. Conventionally, in the PCA reported below, I have focused largely on firms with high positive loadings on a component.
- *Relating cities to common strategies.* In Table 7.3(b) this relation is given as the firms' strategies from Table 7.3(a) because they exactly

Table 7.3   Identifying common location strategies

(a) A basic data matrix

City	Firms' location strategies									
	Firm 1	Firm 2	Firm 3	Firm 4	Firm 5	Firm 6	Firm 7	Firm 8	Firm 9	Firm 10
London	3	2	4	2	3	3	3	4	2	2
New York	5	2	3	3	5	4	5	3	2	2
Hong Kong	2	4	2	2	2	2	2	2	2	4
Paris	2	2	5	2	2	0	2	5	2	2
Singapore	2	4	2	2	2	4	2	2	3	4
Tokyo	2	5	2	2	2	2	2	2	0	5
Shanghai	2	4	2	3	2	3	2	2	3	4
Chicago	4	2	0	1	4	2	4	0	2	2
Dubai	0	2	0	5	0	2	0	0	2	2
Sydney	3	3	2	3	3	5	3	2	1	3
Milan	2	0	4	1	2	2	2	4	5	0
Los Angeles	4	2	2	2	4	3	4	2	2	2

(b) Common and idiosyncratic strategies

City	Common strategies			Idiosyncratic strategies		
	I – American	II – Asian	III – European			
	Firms 1, 5, 7 = 30% variance	Firms 2, 10 = 20% variance	Firms 3, 8 = 20% variance	Firms 4, 6, 9 = 30% variance unaccounted		
London	3	2	4	2	3	2
New York	5	2	3	3	4	2
Hong Kong	2	4	2	2	2	2
Paris	2	2	5	2	0	2
Singapore	2	4	2	2	4	3
Tokyo	2	5	2	2	2	0
Shanghai	2	4	2	3	3	3
Chicago	4	2	0	1	2	2
Dubai	0	2	0	5	2	2
Sydney	3	3	2	3	5	1
Milan	2	0	4	1	2	5
Los Angeles	4	2	2	2	3	2

match. In actual analyses such perfect matches do not occur, instead *component scores* are calculated that produce a sort of average for all firms in a city weighted by their loading on a given component. Scores are presented as standardized variables; in this context it means they have a zero mean and scores with high positive values are deemed to indicate cities that are particularly important in a given common strategy. In Table 7.3(b) for the first strategy, New York would be computed with the highest positive score and Dubai with the lowest negative score.

In interpreting results, the component loadings for firms and component scores for cities are used to interpret and *label* the common strategies. For instance, if Firms 1 and 5 in Table 7.3(a) were banks and Firm 7 was an insurance agency, then that common strategy I would be identified as being constituted by financial service firms. Looking at the highest scores for common strategy I in Table 7.3 (b), New York, Chicago and Los Angeles score highest and therefore these financial services firms are pursuing a strategy focusing on US cities. Hence common strategy I is labelled 'American' in Table 7.3(b). Using the same logic the other two common strategies are labelled 'Asian' and 'European' in Table 7.3(b).

One final point should be made before the results are presented. It has been found in previous studies that principal components analyses are sensitive to sparse matrices, arrays including large numbers of zeros. Thus to avoid results being dominated by cities where firms do not have offices, only 138 cities of the 526 cities in the data are included, inclusion being restricted to cities having presences of at least 35 of the 175 firms.

The basic results showing ten components are presented in Table 7.4. The component labels are derived using standard interpretations: the threshold for meaningful components is set at 0.4 and above, for meaningful scores it is set at 0.5. In addition cities with high negative scores are also noted; although defining strategies leads us to search out positive scores – foci of important offices – some cities are conspicuous by their absence in a given common strategy. Absences have proven to be quite instructive in some of component interpretations; the largest examples are presented in Table 7.5, showing the 11 lowest component scores (all below –2), to which reference will be made as and when necessary in discussion of *extreme excluded cities* in the various common strategies below.

Returning to Table 7.4, the ten components define ten distinctive common location strategies. This reduction from 175 firms' individual strategies to ten common strategies incorporates slightly under 55 per cent of the initial data variance (i.e. the sum of column 2) and their labels are derived from cities with high scores as detailed below. Statistically, this result represents a very good data reduction outcome. As is usual in this type of analysis, components are listed in rank order in terms of the amount of data variance they incorporate. On this criterion the components fall into three groups: the two most important overlap in the long-term centre

Table 7.4 Ten principal components

Principal component	Percentage of variance	Given label (strategies)
1	12.29	USAL: intensive globalization
2	9.57	USAL: extensive globalization
3	6.64	Pacific Asia
4	6.08	Americas
5	6.07	Europe
6	3.66	Australasia/ Commonwealth
7	2.73	Latin America
8	2.47	Canada/ Commonwealth
9	2.30	Scandinavia
10	2.29	China

Note: USAL – USA plus London.

Table 7.5 Extreme excluded cities: cities with negative scores below −2

Scores	City	Component	Strategy
−3.96	Chicago	7	Latin America
−2.63	Mumbai	9	Scandinavia
−2.46	Tokyo	10	China
−2.44	Miami	8	Canada/Commonwealth
−2.25	Palo Alto	4	Americas
−2.21	New Delhi	9	Scandinavia
−2.20	Toronto	6	Australasia/Commonwealth
−2.17	Baltimore	2	Extensive globalization
−2.13	Beijing	7	Latin America
−2.10	Boston	9	Scandinavia
−2.08	Toronto	5	Europe

of the world-economy (the US plus London, which we call USAL), the next three compose a middle group with home-regions equating to the dominant world-regions in globalization processes (American, European and Pacific Asian); and five are relatively minor components each relating to relatively narrower home-regions. These three levels of importance should be kept in mind in descriptions of components below but I choose to organize the discussion in more geographical terms. The ten strategies fall neatly into five pairs with varying degrees of overlap: the two USAL strategies, Pacific Asia and China strategies, Americas and Latin America strategies, Europe and Scandinavia strategies and the two Commonwealth strategies. Since these overlaps represent much of the messiness that is a key feature of this particular global regionalization, they guide interpretation of the PCA below.

Before presenting the results there is a new feature in addition to the PCA, one that enhances interpretation: I add a second geography. As well as the component scores on the cities providing the usual geography of the servicing for each common strategy, there is an extra geography: the geography of the decision making that has produced the strategy is added. This is derived from the headquarter locations of the firms that contribute to a given component. Weighted by their loadings and summed to cities, these provide a measure of the headquarter functions behind each common strategy. Those cities measuring 0.5 or over on this summation are designated *command cities* and these have been identified for all ten common strategies in Table 7.6. We are now ready to consider each pair of common location strategies in detail.

USAL Strategies: Intensive and Extensive Globalizations

The combination of US cities and London has been central to the construction of economic globalization and its current crisis (Wójcik 2011). I have combined them in interpreting the home-region of the two most important components because London has a component score and a HQ sum of over 1.5, like New York and Chicago, in both location strategies (Table 7.6). Such combinations of scores and sums are rare: there are only four other examples in the whole of the rest of the analysis all denoting the key cities in a home-region (Tokyo and Beijing in Pacific Asia, and Sydney and Toronto in their respective Commonwealth components).

USAL is the home-region for these two components that account for over 20 per cent of the variance in the data between them. Their service geographies are given in Figure 7.1(a) and 7.1(b), and their constituent loadings are to be found in Table 7.7. Note that it is London alone and not UK cities in general that feature in Figure 7.1(a) and 7.1(b). That this north Atlantic connection, a long-term central link of the world-economy, defines the home-region for today's most important common strategies is in keeping with the Americanization of the mid-twentieth century being the precursor of globalization in the late twentieth century. This is because London was integral to this process: in hindsight we can see that the City of London's invention of the Eurodollar market in 1957 (Burn 2000;

Table 7.6   Headquarter scores for location strategies

HQ cities	1	2	3	4	5	6	7	8	9	10
Atlanta				0.5						
Baltimore	0.5									
Beijing			1.9							0.5
Boston	1.1			0.5	1			0.6		
Brasília							0.7			
Brussels				0.5						
Charlotte				0.5						
Chicago	4.8	1.9		0.6						
Columbus	0.6									
Detroit	0.6									
Dublin				0.6						
Frankfurt					0.5					
Istanbul					0.5					
Johannesburg						0.5				
London	1.9	3.3	0.9		3.1	0.5				
Los Angeles	1.4									
Madrid					1		0.9			
Melbourne			0.5			1.3				
Miami	0.7									
Milan					1.1					
Mumbai								5		
Munich					0.7	0.6				
New York	9.8	8.2		4.7						
Oslo									0.5	
Paris		1.1	0.5		0.5					
Philadelphia	0.8									
Pittsburgh	1.4									
San Francisco	0.5									
São Paulo							1.3			
Seoul			1.2							
Shanghai										0.7
Shenzhen										0.7
Singapore			0.7							
Stockholm									1.3	
Sydney						1.5				
Tokyo			5.3							
Toronto	1.3			1				1.6		
Trieste					0.5					
Turin					0.5					
Washington	0.7									
Zurich				0.5						

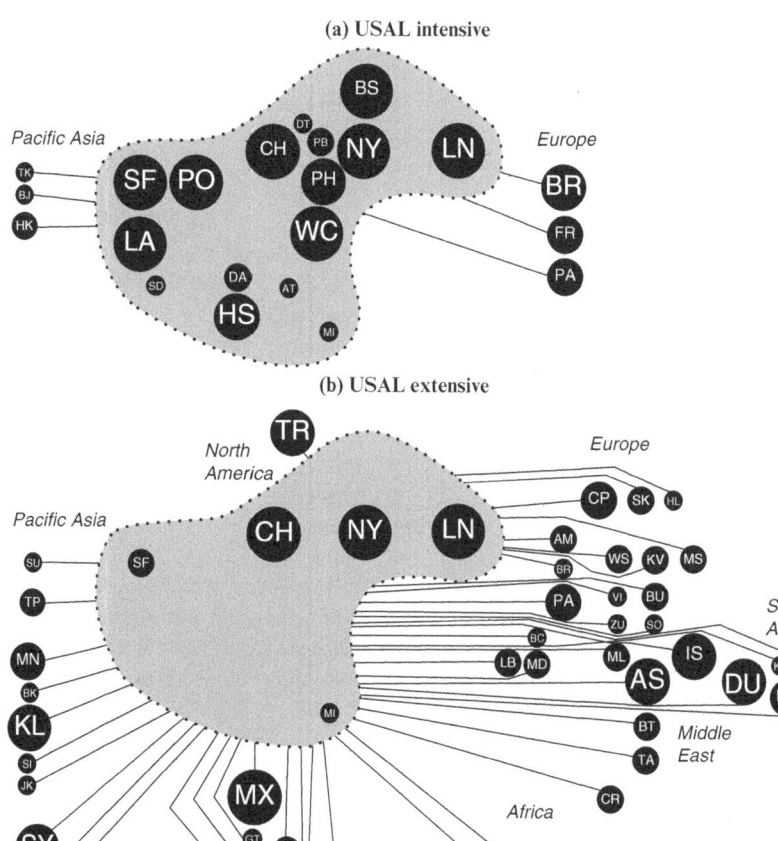

(a) USAL intensive

(b) USAL extensive

Note: Codes used for cities in the analysis are as follows:

AA	Amman	CR	Caracas	LG	Lagos	PX	Phoenix
AD	Abu Dhabi	CS	Casablanca	LM	Lima	RI	Riga
AK	Auckland	CT	Cape Town	LN	London	RJ	Rio de Janeiro
AL	Almaty	CV	Cleveland	LX	Luxembourg	RM	Rome
AM	Amsterdam	DA	Dallas	MB	Mumbai	RY	Riyadh
AN	Antwerp	DB	Dublin	MC	Manchester	SA	Santiago
AS	Athens	DH	Doha	MD	Madrid	SD	San Diego
AT	Atlanta	DS	Düsseldorf	ME	Melbourne	SE	Seattle
BA	Buenos Aires	DT	Detroit	MI	Miami	SF	San Francisco
BB	Brisbane	DU	Dubai	ML	Milan	SG	Stuttgart
BC	Barcelona	DV	Denver	MM	Manama	SH	Shanghai

BD	Budapest	ED	Edinburgh	MN	Manila	SI	Singapore
BE	Belgrade	FR	Frankfurt AM	MO	Monterrey	SJ	San José
BG	Bogotá	GL	Glasgow	MP	Minneapolis	SK	Stockholm
BI	Birmingham	GN	Geneva	MS	Moscow	SL	Saint Louis
BJ	Beijing	GT	Guatemala City	MT	Montréal	SN	San Juan
BK	Bangkok	GZ	Guangzhou	MU	Munich	SO	Sofia
BL	Berlin	HA	Hanoi	MV	Montevideo	SP	São Paulo
BM	Baltimore	HC	Ho Chi Minh	MX	Mexico City	ST	Santo Domingo
BN	Bangalore	HK	Hong Kong	NC	Nicosia	SU	Seoul
BR	Brussels	HL	Helsinki	ND	New Delhi	SY	Sydney
BS	Boston	HB	Hamburg	NR	Nairobi	SZ	Shenzhen
BT	Beirut	HS	Houston	NY	New York	TA	Tel Aviv
BU	Bucharest	IS	Istanbul	OK	Osaka	TK	Tokyo
BV	Bratislava	JB	Johannesburg	OS	Oslo	TM	Tampa
CA	Cairo	JD	Jeddah	PA	Paris	TP	Taipei
CC	Kolkata	JK	Jakarta	PB	Pittsburgh	TR	Toronto
CG	Calgary	KC	Kansas City	PD	Portland	TU	Tunis
CH	Chicago	KL	Kuala Lumpur	PE	Perth	VI	Vienna
CI	Cincinnati	KR	Karachi	PH	Philadelphia	VN	Vancouver
CL	Charlotte	KU	Kuwait	PL	Port Louis	WC	Washington
CN	Chennai	KV	Kiev	PN	Panama City	WS	Warsaw
CO	Cologne	LA	Los Angeles	PO	Palo Alto	ZG	Zagreb
CP	Copenhagen	LB	Lisbon	PR	Prague	ZU	Zurich

Component scores

≥1.50   1.25 to 1.49   1.00 to 1.24   0.75 to 0.99   0.50 to 0.74

Home-region   Global
                        outreach

Source: Taylor et al. (2013).

Figure 7.1   USAL globalization strategies

Kynaston 2011) was a true pioneer of contemporary globalization with London's deregulation – 'big bang' – in 1986 consolidating the process.

In keeping with being the largest component, the intensive globalization strategy has by far the most contributing firms, mainly US law firms, banks and management consultancies (Table 7.6, Table 7.7). The decision-making geography of these firms is dominated by New York, with Chicago also very important and London in third place ahead of ten US cities and one Canadian city (Table 7.6). The servicing geography is largely restricted to USAL and here there are eight cities leading the provisioning: Boston, Chicago, London, Los Angeles, New York, Palo

Table 7.7   Service sectors and common location strategies

Strategies	ACC	ADV	FS	LAW	MC
Intensive globalization	0	2	15	23	10
Extensive globalization	4	19	1	0	2
Americas	2	1	9	2	8
Latin America	0	0	5	0	0
Pacific Asia	0	3	16	0	0
China	0	0	5	0	0
Europe	0	0	9	6	5
Scandinavia	0	0	3	0	0
Australasia/CW	0	0	7	0	1
Canada/CW	0	0	5	0	0

Notes: ACC – accountancy; ADV – advertising; FS – financial services; MC – management consultancy.

Alto, San Francisco and Washington, DC, ahead of eight other US cities (Figure 7.1a). But this is not a simple detached home-region; these firms' strategies reach out to the rest of the world-economy, but with a very selective global outreach, focusing on only the most important cities in the two other key global regions. Thus there are three outreach cities in Europe – Brussels, Frankfurt and Paris – and three in Pacific Asia – Beijing, Hong Kong and Tokyo. It is this extreme selectivity, a global outreach of just six major cities beyond USAL, which warrants the labelling of this strategy as intensive globalization.

The extensive globalization strategy is a very different component. It is largely constituted by advertising agencies (Table 7.7) and these firms typically have large worldwide office networks. This is reflected in the geography of the servicing (Figure 7.1(b)), which features far more cities than intensive globalization: its global outreach covers all regions of the world. The USAL home-region has three of the five leading service provision cities – Chicago, London and New York – but includes only two other cities. In fact the home-region includes an extreme excluded city, as defined and listed in Table 7.5: Baltimore represents the hollowing out of the US in this strategy wherein most US cities are missing. In the global outreach, Johannesburg and Mexico City are the other two leading cities and the remaining cities are spread across Europe (19), Latin America (seven), Pacific Asia (seven), Africa/Middle East (four), South Asia (four), and Australasia (three). However, the decision-making geography of this strategy is much more concentrated than intensive globalization: only four cities feature (Table 7.6). New York still dominates, but London has overtaken Chicago, which this time is the only other US city. Paris features here (as the last command city) on account of its traditional servicing prowess in advertising.

The intriguing finding is having London located in the home-region in what are otherwise American location strategies. Clearly the original locus of contemporary globalization, USAL, has been where these most important global strategies are generated – one highly concentrated in its servicing and command plus a selective global outreach, the other with an impressively worldwide global outreach but with a more select command city geography. It seems that even the globalization emanating from the economic heartland of the world-economy refutes any notion that there is a single global process homogenizing the world.

American Strategies: Regional and Inter-regional Geographies

The components centred on USAL are not the only common strategies emanating from US command and service provision. There is an additional strategy that encompasses other parts of the Americas, that excludes London, and in which the role of New York is less central. In addition there is a minor strategy that emanates from South America but strongly uses London and New York in its servicing provision.

The Americas common strategy (Table 7.7) is largely the product of US consultancy firms and financial services with less of an input from law firms than the intensive globalization strategy. However, once again New York dominates the command cities (Table 7.6) but without London, and with Chicago ranked third. Toronto is the second most important command city and there are three other US cities, plus three Western European cities. The relative importance of Toronto in this strategy is confirmed by the service provision geography, which features all four Canadian cities in our data, with three being highest category cities (Figure 7.2(a)). The US has 17 cities included in this strategy with four in the highest category. But the latter are very different from the USAL service geographies; they are Boston and three southern cities – Atlanta, Dallas and Miami. New York, like London, does not even feature in this geography. And there is an extreme excluded US city: the high-tech centre of Palo Alto is most certainly not part of this strategy (Table 7.5). In addition there are four Latin American cities in the servicing geography that, with the Canadian cities, warrants the inter-regional label of Americas as home-region. This common strategies' global outreach is largely to Europe with nine cities (strongly featuring Dublin and Zurich) and Pacific Asia with seven cities (strongly featuring Singapore). There are also two cities each from South Asia and Australasia (with Sydney featuring strongly in the latter).

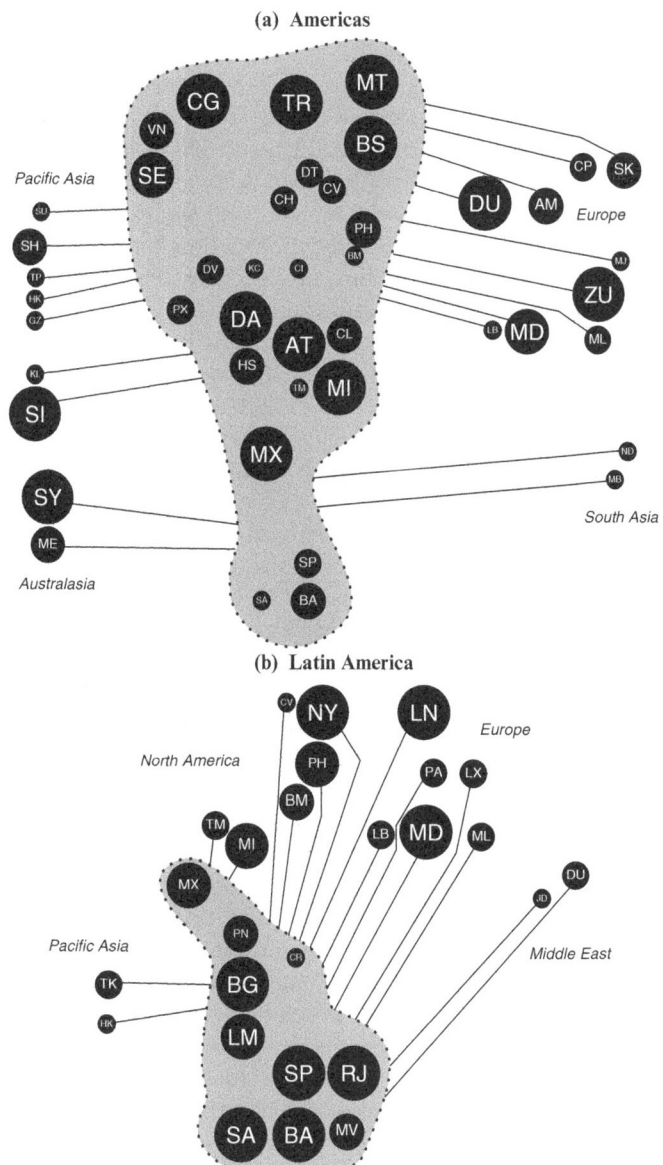

(a) Americas

(b) Latin America

Note: For city codes, see Figure 7.1.

Source: Taylor et al. (2013).

Figure 7.2 Americas strategies

The smaller and more specific Latin American common strategy is constituted by financial service firms (Table 7.7) from two Brazilian command cities – São Paulo and Brasília – plus Madrid (Table 7.6). The resulting service geography is strongly focused on the South America home-region in which all ten cities in the data are featured, five of them with highest category scores: Bogotá, Buenos Aires, Rio de Janeiro, Santiago and São Paulo (Figure 7.2(b)). There are three highest category cities in the global reach: London and New York as mentioned previously, plus Madrid. Miami and Philadelphia also feature prominently among five other US cities in this service geography, and there are also four other cities in Europe, all from Western Europe. Elsewhere just four other cities feature in this geography, two from Pacific Asia and two from the Middle East. Finally, this strategy has two extreme excluded cities both of which are interesting: Chicago, confirming this city's restriction to a USAL role, and Beijing, confirming the relative weakness of this strategy in the important global zone of Pacific Asia.

The addition of these American common strategies to the USAL strategies illustrates the complexity of this regional geography with its extreme excluded US cities and the different uses of New York and London. But all this is in keeping with the US role in generating and promoting economic globalization. However, there are more common strategies not including the US as part of a home-region, six out of ten, showing that globalization is geographically so much more than prior Americanization of the world-economy.

Asian Strategies: a New Distinctive China Initiative

Spinning around to the other side of the globe there are two intriguing common strategies that are even more contrasting than those of the previous discussions. The Pacific Asia component is a well-established common strategy and has featured prominently in previous analyses of service values matrices. In contrast, this is the first such analysis that has identified a specific China strategy. Studies of network connectivity have shown the increasing importance of Chinese cities, specifically Beijing and Shanghai in 2004 (Taylor and Aranya 2008) and in 2008 (Derudder et al. 2010), and it appears that this has finally developed into a distinctive common strategy in 2010. One result of the quite different provenances of these two strategies is that they are very different in size: Pacific Asia ranks third in importance and China enters the list in tenth place (Table 7.4).

The Pacific Asia common strategy is constituted largely by Japanese banks and advertising agencies (Table 7.7). This is reflected by the massive dominance of Tokyo among command cities, above other home-region cities – Beijing, Seoul and Singapore (Table 7.6). It is noteworthy that the list of command cities also includes three cities from the global outreach (London, Paris and Melbourne). However, in the geography of the actual service provisioning, this common strategy totally covers its home-region where every city is strongly featured: of the 16 Pacific Asian cities included in the analysis, fully 12 of them are in the highest component scores category (Figure 7.3(a)). In contrast there is only one global-outreach city in this highest category (Los Angeles). But there are ten further outreach cities and they show a quite distinctive and relatively even global geography. Four are elsewhere in Asia (two in South Asia, two in the Middle East), three are in Europe (two western – Frankfurt and Luxembourg, one eastern – Moscow), one other in North America (Toronto), one in Latin America (São Paulo), and one in Australasia (Sydney). This is globalization Pacific-Asian style in 2010.

The China common strategy is based on just five firms all from financial services (Table 7.7). There are just three command cities, all Chinese (Table 7.6). In the geography of servicing provision all five Chinese cities fall into the highest component score category (Figure 7.3(b)). This is a China-only home-region and its separation from the rest of Pacific Asia is shown by the fact that with only one exception, Pacific Asian cities do not even feature in the global outreach. This is emphasized by the fact that Tokyo, the leading city of the Pacific Asia common strategy, features as an extreme excluded city in this strategy (Table 7.5). Taipei, a Chinese world city but not administered by China has a minus score. The China strategy also differs sharply from the Pacific Asia strategy in the size of its global reach, 21 cities, which is almost twice the number in the Pacific Asia strategy. The China global reach is concentrated in the US where both New York and Miami feature as highest component score cities. In the latter case this may represent an alternative Latin American penetration since no cities from that region feature in this service geography. In Western Europe there is just London featured (remember that neither London nor New York are in the Pacific Asia service geography). However Eastern Europe is represented by five cities, South Asia by three cities, and Africa by one city, Johannesburg, which is notably important as the only second highest component score category city in this geography. Clearly a very distinctive servicing geography, it appears to reflect Chinese overseas past, present and possible future investments.

The discovery of this Chinese common strategy in 2010 is an intriguing finding that may well portend a much more important strategy in future world city network development. This is a clear case of overlapping regions since all the Chinese cities are featured in the Pacific Asia home-region, while also constituting their own home-region. By carving out its

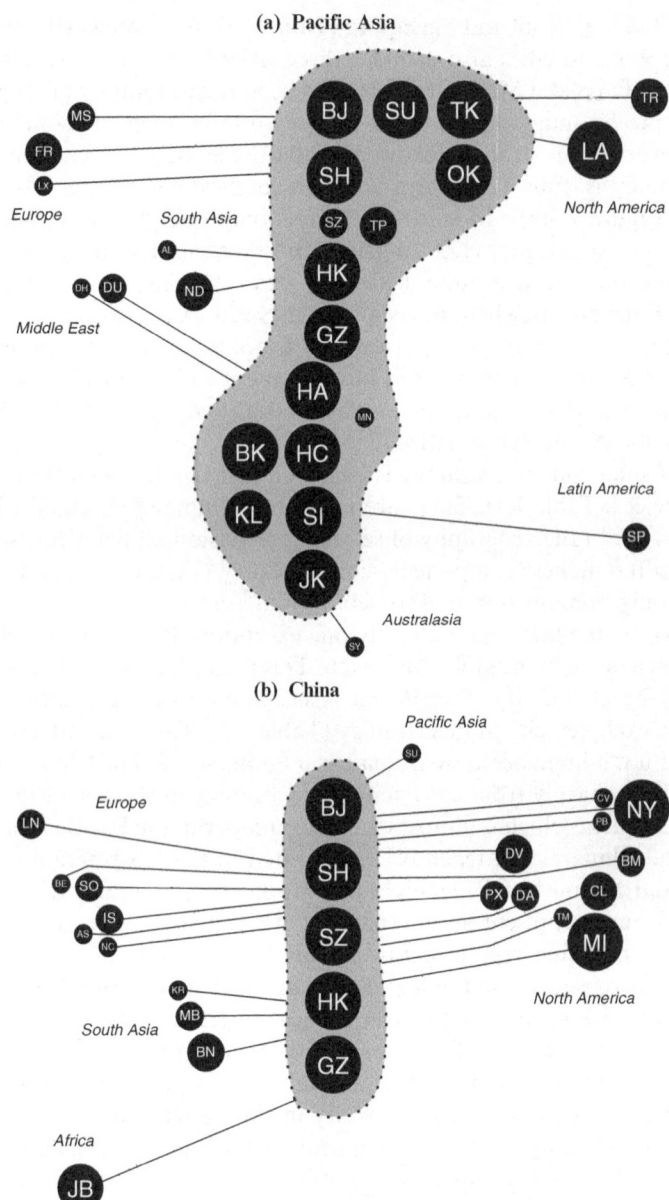

(a) Pacific Asia

(b) China

Note: For city codes, see Figure 7.1.

Source: Taylor et al. (2013).

Figure 7.3   Asia strategies

own strategic geography of home-region and global reach, this suggests that China is not simply another Pacific Asian 'development state' to come to the fore in a globalizing world economy. Neither is it simply a rival to Japan in the Pacific Asian regional-economy; rather it represents a new intervention in the world city network that transcends Pacific Asia perhaps even suggesting a possible future rival of USAL.

European Strategies: Mainstream and Northern

Back in the traditional centre of the world-economy, indeed its initial core zone, Europe is represented by two common strategies. However they are not as might be predicted. In general, there are two familiar regional divisions of Europe: an East–West contrast that historically culminated in the Cold War division; and an equally old North–South division, with the latter consisting of the Mediterranean regions. Both of these divisions have been based upon roughly equal parts of Europe. Not so our identification of contemporary global strategies wherein the two home-regions are of very different magnitudes (Table 7.4) as reflected in their labels: an almost inclusive Europe strategy and a small Scandinavian strategy.

The Europe strategy is constituted by London law firms and more broadly European financial services and European consultancies (Table 7.7). This is reflected in the command cities where London dominates but eight other European cities appear from across the continent (Table 7.6). This widespread home-region pattern is confirmed and elaborated in the service provision geography (Figure 7.4(a)). Here we find a German city concentration (five of seven German cities in the data) in the highest scoring category plus Madrid, Milan and Rome from the South and Moscow from the East. In addition there is one highest category city in the global outreach: Shanghai. This city indicates a location strategy that focuses on China – Beijing and Hong Kong are included – and with further links into South Asia (Mumbai), the Arab Gulf (Abu Dhabi and Dubai), South America (São Paulo) and North America (Boston). This last city's position is somewhat intriguing, suggesting connections that confirm Boston as the most 'European' US city. In contrast, just across the border in Canada, Toronto is an extreme excluded city for the European firms in this component (Table 7.5).

The Scandinavia common strategy is a minor one (Table 7.4) constituted by just three firms, all northern European banks (Table 7.7). The result is just two command cities: Stockholm and Oslo (Table 7.6). The geography of this service provision is very distinctive including 12 highest category cities (Figure 7.4(b)). These include the five home-region cities in the data (three strictly Scandinavian: Copenhagen, Oslo and Stockholm;

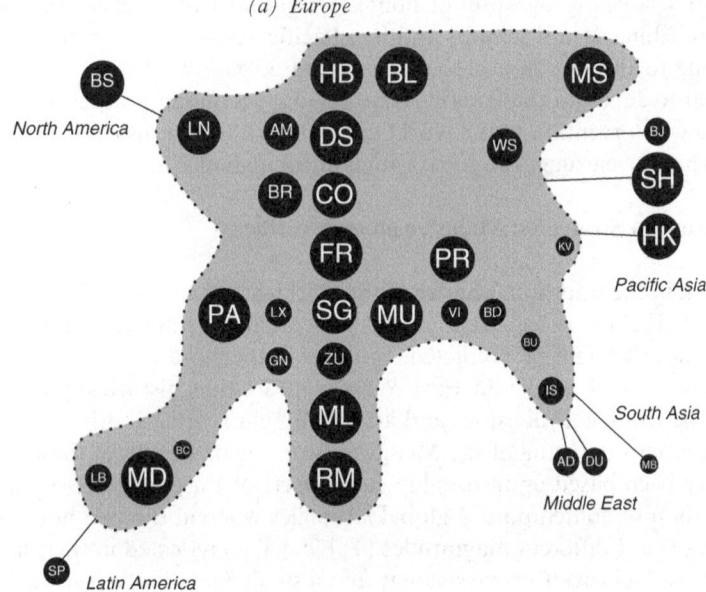

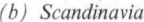

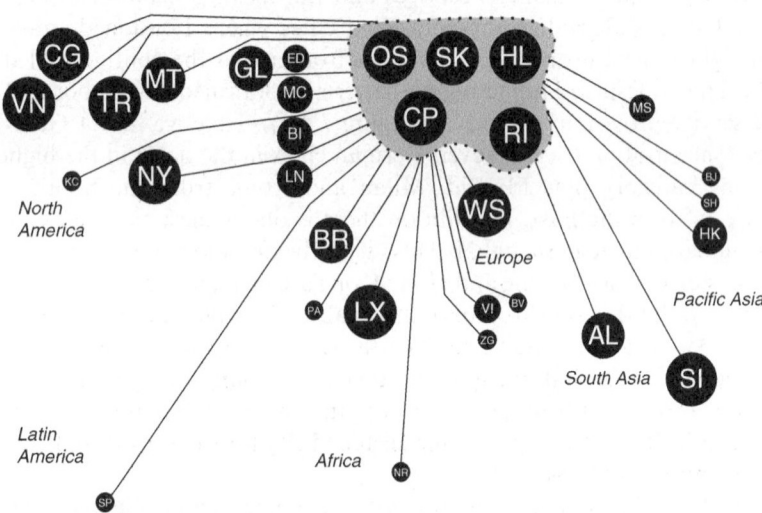

Note: For city codes, see Figure 7.1.

Source: Taylor et al. (2013).

Figure 7.4   Europe strategies

and two Baltic: Helsinki and Riga). The highest category cities extend this 'northern rim' pattern to the Americas to include three Canadian cities (Calgary, Toronto and Vancouver) in its global outreach. The category also includes New York, Luxembourg and Singapore. There is less representation in other continents; the most interesting is Nairobi, a key NGO centre (Taylor 2005) for Scandinavian international development policies. It is also noteworthy that this component has most extreme excluded cities in Table 7.3: these Scandinavian financial services firms are seriously deficient in their servicing in India (Mumbai and New Delhi) and Boston.

It is not entirely clear why these two different strategies have developed in Europe. Although there is some overlap, it is the separation between the service maps that is most striking: the European strategy misses out Scandinavian cities and the Scandinavia strategy misses out German and southern European cities.

Alternative Commonwealth Strategies

One of the surprises in the initial analyses of service values matrices was the appearance of a Commonwealth component (Taylor 2004). Not generally associated with business services, this political relict of British imperialism does actually incorporate continuing cultural links that are reflected in early internationalizing business strategies now enveloped by contemporary globalization. In this latest analysis, we find two Commonwealth strategies associated with erstwhile British dominions at opposite ends of the Earth. Both common strategies are minor ones (Table 7.4), but still interesting in their expression of historical connections.

The Australasia/Commonwealth strategy is the larger of the two (Table 7.4) and is constituted largely by financial services firms (Table 7.7). As would be expected, its two main command cities are Sydney and Melbourne; interestingly, the other command city is Johannesburg (Table 7.6). The servicing geography is very straightforward (Figure 7.5(a)): as well as all five home-region cities in the data in the highest service category scores, the global outreach includes other important Commonwealth cities from across the world – Birmingham, Cape Town, Hong Kong, London, Mumbai, Singapore – except for Canada. North America is only represented weakly in one city, New York. All UK cities in the data are included in this geography but no other European cities. In contrast, Toronto is found to be an extremely excluded city for this component.

The Canada/Commonwealth strategy is also the product of financial services firms (Table 7.7). In this case Toronto dominates as command city: the other command city of interest is Mumbai (Table 7.6). All four home-region cities in the data have highest category scores, and in the

(a) Australasia Commonwealth

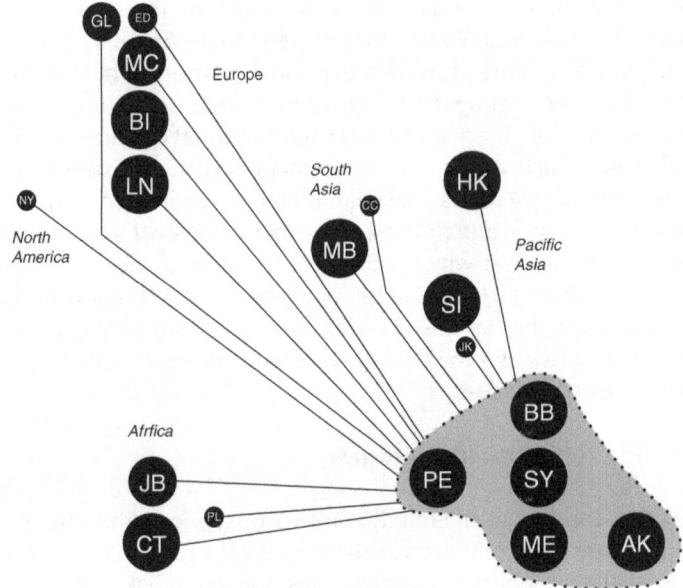

(b) Canada Commonwealth

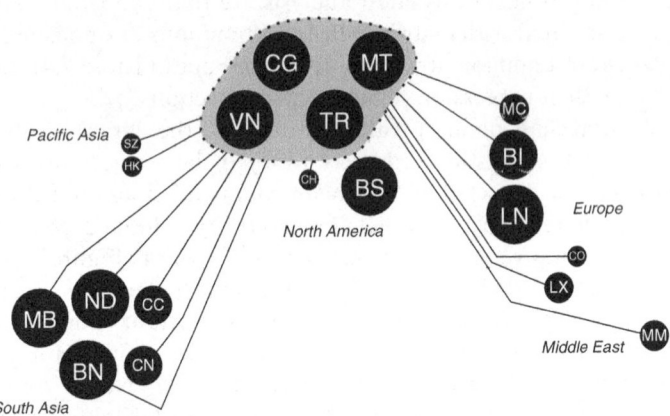

Note: For city codes, see Figure 7.1.

Source: Taylor et al. (2013).

Figure 7.5   Commonwealth strategies

global outreach, Boston and London are in this category along with three Indian cities (Bangalore, Mumbai and New Delhi) (Figure 7.5(b)). With the two other Indian cities in the data being included in this servicing geography, this strategy differs from the Australian one through its more spatially concentrated pattern. There is no representation in Australasia or Africa, only Chicago features weakly in the rest of the Americas (Miami appears as an extreme excluded city (Table 7.5)), there is also only Manama featuring weakly in the Middle East, and although Pacific Asia includes two cities these are also weakly featured. In the UK only English cities are included in the servicing geography but there are two other European cities weakly featured, including Luxembourg.

Having Commonwealth common strategies still seems surprising, even more so in 2010 through discovering two quite distinct examples. This provides a reminder that business location strategy is never a simple matter of economic advantage, other types of connection have roles to play in constructing economic opportunities to which business can respond.

Comparing Geographies

The method of paired comparisons is particularly insightful for the 2010 PCA results, but there are additional things to be said using overall comparisons across the ten common strategies. Table 7.8 has been constructed for this task. For each common strategy, cities are divided between home-region and global outreach and their scores compared. In addition for the home-regions, the total number of cities is given to show the degree to which each location strategy is inclusive of its home-regional cities. However the main purpose of this table is to show variations in the amount of servicing carried out in the home-region relative to the global outreach for each common strategy.

The first point to make is that global outreach is not a minor geographical add-on to an otherwise 'traditional' set of home-regions: the final column of Table 7.8 indicates that global outreach contributes more servicing than home-region in a majority of the common strategies. Even the lowest proportion of servicing for global outreach is nearly 15 per cent, which is by no means insignificant. Looking at the range of values, the three lowest percentages for global outreach represent what have been identified as the key 'globalization arenas' in the making of a globalizing world (USAL intensive, Pacific Asia, Europe) (Taylor 2004). These are regions with their own major advanced producer service firms strongly ensconced in their own important world-region. In contrast the highest percentages for global outreach are largely for strategies from smaller home-regions: the two Commonwealth strategies and Scandinavia.

Table 7.8 *Geographical comparisons between common strategies*

Common strategy	Home-region				Global outreach		
	Cities	Service cities	Average service (score)	Percentage total service	Service cities	Average service (score)	Percentage total service
USAL intensive	28	16	2.09	85.21	6	0.97	14.79
USAL extensive	28	5	1.42	14.18	47	0.92	85.82
Americas	45	25	1.25	61.56	20	0.98	38.44
Latin America	13	10	1.88	48.89	16	1.23	51.11
Pacific Asia	16	16	2.15	77.41	11	0.91	22.59
China	5	5	3.46	46.20	21	0.96	53.80
Europe	38	28	1.48	84.67	7	1.07	15.33
Scandinavia	5	5	2.44	27.44	26	1.24	72.56
Australasia/ Commonwealth	5	5	3.41	14.09	14	1.49	85.91
Canada/ Commonwealth	4	4	2.65	30.52	15	1.61	69.48

Note: USAL – USA plus London.

However, there is one major exception: the second largest percentage of servicing from the global outreach is for USAL extensive; this is a very distinctive location strategy in many ways, and seems to represent a particularly strong move to globalization from the traditional central region of the world-economy.

Conversely we should not under-value the home-region in these globalization strategies: for all common strategies the average service value for home-region cities is larger than for global-reach cities. This is particularly the case for the four smallest home-regions where all regional cities provide high levels of service. Thus overall the message of these comparisons is to confirm the importance of both home-region and global outreach. Between them they constitute integrated spatial strategies that divide globalization processes into a new regional formation.

What does this all add up to? How does it relate to our previous discussions of city networks? As before, what we have been describing is an unusual network in that it is not the nodes (city guardians) that are the network makers, but agents within the nodes, commercial firms. And it is these that ensure the network is based upon complementarities rather than competition. This does not mean there is no competition but this feature is more contingent and involves specific state effects. Where there were states with two leading cities in their 'national economies', globalization has tended to result in one of them leading the way through their service sector in the world city network. Thus have Sydney, São Paulo, Tokyo and Toronto become relatively more important than Melbourne, Rio de Janeiro Osaka and Montréal respectively.

In terms of import replacement there seems to be two forms operating. With the intensive and extensive globalizations US (and London) firms are investing in other major cities in the world-economy and in the process are creating an inward investment form of import replacement. For instance, a London law firm opening a major new office in Singapore is introducing advanced legal services to the city that previously would have had to have been imported from London. But the other more regionally focused strategies represent the usual form of 'indigenous' import replacement as described by Jacobs (1969). A new and growing São Paulo advertising agency can replace work that was previously done in their city by New York advertising agencies (Faulconbridge et al. 2011). Both forms of import replacement make economic space for import shifting and consequent economic expansion. In other words, Sassen's global cities and, more generally, the better-connected cities within the world city network, are contemporary instances of Jacobs' dynamic cities.

CITIES IN GLOBALIZATION II: MEGA-CITIES

As well as the world city network formation, the twentieth century bequeathed a very different but equally important global urban process: mega-city formation. The concept of mega-city is a very simple one. Developed by UN institutions to describe ever-larger urban agglomerations, they are defined as cities with populations above a given high threshold. The latter has increased as city sizes have grown and at the time of writing the threshold is ten million. This figure defines 26 cities as 'mega' and these are listed in Table 7.9. To put this into historical perspective, in 1900 there were no cities with a population of 10 million. In fact there were only 16 cities with populations over one million (Chandler 1987, p. 492); today there are 477 such 'millionaire cities' (www.citypopulation. de, accessed 21 February 2011)!

The New Geography of Large Cities

Clearly the twentieth century was a period of massive urbanization. But it is not just the sizes of cities that have changed; the world geography of largest cities has fundamentally altered. Of the 16 millionaire cities in 1900, half were from the UK and US (four each), with three more from continental Western Europe, two from Russia, and one each from China, India and Japan. In Table 7.9 only six cities are from this old economic core-region of the world-economy (two each from US, Western Europe, and Japan): half of today's mega-cities are in the developing countries of Asia (13), with the remainder from Latin America (four), Africa (two) and Russia. Of course this geographical realignment has been long recognized and has been associated with a break in the determinants of large urban population growth (Castells 1978). In the historical narratives above the population size of cities has been used as a surrogate for their economic dynamics. And this was how contemporaries interpreted the great urbanization of the nineteenth century: Weber (1899) identified this period of massive urbanization as a consequence of large-scale industrialization. But large city growth in the twentieth century displayed a disjuncture between demographic growth and economic development: most of the cities listed in Table 7.9 are not the important hubs of the world-economy described previously as the world city network. This 'causal break' where population growth does not reflect economic growth is usually dated to around the middle of the twentieth century. It is this new process, mega-city formation, that has led to the situation in the early twenty-first century where urban dwellers constitute a majority of humanity.

As a generic city-ness process within a specific modern world systemic

Table 7.9   *Mega-cities (as of 1 January 2011)*

Rank	City	Population (millions)
1	Tokyo	34.2
2	Guangzhou	24.5
3	Seoul	24.5
4	Delhi	23.9
5	Mumbai	23.3
6	Mexico City	22.8
7	New York	22.2
8	São Paulo	20.8
9	Manila	20.1
10	Shanghai	18.8
11	Jakarta	18.7
12	Los Angeles	17.9
13	Osaka	16.8
14	Karachi	16.7
15	Kolkata	16.6
16	Cairo	15.3
17≈	Buenos Aires	14.8
17≈	Moscow	14.8
19	Dhaka	14.0
20	Beijing	13.9
21	Tehran	13.1
22	Istanbul	13.0
23≈	London	12.5
23≈	Rio de Janeiro	12.5
25	Lagos	12.1
26	Paris	10.5

Source: The Principal Agglomerations of the World (www.citypopulation.de/world/Agglomerations, accessed 21 February 2011).

process, mega-city formation in the twentieth century and today is the result of a critical intersection of two key processes. Looking back to Chapter 2 (Figure 2.3), mega-cities result from a combination of massively enhanced demand on primary supply regions and strong push factors favouring clearances of unwanted rural labour. For all of its history the modern world-system has undermined peasant economies as cities continually remake the world for their ever-changing needs (Vanhaute 2008). It is this 'creative destruction' of the 'rural' that has come to a head in the last half-century to create the unparalleled phenomenon of numerous mega-cities.

The key point for this final 'global' remaking of the rural is the geographical separation of the cities that are primarily responsible for the ever increasing demand, from the world regions required to satisfy the demand. When this process intersects with the inter-state system the result is that the consequent rural–urban migration is primarily not to the rich cities in the core of the world-economy but rather to cities within the poorer states of non-core regions. Therefore the economic growth in core cities has become detached from the rural upheaval it has caused in non-core supply regions. The end result is the creation of mega-cities in leading cities of poor countries. And whatever local city dynamism exists in these countries, it cannot keep up with (i.e. produce enough jobs for) the colossal level of rural–urban migration being created by outside forces. This is commonplace rural–urban migration but on a new level: the 'unprecedented upheaval in the global countryside' (Davis 2006, p.16). A hollowing out of the rural world is happening with terms such as de-agrarianization, de-peasantization and, more generally, de-ruralization being widely used (Wallerstein 1999). This is an immense mega-migration flow. Across the world, the reasons for these great flows of people are manifold and vary greatly but rampant market forces disadvantaging small farmers, imposed structural adjustment programmes, plus savage military conflicts, are each very important. In Davis' words: 'Cities ... have simply harvested this world agrarian crisis' (p. 16).

Worlds of Despair, Worlds of Hope

Most of the research and discussion on mega-cities has been under the auspices of the United Nations. As previously noted they have decided the increasing size threshold for membership and this interest is related to their Habitat programme that is concerned with the severe problems of living in large poor cities. In this case size and rapid growth throw up myriad crises relating to housing, water, security and other basic services. This was a continuation of seeing 'cities as problems' that dominated the 1970s and 1980s and earlier eras. In fact terminology from the past was revived with the identification of 'mega-slums'. However, as reported in Chapter 1, the idea of 'cities as solutions' reached United Nations agencies by the turn of the century. Thus there has been appreciation and recognition of these large, dense, concentrations of people as sites for renewed creativity, albeit in very difficult circumstances. There is both creativity for economic survival and creativity for economic growth.

Mega-city slums as documented by UN-Habitat (2003) and interpreted by Mike Davis (2006) as a sort of 'surplus humanity' are worlds of despair. The term slum was coined in the late nineteenth century to describe the poor housing conditions in the growing cities of Europe and North

America. But what is happening today in the poorer countries of the world is at a completely different scale. As Davis (2006) shows so vividly, today there are mega-cities largely constituted of mega-slums. The growth of urbanization in the periphery has been unparalleled in creating mega-cities but that demographic growth rate has itself been easily outpaced by the growth rate of slums – as one Indian observer has put it: 'If such a trend continues unabated we will have only slums and no cities' (Davis 2006, p.18). Already in a few countries slum-dwellers account for almost all the urban population. (Cities in Chad and Ethiopia are ranked first equal with an amazing 99.4 per cent of city dwellers classified as slum-dwellers (p.23).) The number of 'millionaire cities' reported for 1900 is about the same as 'millionaire slums' today: Davis lists 14 slums each housing over a million people (p.28). There are currently estimated to be 200000 slums across the world (p.26): this is an urban phenomenon, and equally as exceptional a component of contemporary globalization as the world city network.

Overall, this pans out as urbanization in its most virulent pernicious form: rich cities are restructuring far-off lands with the consequent herding of people into poor (job-scarce) cities. With inadequate economic growth and formal work declining, informal work becomes the norm but can no longer be a stepping-stone to the formal sector. According to Brand (2010, p.42) 'squatters are now the predominant builders of cities in the world', so that, rather than steel and glass towers of the world city network, the emblematic city of the future is more likely to be made of discarded plastic and wattle: Davis' (2006) 'planet of slums'. Additional jobs are being created through the fragmentation of existing informal work (pp.181–2). But this survival strategy is the very opposite of Jacobs' (1969) 'new work' that expands economies. Jacobs' new work leads to a more complex division of labour as in world city network formation; in mega-city formation, work fragmentation merely divides existing old work in a stagnant or declining market: it is a downward spiral of increasing poverty.

But creativity is creativity, even if primarily used to generate an economics of survival. I would judge that more creativity is required to survive in Kinshasa or Karachi than is needed to generate banking profits in London or New York. Thus Davis' (2006) despairing prognosis is not the only way to interpret the economics of mega-slums. For Brand (2010, p.36) 'squatter cities are vibrant', so that these 'slums are the scene of a world-changing economic event' (p.43). There is growing evidence that new waves of economic growth are being generated in these seemingly inhospitable places: Neuwirth (2006) shows the new urban creativity in a much more positive economic light; Brugmann (2009) sees the making of new urban revolutions. From the perspective of this book we can argue that this is a contest between Jacobs' generic urban process and Wallerstein's specific structural peripheral process. If the evidence continues to grow that Jacobsean processes are happening in these least likely places in the capitalist world-economy, this would signal a critical erosion of the modern world-system's ordinary reproduction and therefore provide clear support for Wallerstein's prognosis that we are in the demise phase of the system, of which more in the next chapter.

TWO ECONOMIC GLOBALIZATIONS: CITIES AND STATES IN THE EARLY TWENTY-FIRST CENTURY

The best refutation that globalization heralds the end of the state is the simple fact that globalization is itself a product of state policies. The global space of flows of recent decades is dependent upon government policies premised on the superiority of private markets over public intervention. Originally associated with two conservative political leaders as Thatcherism and Reaganomics, these ideas were to become truly global in two steps. First, in the 1980s and 1990s the 'Washington consensus' doled out a very strict economic medicine to ailing poor countries – IMF structural adjustment programmes that imposed free trade, reduced budgets, financial deregulation, and privatization of state assets – to perpetuate their role as supply regions for rich countries. Second, the World Trade Organization (WTO) came into existence in 1995 with prime aims of promoting trade liberalization and economic competition. It now has over 150 states as members including China who joined in 2001. In short, this represents a global *modus operandi* between states and multi-national corporations, who reportedly have morphed into global corporations.

The common name for this policy nexus is neoliberalism. The original nineteenth-century economic liberalism promoted the 'nightwatchman state', reducing state actions largely to the protection of private property; contemporary neoliberalism promotes a 'nightwatchman' global governance regime that protects private property (global corporations) internationally. We can trace this back to the late 1970s when economic stagnation was blamed on Keynsian economic policies and the growing welfare state (Harvey 2005). Not coincidentally, the political turn to neoliberalism coincided with two equally profound changes. First, the 1970s saw the combination of two hitherto distinct industries – computers and communication – to usher in a new connectivity revolution that has culminated in the global Internet. This provided the electronic infrastructure for level one space of flows in Castells' network society. More generally, it has been the enabling piece of the jigsaw for the neoliberal ideology to be equated with a globalizing economy as neoliberal globalization. Second, communist China embarked on its post-Mao journey towards WTO membership with liberal economic reforms starting in 1978. This opening of China to the capitalist world-economy is remarkable on many levels, not least its phenomenal economic success.

The interplay between these critical changes is complex and truly multifarious. We have a little hindsight, some three decades of experience, so please excuse my indulgence, I will do a little speculation on what their ultimate meanings – what their relative saliencies might become – in this section of the chapter, as a portend of more speculation in the next chapter. I have noted that the first two changes, neoliberalism and the electronic communication revolution, have been widely interpreted as twin processes. However I note further that the global economic crisis starting in 2008 has severely undermined the neoliberal side of the equation without any diminution of global connectedness. Thus the neoliberal globalization label may well be an important contemporary conceptual combination that will have less resonance for the future. My thesis is that while the West was congratulating itself for its supposed progressive neoliberal globalization, there was another process, China globalization, proceeding apace that will turn out to be much more important in the rest of the twenty-first century. I will treat each globalization process in turn.

Neoliberal Globalization as Class Victory

Viewed from the core countries, before the economic crisis that began in 2008, the world-economy seemed to be doing remarkably well. Apart from the odd hiccup, there even seemed to be the promise of continuous growth. Notoriously, Gordon Brown, in charge of the British economy for over decade, declared that the times of boom and bust were over. Neoliberal globalization had, it seemed, eliminated cyclical time! In this post-economics euphoria with global banks employing the cleverest mathematicians to devise their products, what could go wrong? In fact, in modern times, the most dangerous guardians are Keynsians who do not believe in cycles. Whether welfare Keynsians (Europe) or military Keynsians (US), they inevitably lead to a debtor's fall: instead of an upturn at the end of a cycle there is a downward spiral, a general crisis. But in the meantime there were many winners: who were they?

It is, of course, no accident that the building of a world city network and the expansion of mega-cities are coincident with the rise of neoliberalism as a dominant ideology guiding recent economic policy. Unknowingly fashioned from Jacobs' (1992) commercial moral syndrome, it became the tool of choice for state elites with political goals to 'roll back the state'.

The resulting global *modus operandi* is a classic 'monstrous hybrid' with guardians forfeiting their national roles to global commercial agents. Brenner and Theodore (2002b) provide two useful analytical tools for understanding 'actually existing neo-liberalism': path dependency and creative destruction. They add the adjective 'actually existing' to make the point that there is no 'pure' neoliberalism, even though the ideology's prescriptions are clear, simple and theoretically universal. Neoliberal policies and practices are applied at different starting points in different places: the slate is never wiped clean even in collapsed states (ex-USSR) and authoritarian military states (Chile). In other words, there are always political, economic and cultural contexts through which neoliberalism policies and practices have to be negotiated. This is path dependency. Within these constraints, neoliberalism aspires to restructure economies through creative destruction. This means getting rid of the old collectivist institutions and ways of thinking and creating new institutional frameworks and ideas to replace them. These processes are usually considered for different countries; I will consider them in terms of cities first in the world city network and then in the world of mega-cities.

The world city network has been created by advanced producer service firms to facilitate the functioning of global capital. Effectively their task is to smooth out global economic space so that corporations can operate in as near a neoliberal world as possible. Thus the network is expressively transnational in structure so as to cope with national path dependencies. This is explicit in the work of global law firms that create contracts in an international world by transcending sovereign legal boundaries through writing in a single source (global) law (in practice this is done in New York and London using either New York State Law or English Common Law). Thus can corporations transcend inter-jurisdictional hurdles in their business operations. Similarly, global accountancy firms facilitate trans-border mergers and acquisitions through their standard auditing, and advertising agencies incorporate cultural sensitivities into global campaigns to ensure maximum realization of capital in consumption. Such reductions of path dependency are augmented by creative-destruction servicing: the classic case is the boom in the work of law firms and management consultancies in the 1990s in eastern Europe to facilitate sales of state assets. More generally, management consultants diffuse union avoidance best practice across countries and banks facilitate the trans-border movement of capital (safe havens, laundering, and so on). These are just some examples of servicing corporations whose purpose is to make 'real existing international space' closer to neoliberalism's ideal business-friendly, 'borderless world'.

Globalization practices and neoliberal needs have placed the managerial, financial, professional and creative staff working for global service firms in a powerful strategic position. There has always been a confused class positioning of cadres employed in the capitalist world-economy to facilitate capital accumulation (Wright 2000): they are paid employees but with class interests aligned to capital. It is this strata of the middle class that globalization/neoliberalism has finally detached from the rest of society and integrated with capital. With very large salaries, big bonuses and generous share options, many global service firm operatives have become members of what Sklair (2002) calls the transnational capitalist class. They live in a rich world of consumption; the world city network is their work habitat (Beaverstock 1994).

The neoliberal project in the periphery is well known and is told in outline by Davis (2006, pp. 151–73). In the mid-1970s the World Bank and IMF changed course to neoliberal prescriptions for poor countries and were able to implement their policies through the debt crisis of the 1980s. Structural adjustment programmes and conditionalities 'opened up' states to global capital and 'closed them off' from local society; for Davis (2006, p. 50) such policy reveals 'states as traitors'. Given the theory that market solutions via retreat of the state will release economic potentials, the 1990s should therefore have been 'the utopian decade' for the periphery (p. 163). Instead, 46 of the poorest countries saw development go into reverse: neoliberalism turned out to be a super-efficient motor for Frank's (1969) 'development of underdevelopment'.

The neoliberal extremity in the periphery has been even more profound than the world city network in its structural upheaval: in the periphery path dependence is represented by diversity of neoliberal practices but the outcomes are simpler and focus particularly strongly on creative destruction (but with the 'creative' dividends felt elsewhere). Global economic competition and the demise of state functions have created two unpredicted new peripheral phenomenon in the wake of destructions. First, the space economies have been turned inside out in a very surprising way: from capital-intensive (industrial) cities surrounded by labour-intensive countryside to labour-intensive (de-industrializing) cities surrounded by capital-intensive agriculture (Davis 2006, p. 16). Second, the decline of formal work has meant that marginalization has reappeared on the agenda. Davis (2006, p. 176) describes the informal economy as returning 'with a vengeance' from 1980 as the neoliberal policies hit the periphery. Cities had always been places of opportunity, migrants may start at the bottom but they had hope, if not for themselves for their children, of a better life. And this historical process appeared to be operating before neoliberalism. But neoliberalism created something new: the cities of despair reported above – people in cities without opportunity whose habitat is the planet of slums.

World city network combined with planet of slums represents a new, very rapid, global economic polarization that reflects a global class victory that is only slowly being recognized. For about a century before the 1970s, inequalities appeared to be lessening across the world. This feature was so strong that it was given law-like status as the Kuznets curve: the process posited that as societies modernized populations became more educated and inequalities narrowed. This was the basis of the optimism behind the whole idea of development: states would become more social democratic as they became more modern, meaning industrialization. And then came what Alderson and Nielson (2002) call the 'great U-turn'.

The fallacy of the Kuznets curve was first recognized for the US and has been subsequently broadened to other core states by Alderson and Nielson (2002): their large-scale statistical analysis showed conclusively that inequalities across OECD countries have been increasing. Furthermore, the increase is invidious: it is not that the rich are just improving their incomes at a faster rate than the poor and hence increasing the income gap between them. No, this is real polarization, absolute polarization. Alderson, Beckfield and Nielsen (2005) show that the rich are getting richer as the poor are getting poorer. We can now see that this is neoliberal globalization's great legacy to 2008; a conservative reversal of a century of social progress. But being a monstrous hybrid, this new *modus operandi* cannot sustain systemic reproduction; hence the current crisis.

World city network and planet of slums are basic geographical artefacts of the great global U-turn. It is part of how neoliberalism has become globally embedded. As always dis-embedding will be difficult but the tools can be found in Jacobs' work – this is explored in the next chapter. For the current situation, I have only told part of the globalization story, the western version. To understand how the world-economy reached its new crisis requires a critical interpretation of the rise of China.

Chinese Globalization as Labour Imperialism

While neoliberalism was destroying jobs, destroying dreams and creating poverty across the world, in China towards half a billion of people were being taken out of poverty. This achievement should be seen in systemic perspective. Evidently, it can be numbered as one of four great risings of ordinary people out of poverty. These routes out of poverty are the results of different forms of the modern *modus operandi*.

- The social democratic route was formulated by the European social-ist movement (trade unions and parties), abetted by social (impe-rial) conservatives, in the late nineteenth century and culminated in welfare states in the post-World War II boom. It is this route, initially diffused across to many poorer countries, that has been the main target of neoliberalism.

- The business concordat route is the American way, pioneered by progressive Republicans in the beginning of the twentieth century, it supplanted Roosevelt's weak social democratic New Deal in the post-World War boom by raising the workers to property-owning, middle-class status; symbolized by the 1947 deal between General Motors and the Auto Workers Union, it generated US mass consumption to provide the demand for US mass production. Under US hegemony this diffused to Europe to merge with the social democratic route.

- The development state route was pioneered by Japan in the post World War II boom and involved the use of the state to promote national industrial development for the world market; it spread first to the four 'flying geese' – Hong Kong, Singapore, South Korea and Taiwan – and then more generally to Southeast Asia from the 1970s. It was this state-led economic success that undermined the salience of the idea of neoliberalism as an appropriate development strategy for poorer countries long before the 2008 crisis.

- The China route is similar to the development state route but much more, made possible by the sheer size of this state. In effect the Chinese state has engineered a process whereby a new 'workshop of the world' has been created on the back of cheap labour with the west providing the necessary demand for its multitude of products. This can be seen as an unfinished project, the next step is to create a large middle class to consume and create a massive domestic market. It is the story of this route that I tell briefly here.

There are two things to note about this list. First, evidently there is no neoliberal route out of poverty. Second, the final route is China's alone; I have not been tempted to use the fashionable BRIC concept, wherein Brazil, Russia and India (and even South Africa in BRICS) are given equal billing. I consider the concept to be chaotic in structure: the Russian economic success is a territorial one based upon raw materials; Brazil and India have successful cities but they do not measure up to China's leading cities (Table 7.1, Table 7.2). And this is what makes the China location strategy in the 2010 world city network analysis so interesting, as something very new and just coming fully into play as a globalization process (Figure 7.2(b)).

The China success story has an unpromising starting point: as a communist state from 1949, China shared a general communist antinomy towards cities, especially large cities. The following quote from Davidovich (1974), a Soviet scholar writing on urban geography, concerns application of 'the law of planned (proportional) development of the national economy' (p. 616, parentheses in the original) and what it means for Soviet cities:

> In the long run, measures will evidently be taken to prevent excessive development of supercities [i.e. Moscow and Leningrad] and to limit the growth of existing large cities. . . . Little by little, part of the population of million-cities will be induced to move with the transfer of enterprises and institutions to other economic regions and to satellite cities. The population of the very big cities will also be reduced by modernization of existing large enterprises and by the increased movement of labor resources towards newly developed regions. (pp. 627–9)

This betrays a total misunderstanding of cities and their economies. But such anti-Jacobs thinking and practice was even stronger in Maoist China, where suspicion of cities as anti-revolutionary locales precipitated the Great Leap Forward in the 1950s and the Cultural Revolution in the 1960s featuring the forced evacuation of cities. Thus while the rest of the 'third world', which China aspired to lead, was massively urbanizing in these decades, uniquely China was de-urbanizing (Lin 2002). This was the context out of which Deng Xiaoping launched the post-Mao reforms in 1978.

Fully engaging with the capitalist world-economy is a very dangerous strategy for poor countries. Peripheralization is the name of the game and they get slotted into supply region status for rich core cities. And in some ways this has happened to China as it became a supply region for cheap industrial goods, but without the obvious ravages bestowed on peripheral zones. We get a hint of this in Davis' (2006) *Planet of Slums*, where China has the fastest and largest rural–urban migration but its cities do not figure in the production of mega-slums. This contradiction can only be understood with reference to state economic power. The city-centric approach taken in this book does not deny the importance of state economic power but treats it as an empirical question not an unexamined assumption: there are the 'development states', notably in East Asia mentioned previously, that have been instrumental in 'creating' their world cities and may even be bucking the great global U-turn (Hill and Kim 2000; Hill and Fujita 2003). Although this state power does not create economic expansion directly, it can strongly facilitate that expansion through its cities. The political ability to achieve such aims varies greatly but appears to have been particularly strong in China since its decision to open its economy in 1978. There have been many interpretations of how and why the Chinese economy has been so successful in pulling so many people out of poverty.

This is a beacon of hope in the otherwise social democratic despair of the great post-Kuznets U-turn. I will provide a world-systems interpretation of this intriguing and incredibly important phenomenon.

Let us begin by making it very clear that contemporary China's economic triumph has been built upon the economic success of its cities. Its unique long-term double-digit economic growth coincides with historically unprecedented levels of rural–urban migration leading to unremitting massive urbanization. According to UN-Habitat (2010, p.92) from 1978 to 2008 the GDP of the country went up 82-fold, urban population increased from 172 million to 606 million (that is from 18 per cent of the population to 46 per cent), and the number of urban jobs grew from 95 million to 302 million. The faster rise in GDP compared to urban jobs is an indication of the immense added value of new work done in cities. China now has over 150 cities with population of a million-plus, many to be found in 12 main concentrations: the three great multi-nodal mega-regions in the east that UN-Habitat describe modestly as 'metropolitan areas' – the Yangtze River Delta, the Pearl River Delta, and Beijing-Tianjin-Hebei – and nine 'urban clusters' identified as 'the mid south of Liaoning Province, the Central Plains of Henan Province, Wuhan of Hubei Province, Changsha-Zhuzhou-Xiangtan of Hunan Province, Chengdu-Chongqing, the Southeast of Fujian Province, the Shandong Peninsular, Guanzhong-Tianshui, and the Beibu Gulf' (p.2). Their roles in Chinese economic expansion is described as follows:

> These metropolitan areas and urban clusters ... have become important economic growth poles ... They have in essence broken the constraints of administrative divisions, realized the integration and consolidation of social and economic activities within vast areas, greatly reduced distance and space between people, and promoted the human movement and economic activities at the regional and national levels. The trans-regional industrial groups, financial networks and trading institutions have developed at a rate and scale unparalleled in history. All these have made it possible for capitals, technologies and information to flow and spread more smoothly around the country, and for metropolitan areas and urban clusters to become pivots to promote the regional economic development of China. (p.2)

This UN-Habitat report captures the way in which metropolitan areas and urban clusters have created a new Chinese space of flows, but it does not provide a strong sense of the relative longevity of the process despite the statistics provided.

I attempt to rectify this in Table 7.10 where average annual city growth rates from 1978 to 2009 are presented. I have been able to obtain continuous statistics over the three decades for just the seven cities in the table; the

Table 7.10   Population growth rates of seven major Chinese cities, 1978–2009

	Guangzhou (%)	Wuhan (%)	Beijing (%)	Chengdu (%)	Hangzhou (%)	Shanghai (%)	Wuxi (%)
1978–79	**2.17**	1.84	**2.46**	1.21	1.24	**3.08**	**2.38**
1979–80	1.72	1.59	1.73	0.82	0.72	1.27	0.80
1980–81	1.72	1.88	1.70	1.32	1.01	1.42	1.05
1981–82	1.64	1.57	1.89	1.18	1.41	1.52	1.13
1982–83	1.52	1.26	1.68	0.66	0.95	1.14	0.48
1983–84	1.68	1.04	1.29	0.61	0.83	0.90	0.38
1984–85	1.75	1.30	1.34	1.02	1.03	0.99	0.64
1985–86	1.91	1.90	1.39	1.40	1.19	1.29	1.15
1986–87	1.74	1.51	1.73	1.44	1.47	1.39	1.37
1987–88	**2.09**	1.97	1.34	1.27	1.33	1.03	1.48
1988–89	1.48	1.80	1.99	1.12	1.05	1.11	1.38
1989–90	1.51	**2.52**	1.09	1.20	0.67	0.54	1.28
1990–91	1.34	1.09	0.71	0.90	0.69	0.30	0.84
1991–92	1.66	1.10	0.52	0.98	0.63	0.17	0.64
1992–93	1.87	1.06	0.60	1.11	0.81	0.42	0.62
1993–94	**2.14**	1.20	1.01	1.38	0.99	0.31	0.42
1994–95	1.52	1.43	0.80	1.17	0.85	0.20	0.20
1995–96	1.44	0.84	0.69	0.94	0.88	0.24	0.38
1996–97	1.59	1.11	0.72	0.86	0.79	0.08	0.34
1997–98	1.15	1.09	0.55	0.79	0.61	0.09	–0.02
1998–99	1.61	1.15	0.76	0.66	0.72	0.50	0.28
1999–00	**2.29**	1.22	0.70	–0.02	0.90	0.65	0.28
2000–01	1.70	1.21	1.34	1.65	1.22	0.42	0.30
2001–02	1.13	1.30	1.25	0.84	1.22	0.53	0.61
2002–03	0.63	1.70	1.10	1.54	0.94	0.57	0.90
2003–04	1.72	0.60	1.23	1.47	1.38	0.79	1.05
2004–05	1.74	1.97	1.53	**2.11**	1.35	0.58	1.26
2005–06	1.36	**2.18**	1.43	1.97	0.89	0.97	1.10
2006–07	1.68	1.14	1.31	0.80	0.91	0.79	0.86
2007–08	1.38	0.61	1.37	1.14	0.79	0.88	0.53
2008–09	1.33	0.28	1.29	1.30	0.85	0.69	0.31
1978–2009	**64.55**	**52.39**	**46.62**	**41.38**	**35.18**	**27.54**	**27.50**

Note: Values in bold type are over 2%; values in italic are between 1 and 1.99%.

data derive from a mixture of national and local bureau of statistics and therefore relate to administrative areas rather than the agglomerations referred to by UN-Habitat. This implies that any errors will be on the low side as new growth may be missed. Even given this caveat the results are remarkable for their high average annual rates; of 217 rates, ten are above 2 per cent and a majority of the remainder are over 1 per cent. Four of the rates above 2 per cent occur in the first year of reform, three of them in the biggest cities (Beijing, Guangzhou and Shanghai), which presumably reflects a pent-up demand for city living finally being released by the new policy. All cities except Hangzhou experience at least one year of above 2 per cent growth, and Guangzhou, the fastest growing city, has three such years. But the key finding of this table is the relentless city growth, covering all the cities and spread across three decades. This ongoing longevity makes China's 'economic miracle' so much more impressive than many earlier reported 'miracles' that often tend to survive for less than a decade. How has China been able to maintain its growth, to transform its success from event (a 'miracle') to a *moyenne durée* phenomenon with potentially *longue durée* implications?

Answering this question requires returning to the basic contradiction of the capitalist world-economy, the relationship between production (supply) and consumption (demand). This was solved in consumer modernity by capital conceding relatively high wages to produce worker-consumers in the core, whilst relying on cheap raw materials and energy from the periphery. As described in the last chapter, this core–periphery model, US hegemony's contribution to modern world-system reproduction, provided the demand to sustain production in rich countries. But globalization undermined this 'Western fix' from the late 1970s with the 'new international division of labour', whereby multinational corporations moved industrial jobs to low-wage areas precipitating de-industrialization in the core. This provided the opening for neoliberalism discussed above, but it also provided the opportunity for China to become the new 'workshop of the world'. The result has been Chinese production to supply the West complemented by Western consumption through demand generating debt. This is China globalization, a process fully revealed by the 2008 debt crisis in the West, when it eclipsed neoliberal globalization. The key process that has made this possible I call 'labour imperialism' (Taylor 2011a).

There has been a basic antinomy at the heart of all Western socialist party government (Wallerstein 1984, pp. 8–11). Although such parties are given meaning through universal ideals, in government they are expected to conduct the special interests of their state. This dilemma has been most acutely felt in foreign policy where realist international relations impose nationalist competitive policies on socialist ministers harbouring cosmopolitan, internationalist principles. Although there has been some unsustained flirting with 'ethical' foreign policy, the main cosmopolitan thrust has been to support universal organizations of states (League of

Nations, United Nations), although these have turned out to be less universal institutions than particular tools to be discarded by major states when national interest requires. In short foreign policy for universalist democratic socialists is impossible, because all policy based upon states is inherently discriminatory. For most of its history the People's Republic of China has not had to deal with this socialist dilemma because it was able to express its universal ideals as revolutionary sociologists. In 1964 during a trip to Africa, Chinese leader Zhou Enlai famously declared that Africa was ripe for revolution; his government's foreign policy was to promote and support anti-imperialist movements. But in 1971 communist China was finally admitted to membership of the United Nations, thereby having such policy against fellow member states proscribed. However since 1978, the reformed Chinese government has developed what can be called a 'labour foreign policy'.

From their origins in nineteenth-century Europe there has always been an uneasy relationship between socialist and labour movements. Although seen as 'natural' allies, in fact the former was universalist whereas the latter constituted a special interest. This alliance worked for domestic policy development (on issues such as job security, health, and housing) but generally not for foreign affairs notably in immigration (for instance, to preserve supporters' jobs the Australian Labour Party supported a 'White Australia' policy in the twentieth century). Stripping off socialist universal ideals, a labour foreign policy has no contradictions, it focuses on economics and promotes domestic jobs. This is a good description of China's post-1978 foreign policy. What has been happening is that Chinese policies have been sucking industrial jobs from all other erstwhile 'third world' countries. Thus although contemporary globalization started with the new international division of labour leading to de-industrialization of large swaths of core countries, it has culminated in a Chinese division of labour leading to de-industrialization of large swaths of non-core countries. This is labour imperialism. This is what keeps China under communist party control. As China scours the rest of the world, notably Africa, for raw materials to fuel its great industrial revolution, one wonders what Zhou Enlai would have made of this last great modern imperialism?

There are two conditions that have made the creation of Chinese labour imperialism possible. First, it derives from the political self-interest of the guardians, the communist party elite. They can only expect to maintain their one-party monopoly through tangible economic results. For Chinese labour this means, above all, jobs. Hence the party's draconian domestic policy of population control, the one-child-per-family prescription to curtail demographic growth. Traditionally high population growth rates are treated positively by states but in this case it was seen as destabilizing since there was no guarantee that job creation would be able to keep pace with massive population increases. Labour imperialism complements this domestic policy of limiting the number of jobs required, with a foreign policy that imports the now manageable number of jobs that are nevertheless still needed. The agency for both policies is guardian self-interest in full employment to produce a relatively quiet political life.

Second, agency is never enough on its own, there has to be a suitable context for the policy to be successful. This is a matter of the policy autonomy that states have within the inter-state system under conditions of contemporary globalization. In their influential book *The Global Trap*, Martin and Schuman (1997) argued that only the US had preserved its national sovereignty. I think that experience since the mid-1990s suggests that their US exceptionalism claim needs revision, China has to be recognized as a second state that has also maintained its national sovereignty, at least in the sense of relative economic autonomy. This appears to be a matter of size, of which more in the concluding discussion. The point to note here is that China has the policy autonomy to take advantage of current globalization processes built upon consumerism. US relative autonomy has been expressed through military adventurism but China has used its power in a completely different way: the erstwhile 'lone superpower' is being confronted by a new 'workshop of the world'. But I do want to imply here that China is directing its economy like the US is directing its wars. Rather, a version of the modern *modus operandi* that all successful modern states have employed has emerged in China. In his detailed review of the role of the state in the economic success of Shanghai, Zhang (2003, p. 1569) concludes:

> Shanghai's experience . . . suggests that a local authority can influence the flow of resources by articulating a broad vision, mobilising political support, attracting inward investment, and providing the necessary infrastructure. But the case of Shanghai also shows that the lack of sophisticated market knowledge and political independence of government decision-makers make it very difficult for them to effect structural transformation in its true sense. On the other hand, the case demonstrates that, while the priorities and macroeconomic policies of the central government can significantly influence opportunities for and conditions of economic development among cities, they cannot override market forces, even in a country such as China.

Lai (2012, p. 1281) supports Zhang's first point by arguing that central laws lack specificity, thereby allowing local leeway in application: 'While the final decision-making is restricted to policy circles in Beijing, authorities in Shanghai have considerable autonomy to interpret and implement them.' Similarly, Fenby (2012, p. 171) supports Zhang's final point emphasizing that 'the process took on a momentum of its own in the 1980s', and even quoting Deng Xiaoping as proof: 'the result was not anything I or any comrades had foreseen; it just came out of nowhere'. And don't doubt that this was a fully-fledged Jacobs process: behind the massive Chinese exports that have been experienced in western countries, some 40 million small and medium-sized firms have been created (Fenby 2012, p. 32). Although this suggests similarities with the Dutch 'merchant state' or Britain's 'nightwatchman state' ideal, the situation is more like President Calvin Coolidge's 'the business of America is business'; in fact 'the business of China is business' could be a slogan that the Chinese guardian communist elite might adopt!

That is the supply story. The demand complement is much better known: neoliberalism meant the West was open for business, mainly as consumers. There was a toxic mixture of arrogant Western guardians mistaking Chinese supply as eradicating economic cycles, and arrogant Western commercial agents thinking that capital could be packaged in such complex ways (derivatives) that the problem of its realization was eradicated (i.e. the ultimate need to show a profit). Here is a succinct statement on the West's incredulous culpability:

> the story everyone has been told for the last decade or so [is] revealed to be a colossal lie. There's really no nicer way to say it. For years everyone's been hearing of a whole host of new, ultra-sophisticated financial innovations: credit and commodity derivatives, collateralized mortgage obligation derivatives, hybrid securities, debt swaps, and so on. These new derivative markets were so incredibly sophisticated that – according to one persistent story – a prominent investment house had to employ astrophysicists to run trading programs so complex that even the financiers couldn't begin to understand them. (Graeber 2011, p. 15)

Supporting academics even 'heralded a looming transformation of the very nature of time' (p. 15). I never said city innovations were always for the good! This was certainly not the case here, and the result is that we find ourselves dealing such large numbers we cannot imagine what they mean. For instance, the World Bank Group provide statistics on the Gross External Debt Position of countries: for the second quarter of 2011 this amounted to $40 748 897 000 000 for the US, Eurozone and UK which is more than 45 times that of China (http://ddp-ext.worldbank.org/ext/ddpreports, accessed 31 January 2012). This is only a very small part of the story, personal debt is not included, but I use it as indicative of the current global situation. Obviously debt is not intrinsically a bad thing, it is a necessity for dynamic commercial work, but this imbalance matters. The West appears to have sleepwalked into a China globalization that will likely dominate much of the twenty-first century.

Whither the Bourgeoisie?

The great irony of the early twenty-first century is that neoliberalism, in the form of austerity programmes (not yet called 'structural adjustment'), has a subordinate role in China's globalization; it is now the means to ease the self-peripheralization of (parts of) the West. In my treatment of the modern world-system I discussed the relative decline of selected core states as part of the rise and fall in hegemonic cycles but there has been no consideration of absolute decline in the core. This zone has been very stable in the geohistory of the system; Western Europe has maintained its status as core zone while the zone has expanded in line with the overall expansion of the world-economy. Evidently dropping out of the core is not a process that has occurred. But it might well be the process that marks the demise of the modern world-system. How can indications of such change be identified?

I will answer by focusing on the geohistory of the bourgeoisie. Although used by Marx to mean a capitalist, an owner of the means of production (factory owner), I will revert to its original meaning as prosperous urban dwellers. The term derives from 'burgher' and 'burgess' from which is also derived 'borough' as an urban administrative area. Thus the bourgeoisie are members of the urban middle class, city dwellers marked by their materialist ambitions. As middle class, they include small factory owners and entrepreneurs, merchants and shopkeepers, managers and administrators in both private and public sectors, and the professions. They are the middle 'organizational' strata between the major deployers of capital in both private and public sectors, and the direct producers. Boundaries are fuzzy and changeable; remember US hegemony was based upon converting direct producers (factory workers) to middle-class membership, and today, as previously noted, professionals organizing finance in global cities have risen above the middle class through their salaries and bonuses.

As prosperous middle-class citizens we have come across them in their hegemonic locales: Dutch burghers in multiple Holland cities, the 'English' middle class in their great Victorian cities, and American suburbanites surrounding dynamic US cities. It is in the latter hegemonic cycle that the middle class has become the majority class through consumer modernity; the middle-class lifestyle is now premised upon mass consumption in cities across the world. However, although the bourgeoisie has grown immensely with the expansion of the modern world-system, it has maintained a distinctive world geography. Successful bourgeoisie are concentrated in the cities of the hegemonic state and cities of coterminous core states emulating it. They are also found in the rest of the world-economy in necessary organizational roles, but here they have been and remain a relatively small minority. Thus today cities in the rich West might have about 80 per cent of their population living middle-class lifestyles of relatively conspicuous consumption, whereas in the cities of the poor South, people living such lifestyles might constitute about 20 per cent of the population. Yet because mega-cities of the South are so large, their middle classes are absolutely sizeable markets; this means that the essential infrastructures of consumerism, notably large shopping malls, are very conspicuous in all major cities across the world.

It follows that if the core zone is characterized by its high proportion of bourgeoisie, then falling out of this zone should be reflected in a relative reduction of the middle class. This is what neoliberal policies of 'rolling back the state' amounts to through destruction of public sector middle-class jobs. In the private sector a whole new profession has been spawned to take out private middle-class jobs: management consultancy. Originating in the mid-twentieth century, these service firms are brought in to rationalize company practices and make them more 'efficient'; the standard result is to hollow out the middle management, provide greater rewards for higher management, and reduce workers' pay (perhaps by relocating). This profession grew immensely towards the end of the twentieth century as a response to the downside of American hegemony. They were thus instrumental in increasing inequality, the demise of the Kutznet cycle, reported earlier. What does this mean for the West? Well, it is becoming more like the South where stark inequalities have always been the rule. Thus the great class victory of the Western rich can now be seen in a different light: it represents incipient peripheralizing processes in traditional core zones.

If the modern world-system is beginning to lose its bourgeoisie in the West, where are new bourgeoisie replacements to be found? Clearly China is the most likely answer to this question. The national government in its latest national plan (2010) has highlighted increasing domestic demand to counter falling consumption in the West. And this certainly does not seem to be moving against global market trends. After their world record in raising people out of poverty, China is ready to set another world record: the rapid rise of a national bourgeoisie. One indicator is the increase in student numbers in higher education: there are now 1090 universities and 2305 institutes of higher education in China teaching a total of 20 million students (http://www.chinaeducenter.com/en/cedu.php, accessed 31 January 2012). This is appreciably more than in the US, the heart of the twentieth-century expansion of higher education (http://www.uis.unesco.org/Library/Documents/ged09-en.pdf, accessed 1 February 2012). Obviously, future decades of this number of highly qualified young people entering the labour market will likely give China the world record alluded to above.

If such an outcome were to come about it really would mark a turnaround in the geography of the modern world-system; the core–periphery structure would remain but the core itself would be geographically shifted. Probably we are not talking here about a wholesale movement of economic activity from West to East – change will be selective (Derudder et. al 2011). In the East, I have argued that Chinese cities will be the main chosen beneficiaries, but what about the West? It seems at the moment that it is Europe (Eurozone and UK) that is best at doing austerity – that is, actively pursuing policies of self-peripheralization. The twenty-first century is looking more and more like being about China versus US within an encompassing world city network.

CONCLUDING REMARKS: HEGEMONIC BATON OR POISONED CHALICE?

The tone of my discussion above is that China and its cities will likely become the leading players as we embark further into the twenty-first century. There are now innumerable books that have considered this scenario in much more detail than I have been able to present above. For some this is a reversal back to the usual scheme of things when China was the 'Middle Kingdom' of the world; this has been theoretically and evidentially argued in their different ways by Gunder Frank (1998) and Giovanni Arrighi (2007) that relate in some ways to my contrasting modernity to 'Normal History'. There are also two post-1949 assessments of current Chinese economic success that also intersect partially with my argument. Minqui Li (2008, p. 176) uses world-systems tools to show that China in alliance with other large semi-periphery states (BRIC?) may represent a fatal challenge to the modern world-system from below. Will Hutton (2007) presents an Enlightenment view arguing that China needs to incorporate more Western (as universal) traits to prevent its authoritarian politics holding it back. I respect all these views but will simplify the situation for my concluding remarks. Accepting that China will be a major player in the twenty-first century, what might be China's role in the ongoing demise phase of the modern world-system?

As hinted on several occasions above, the 'sheer scale' of China's growth (Fenby 2012, p. 32), specifically through its large cities, makes this country special. As we have seen in the previous chapter, economic success such as China's might be expected to usher in a new hegemonic cycle in the modern world-system, and size initially appears relevant to this. The sequence of hegemonic states is one of increasing size: from a small United Provinces, to a medium-sized United Kingdom, to a continental US.

Looked at this way, China is possibly the only state that could realistically continue the pattern. But there are many obstacles in the way; Li (2008) only sees China's potential in semi-periphery terms, and Hutton's (2007) concerns are important because hegemonic states are liberal champions within the system. In any case in Wallerstein's demise of the modern world-system there is simply no time left for another sequence of reproduction through hegemony. There can be no fourth hegemony, by China or whoever.

But China remains a critical player. I agree with Arrighi's (2010, pp. 382–3) neat summary of the situation:

> . . . given China's demographic size, its economic expansion is far more subversive of the global hierarchy of wealth than all previous East Asian economic 'miracles' put together. For all these miracles (the Japanese included) were instances of upward mobility within a fundamentally stable hierarchy. The hierarchy could and did accommodate the upward mobility of a handful of East Asian states (two of them city-states) accounting for about one twentieth of the world population. But accommodating the upward mobility of a state that by itself accounts for about one fifth of the world population is an altogether different matter. It implies a fundamental subversion of the very pyramidal structure of the hierarchy.

As a 'subversion' this implies the opposite of hegemonic reproduction, China is implicated in the demise processes of the modern world-system. This is what my analysis above has indicated. But it means that China and its cities move to core position in a world-system in crisis; it is not clear if there are many benefits to accrue for being so important at this specific time. Certainly it is not as clear-cut as with the benefits of hegemonic leadership. Further, as well as having to cope with symptoms of system decline there is also the looming possibility of catastrophic climatic change as the result of phenomenal waste from the capitalist world-economy's phenomenal economic expansion. China's prize might well be a poisoned chalice. This all needs another chapter to wrap up my narrative.

8.   Towards green networks of cities for the twenty-first century

INTRODUCTION

In the twenty-first century humanity will need its cities more than ever; they really will have to be extraordinary. Their task may be nothing less than saving the planet as a home for humanity. Please excuse the hyperbole, but things may get that serious in the lifetimes of people living today. However not everyone sees it this way. There is a long-term anathema to big cities by guardian elites that can be traced back at least as far as classical Greece and continues today.

In times of challenge and stress it is understandable that people should look to a supposed simpler past at a presumed smaller scale. Trying to regain some control in a rapidly changing world, a return to the local, has been alluringly attractive. This was a common reaction to industrialization in the nineteenth century from both conservative and radical perspectives (Hunt 2004). Elisée Reclus, the communard and influential anarchist–geographer, warned his comrades off this anti-city policy:

> Yet it is easy to show that this monster growth of the city, the complex outcome of a multiplicity of causes, is not altogether a morbid growth. If, on the one hand, it constitutes, in some of its incidents, a formidable fact for the moralist, it is, on the other hand, in its normal development, a sign of healthy and regular evolution. Where the cities increase, humanity is progressing; where they diminish, civilization itself is in danger. (Reclus 1895, p. 246)

While fellow anarchists were promoting small-scale rural living, he realized that any radical movement's starting point has to be the contemporary situation, however unpalatable – in his case, the rise of great industrial cities. In the early twenty-first century the latest 'monster growth' has produced world cities, global cities and mega-cities. And guardian responses, and some radical reaction, are repeating themselves.

Edward Glaeser (2011, pp. 213–17) encapsulates the contemporary version of this perennial modern debate by contrasting the views of Charles Windsor, Prince of Wales, Duke of Cornwall and much else, against Ken Livingston, erstwhile Mayor of London. He describes both as 'die-hard greens' (p. 216), pointing out that they agree climatic change is the critical issue for humanity's future; but their presciptions could hardly be further apart. Windsor's green vision is traditional as illustrated by the building of Poundbury as an 'ecotown' urban extension on his land. Livingston's green vision is illustrated by his imposition of congestion charges for traffic in central London. In addition this radical socialist has had to come to terms with the fact that 'cities must compete in a globalized world' (p. 216) and therefore he has revised his opinion on the need for high-rise office development to accommodate London's highly success-ful financial services industry. Glaeser's describes his own stance on these positions is a quite humorous manner:

> If people really could be counted upon to act like fifteenth-century peasants, then rural ecotowns could be extremely green. But people don't want to live like medieval serfs. If they end up living in a low-density area, they'll drive a lot, and they'll want big houses that are comfortably cooled and heated. In cities, however, people end up sharing common public spaces, like restaurants, bars and museums. The urban model is green when used by real people. (p. 217)

This is to accept the existence of contemporary globalization, which is not the same as condoning it. We live in a world of powerful global forces that did not just emerge from nowhere. Our present is path dependent, we cannot go back and change track but we can try and change future direc-tion. The temptation of simple localism is obvious but it carries one rather serious flaw: there are going to be somewhere between eight and ten billion people living on our planet later in the century and there is no way they are all going to be sustained through the building of many thousands of little Poundburys. As architect Peter Calthorpe (2011, p. 3) says, 'Like it or not, the globe has an urban future'. It further follows that 'if the global future is urban, as every indication suggests it is, we need to take an urgent look at what this means' (Steel 2008, p. 10). That is the purpose of this chapter.

I have argued previously that the modern world-system is a social engagement which has resulted in a relentless diminution of the world's peasantry. However, Brand (2010, p. 73) has added a caveat: 'Peasant life is over unless catastrophic climate change drives us back to it'. In my terminology this means back to world-empire, the world-system girded by peasant production. There is a precedent. In the beginnings narrative (Part II) early city dwellers had to invent not just the new work of agriculture but specifically this work had to be sustainable. Urban growth without sustainable agriculture created 'empty quarters', a desiccated environmen-tal outcome that is a lesson for our times: ultimately all new city work has to be sustainable. In the context of my cities' perspective in the experiment that is this book, this means that we should be thinking not just about what it is to be a 'green city', rather the guiding concept should be 'green networks of cities'. In simplest terms, this requires that we go further than just considering environmental footprints as an areal measure, a guardian concept premised upon spaces of places. There is an additional requirement for some notion of environmental *net-prints* as a network measure, a commercial concept premised upon spaces of flows. Once again following Jacobs, this is not a matter of choosing between the two types of agents leaving their marks, rather it is a question of how they might be practically harnessed through a new geohistorical tango to create a non-catastrophic future.

This chapter is divided into four main sections. I begin by rehearsing the arguments for understanding the twenty-first century as an era of crisis. This sets the scene; delineating what appear to be the challenges that will necessitate green networks of cities. But the route towards a green network of cities is difficult both practically and conceptually, and I have chosen to begin at the local scale rather than the global. Although this may appear unexpected given description of the contemporary situation in the last chapter, it should be remembered that the core idea from Chapter 2 is humanity's ability to draw on local and non-local resources, with city networks derived from non-local trade. Thus Glaesner's admonishment of Windsor's top-down localism should not be interpreted as an indictment of all local-scale proposals. In the second and third sections, I critically review, in a reasonably friendly manner, two fascinating practices and literatures on local initiatives to counter environmental catastrophe, first the 'transition town' initiative in which the position of cities is a rather uncomfortable one, and second 'green cities' in which the nature of individual cities is central. I accept that small geographical communities, whether urban neighbourhoods or rural villages, must be integral to any relevant practice because this is where most face-to-face relations occur throughout our lives: the local matters. But it must be seen in relation to wider scales as they exist today described in the previous chapter. It is only after interrogating the local and its context that I return to the urgent need for city creativity whereby we should go beyond 'greening' our cities and consider the 'greenness' of inter-city relations. Remember that Jacobs' (1969) model of economic growth is about local and non-local procurement of production, and I now bring this back into the argument in the fourth section: I make the surprising claim that sustainable city networks and rapid economic growth are both dependent on the same process: import replacement. I am personally surprised by this optimistic and constructive outcome to my city-centric intellectual experiment. I reconsider commercial/guardian relations in a short concluding argument on the need for guardian stewardship of commercial networks: another unforeseen ending.

TWENTY-FIRST CENTURY AS CRISIS CENTURY

Immanuel Wallerstein's world-systems analysis was devised to argue against the progressive/developmentalist ideology of perpetual economic growth inevitably leading to a better standard of living for all humanity. This optimism is simply countered by the historical nature of all world-systems: they have a beginning that sets up the social logic of system, a period of ongoing reproduction of that social logic, and a demise when the social logic unravels. That is what we learned from Wallerstein (1979; 1984; 2004) as laid out in Chapter 2. This applies to the modern world-system, and Wallerstein considers we have are living through the demise phase – the crisis of the system – which began in the second half of the twentieth century and will be finally resolved in the twenty-first century. I call this the endogenous limits to our system, which is the first topic I deal with using two arguments. First I specify the demise in world-systems terms; second I suggest some empirics to indicate what demise might mean locally, using the collapse of both guardian and commercial work in Mexico's Ciudad Juárez as my case study.

But there is an important omission in Wallerstein's argument that must be addressed. Wallerstein (2004, pp. 81–2) mentions contemporary environmental issues as 'hidden costs' of capital, specifically the dumping of waste and the exploitation of raw materials. Treating these as costs to capital within the social logic of the system completely misses out their potential catastrophic effects on macro-social change: Wallerstein's future chaos may be much more chaotic than we can imagine. The exhaustion of carbon-based energy sources can be accommodated in Wallerstein's model: changing energy sources has been central to the story of the modern world-system, but I fear this may be a step too far for an ever-intensifying capitalism. However, environmental dumping is of an entirely different order, with CO_2 dumping seemingly affecting global climate. Although the ultimate cause of climatic change can be traced to the social logic of ceaseless capital accumulation, it is not encompassed in the purpose of capitalist agents; rather it is a huge global unintended consequence. As such, it is governed by its own, autonomous, ecological process, and it may be beyond humanity's ability to control the conse-quent outcomes. Ecological time leading to a catastrophic tipping point bears no direct relation to cyclical times of routine social reproduction. It is for this reason that I have designated this an exogenous limit to our system: it may lead to a very different twenty-first century crisis than that envisaged by Wallerstein.

Endogenous Limits to our World System

Wallerstein (1984, p. 23; 2004. p. 76) has always been careful in his use of the concept of crisis, a term widely employed to denote any set of severe problems. Wallerstein specifically means a situation where there can be no resolution through the ordinary workings of the system. Thus the downturns in the system cycles are not crises because they are resolved in the making of the next upturn. Crises are what occur at the end of a system when the resolution requires such fundamental change that a new system (or systems) results.

Crises denote endogenous limits to geohistorical systems because they derive from contradictions within the normal workings of the system. For instance, in world-empires the guardian logic requires continual territorial expansion that eventually reaches logistic buffers and consequent dismemberment of the empire. For our modern world-system the contradictions are to be found in the commercial logic of a capitalist world-economy. This has also entailed geographical expansion but in this case logistic problems have been overcome, hence the elimination of all other systems in the process to become the one and only global-scale system. But the capitalist social logic has engendered new guardian contradictions alongside its commercial contradictions.

The capitalist world-economy has developed through a mixture of cycles and trends. It is amongst the trends that contradictions are found. Trends can be of two types, sustainable and unsustainable. Increasing mechanization is an example of the former. Not a smooth trend and intimately related to the growth phases of cycles, nevertheless the increased mechanization of production from Dutch windmills through steam engines to contemporary electronics has been a hallmark of modernity, resulting from its undoubted prowess in technological innovation. But systems don't live by technology alone. The social construction of modernity as capitalism has created trends that are asymptotic; they have real limits that cannot be transcended within the system. One of the key trends that Wallerstein (1984) identifies is what he terms the proletarianization of labour. This is related to mega-city growth but Wallerstein emphasizes the de-peasantization side of the process. From his perspective peasants have constituted a potential urban workforce that is converted to actual cheap labour as part of the solution to economic downturns. But this is obviously a diminishing source of new labour that is now coming to an end; this option for expansion has been largely used up. It is not clear whether the resulting informal workers in the mega-cities can play the same role.

Initially Wallerstein (1979, p. 35) identified two basic contradictions, one relating to economic process (making a commercial profit) and the other to political process (keeping guardian control); more recently Wallerstein (1984) has presented them by emphasizing their entwining in capitalist social logic. The social logic of the modern world-system is ceaseless capital accumulation, which makes capitalists – the owners and deployers of capital – the key agents as others respond to their demands and needs. There is a contradiction that derives from their quest for profit: basically there are just two ways of achieving this, by rising prices or by lowering costs. Rising prices is constrained by competition among capital-ists that is only temporarily resolved by the tendency towards economic monopoly. This leaves lowering costs, which can be achieved by lowering labour wages, by mechanization (using less labour) or by moving produc-tion (searching out new cheaper labour). But both these ways only address the supply side of the commercial process, and both will reduce demand. This is most obviously the case for rising prices, but workers are also con-sumers and are necessary for an effective demand that can sustain cease-less capital accumulation. The contradiction is that individual capitalists want low wages for their labour, but not for labour overall. But changing income distributions across and within countries is beyond their direct control. Enter the state, originally regulating for capital, Marx's 'organi-zation committee for the bourgeoisie': from the late nineteenth century it took over a social reproduction role covering such matters as employment security and old age security. But here we find another contradiction. As people have moved into cities they have generated political movements leading to much political innovation that collectively create the modern concept of citizenship. The many rights this confers vary between coun-tries but all are subsequently a cost to capital in terms of taxes, directly on capital and in reducing consumption of workers. Of course, neoliberalism and the Washington consensus were all about reducing these latter costs, but looked at broadly, it is surprising how little they have been able to 'roll back the state' except in the poorest countries. This fits Wallerstein's (2004) argument that neoliberalism has come far too late to restore the capitalist world-economy. This intensification of the social logic of capi-talism is happening in the unstable throes of a transition; the question now is less about roll back and more about what will follow the current system.

Wallerstein (1996; 2004) describes the current transition as a mixture of chaos (systemic uncertainties), but with choices (autonomy of the future), along the lines of a bifurcation (rival alternative outcomes). We can glimpse this coming bifurcation at new guardian meeting grounds for discussing alternative futures: the neoliberals and globalizers at the World Economic Forum at Davos and the social and environmental movements at the World Social Forum, initially at Porto Alegre. According to Wallerstein (2004, p. 87) 'the world is facing increasingly a struggle on many fronts between the spirit of Davos and the spirit of Port Alegre'. Although the final outcome is today uncertain, some time in the twenty-first century, the system will eventually 'lean in one direction' and 'at some point . . . there is a clear outcome and . . . we find ourselves ensconced in a different historical system' (p. 77). It would seem from the 'great U-turn' documented in the last chapter that the Davos spirit has at least won the early battles in this global class war.

I broadly accept this world-systems analysis of twenty-first century as crisis century. However, my basic description of Wallerstein's view of the transition from the capitalist world-economy does not do justice to his understanding of the chaos that will ensue in system-breakdown. Norms and patterns built up over half a millennium will be smothered in doubt as things turn out in ways that they shouldn't. This is, of course, the Chinese curse of 'living in interesting times'; a fate that appears to await the peoples of the twenty-first century. Failed states, including failed liberal states, will likely become increasingly common leaving cities in limbo as their top-down guardian buttresses are removed before bottom-up replacements are invented.

We can perhaps glimpse this today in Ciudad Juárez, which Charles Bowden (2010) dubs 'Murder City'. This Mexican border city seems to be an early candidate for the role of the 'shock city' of twenty-first-century demise, totally divergent from the hegemonic cases of Amsterdam in the seventeenth century, Manchester in the nineteenth century and Los Angeles in the twentieth century. With drug routes to North America moving from Caribbean islands to Mexico, Bowden describes a situation where governance has broken down; the new commerce is economically so successful that a hybrid has been created of truly monstrous proportions. The resulting break down of order in the city and state portends a new world: 'The future here is now, the moment is immediate, and the message is the crack of automatic weapons' (p. 118). What makes this so shocking is that it appears everybody, including drug lords and the Mexican military, have lost the power to influence their destinies: 'once, their worse nightmare was that they were not in control. Now, their real nightmare is that no one is in control' (p. 171). Bowden suggests a complete rethink as to what power means in this circumstance:

We insist that power must replace power, that structure replaces an earlier structure. And we insist that power exists as a hierarchy, that there is a top where the boss lives and a bottom where the prey scurry about in fear of the boss. Also, we believe that state truly owns power and violence, and that is why any nonstate violence by people earns them the name of outlaws. Try for a moment to imagine something else, not a new structure but rather a pattern, and this pattern functionally has no top or bottom, no center or edge, no boss or obedient servant. Think of something like the ocean, a fluid thing without king and court, boss and cartel. Give up all normal way of thinking. (p. 104)

Here is a new world; one totally transcending the way the modern world-system has reproduced itself over the centuries. It is not that this is the first case of societal breakdown; all wars generate such circumstances and indeed the inter-state system derived from such a breakdown in the Thirty Years war that led to the Treaty of Westphalia. And when parts of the inter-state system break down, 'war lords' (people creating alternative spaces of places), have continued to wreak social havoc up to the present, as represented by Somalia today. But the Ciudad Juárez example is different. It is based upon trade where spaces of flows are dominating spaces of places – states – in such a manner that the latter, represented by Mexico, are beginning to disintegrate. This is a very twenty-first-century chaos.

Exogenous Limits to our World-system

Cities are beginning to feature prominently in discussions of climatic change; I draw on two OECD working papers (Corfee-Morlot et al. 2009; Kamal-Chaoui and Robert 2009) to evidence this here. Typically cities are allocated three roles; as victims, as regressive loci of risk; and as solutions. I will briefly consider each in turn.

Cities are considered to be highly vulnerable to climatic change: rising sea levels, extreme storms, and extreme heat events are specifically threatening (Kamal-Chaoui and Robert 2009, p. 51). Most major cities in the world are in low-lying areas (ports, low riverine locations) that results in them being vulnerable to quite small rises in sea level. For instance, a 50 cm rise by mid-century is reported as leading to severe destruction of capital assets (for example, in Guangzhou, Kolkata, Miami, Mumbai, New York, Shanghai), and exposure of large populations to flooding (for example, in Bangkok, Dhaka, Ho Chi Minh City, Mumbai, Ningbo) (p. 54). This also makes cities vulnerable to increasing numbers of hurricanes and typhoons, especially associated with storm surges; Hurricane Katrina's devastation of New Orleans in 2005 is viewed as a possible portend for the future (Corfee-Morlot et al. 2009, p. 18). In addition, cities have long been identified as 'heat islands', warmer than their rural surrounds, and this microclimate makes them particularly vulnerable in extreme heat events; Paris in the European heat wave of 2003 is viewed as a possible portend for the future (Corfee-Morlot et al. 2009, p. 18).

But within cities, it is the poor who are most vulnerable: New Orleans' Ninth Ward remains the classic case and is viewed as a likely scenario for the future (Corfee-Morlot et al. 2009, p. 19). More generally exposure to climatic change intersects with the mega-city/mega-slum discussion because illegal settlements are condemned to be on the least desirable urban land, encompassing both floodplains and hillsides. For instance, that most famous slum, Dharavi in Mumbai, is in a floodplain and thereby is specifically vulnerable (Corfee-Morlot et al. 2009, p. 19).

However, there is a positive side to this city/climate interaction that takes two forms. First, various practices of local mitigation have important co-benefits that will allay the typical large costs that are required (Corfee-Morlot et al. 2009, pp. 21, 23). In any case, it is argued that inaction is not an option because the indirect impacts on economic activity will be so large (Kamal-Chaoui and Robert 2009, p. 61). Second, there is recognition in an urban future cities will be the locus of necessary innovation so as to become the 'policy laboratories for action on climatic change' (OECD 2009, p. 2).

Within urban studies, Calthorpe (2011, p. 8) summarizes the general research and policy reaction quite nicely:

> I take as a given that climate change is an imminent threat and potentially catastrophic – the science is now clear that we are day to day contributing to our own demise. In addition, I believe that an increase in fuel costs due to declining oil reserves is also inevitable. The combination of these two global threats presents an economic and environmental challenge of unparalleled proportions – and, lacking a response, the potential or dire consequences. These challenges will in turn bring into urgent focus the way our buildings, towns, cities, and regions shape our lives and our environmental footprint. Beyond a transition to clean energy sources, I believe that urbanism – compact, diverse, and walkable communities – will play a central role in addressing these twin threats. In fact, responding to climate change and our coming energy challenge without a more sustainable form of urbanism will be impossible.

I agree with this statement but think it does not go far enough – there is a definite suggestion that solutions can be found through internal urban relations, city by city, without concern for relations between cities. This is also true of policy and practice suggestions in the OECD working papers. Although there is some treatment of infrastructures this remains local; there is no consideration of local/non-local distinctions in flows that are the hallmark of this book.

Further, the social impacts that are discussed as consequent on climate change come with no social framework on how environmental change will be received by existing social structures. This is true of Calthorpe, even though he is explicit on the possible dire consequences of climate change as an economic challenge. The same thing is missing from Corfee-Morlot et al.'s (2009, p. 18) treatment of 'impacts on cites'. They describe these impacts as three types, relating to 'climate mean changes', to 'climate variability changes', and to 'catastrophic changes'. The latter produces 'massive asset losses' and 'cultural losses'. But this is to look at the situation from an environmental perspective. From a social perspective, a catastrophe for both commercial and guardian practices may well occur much before environmental catastrophe. In fact the twenty-first century is exactly the wrong time for humanity to face the economic challenge Calthorpe identifies; in its demise phase the modern world-system is at its least resilience. Thus mean changes and variability changes may well be enough to generate a real social catastrophe. And this might occur before the resolution to Wallerstein's bifurcation has been fought out; or it might speed it up bringing it to a rapid conclusion. In other words, in my interpretation of the impact of climate change I have a theoretical position that enables me to generate a social science approach, one which makes dealing with this all-important policy issue much more urgent than purely environmental policy approaches suggest.

RETURN TO THE LOCAL I: TRANSITION TOWNS

Consideration of the local brings us back to my initial identification of humanity as *homo geographicus*, the only species that draws on non-local resources for its social reproduction. But this unique behaviour gives humans the unique capacity to keep growing and growing economies until eventually destroying the Earth as the home of humanity. In the Cold War era and the nuclear standoff, William Bunge (1986) warned us that the Earth is too small for war; today it is becoming too small for ceaseless capital accumulation, in other words we face the demise of the modern world-system. Only humans as animate agents can annihilate global ecology. Thus are economic growth and sustainability commonly seen as incompatible: the Earth is proving to be not big enough for *homo geographicus*! Hence the Brundtland Commission's 'sustainable development' has come to be seen as an oxymoron: this optimistic report has been overtaken by events, notably the threat of 'global warming'. In this new context I am trying to construct a rapprochement between the processes that generate economic growth and human sustainability and/or resilience in the wake of environmental change. The distinction between local and non-local is at the heart of this argument; my purpose is to plot a route to local futures while maintaining humanity's non-local (cosmopolitan) quintessence.

There have been many recent proposals for moving towards more local economic activities (e.g. Girardet 2008; Steel 2008) but here I will focus upon one particular call for localization – the work of Rob Hopkins (2008). He has successfully created an international movement, the Transition Initiative, which promotes small towns as prime units of transition to a sustainable future. I have chosen to focus on this example of localization because it seems to me that this movement, or something very like it, is a necessary proactive response to the challenges of the twenty-first century. My purpose is to explore ways in which this very successful initiative can be made compatible with a world of large cities. My job appears to be quite difficult – a squaring of the circle in terms of very different scales of settlement. Drawing on Taylor (2012b) my means to achieve this end is to interrogate the concept of 'local' to make it more strategically amenable to analysing multiple-scale living, and concomitantly, to recognize and reaffirm the importance of non-local spheres of behaviour.

The Transition Initiative is one of the most impressive and important social/community movements of the early twenty-first century. Starting in 2005 in Totnes, England – a small town of some 8000 population – it has grown exponentially so that by early 2011 it comprised 714 separate initiatives in places across 31 countries (www.transitioninitiative.org, accessed 3 April 2011). Its success has been facilitated by a well crafted 'start-up manual', *The Transition Handbook* (Hopkins 2008), that provides both a convincing rationale and a proactive programme of activities. The rationale is very clever in combining concern for oil dependency with climatic change; the former provides a narrative that speaks directly to current everyday life, which is rendered transient by the 'peak oil' argument, and thereby demands actions that have direct resonance for the more abstract (temporarily remote) threats posed in climatic change narratives. But the key to the movement's popularity is its very practical, bottom-up approach to the threats identified. A very positive outlook is provided – something can still be done – through 'a replicable strategy for harnessing the talents, vision, and goodwill of ordinary people' (Heinberg 2008, p. 9). The challenge is for local communities to change their ways and create more resilient places for living. That so many have taken up the challenge in such a short time is testimony to both supply – the inspiration of the original thinking – and demand – a widespread feeling that we need to act now in the face of such daunting threats to humanity's future.

The Transition approach does not pretend or claim to be the sole solution to the issues it raises. For instance, on the question of top-down or bottom-up initiatives, Hopkins (2008, p. 75) argues the need for a 'combination of responses' which he interprets in a conventional three-scale ordering: international, national and local with the former two identified as important for drawing up formal agreements and protocols which allow local actions to be meaningful. And it is at this local level that Transition Initiatives provide a way forward. In developing a friendly critique of this approach I start by interrogating the way Hopkins (2008) uses the concept of the 'local'.

Local: 'Ideal Scale' or Systems?

In the early development of the approach the Initiative was referred to as Transition Towns – Totnes was the first 'Transition Town' – but this was changed to Transition Initiatives when other types of places came on board: Hopkins (2008, p. 134) lists 'transition cities, boroughs, valleys, peninsulas, postcodes, villages, hamlets and islands'. This variety of what is local is further discussed through the concept of 'ideal scale' where Hopkins reverts to the origins of the approach by identifying market towns with their surrounding hinterlands as the clear example of the ideal (p. 143). However he also mentions islands as ideal because they have clearly defined boundaries (p. 143). But the key point is that Hopkins is not prescriptive on the issue of scale:

> I have come to think that the ideal scale for a Transition Initiative is one over which you feel you can have an influence. A town of 5000 people, for example, is one that you can relate to; it is one with which you can become familiar. (p. 144)

Thus he argues 'there is no magic formula for the question of scale' (p. 144) and followers are invited to use their 'instinct' in designating places for transition.

This very practical approach can be evaluated alongside a theoretical discussion on 'why small is inevitable' that Hopkins (2008, p. 68) introduces through the process of 'relocalisation'; he refers to 'region, county, city or even neighbourhood'. But he does not relate this argument to an earlier, more fundamental, theoretical discussion on resilience where he states that to understand the latter concept requires systems-thinking (pp. 54–6). Here the goal is 'increased resilience and a stronger local economy' with specific reference to 'towns and cities' (p. 55). In this part of his argument the local appears as smaller feedback loops that make the consequences of actions more obvious, being closer to home (p. 56). Perhaps the 'familiarity' and 'instinct' in choosing an ideal scale will equate with a local economic system but this is by no means certain.

Rather there appears to be a lack of spatial congruence between ideal scale and resilient system. More generally, the matter-of-fact flexibility in choosing scale has a price to pay by potentially divorcing the practice from the theory. As previously discussed and illustrated many times in previous chapters, sub-national economic systems are usually equated with cities and city-regions. But in Hopkins' (2008) argument, cities *per se* are not systematically discussed; they most certainly do not appear as the ideal scale. The reason for this appears to lie, in part, in the vision behind the Transition Initiative.

A Limiting Vision: Where are the Cities?

Hopkins (2008) devotes a chapter to his 'vision for 2030' describing the fundamental changes made in the UK assuming a transition has successfully taken place. Although the UK is one of the most urbanized of countries, cities do not feature prominently in this vision. Commonly the phase used is 'towns and cities' thereby conflating, for instance, country towns like Totnes with great cities including London; remember, the need for separate considerations of towns and cities is a major feature of our cities' tool-box in Chapter 2. In Hopkins' urban vision, towns and cities feature together under the headings 'food and farming', 'economy' and 'transport'. These deal with, respectively, 'urban agriculture' (p. 109), local currencies (p. 112), and the demise of car and air travel consequent on pedestrianized urban streets and commercial sail-power (p. 113). On the rare occasions where cities are mentioned without towns, a rather jaundiced view is fleetingly revealed: with urban agriculture as a 'priority for urban planners' we find that 'cities have been redesigned as productive places' (p. 109) hinting that only production from land counts; and cities have to be transformed from 'large, bland places with few "entertainment" venues, into diverse places with gardens, ponds, artworks' (p. 113) – has the author never been to London? But to flesh out the position of cities in the transition vision we have to glean further evidence from other chapters of the *Handbook*.

As was noted previously, cities were one of the places designated as transition candidates with the move beyond transition referring to towns only. Transition Bristol was the first 'city-scale initiative' (p. 144). This works at two levels. At the citywide level there appear to be two main functions: first 'it seeks to inspire, train and enable, and to support emerging neighbourhood-scale initiatives' (p. 144), and second it is producing 'an Energy Descent Plan for the city as a whole' (p. 208). The latter is interesting in admitting of a citywide need, but overall there appears to be more weight given to 'village-scale' (neighbourhood) initiatives (p. 208). Here we find a clue to the way cities are viewed when Bristol is interpreted as generic:

> Bristol, like all cities, is formed from a collection of 'villages', each area having a distinct identity and this feels like the ideal scale for much of this work. (p. 208)

This very 'Balkanized' vision of the city leaves little or no room for the idea of the city as an integrated urban economy. And yet there is a direct link to the radical urban economics literature through Hopkins' (2008, p. 112) proposal for local currencies.

In the very first Transition Initiative, he describes an experiment with the 'Totnes pound', which he deems to be a successful endeavour in the sense of having a reasonable take-up among local businesses (pp. 197–200). The economic reason he gives for this local currency is to stop money pouring out of 'the community in much the same way as water pours from a leaky bucket' (p. 197). But this misses the critical purpose of a currency: if it is allowed to float, its changing value provides a feedback loop on how an economy is doing (Jacobs 1984). This only works with the economy designated as a system, and at the local level this means a city or city-region economy. In other words, if the transition approach is about 'designing for economic renaissance, albeit a local one' (p. 135), you will only know if a renaissance is happening if the currency works at a city or city-region scale.

The relative neglect of cities in the Transition Initiative is unfortunate given that twenty-first century is shaping up to be a century of ever larger and larger cities. Even today, cities with over a million population are becoming commonplace but these are particularly difficult to fit into the transition vision (Bristol's population is just 400 000). This issue is directly addressed on the Initiatives' website with a Forum topic entitled 'What strategies are working in big cities?' This turns out to be an unproductive dialogue between Hamburg and Barcelona transition people that finds no way forward for cities with more than a million population (www. transitioninitiative.org, accessed 3 April 2011). Most of the latter are, in any case, in the three poorer continents and it is indicative that the world map of transition initiatives records only three in Latin America, two in Asia and one in Africa (www.transitioninitiative.org, accessed 3 April 2011). The vision appears to be producing an international practice (31 countries) but hardly a global one.

What is the source of this vision that neglects cities and finds it difficult to become global? We get a hint of an answer when Hopkins (2008, pp. 136–41) lays out the 'philosophical underpinnings' of the transition approach. He begins with the statement that 'one of the principal foundations of the transition concept is permaculture' (p. 136) but in fact this is the only topic broached as input into his philosophical position. Permaculture is essentially a comprehensive approach to rural land use – 'permanent agriculture' – that replaces conventional monoculture and annual cropping with 'multi-layered systems making use of productive and useful trees and perennial plants' (p. 137). In effect this is replacing agricultural simplicity by an ecologically complex process. These principles for sustainable food production have been extrapolated to 'other elements that make up society – economics, building, energy and so on' (p. 140). Thus Hopkins, a teacher of permaculture, uses 'permaculture design principles' 'as the design "glue" and the ethical foundations we use to underpin Transition work, to stick together all the elements of a post-peak settlement' (p. 137).

Once again this is systems thinking from ecology, and highlights the need for integration, diversity, maximizing self-sufficiency, and creativity to go with the presumptive small-scale.

The key point from my perspective is, of course, that these complex ecological principles of resilience are to be found in abundance in cities; that is what this book has been all about. Hopkins' *Transition Handbook* (2008) is imbued with concepts and ideas that I find central to how cities operate such as: 'sufficient creativity and imagination' (p. 53), 'diversity of functions' (p. 55), 'more opportunities for meeting and working with people' and 'self-reliant community' (p. 69). I do not argue that creativity is a monopoly of cities but I do strongly believe that the evidence shows this is where such behaviour has been concentrated in geohistory. And, most obviously, large cities are invariably much more economically diverse and self-reliant than small towns. In the case of the latter, as a long-standing literature on so called basic/non basic economic activities (basic means exports in this traditional economics) has shown, the larger the urban place the more work is done supplying the local market thus requiring relatively less imports. All this adds up to is that if Hopkins' (2008) valuing of diversity, creativity and self-reliance is right – and I am in full agreement with him here – then he should pay much more attention to cities, especially large cities.

RETURN TO THE LOCAL II: GREEN CITIES

Cities can also be interpreted as representing the local, still encompassing everyday familiarity and a degree of control, albeit not at the immediate level with its habitual face-to-face contacts of small towns. But what is lost through size is more than compensated for by the additional potential benefits as just described above and throughout this book. Thus whereas for

Hopkins (2008) Bristol and their ilk are largely just a useful organizational level, there is a literature on 'green cities' that, as the name suggests, bring cities to the centre of environmental debates.

There are two basic reasons why cities should be central to our concerns for future sustainability and they are encapsulated in the subtitles of two recent, relevant books. David Owen's (2009) *Green Metropolis* has as its subtitle 'why living smaller, living closer, and driving less are the keys to sustainability'. This is to argue that cities as population concentrations are inherently greener than dispersed suburbia and rural living. To reinforce this argument he begins by shocking his readers: 'New York is the greenest community in the United States' (p. 9). Edward Glaeser's (2011) *Triumph of the City* is subtitled 'How our greatest invention makes us richer, smarter, greener, healthier and happier'. Here greenness is linked to other properties of city living, many of which I have chronicled earlier. Calthorpe (2011, p. 10) describes this as an urban premium: on top of gains made from city living, 'urbanism generates a fortuitous web of co-benefits – it is our most potent weapon against climate change because it does so much more'. Obviously the two arguments are closely related but I will briefly illustrate each in turn before critiquing the concept of green cities.

How Green are our Cities? A US Case Study

Calthorpe (2011, p. 4) states:

> Certainly cities are green. On a per capita basis, they require less land, less auto travel, and less energy, and they emit less carbon.

But some cities are greener than others. I know of only one serious attempt to measure impacts of cities on the environment across a range of cities: Glaeser and Kahn (2008) have estimated carbon emissions for the 66 largest US cities. This study helps us understand what is going on in cities that affects their urban sustainability. Although cities are inherently more sustainable than non-urban living there are important differences between them. This is largely based on the urban structure, which in turn reflects differences in cities' growth periods. Newer cities have grown when the car is the main mode of transport resulting in large spread-out cities, the derogatory term for this is 'urban sprawl'. This contrast is very clear in the US as we shall see.

I have summarized part of Glaeser and Kahn's (2008) results in Table 8.1 focusing on just ten major cities spread across the country. The first column shows the variable effect of car travel in terms of CO_2 emissions. The greenness of New York is reflected in having by far the lowest

Table 8.1   Sustainable living in leading US cities

City	Emissions from driving*	Emissions from public transport*	Emissions from home heating*	Electricity**	Sustainability ranking
Atlanta	29425	1121	8851	14.63	57
Boston	22870	2276	14019	7.92	9
Chicago	24278	5221	10374	9.83	39
Dallas	27323	1723	6100	17.81	61
Houston	27333	1447	5344	18.74	62
Los Angeles	23553	1062	6439	8.43	5
New York	18081	6386	12503	7.83	21
Miami	24187	4689	896	17.92	38
San Francisco	23970	1675	6784	7.03	2
Washington, DC	25918	4729	5674	13.72	49

Notes:
*   lbs of CO_2.
**   megawatt hours.

Source: Glaeser and Kahn (2008).

emissions; in contrast the three growth cities of the South – Atlanta, Dallas and Houston – have the largest emissions. But this does not mean New York is America's greenest city as Owen (2009) has asserted and is quoted above. Glaeser and Kahn measure three other contributions to CO_2 emissions. In the second column of Table 8.1 public transport emissions are listed and New York has the highest rate, but the key point is that these emissions are at a much lower level than those in column 1. The third column shows CO_2 emissions from home heating and this is largely a climatic effect – Glaeser and Kahn show it is correlated with January temperatures. Thus, not surprisingly, in this case the three most northern cities – Boston, Chicago and New York – have highest emissions, and Miami with its mild winters has by far the lowest. In the fourth column Glaeser and Kahn's results show electricity consumption whose variability is largely the result of air conditioning – they show it to be correlated with July temperatures. Again not surprisingly, it is the five southern cities that feature high on this measure. The final column sums up the results as overall sustainability rankings and the geography is very clear: the two Californian cities are the most sustainable; the two northeast cities come next. Most alarmingly, the three boom cities of the South – Atlanta, Dallas and Houston – are right near the bottom of the ranking. In other words current US urban growth is occurring in a most unsustainable way exemplified by boom towns of the South: the cities ranked below Dallas and Houston in Glaeser and Kahn's full results are, from the bottom up, Memphis, Oklahoma City, Nashville and Birmingham.

From an environmental perspective recent US urban growth is clearly dysfunctional. This chimes with deeper explorations of how US metropolitan regions are being developed. Paul Knox (2008, p. 66) identifies this as a 'developer's utopia' that calls itself the New Urbanism, commonly encompassing '"green" communities or "sustainable" developments' (p. 85). In a devastating critique he refers to this being only a 'rhetoric of sustainability' behind which hides an 'anti-urban', 'anti-intellectual' discourse that is intrinsically about development in accordance with the 'sumptuary codes' of the rich and resulting 'consultant's fees' (p. 110). More generally, the degree to which the rest of the world is copying current US growth processes that cater for cars and air conditioning units – in China and India, for example – the more unlikely it is that we will be able to do anything practical to prevent catastrophic climatic change.

Green Cities: What Can They Do?

But what if all cities were satisfactorily 'green' using measures such as Glaeser and Kahn's, can they be more proactive in advancing green agendas? From our knowledge of cities this should be an obvious possibility and is explored in the green city literature. For example, Calthorpe (2011, p. 124) muses:

> There is a special kind of wisdom in our cities born of the shifting forces of time. Each age rings with it a new set of priorities to which the city responds by constantly modifying and adjusting its form and character.

He is looking forward to a post-cheap energy age, as envisaged by Hopkins in his conception of transition towns, but for larger cities. This follows Jacobs' (1969) classic position that problems are created in cities, and are then solved in cities, which is how urban creativity has always been harnessed. However Calthorpe (2011, p. 125) admits that although 'many economists and environmentalist are writing about a "green" future, . . . its shape, narrative, and balance points are yet to emerge'. In fact it is worse than this; there are plain contradictions about what is best. According to Calthorpe 'urbanism naturally tends towards a "small is beautiful" philosophy' (p. 11), and yet Stuart Brand (2010, p. 33) while agreeing that 'city growth creates problems, and then city innovation speeds up to solve them' concludes that 'the secret to creating a more environmentally sustainable society is making our cities bigger'. This difference derives from contrasting geographical foci: Calthorpe's US cities are being confronted by Brand's (2010, p. 42) mega-cities with their 'mega-slums' where 'squatter cities are green' (p. 67). I think this contradiction can be resolved, at least in part, through the difference in timing between greening modernity, and transcending modernity to an alternative sustainable world-system. Today cities in core regions remain the main centres for innovation but it is the cities of the non-core world that are the massive centres of improvization. While the modern world-system's core–periphery structure is still firmly in place, then the former will remain most important, but ultimately a sustainable future, if it is to be created, will likely come from the megacities bereft of core–periphery confinement. I will explore this idea further in terms of green networks of cities below.

Jacobs' (1969) view of cities as inherently inefficient results from the inevitable time lag between being afflicted by a problem, and finding a solution and putting it into operation. This is most clearly the situation with major infrastructure investments as I have previously discussed. Bogart (2006, pp. 5–7) discusses this explicitly for existing metropolitan structure, contrasting cities built for mass transit to more recent urban sprawl that accommodates cars. As problems deriving from post-peak oil and climate change come to a head, we can expect both types of city to respond, albeit in different ways. For now there is a generalized concern for these issues that are generating new technologies especially for energy provision: capturing biomass, geothermal, solar, wave and wind energies are all being pursued. Their costs relative to traditional carbon-based sources of energy are still very high and therefore this is an industry largely reliant on state subsidy. This can be considered a beginning to the greening of modernity, a technological fix being actively pursued in energy technology clusters across cities in the richer parts of the world. But this city process is sometimes misconstrued. For instance, Owen (2009, p. 59) offers the following argument:

> There has been much talk of reviving the economy with green jobs and green industries, but that won't be as easy as it might sound. Creating green jobs is different from creating new jobs, since green jobs, if they're truly green, displace non-green jobs – wind turbines instead of oil-rig roughnecks – probably a zero-sum game, as far as employment is concerned.

This is a classic example of misunderstanding city-ness based upon continual replacement of old work by new work. Technologies are always being superseded but this is only a zero-sum game if the process is viewed as effectively static, one technology in one city at a time. New technologies in any sector will usually be concentrated in a limited number of cities, and these will not always be in the city whose work is superseded. But cities are always part of larger networks with multiple other opportunities. And anyway, vibrant cities encompass large complex economies that can survive losses in any given sector; this is what makes cities so resilient.

The basic lesson to be drawn from this discussion is that guardian-promoted city policies that do not appreciate the centrality of 'commercial' city-ness in macro-social change are doomed to essential superficiality, a modern ostentation of being seen to be doing something but with no firm handle on process. I see this in the many city-centred policies that were stimulated by the 1992 Rio de Janeiro sustainability conference. Bringing cities to centre-stage is of limited utility if this does not include an understanding of city-ness. Thus both the Arup Report (2011) on city policies that identifies 4734 'climatic actions' (with another 1465 under consideration) in 36 mega-cities, and the 'dozens' of 'internationally agreed commitments that directly concern cities' identified by the UNCSD (2012), encompass guardian practices with little or no reference to the creativity inherent in large cities. City-ness is being ignored just when it it is most needed.

Green Cities in Context

My starting position that green cities should not be considered singly is by no means an untypical position to take. Here are three typical examples. According to Owen (2009, p.40):

> The crucial fact about sustainability is that it is not a micro-phenomenon: there can be no such thing as a 'sustainable' house, office building, or household appliance, for the same reason there can be no such thing as a one-person democracy or a single company economy. Every house, office building, and appliance, no matter where its power comes from or how many of its parts were made from soya beans, is just a single small element in a civilization-wide network of deeply interdependent relationships, and it's the network, not the individual constituents, on which our future depends. Sustainability is a context, not a gadget or a technology. This is the reason that dense cities set such a critical example: they prove that it's possible to arrange large human populations in ways that are inherently less wasteful and destructive.

Calthorpe (2011, p. 16) emphasizes new relationships:

> At this point in history, most of our key economic, social, and environmental networks extend well beyond individual neighbourhoods, jurisdictions, or even cities. . . . The tradition of urbanism must be extended to an interconnected and interdependent regional network of places, creating polycentric regions rather than a metropolis dominated by the old city/suburb schism.

And Wall and colleagues (2007, p.12) extends its implications for practitioners:

> The emergence of globalization and urban networks should compel policy makers and planners to reconsider the reach of their professions.

These positions are all laudable but there remains the problem of how to satisfactorily offer practically relevant and theoretical sound ways forward.

The urgency for moving away from single-project, one-city approaches – environmentalism without context – has been illustrated by Glaeser (2011) in his comparisons of urban growth in California and the American South. Migration streams have turned around in the US; after more than a century of 'Go West, Young Man', in the second half of the twentieth century cities in the American South became the fastest growing. Glaeser's explanation for this relates to the economics of the average middle-class American family (pp.183–93). Now priced out of housing in California, high-quality affordable housing in cities like Houston has meant the American Dream can only be fulfilled for the mass of ordinary people in the American South. How and why? Pro-development policies (Houston is the only city in the US without a zoning code) allow for unrestricted new building and thus housing supply keeps housing prices down:

> More than in any other place, Houston's developers have successfully argued that restrictions on development will make the city less affordable to the less successful. These arguments are patently self-interested, but they are also correct. Houston's free-wheeling growth machine has actually done a better job of providing affordable housing than all of the progressive reformers on the American East and West coasts. (p.192)

Thus, 'for millions of Americans, the decision to move to Houston', and other southern cities, 'makes clear economic sense' (p.187). But we have seen in Table 8.1 that it is precisely these cities that are producing the most carbon emissions. And it is the Californian cities with least emissions in Table 8.1 (San Diego ranks first in Glaeser's full analysis) that have forfeited the urban growth that the South has reaped. This is an unintended national consequence of Californian environmental NIMBYism ('not in my backyard') long ago chronicled and criticized by Mike Davis (1990). Glaeser's (2011, p.212) even more damning indictment is that '[b]y using ecological arguments to oppose growth, California environmentalists are actually ensuring that America's urban footprint will rise, by pushing new housing to less temperate climates'.

There can be no clearer example of why serious environmental thinking has to encompass the big picture. Glaeser's argument points towards the dangers of localism. This is not to say that transition towns, for example, are not good environmental practice, far from it, but it does mean that all environmental projects ought to be as outward-looking as they are inward-looking: they must always have to show that their environmentally positive practices are not just transferring environmental negatives elsewhere. Outward-looking to where? To places with which they have economic relations, which means city networks.

Let us now take stock briefly of where green arguments have led us. There are three basic scales of activity that need to be modified in any comprehensive resilient route forward.

The transition town scale based upon familiarity and a sense of being able to have a direct influence is the level for individual and group mobilization; but a mosaic of transition communities – green neighbourhoods and green villages – is not a sufficient future vision.

The green cities scale is a transition-enabling scale but it can and should be much more than this; this is where we can expect to find creativity and resilience coming together first to innovate greening the modern, and subsequently, second to solve the acute problems arising in transcending the modern. But individual green cities dotted across the landscape are not a sufficient future vision.

Green cities in context point towards cities operating through networks as the key scale. Bringing city-ness into the argument means that we should build our definitive vision of the future on green networks of cities. This scale does not replace the national scale but complements it as long as the latter remains the key level of decision-making. As the US case study has indicated, for the larger countries there is a need to recognize that their economic space should operate through a green network of cities. But ultimately we need to be thinking in terms of a green world city network.

In the next section I focus on level 3 but with continuing references to the other scales.

GREEN NETWORKS OF CITIES: MODERN AND BEYOND MODERN

In his Transition initiative, Hopkins (2008, p. 197) recognizes economics as a 'key challenge' for his approach, which he describes as 'designing for economic renaissance, albeit a local one' (p. 135). However he does not provide a systematic description of how this will work – references to economic processes are scattered throughout his text. But we can find a very important point he makes in relation to the nature of his localism:

We aren't looking to create 'nothing in, nothing out' economy, but rather to close economic loops where possible and to produce locally what we can. (p. 68)

So no simple 'delinking': local autarchy is not envisaged. And elsewhere he goes a step further:

Increased resilience and a stronger local economy does not mean that we put a fence up around our towns and cities and refuse to allow anything in or out. It is not a rejection of commerce or somehow a return to a rose-tinted version of some imagined past. What it does mean is being more prepared for a leaner future, more self-reliant, and prioritising the local over the imported. (p. 55)

The last phrase clearly resonates with Jacobs' import replacement mechanism.

Thus transition economics does prompt two important aspects of relationships between the local and the non-local. I will interpret them as follows. First, the containing nature of the local I will treat as leading towards a possible modern handling of how to make green networks. Second, the introduction of 'prioritizing the local' – something like import replacement – I will use to set up contradictions that can lead to ideas on a greening of networks beyond the modern.

Towards a Modern Green Network of Cities: Modularity

Whereas Glaeser warns of the negative aspects of localism at the city scale, Hopkins (2008, p. 55) illustrates the positive aspects of localism at the town level. He uses the concept of modularity, by which he means a particular patchwork structure within a system rather than a tightly integrated system. This is identified as an important feature that makes systems resilient. He thinks this is a 'key' issue because:

A more modular structure means that the parts of the system can more effectively self-organise in the event of shock (so that) maximising modularity with more internal connections reduces vulnerability to any disruptions of wider networks. (p. 56)

It is here that Hopkins criticizes contemporary globalization using examples from finance and the food industry. He argues that:

... the globalised networks, often trumpeted as one of globalisation's great strengths, can in fact also be one of its great weaknesses. The over-networked nature of modern, highly connected systems allow shock to travel rapidly through them, with potentially disastrous effects. (p. 56)

Although we might argue that modularity at the scale of a small town is unlikely to be effective given their excessive dependence on the non-local – of which more in the next section – his modular argument is important not least because large networks do not have to be so integrated. In fact, as shown in the last chapter, the contemporary world city network is highly regionalized. Let us explore this as modularization.

According to Jacobs (1984, p. 135) 'backward cities need one another', suggesting that cities in poorer countries in general need to be insulated from wider networks that include richer cities through which they may be exploited. In other words she is advocating modular protection. But she has another new argument for advocating a more segmented network structure, specifically in national terms, whereby cities not growing rapidly can be aided by those experiencing explosive growth:

> Some places in the nation, such as stagnant regions or declining cities, may show no growth at all ... Other places – cities with the most rapidly growing economies – have a much higher rate of economic growth ... Of course the same cities are not continually and steadily doing most to raise the (national) net growth rate – only those growing explosively at the time. Not all cities of a rapidly expanding (national) economy are simultaneously replacing imports rapidly. The economy is a little like a corn popper in which not all the kernels are popping simultaneously; but all the time the corn is popping. (Jacobs 1969, p. 167)

The lesson here is clear: if all kernels pop in unison a situation will arise when none is popping. In other words a network of simultaneously successful cities is especially vulnerable to cyclical economic change because one downturn could eliminate all the 'urban sparks' thereby nullifying an economic upturn. The degree to which today's world city networks are tending towards such dynamic coincidence, the more the likelihood that a clear route towards a very unresilient global system is being taken.

Fortunately globalization is not always as global as it appears or as its advocates would have us believe. Finance and its recent global crisis are the counter case and there are moves to separate retail and wholesale banking functions to lessen the global network dangers. But in fact the effects of the financial crisis were anything but geographically homogeneous: some world regions were much more resilient than others. In general this marked a shift in financial power from West to East (Derudder et al. 2011). This outcome appears to reflect the inherent regionality of the world city network despite its global scope. The globalization is uneven and diverse so that even in finance there is a complex variety in the geography of effects from the severe shock of 2008. Thus global financial networks appear more resilient than expected: after the initial shock and bail outs from the state public sector, there has been a return to normal with many banks continuing with their high profits and bonus culture leaving economic austerity behind in the public sector of, mainly, western states. The crisis of the banks has been converted into a crisis of states, mainly states in the West as discussed in the last chapter.

What specifically is this contemporary world city network modularity? As we have seen, it is based upon world regions and larger nation states. The former have many different historical trajectories to contemporary globalization and this produces a wide variety of ways in which cities are integrated into global networks. In a recent study, such regional concentrations of city processes for nine world regions were investigated (Taylor et al. 2011, pp. 67, 81–2, 90, 100, 110, 130–31, 144, 163–4, 182). And within these big regions there are a small number of states whose economic jurisdictions are distinctive and important. As expected, two in particular are critical: the US and China. In world city network studies US cities always appear as a distinctive block, an American exceptionalism wherein intra-nation links are unusually important relative to foreign links. There are recent indications that Chinese cities might be developing in the same way because of their country's unique late and dramatic entry into globalization. For instance, of 525 cities worldwide, the ranking of cities for relative concentration of links within their own country featured only US and Chinese cities in the top 27 places (22 from the US, five from China) (Taylor et al. 2011, pp. 208, 260, 334). This partly reflects the sizes of these two economic jurisdictions – they have more cities in their own country to link to – but the degree of difference between the cities of these two countries and the rest suggests rather deep national modularities are being created here.

Of course, these modularities, both regional and national, are not exactly the same as Hopkins (2008) envisages in his transition approach. He argues for engaging 'with the wider world but from an ethic of networking and information sharing rather than of mutual dependence' (p. 56). The mutuality in world city networks encompasses this ethic but emphasizes 'inter-dependence', which suggests a more integrated network process than Hopkins suggests. Certainly there is no consistent patterning of modularity, rather in world city networks it reflects contingent economic and political factors – cities in richer regions and in smaller states tend to have more and wider connections. Such historical serendipities may create modularities but not necessarily the ones suitable for controlling shocks. A green network of world cities would have a specific modularity that maximizes city network resilience.

Modern green networks of cities will have to be based on a greening of existing services: green financial services, green accountancy, green advertising and so on. But what does this mean? I'm not really sure but it must engage with current world city network agents. Girardet (2008, p. 269) addresses precisely this point in discussion of his generic sustainable city, EcoPolis, but it is not clear how to generate such new practices beyond his exhortations (pp. 261, 294). Put simply there is a critical research and practice agenda that is necessary and urgent to go beyond government-sponsored 'eco-towns,' or even 'a truly green city' (p. 289) such as China's Dongtan, and to consider seriously how a green network of cities might function and how we can make them come to pass. For a start there is a need to go beyond the basic concept of non-local; this has been crucial to understanding economic change but is less suitable for considerations of sustainability and resilience. If network agents in Shanghai replace imports from Beijing and Osaka, this is no different from them replacing imports from Paris and Chicago in terms of Shanghai's economic growth: it matters not from whence imports are replaced except that they be non-local. However there are huge differential impacts here in terms of commodity-miles to generate this city change: not all non-local interaction is environmentally equal. This implies that we ought to prevent the global reach of trade, but this is impracticable: long-distance, non-local trade may be necessary depending on the geographies of input into production (specific raw materials, customized equipment, specialist labour). City niches, and therefore trade, are integral to the modern world-system but their scope can be controlled through application of a strict *intervening opportunities* metric. Originally devised to study migration by Stouffer (1940), this method replaces physical distance by the number of possible alternative destinations between origin and actual destination. For usage here, origin is the location of consumption and destinations are source locations for a commodity. This would mean that the theoretical non-local is interpreted practically as the nearest non-local. This is an example of thinking beyond reducing a single city's ecological footprint, to focus on reducing many cities' ecological netprints collectively, thereby creating greener networks of cities.

Towards a Green Network of Cities Beyond Modernity: Alternative Import Replacements

We have returned to the import replacement mechanism for greening modern networks of cities but careful contemplation of this process in relation to sustainability reveals a critical contradiction in the approach. I use this to open up consideration of green networks of cities beyond modernity. The key argument in Jacobs' (1969) model is that economic expansion occurs rapidly within cities through replacing and shifting imports. The cumulative result is that trade is not expanded, but production is. As shown in Chapter 2, this can be interpreted as growing cities becoming increasingly self-sufficient in their needs; as a trade theory, this is the very opposite of economists' comparative advantage model that minimizes self-sufficiency. In Jacobs' thinking the key index is the ratio between trade and production: the larger the settlement, the less trade relative to production: *ipso facto* city development is the route to societal sustainability. In contrast, rural areas, with their farms, villages and small towns, export most of what they produce and import most of what they need: rural development is the route to societal unsustainability. This is where small does not look quite so beautiful!

It is hard to imagine a more controversial argument: not only is Jacobs' economic growth deemed good for sustainability, economic growth actually is sustainability. Obviously this does not make sense in terms of resource limits for ceaseless capital accumulation: the Earth is too small for non-stop city import replacement as a commercial process. In the current model continual renewal of the city network is through innovation and its diffusion as imitation. Therefore one way that the city process can be stopped is by purging innovation from society; a strict traditionalism imposed on humanity by neo-Luddite guardians would mark a transition to a new world-system. The result would be no new ideas entering the network to be imitated and replaced as imports. This is equivalent to the classic Ethiopian historical urban demise described in Chapter 2: all cities would gradually become economically identical as existing innovations are used up through the final throes of import replacement. Then, inter-city trade would become unnecessary, networks would collapse, and we finish with a world of duplicate 'subsistence cities'. This trail of thought sacrifices the potential for human creativity for the promise of sustainable survival. Instead of greening city networks, they are simply eliminated.

Is this the sort of trade off we can ever be satisfied with? Is this the only way for cities beyond modernity, to become 'un-dynamic'? It would be the greatest of ironies if the legacy of the great creative historical interlude that is modernity turned out to be the destruction of human creativity. It is time for alternative forward thinking drawing on previous discussions. Two notions spring to mind, one from Wallerstein and one from Jacobs, both first broached in Chapter 2. Starting with the former I focus on his separating of market from capitalism (using Braudel 1982); this is to disconnect everyday commercial practice (generic) from capitalism with its systemic accumulation imperative (specifically modern). This is, of course, the basis for studying commerce in Chapter 5 as part of Normal History (using Sanderson 1995), and confirms that commerce does not have to be destructive capitalism. Therefore there may be a different type of relation between guardians and commerce from the modern *modus operandi*, that can maintain dynamic cities but without ceaseless capital accumulation. Wallerstein (1991) suggests such a possibility:

> Braudel's 'liberatory' market is not what we have come to recognize as a market in the real world. It is truly competitive, in that supply and demand really do determine the price, that is, potential (or fully realized) supply and demand. The 'profits', it would follow, would be miniscule, in effect, a wage for the work. Whether such a system is historically viable remains a question. (pp. 216–17)

It follows that the 500-year modern interlude is indicted as 'the constant defeat of this market' and therefore:

> It may be that the triumph of the market (in Braudel's sense), no longer being the sign of the capitalist system, turns out to be the sign of world socialism. (p. 206)

The latter is not specified beyond 'the egalitarianization of the world' as 'the struggle for human liberties' (p. 206) but as a replacement for ceaseless capital accumulation it would certainly portend a sustainable world of commercial cities. If this were to happen, then Arrighi (2007) places its origins firmly in China. In his world-systems analysis he looks forward to:

> an East Asia-centered world market society based upon mutual respect of the world's cultures and civilizations . . . such an outcome presupposes a radically different model of development that . . . is socially and ecologically sustainable. (Arrighi 2010, p. 385)

This is commerce without capitalism.

Jacobs adds commerce without commerce! In Chapter 2, in commenting on Jacobs' (1992) labelling of her two moral syndromes, I indicated that I thought 'commercial' to be a little restrictive since she included work outside the market. This opens a window to an alternative to Jacobs' (1969) initial focus on economic growth, through her unorthodox economic way of thinking. At the centre of Jacobs' economics we find work – people have always been attracted to cities because they offer a better livelihood, either through existing jobs or the opportunity of making jobs (seeking out a living). Thus the invisible hand of the market is replaced by the very visible complexity of the city at the centre of the analysis. Markets can play an important role in her thinking as firms compete, of course, but these are not the only agents that make city complexity. Here is Jacobs (1969, pp. 54–5) on the new work deriving from old (i.e. parent) work creating a more complex division of labour:

Nor is the process by which one thing leads to another confined to profit-making enterprises. A hospital outpatient department is starting a home care service; a library is starting a program of art exhibits; an art museum is starting a library. Nor is it . . . confined to useful, legal or innocuous work. . . . police sometimes add burglarizing to their work of patrolling, and other divisions of labour to dispose of the goods. . . . of course nothing precludes a society from suppressing certain kinds of new activities while permitting and encouraging others. Indeed, a society must do that or else risk nurturing activities and organizations that will devote themselves to outright destruction of useful activities and also to preventing or hampering the emergence of new and useful goods and services.

This provides clear hints of alternative importing or import replacing among cities. We can glimpse such a possibility in the global networks of cities created by non-governmental organizations (NGOs). These are non-market agents who use cities in their work; they are global networkers as represented by their multiple offices worldwide (Taylor 2005). Nairobi, for instance, is a major world city for NGO work and as NGOs grow in the city they take on more functions locally, which is creating new work through import replacement. Of course, this particular sector is minute as a global player compared to the global corporations that currently dominate the modern world-system but NGOs could be harbingers of a green network of cities beyond modernity. The Jacobs quote above also heralds the means to this alternative greening in reference to 'society' (i.e. the state) 'suppressing', 'permitting' and 'encouraging' new work. This portends a return of the guardians, but with different emphases in their practice.

To summarize: a process of green networks of cities, enabling creative dynamism for a sustainable and resilient world, should not be beyond the wit of urban humanity.

CONCLUDING WITH THE LAST TANGO: WHAT NEW *MODUS* FOR CITY/STATE RELATIONS?

This book has ended by introducing the concept of green networks of cities. The chapter heading started with 'Towards', indicating a final narrative becoming increasingly different from narratives in Parts II and III as we moved from what is known about contemporary actual city networks to more speculative, sometimes verging on the normative, ideas on future twenty-first-century urban development. Obviously this reflects that this urban future has still to be made and therefore cannot be properly specified. But there are degrees of 'unknowability'. Thus I divided my speculations into modern and beyond modern with the former being much the firmer of the two. This is because comprehension can be built upon specific knowledge of the modern present from which this future will derive. Beyond modern is another case completely, since I am looking towards a new world-system (or even to a world of multiple world- or mini-systems) that cannot be discerned from today's specifics. But we do have generic concepts that have served humanity thus far through various geohistorical world-systems and can be expected to continue their salience beyond the modern interlude. I will finish by deploying these tools to 'beyond modern' speculation.

In a possible transition to a sustainable world-system the moral syndromes model suggests where to look for creators of this new world. It appears that those making a commercial living might well be orientated towards their *individual* futures but it is from the ranks of guardians that we can expect to find explicit concern for our *collective* futures. This is because stewardship, in Jacobs' terms honouring predecessors and thinking of posterity (Lawrence 1989b, p. 200), is self-evidently associated with guardian morals and practices. To be sure there is commercial stewardship notably in sustainable forestry, but note this is commercial practice on land production, where commercial practices commonly elide into guardian practices. Historically, stewardship has been inherently territorial in focus, hence its guardian nature. But flows as well as places require long-term maintenance: where are the network stewards? Usually involving large-scale infra-structural improvements, these are also traditionally the responsibility of guardians operating first through world-empires and latterly through modern states. It has been a common theme in Marxist thinking that capital will 'destroy itself' (i.e. is unsustainable) unless saved 'from itself' by the state (e.g. Holloway and Picciotto 1978); in world-systems analysis it is in hegemonic states that innovative infra-structures have been invented. Jacobs (1992) always insisted that societies need both commercial and guardian practices, I have suggested the balance between the two changed in the transition to modernity – in the transition from modernity it appears a reversal will ensue.

It would be too simplistic to suggest that a future transition will mark the return of world-empire, global or otherwise. After all, I have also used Jacobs' economics to argue that commercial work can be a key part of the solution through import replacement in cities. Combining guardian stewardship with dynamic radical commercial practice suggests that the new system while not continuing the modern *modus operandi*, does not necessarily fit with a revived *modus vivendi*. Some new original mixture of the two syndromes needs to be invented. We do not know what this is to be but we can say that guardians will be indispensable to thinking about reaching a sustainable future. Guardians may work through multiple new states, or through just one global state, or through a new form of global governance not yet foreseeable. We can say that whatever the governance, it is likely to be invented in and derived from problems generated in twenty-first-century cities in societal crisis. There will be some equivalence to the rapid throwing up of city walls that marked the invention of enhanced guardian apparatus that was the state and became world-empire in Mesopotamia 5000 years ago. The world is saved; guardians are heroes.

I remarked in the introduction of this chapter that the optimistic outcome of my analysis was somewhat surprising. This might be wishful thinking. Guardians-as-stewards could turn out to be far less common than the familiar guardians-as-warriors; this may well be the final form that Wallerstein's demise bifurcation takes. And in any case, there is the no small matter of non-synchronization between ecological time and social time; the social change processes I identify may not have the time to come to fruition. At the very least we can hope that humanity has the chance to start again, from new city beginnings, so as to build upon its extraordinary collective potential, but with one key proviso: maintaining a strong collective myth exhorting the need for universal stewardship of the Earth.

And finally: given the amount of text already amassed in this book, I have resisted the temptation of bringing ideas together in an epilogue. Enough is enough. All I want to say is that I hope the reader takes away a critical sense of two experiments I have been engaged with. First, there is the city-centric intellectual experiment expressed through the book; will this contarian social science work in the sense of generating new cumulative thinking? Second, this work is embedded in the great social experiment we call modernity; will this abnormal world-system work in the sense of generating a resilient posterity?

References

Abbott, C. (1999) *Political Terrain: Washington, DC, from Tidewater Town to Global Metropolis*. Chapel Hill, NC: University of North Carolina Press.

Abrutyn, S. and K. Lawrence (2010) 'From chiefdom to state: toward an integrative theory of the evolution of polity', *Sociological Perspectives* **53** (3), 419–42.

Abu-Lughod, J.L. (1989) *Before European Hegemony: The World System, AD 1250–1350*. New York: Oxford University Press.

Adams, R.M. (1966) *The Evolution of Urban Society: Early Mespotomia and Prehispanic Mexico*. Chicago, IL: Aldine.

Agnew, J. (1993) 'The territorial trap: the geographical assumptions of international relations theory', *Review of International Economy* **1**, 53–80.

Alderson, A.S. and F. Nielson (2002) 'Globalization and the great U-turn: income inequality trends for 16 OECD countries', *American Journal of Sociology* **107**, 1244–99.

Alderson, A.S., J. Beckfield and F. Nielson (2005) 'Exactly how has income inequality changed?', *International Journal of Comparative Sociology* **46**, 405–23.

Alexiou, A.S. (2006) *Jane Jacobs: Urban Visionary*. New Brunswick, NJ: Rutgers University Press.

Algaze, G. (2005a) *The Uruk World System: The Dynamics of Expansion of Early Mesopotamian Civilization*, second edition. Chicago, IL: University of Chicago Press.

Algaze, G. (2005b) 'The Sumerian take-off', *Structure and Dynamics: eJournal of Anthropological and Related Sciences* **1** (1), Article 2, http://repositories.cdlib.org/imbs/socdyn/sideas/vol1/iss1/art 2 (accessed 6 August 2012).

Amen, M., N.J. Toly, P.L. McCarney and K. Segbers (eds) (2011) *Cities and Global Governance*. Farnham: Ashgate.

Amin, S. (1990) *Delinking*. London: Zed Books.

Amin, A. and N.J. Thrift (1992) 'Neo-Marshallian nodes in global networks', *International Journal of Urban and Regional Research* **16**, 571–81.

Arrighi, G. (1990) 'The three hegemonies of historical capitalism', *Review* **13**, 365–408.

Arrighi, G. (1994) *The Long Twentieth Century*. London: Verso.

Arrighi, G. (2007) *Adam Smith in Beijing: Lineages of the Twenty First Century*. London: Verso.

Arrighi, G. (2010) 'Postscript to the second edition', in G. Arrighi, *The Long Twentieth Century*. London: Verso, pp. 371–86.

Arup (2011) *Climate Action in Megacities*, www.c40cities.org (accessed 1 June 2012).

Attarian, C.J. (2003) 'Cities as a place of ethnogenesis: urban growth and centralization in the Chicama Valley, Peru', in M.L. Smith, (ed.) *The Social Construction of Ancient Cities*. Washington, DC: Smithsonian Books, pp. 184–211.

Bairoch, P. (1988) *Cities and Economic Development*. Chicago, IL: University of Chicago Press.

Balter, M. (1998) 'The first cities: Why settle down? The mystery of communities', *Science* **282**, November, 1442.

Balter, M. (2005) *The Goddess and the Bull. Çatalhöylük: An Archaeological Journey to the Dawn of Civilization*. New York: Free Press.

Barbour, V. (1963) *Capitalism and Amsterdam in the Seventeenth Century*. Ann Arbor, MI: University of Michigan Press.

Barraclough, G. (1979) *The Times Atlas of World History*. London: Times Books.

Bathelt, H., A. Malmberb and P. Maskell (2004) 'Clusters and knowledge: local buzz, global pipelines and the process of knowledge creation', *Progress in Human Geography* **28**, 31–56.

Bauman, Z. (1991) *Modernity and Ambivalence*. Cambridge: Polity.

Beaverstock, J.V. (1994) 'Re-thinking skilled international labour migration: world cities and banking organisations', *Geoforum* **25**, 323–38.

Beaverstock, J.V., M. Hoyler, K. Pain and P.J. Taylor (2001) *Comparing London and Frankfurt as World Cities: A Relational Study of Contemporary Urban Change*. London: Anglo-German Foundation.

Begg, I (1999) 'Cities and competitiveness', *Urban Studies* **36**, 795–809.

Belich, J. (2009) *Replenishing the Earth: The Settler Revolution and the Rise of the Anglo-World, 1783–1939*. Oxford: Oxford University Press.

Bell, D.A. and A. de-Shalit, A (2011) *The Spirit of Cities. Why the Identity of a City Matters in a Global Age*. Princeton, NJ: Princeton University Press.

Berg, L., E. Braun, J. Meer and G. Mingardo (2006) 'The urban dimension in European policy: history, actors and programmes', in L. Berg, E. Braun and J. Meer (eds) *National Policy Responses to Urban Challenges in Europe*. Aldershot: Ashgate.

Berman, M. (1988) *All that is Solid Melts into Air: The Experience of Modernity.* New York: Penguin.

Berry, B. J. L. (1961) 'City size distributions and economic development' *Economic Development and Cultural Change* **9**, 573–88.

Berry, B.J.L. (1964) 'Cities as systems within systems of cities', *Papers of the Regional Science Association* **13**, 147–63.

Berry, B.J.L. and F.E. Horton (1970) *Geographic Perspectives on Urban Systems.* Englewood Cliffs, NJ: Prentice-Hall.

Blaut. J.M. (2000) *Eight Eurocentric Historians.* New York: Guilford Press.

Bogart, W. T. (2006) *Don't Call It Sprawl: Metropolitan Structure in the Twenty First Century.* Cambridge: Cambridge University Press.

Boogman, J.C. (1978) 'The *raison d'état* politician Johan de Witt', *Low Countries History Yearbook 1978*, 55–78.

Boogman, J.C. (1979) 'The Union of Utrecht: its genesis and consequencies', *Bijddragen Mededlingen Detreffende de Geschiedenis der Nederlanden* **94**, 277–407.

Borchert, J.R. (1967) 'American metropolitan evolution', *Geographical Review* **62**, 320–45.

Bourne, L.S. (1975) *Urban Systems: Strategies for Regulation.* Oxford: Clarendon Press.

Bourne, L.S. and Simmons, J.W. (eds) (1978) *Systems of Cities.* New York: Oxford University Press.

Bowden, C. (2010) *Murder City: Ciudad Juárez and the Global Economy's New Killing Fields.* New York: Nation Books.

Brand, S. (2010) *Whole Earth Discipline.* London: Atlantic Books.

Braudel, F. (1972a) 'History and the social sciences: the *longue durée*', in P. Burke (ed.) *Economy and Society in Early Modern Europe.* London: Routledge and Kegan Paul, pp. 25–53.

Braudel, F. (1972b) *The Mediterranean and the Mediterranean World in the Age of Phillip II*, volume 1. London: Collins.

Braudel, F. (1980) *On History.* Chicago, IL: University of Chicago Press.

Braudel. F. (1981) *The Structures of Everyday Life.* London: Collins.

Braudel, F. (1982) *The Wheels of Commerce.* London: Collins.

Braudel, F. (1984) *The Perspective of the World.* London: Collins.

Brenner, N. (2004) *New State Spaces: Urban Governance and the Rescaling of Statehood.* Oxford: Oxford University Press.

Brenner, N. and Theodore, N. (eds) (2002a) *Spaces of Neoliberalism: Urban Restructuring in North America and Western Europe.* Oxford: Blackwell.

Brenner, N. and N. Theodore (2002b) 'Cities and the geographies of "actually existing neoliberalism" ', in N. Brenner and N. Theodore (eds) *Spaces of Neoliberalism: Urban Restructuring in North America and Western Europe*. Oxford: Blackwell, pp. 2–32.

Brenner, N., B. Jessop, M. Jones, and G. MacLeod (eds) (2003) *State/ Space: A Reader*. Oxford: Blackwell.

Brook, T. (2008) *Vermeer's Hat: The Seventeenth Century and the Dawn of the Global World*. New York: Bloomsbury Press.

Brugmann, J. (2009) *Welcome to the Urban Revolution*. New York: Bloomsbury Press.

Brulez, W. (1973) 'Bruges and Antwerp in the 15th and 16th centuries: an antithesis?', *Acta Historiae Needlandica* **6**, 1–26.

Bunge, W. (1966) *Theoretical Geography*. Lund, Sweden: Gleerup.

Bunge, W. (1986) 'Epilogue: Our planet is big enough for peace but too small for war', in R.J. Johnston and P.J. Taylor (eds) *A World in Crisis: Geographical Perspectives.* Oxford: Blackwell.

Burn G. (2000) 'The state, the City and the Euromarkets', *Review of International Political Economy* **6**, 225–61.

Butlin, R.A. (1977) 'Urban and proto-urban settlements in pre-Norman Ireland', in R.A. Butlin (ed.) *The Development of the Irish Town*. London: Croom Helm.

Calthorpe, P. (2011) *Urbanism in an Age of Climatic Change*. Washington, DC: Island Press.

Carmona, S. and M. Ezzamel (2009) 'Ancient accounting', in J.R. Edwards and S.P. Walker (eds) *The Routledge Companion to Accounting History*. London: Routledge, pp.73–94.

Carneiro, R.L. (1978) 'Political expansion as an expression of the principle of competitive exclusion', in R. Cohen and E.R. Service (eds) *Origins of the State: The Anthropology of Political Evolution*. Philadelphia, PA: ISHA.

Carneiro, R.L. (1970) 'A theory of the origin of the state', *Science* **169**, 733–8.

Cartledge, P. (2009) *Ancient Greece: a History of Eleven Cities*. Oxford: Oxford University Press.

Castells, M. (1978) *The Urban Question*. Oxford: Blackwell.

Castells, M. (1989) *The Informational City*. Oxford: Blackwell

Castells, M. (1996) *The Rise of Network Society*. Oxford: Blackwell.

Castells, M. (1999) 'Grassrooting the space of flows', *Urban Geography* **20**, 294–302.

Castles S. and M.J. Miller (2003) *The Age of Migration*. Basingstoke: Palgrave Macmillan.

Chakrabarti, D.K. (2000) 'Mahajanapada states of early historic India', in M.H. Hansen (ed.) *A Comparative Study of Thirty City-State Cultures*.

Copenhagen: Historisk-filosofiske Skrifter 21 (Royal Danish Academy of Sciences and Letters), pp. 375–91.

Chandler, T. (1987) *Four Thousand Years of Urban Growth: An Historical Census*. Lewiston, NY: Edwin Mellen Press.

Charlton, T.H. and D.L. Nichols (1997a) 'The city-state concept: development and application', in D.L. Nichols, and T.H. Charlton (eds) *The Archaeology of City-states: Cross-Cultural Approaches*. Washington, DC: Smithsonian Institution Press, pp. 1–14.

Charlton, T.H. and Nichols, D.L. (1997b) 'Diachronic studies of city-states: permutations on a theme. Central Mexico from 1700 B. C. to A. D. 1600', in D.L. Nichols, and T.H. Charlton (eds) *The Archaeology of City-states: Cross-Cultural Approaches*. Washington, DC: Smithsonian Institution Press, pp. 169–207.

Chase-Dunn, C. (1985) 'The system of world cities: AD 800–1975', in M. Timberlake (ed.) *Urbanization in the World Economy*. New York: Academic Press, pp. 269–92.

Chase-Dunn, C. (1989) *Global Formation: Structures of the World-Economy*. Oxford: Blackwell.

Chase-Dunn C. and T.D. Hall (1995) 'Cross world-system comparisons: similarities and differences', in S.K. Sanderson (ed.) *Civilizations and World-Systems*. Walnut Creek, CA: AltaMira.

Chase-Dunn, C. and T.D. Hall (eds) (1997) *Rise and Demise: Comparing World-Systems*. Boulder, CO: Westview.

Chase-Dunn, C. and A. Willard (1993) 'Systems of cities and world-systems: settlement size hierarchies and cycles of political centralization, 2000 BC–1988 AD', http://irows.ucr.edu/papers/irows5.htm (accessed 12 September 2009).

Chase-Dunn, C, R. Niemeyer, A. Alvarez and H. Inoue (2009) 'Scale transitions and the evolution of global governance since the Bronze Age', in W.R. Thompson (ed.) *Systemic Transitions: Past, Present, and Future*. New York: Palgrave Macmillan.

Chase-Dunn, C., D. Pasciuti, A. Alvarez and T.D. Hall (2006) 'Growth/decline phases and semi-peripheral development in the Ancient Mesopotamian and Egyptian world-systems', in B.K. Gills and W.R. Thompson (eds) *Globalization and Global History*. London: Routledge.

Chichello, A. (1989) 'In defense of Jane Jacobs: an appreciative overview', in F. Lawrence (ed.) *Ethics in Making a Living: The Jane Jacobs Conference*. Altanta, GA: Scholars Press, pp. 99–168.

Childe, V.G. (1950) 'The urban revolution', *Town Planning Review* 21, 3–17.

Christaller, W. (1966) *Central Places in Southern Germany*. Englewood Cliffs, NJ: Prentice Hall.

Clark, P. (2009) *European Cities and Towns, 400–2000*. Oxford: Oxford University Press.

Coe, M.D. (2005) *The Maya*. London: Thames & Hudson.

Cohen, N. (2007) *What's Left: How Liberals Lost Their Way*. London: Fourth Estate.

Collis, J. (2000) ' "Celtic" oppida', in M.H. Hansen (ed.) *A Comparative Study of Thirty City-State Cultures*. Copenhagen: Historisk-filosofiske Skrifter 21 (Royal Danish Academy of Sciences and Letters), pp. 229–39.

Coquery-Vidrovitch, C. (2005) *The History of African Cities South of the Sahara: From Origins to Colonization*. Princeton, NJ: Markus Wiener.

Corfee-Morlot, J., L. Kamai-Chaoui, M.G. Donovan, I. Cochran, A. Robert and P.J. Reasdale (2009) *Cities, Climate Change and Multilevel Governance*. Paris: OECD.

Corráin, D.O. (2005) 'Ireland in 800: aspects of society', in D.O. Cróninín (ed.) *A New History of Ireland: I Prehistoric and Early Medieval Ireland*. Oxford: Oxford University Press, pp. 549–608.

Cosmo, N.D. (2000) 'Ancient city-states of the Tarim Basin', in M.H. Hansen (ed.) *A Comparative Study of Thirty City-State Cultures*. Copenhagen: Historisk-filosofiske Skrifter 21 (Royal Danish Academy of Sciences and Letters), pp. 393–407.

Cowgill, G.L. (2003) 'Teotihuacán: cosmic glories and mundane needs', in M.L. Smith (ed.) *The Social Construction of Ancient Cities*. Washington, DC: Smithsonian Books, pp. 37–55.

Crawford, H. (2004) *Sumer and the Sumerians*. Cambridge: Cambridge University Press.

Curtin, P.D. (1984) *Cross-Cultural Trade in World History*. Cambridge: Cambridge University Press.

Davidovich, V.G. (1974) 'On patterns and tendencies of urban settlement in the USSR', in G.J. Demko and R.L. Fuchs (eds) *Geographical Perspectives in the Soviet Union*. Columbus, OH: Ohio State University Press.

Davis, M (1990) *City of Quartz*. London: Verso

Davis, M. (2006) *Planet of Slums*. London: Verso.

de la Court, P. (1972) *The True Interests and Political Maxims of the Republic of Holland*. New York: Arno (unauthorized publication 1662; enlarged and revised 1669; English translation 1746).

Denemark, R.A., J. Friedman, B.K. Gills and G. Modelski (eds) (2000) *World System History: The Social Science of Long-Term Change*. London: Routledge.

Derudder, B., M. Hoyler and P.J. Taylor (2011) 'Goodbye Reykjavik:

international banking centres and the global financial crisis', *Area* **43**, 173–82.

Derudder, B., M. Hoyler, P.J. Taylor and F. Witlox (eds) (2012) *International Handbook of Cities and Globalization*. Cheltenham, UK and Northampton, MA, USA: Edward Elgar.

Derudder, B., P.J. Taylor, P. Ni, A. de Vos, M. Hoyler, H. Hassens, D. Bassens, J. Huang, F. Witlox and X. Yang (2010) 'Pathways of growth and decline: connectivity changes in the world city network, 2000–2008', *Urban Studies* **47**, 1861–77.

de Sousa Santos, B. (1995) *Towards a New Common Sense*. London: Routledge.

de Vries, J. (1981) *Barges and Capitalism: Passenger Transport in the Dutch Economy, 1632–1839*. Utrecht, Netherlands: HES Publishers.

de Vries, J. (1984) *European Urbanization, 1500–1800*. London: Methuen.

Dicken, P. (2005) *Global Shift*. London: Paul Chapman.

Dincauze, D.F. and R.J. Hasenstaub (1989) 'Explaining the Iroquois: tribalization on a prehistoric periphery', in T.C. Champion (ed.) *Centre and Periphery: Comparative Studies in Archaeology*. London: Unwin Hyman, pp. 67–87.

Dobb, M. (1946) *Studies in the Development of Capitalism*. London: Lawrence & Wishart.

Dodgshon, R.A. (1998) *Society in Time and Space*. Cambridge: Cambridge University Press.

Doherty, C. (1985) 'The monastic town in early medieval Ireland', in H.B. Clarke and A. Simms (eds) *The Comparative History of Urban Origins in non-Roman Europe*, BAR International Series no. 255, Oxford: British Archaeological Reports, pp. 66–7.

Düring, B.S. (2007) 'Reconsidering the Çatalhöyük community: from households to settlement systems', *Journal of Mediterranean Archaeology* **20** (2).

Edwards N. (2005) 'The archaeology of early Medieval Ireland, c. 400–1169: settlement and economy', in D.O. Crónínín (ed.) *A New History of Ireland: I Prehistoric and Early Medieval Ireland*. Oxford: Oxford University Press, pp. 235–300.

Emberling, G. (2003) 'Urban social transformations and the problem of the "first city": new research from Mesopotamia', in M.L. Smith (ed.) *The Social Construction of Ancient Cities*. Washington, DC: Smithsonian Books, pp. 254–68.

Epstein, S.A. (1996) *Genoa and the Genoese, 958–1528*. Chapel Hill, NC: University of North Carolina Press.

Esin, U. and S. Harmankaya (1999) 'Aşikli', in M. Özdoğan and

N. Başgelen (eds) *Neolithic in Turkey: The Cradle of Civilization: New Discoveries*. Istanbul, Turkey: Arkeoloji ve Sanat Yayinlari.

Faulconbridge, J., J.V. Beaverstock, C. Nativel and P.J. Taylor (2011) *The Globalization of Advertizing: Agencies, Cities and Spaces of Creativity*. London: Routledge.

Feinman, G.M. and J. Marcus (eds) (1998) *Archaic States*. Sante Fe, NM: School of American Research Press.

Fenby, J. (2012) *Tiger Head, Snake Tails*. London: Simon & Schuster.

Flannery, K.V. (1998) 'The ground plans of archaic states', in G.M. Feinman and J. Marcus (eds) *Archaic States*. Sante Fe, NM: School of American Research Press, pp. 15–57.

Frank, A.G. (1969) *Latin America: Underdevelopment or Revolution*. New York: Monthly Review Press.

Frank, A.G. (1998) *ReOrient: Global Economy in the Asian Age*. Berkeley, CA: University of California Press.

Frank, A.G. and B.K. Gills (eds) (1993) *The World System: Five Hundred Years or Five Thousand?* London: Routledge.

Frank, A.G. and W.R. Thompson (2005) 'Early iron age economic expansion and contraction revisited', in B.K. Gills, and W.R. Thompson (eds) *Globalization and Global History*. London: Routledge.

Frank, A.G. and W.R. Thompson (2006) 'Bronze age economic expansion and contraction revisited', *Journal of World History* **16**, 115–72.

Freeman, M. (1986) 'Transport', in J. Langton and R.J. Morris (eds) *Atlas of Industrializing Britain, 1780–1914*. London: Methuen, pp. 80–93.

Freund, B. (2007) *The African City: A History*. Cambridge: Cambridge University Press.

Friedmann, J. (1986) 'The world city hypothesis', *Development and Change* **17**, 69–83.

Friedman, J. and C. Chase-Dunn (eds) (2005) *Hegemonic Declines: Past and Present*. Boulder, CO: Paradigm.

Frobel, F., J. Heinrich and O. Kreye (1980) *The New International Division of Labor*. Cambridge: Cambridge University Press.

Fujita, M. and J-F. Thisse (2002) *Economics of Agglomeration*. Cambridge: Cambridge University Press.

Fukuyama, F. (1992) *The End of History and the Last Man.* New York: Free Press.

Gamble, C. (2007) *Origins and Revolutions: Human Identity in Earliest Prehistory*. Cambridge: Cambridge University Press.

Giddens, A. (1985) *The Nation-state and Violence*. Cambridge: Polity.

Giddens, A. (1990) *The Consequencies of Modernity*. Cambridge: Polity.

Gills, B.K. and A.G. Frank (1993a) 'The cumulation of accumulation', in

A.G. Frank and B.K. Gills (eds) *The World System: Five Hundred Years or Five Thousand?* London: Routledge.

Gills, B.K. and A.G. Frank (1993b) 'World system cycles, crises, and hegemonic shifts, 1700 BC to 1700 AD', in A.G. Frank and B.K. Gills (eds) *The World System: Five Hundred Years or Five Thousand?* London: Routledge.

Gills, B.K. and W.R. Thompson (eds) (2006) *Globalization and Global History*. London: Routledge.

Girardet, H. (2008) *Cities People Planet: Urban Development and Climate Change*. Chichester: Wiley.

Glaeser, E.L. (2000) 'Cities and ethics: an essay for Jane Jacobs', *Journal of Urban Affairs* **22**, 473–93.

Glaeser, E.L. (2011) *Triumph of the City*. London: Macmillan.

Glaeser, E.L. and M.E. Kahn (2008) 'The greenness of cities: carbon dioxide emissions and urban development', working paper series. Los Angeles, CA: California Center for Population Research (UCLA), escholarship.org/uc/item/2pk7j5cp (accessed 1 May 2011).

Glaeser, E.L., H.D. Kalial, J.A. Scheinkman and A. Schleifer (1992) 'Growth in cities', *Journal of Political Economy* **100**, 1126–52.

Goldstein, J, (1988) *Long Cycles: Prosperity and War in the Modern Age*. New Haven, CT: Yale University Press.

Gottmann, J. (1984) *Orbits: the Ancient Mediterranean Tradition of Urban Networks*. Oxford: Leopard's Head.

Graeber, D. (2011) *Debt: The First 5000 Years*. New York: Melville House.

Graham, S. (ed.) (2004) *Cities, War, and Terrorism: Towards an Urban Geopolitics*. Oxford: Blackwell.

Griffeth, R. (2000) 'The Hausa city-states from 1450 to 1804', in M.H. Hansen (ed.) *A Comparative Study of Thirty City-State Cultures*. Copenhagen: Historisk-filosofiske Skrifter 21 (Royal Danish Academy of Sciences and Letters), pp. 483–506.

Grimal, P. (1983) *Roman Cities*. Madison, WI: University of Wisconsin Press.

Grube, N. (2000) 'The city-states of the Maya', in M.H. Hansen (ed.) *A Comparative Study of Thirty City-State Cultures*. Copenhagen: Historisk-filosofiske Skrifter 21 (Royal Danish Academy of Sciences and Letters), pp. 547–65.

Hagen, von A. and C. Morris (1998) *The Cities of the Ancient Andes*. London: Thames & Hudson.

Hall, P. (1998) *Cities in Civilization*. London: Weidenfeld & Nicolson.

Hall, P. and K. Pain (2006) *The Polycentric Metropolis*. London: Earthscan.

Hansen, M.H. (ed.) (2000a) *A Comparative Study of Thirty City-State*

Cultures. Copenhagen: Historisk-filosofiske Skrifter 21 (Royal Danish Academy of Sciences and Letters).

Hansen, M.H. (2000b) 'Introduction: the concepts of city-state and city-state culture', in M.H. Hansen (ed.) *A Comparative Study of Thirty City-State Cultures*. Copenhagen: Historisk-filosofiske Skrifter 21 (Royal Danish Academy of Sciences and Letters), pp. 11–34.

Hansen, M.H. (2000c) 'The Hellenic *polis*', in M.H. Hansen (ed.) *A Comparative Study of Thirty City-State Cultures*. Copenhagen: Historisk-filosofiske Skrifter 21 (Royal Danish Academy of Sciences and Letters), pp. 141–87.

Hansen, M.H. (2002) *A Comparative Study of Six City-State Cultures*. Copenhagen: Historisk-filosofiske Skrifter 27 (Royal Danish Academy of Sciences and Letters).

Harris, C.D. and E.L. Ullman (1945) 'The nature of cities', *Annals of the American Academy of Political and Social Sciences* **242**, 7–17.

Harris, R. (2011) 'The magpie and the bee: Jane Jacobs's magnificent obsession', in M. Page and T. Mennel (eds) *Reconsidering Jane Jacobs*. Chicago, IL: Planners Press.

Harvey, D. (1990) *The Condition of Postmodernity*. Oxford: Blackwell.

Harvey, D. (2005) *A Brief History of Neoliberalism*. Oxford: Oxford University Press.

Havighurst, A.F. (1976) *The Pirenne Thesis: Analysis, Criticism, and Revision*. Boston, MA: Heath.

Haywood, J. (2005) *The Penguin Historical Atlas of Ancient Civilizations*. London: Penguin.

Heinberg, R. (2008) 'Foreword', in R. Hopkins *The Transition Handbook*. Totnes: Green Books, pp. 8–10.

Herz, J. H. (1957) 'Rise and demise of the territorial state' *World Politics* **9**, 473–93.

Hill, R.C. and K. Fujita (2003) 'The nested city: introduction', *Urban Studies* **40**, 207–17.

Hill, R.C. and J.W. Kim (2000) 'Global cities and developmental states', *Urban Studies* **37**, 2167–98.

Hilton, R. (1976a) *The Transition from Feudalism to Capitalism*. London: Verso.

Hilton, R. (1976b) 'Introduction', in R. Hilton (ed.) *The Transition from Feudalism to Capitalism*. London: Verso, pp. 9–30.

Hodder, I. (2006) *Çatalhöyük: The Leopard's Tale*. London: Thames & Hudson.

Hodge, M.G. (1997) 'When is a city-state? Archaeological measures of Aztec city-states and Aztec city state systems', in D.L. Nichols and T.H. Charlton (eds) *The Archaeology of City-states: Cross-Cultural*

Approaches. Washington, DC: Smithsonian Institution Press, pp. 209–27.

Holloway, J. and S. Picciotto (eds) (1978) *State and Capital: a Marxist Debate*. London: Arnold.

Hopkins, R. (2008) *The Transition Handbook. From Oil Dependency to Local Resilience*. Totnes: Green Books.

Hopkins, T. R. and I. Wallerstein (eds) (1996) *The Age of Transition: Trajectory of the World-System, 1945–2025*. London: Zed Books.

Hourani, A. (1991) *A History of the Arab Peoples*. London: Faber & Faber.

Houston, S.D., H. Escobedo, M. Child, C. Golden and A.R. Munuz (2003) 'The moral community: Maya settlement transformation at Piedras Negras, Guatemala', in M.L. Smith (ed.) *The Social Construction of Ancient Cities*. Washington, DC: Smithsonian Books, pp. 212–53.

Hudson, M. (1996) 'Sannai Maruyama: a new view of prehistoric Japan', *Asia-Pacific Magazine* **2** (May), 47–8.

Hughes, K. (2005) 'The church in Irish society, 400–800', in D.O. Cróninín (ed.) *A New History of Ireland: I Prehistoric and Early Medieval Ireland*. Oxford: Oxford University Press, pp. 301–30.

Hunt, T. (2004) *Building Jerusalem: The Rise and Fall of the Victorian City*. London: Weidenfeld & Nicholson.

Hutton, W. (2007) *The Writing on the Wall: China and the West in the 21st Century*. London: Little, Brown.

Hymer, S. (1972) 'The multinational corporation and the law of uneven development', in J. Bhagwati (ed.) *Economics and World Order from the 1970s to the 1990s*. London: Collier-Macmillan.

Isin E.F. (ed.) (2000) *Democracy, Citizenship and the Global City*. London: Routledge.

Israel, J.I. (1990) *Empires and Entrepots*. London: Hambledon.

Israel, J.I. (1995) *The Dutch Republic. Its Rise, Greatness and Fall, 1477–1806*. Oxford: Clarendon Press.

Jacobs, J. (1960) *The Death and Life of Great American Cities*. New York: Vintage.

Jacobs J. (1969) *The Economy of Cities*. New York: Vintage.

Jacobs J. (1984) *Cities and the Wealth of Nations*. New York: Vintage.

Jacobs, J. (1989a) 'Systems of economic ethics, part one', in F. Lawrence (ed.) *Ethics in Making a Living: The Jane Jacobs Conference*. Altanta, GA: Scholars Press, pp. 211–50.

Jacobs, J. (1989b) 'Systems of economic ethics, part two', in F. Lawrence (ed.) *Ethics in Making a Living: The Jane Jacobs Conference*. Altanta, GA: Scholars Press, pp. 251–86.

Jacobs J. (1992) *Systems of Survival*. New York: Vintage.

Jacobs J. (2000) *The Nature of Economies*. New York: Vintage.

Jacobs J. (2004) *Dark Age Ahead*. New York: Vintage.

Jacobsen, T. (1970) *Toward the Image of Tammuz*. Cambridge, MA: Harvard University Press.

Janelle. D.G. (1969) 'Spatial reorganization: a model and a concept', *Annals of the Association of American Geographers* **59**, 348–64.

Johnson, J.H. (1967) *Urban Geography: An Introductory Analysis*. Oxford: Pergamon.

Johnston, R.J. (1982) *The American Urban System*. London: Longman.

Kamal-Chaoui, L. and A. Robert (eds) (2009) *Competitive Cities and Climatic Change*. Paris: OECD.

Kardulias, P.N. (ed.) (1999) *World-Systems Theory in Practice: Leadership, Production and Exchange*. Boulder, CO: Rowman & Littlefield.

Kea, R.A. (2000) 'City-state culture on the Gold Coast: the Fante city-state federation of the seventeenth and eighteenth centuries', in M.H. Hansen (ed.) *A Comparative Study of Thirty City-State Cultures*. Copenhagen: Historisk-filosofiske Skrifter 21 (Royal Danish Academy of Sciences and Letters), pp. 519–30.

Keally, C. T. (2005) 'Japanese archaeology: Jomon culture', www.mnsu. edu/emuseum/prehistory/japan/jomon/jomon_culture (accessed 12 September 2007).

Keeley, R.C. (1989) 'An interview with Jane Jacobs', in F. Lawrence (ed.) *Ethics in Making a Living: The Jane Jacobs Conference*. Altanta, GA: Scholars Press, pp. 1–28.

Keith, K. (2003) 'The spatial patterns of everyday life in Old Babylonian neighborhoods', in M.L. Smith (ed.) *The Social Construction of Ancient Cities*. Washington, DC: Smithsonian Books, pp. 56–80.

Kelley, J.E. (1991) 'Cahokia and its role as a gateway center in interregional exchange', in T.E. Emerson and R.B. Lewis (eds) *Cahokia and its Hinterlands: Middle Mississippian Cultures of the Midwest*. Urbana, IL: University of Illinois Press.

Kennedy, R.G. (1994) *Hidden Cities: The Discovery and Loss of Ancient North American Civilization*. New York: Free Press.

Kenoyer, J.M. (1997) 'Early city-states in South Asia: comparing the Harappan Phase and the Early Historic Period', in D.L. Nichols and T.H. Charlton (eds) *The Archaeology of City-states: Cross-Cultural Approaches*. Washington, DC: Smithsonian Institution Press, pp. 51–70.

Kenyon, K. (1960) *Archaeology in the Holy Land*. London: Ernest Benn.

Kern, P.B. (1999) *Ancient Siege Warfare*. Bloomington, IN: Indiana University Press.

Kindleberger, C.P. (1993) *A Financial History of Western Europe*. New York: Oxford University Press.

King, A.D. (1990) *Global Cities: Post-Imperialism and the Internationalization of London*. London: Routledge.

Knight, R.V. (1989) 'City building in a global society', in R.V. Knight and G. Gappert (eds) *Cities in a Global Society*. Newbury Park, CA: Sage, 326–34.

Knight, R.V. and G. Gappert (eds) (1989) *Cities in a Global Society*. Newbury Park, CA: Sage.

Knox, P.L. (2008) *Metro-Burbia, USA*. New Brunswick, NJ: Rutgers University Press.

Kolata, A.L. (1997) 'Of kings and capitals: principles of authority and the nature of cities in the Native Andean State', in D.L. Nichols and T.H. Charlton (eds) *The Archaeology of City-states: Cross-Cultural Approaches*. Washington, DC: Smithsonian Institution Press, pp. 245–54.

Kossmann, E.H. and A.F. Mellick (eds) *Texts Concerning the Revolt of the Netherlands*. Cambridge: Cambridge University Press.

Krugman, P. (1995) *Development, Geography, and Economic Theory*. Cambridge, MA: MIT Press.

Kynaston, D. (2011) *City of London. The History*. London: Chatto & Windus.

LaBianca, O.S. and S.A. Scham (eds) (2006) *Connectivity in Antiquity: Globalization as Long-term Historical Process*. London: Equinox.

Lai, K. (2012) 'Differentiated markets: Shanghai, Beijing and Hong Kong in China's financial centre network', *Urban Studies* **49**, 1275–96.

Larsen M.T. (2000a) 'The old Assyrian city-state', in M.H. Hansen (ed.) *A Comparative Study of Thirty City-State Cultures*. Copenhagen: Historisk-filosofiske Skrifter 21 (Royal Danish Academy of Sciences and Letters), pp. 77–87.

Larsen, M.T. (2000b) 'The city-states of the early Neo-Babylonian period', in M.H. Hansen (ed.) *A Comparative Study of Thirty City-State Cultures*. Copenhagen: Historisk-filosofiske Skrifter 21 (Royal Danish Academy of Sciences and Letters), pp. 117–27.

Lash, S. and J. Friedman (1992) 'Introduction; subjectivity and modernity's other', in S. Lash and J. Friedman (eds) *Modernity and Identity*. Oxford: Blackwell.

Lattimore, O. (1962) *Studies in Frontier History*. London: Oxford University Press.

Lawrence, F. (ed.) (1989a) *Ethics in Making a Living*. Atlanta, GA: Scholars Press.

Lawrence, F. (1989b) 'Systems of economic ethics: a response', in

F. Lawrence (ed.) *Ethics in Making a Living: The Jane Jacobs Conference*. Altanta, GA: Scholars Press, pp. 191–202.

Lees, A. and L.H. Lees (2007) *Cities and the Making of Europe, 1750–1914*. Cambridge: Cambridge University Press.

LeGates, R.T. and F. Stout (eds) (2000) *The City Reader*, second edition. London: Routledge.

Leick, G. (2001) *Mesopotamia. The Invention of the City*. London: Penguin.

Lerner, D., J.S. Coleman and R.P. Dore (1968) 'Modernization', in D. Sills (ed.) *International Encyclopedia of Social Sciences*. New York: Macmillan.

Lerner, G. (1986) *The Creation of Patriarchy*. New York: Oxford University Press.

Lesger, C. (2006) *The Rise of the Amsterdam Market and Information Exchange*. Aldershot: Ashgate.

Lewis, M.E. (2000) 'The city-state in Spring-and-Autumn China', in M.H. Hansen (ed.) *A Comparative Study of Thirty City-State Cultures*. Copenhagen: Historisk-filosofiske Skrifter 21 (Royal Danish Academy of Sciences and Letters), pp. 359–73.

Li, M. (2008) *The Rise of China and the Demise of the Capitalist World-Economy*. New York: Monthly Review Press.

Lin, G.C.S. (2002) 'The growth and structural change of Chinese cities: a contextual and geographic analysis', *Cities* 19, 299–316.

Liu, L. (2004) *The Chinese Neolithic: Trajectories to Early States*. Cambridge: Cambridge University Press.

Liu, L. (2009) 'State emergence in early China', *Annual Review of Anthropology* 38, 217–32.

Limberger, M. (2001) '"No town in the world provides more advantages": economies of agglomeration and the golden age of Antwerp', in P. O'Brien, D. Keene, M. 't Hart and H. van der Wee (eds) *Urban Achievements in Early Modern Europe: Golden Ages in Antwerp, Amsterdam and London*. Cambridge: Cambridge University Press.

Lukermann, F. (1966) 'Empirical expressions of nodality and hierarchy in a circulation manifold', *East Lakes Geographer* 2, 17–44.

Magnusson, W. (2011) *Politics of Urbanism: Seeing like a City*. London: Routledge.

Manguin, P-Y. (2000) 'City-states and city-state cultures in pre-15th-century Southeast Asia', in M.H. Hansen (ed.) *A Comparative Study of Thirty City-State Cultures*. Copenhagen: Historisk-filosofiske Skrifter 21 (Royal Danish Academy of Sciences and Letters), pp. 409–16.

Mann, M. (1986) *The Sources of Social Power*. Volume 1. Cambridge: Cambridge University Press.

D.L. Nichols and T.H. Charlton (eds) *The Archaeology of City-states: Cross-Cultural Approaches*. Washington, DC: Smithsonian Institution Press, pp. 91–105.

Mumford, L. (1961) *The City in History*. London: Harcourt.

Myrdal, G. (1957) *Economic Theory and Under-Developed Regions*. London: Duckworth.

Needham, J (1954) *Science and Civilization in China*. Cambridge: Cambridge University Press.

Neimeyer, H.G. (2000) 'The early Phoenician city-states on the Mediterranean: archaeological elements in their description', in M.H. Hansen (ed.) *A Comparative Study of Thirty City-State Cultures*. Copenhagen: Historisk-filosofiske Skrifter 21 (Royal Danish Academy of Sciences and Letters), pp. 89–115.

Neuwirth, R. (2006) *Shadow Cities: A Billion Squatters, a New Urban World*. London: Routledge.

Nichols, D.L. and T.H. Charlton (eds) (1997) *The Archaeology of City-States*. Washington, DC: Smithsonian Institution Press.

Nissen, H.J. (1986) 'The archaic texts of Uruk', *World Archaeology*, 17, 317–34.

Nissen, H.J. (1988) *The Early History of the Ancient Near East, 9000–2000 BC*. Chicago, IL: University of Chicago Press.

Nissen H.J., P. Damerow and R.K. Englund (1993) *Archaic Bookkeeping: Early Writing and Techniques of Economic Administration in the Ancient Near East*. Chicago, IL: University of Chicago Press.

Norwich J.J. (1982) *A History of Venice*. London: Penguin.

Norwich, J.J. (ed.) (2009) *The Great Cities in History*. London: Thames & Hudson.

Nowlan, D. (1997) 'Jane Jacobs among the economists', in M. Allen (ed.) *Ideas that Matter: The Worlds of Jane Jacobs*. Owen Sound, ON: Ginger Press, pp 111–13.

Nyerere, J. (1968) *Ujamaa: Essays in Socialism*. London: Oxford University Press.

OECD (2009) *Cities and Climate Change*. Paris: OECD.

O'Brien, P. (ed.) (2001) *Urban Achievement in Early Modern Europe: Golden Ages in Antwerp, Amsterdam and London*. Cambridge: Cambridge University Press.

Ogborn, M. (1998) *Spaces of Modernity: London's Geographies 1680–1780*. New York: Guilford.

Oliver, R. and J. D. Fage (1988) *A Short History of Africa*. London: Penguin.

Owen, D. (2009) *Green Metropolis: Why Living Smaller, Living Closer, and Driving Less are the Keys to Sustainability*. New York: Riverhead Books.

Özdoğan, A. (1999) 'Çayönü', in M. Özdoğan and N. Başgelen (eds) *Neolithic in Turkey: The Cradle of Civilization: New Discoveries*. Istanbul, Turkey: Arkeoloji ve Sanat Yayinlari.

Özdoğan, M. and N. Başgelen (eds) (1999) *Neolithic in Turkey: The Cradle of Civilization: New Discoveries*. Istanbul, Turkey: Arkeoloji ve Sanat Yayinlari.

Parker, G. (2004) *Sovereign City: The City-State through History*. London: Reaction Books.

Parkinson, M., T. Champion, J. Simmie, I. Turok, M. Crookston, B. Katz and A. Park (2006) *State of the English Cities*. Office of the Deputy Prime Minister, London.

Pauketat, T.R. (2004) *Ancient Cahokia and the Mississippians*. Cambridge: Cambridge University Press.

Pearce F. (2010) *Peoplequake: Mass Migration, Ageing Nations and the Coming Population Crash*. London: Transworld.

Pearson, M.P. (2009) 'Stonehenge Riverside Project: 2007 Excavation II', www.shef.ac.uk/archaeology/research/stonehenge/stonehenge07-02 (accessed 2 June 2009).

Pearson, R. (2003) 'Insurance', in J. Mokyr (ed.) *The Oxford Encyclopedia of Economic History*, Volume 1. Oxford: Oxford University Press, pp. 83–7.

Peel, J.D.Y. (2000) 'Yoruba as a city-state culture', in M.H. Hansen (ed.) *A Comparative Study of Thirty City-State Cultures*. Copenhagen: Historisk-filosofiske Skrifter 21 (Royal Danish Academy of Sciences and Letters), pp. 507–17.

Peregrine, P.N. (1992) *Mississippian Evolution: A World-systems Perspective*. Madison, WI: Prehistoric Press.

Pike, R. (1966) *Enterprise and Adventure: The Genoese in Seville and the Opening of the New World*. Ithaca, NY: Cornell University Press.

Pirenne, H. (1969) *Medieval Cities: Their Origins and the Revival of Trade*. Princeton, NJ: Princeton University Press.

Pirenne, H. (1962) 'Stages in the social history of capital', in R. Bendix and S. Lipset (eds) *Class, Status and Power: A Reader in Social Stratification*. Glencoe, IL: Free Press, pp. 501–17.

Pocock, J.G.A. (1992) 'The Dutch republican tradition', in M.C. Jacobs and W.W. Mijnhardt (eds) *The Dutch Republic in the Eighteenth Century*. Ithaca, NY: Cornell University Press.

Pomeranz, K. and Topik, S. (1999) *The World that Trade Created: Society, Culture, and the World Economy, 1400–the Present*. Armonk, NY: M.E. Sharpe.

Poovey, M. (1998) *A History of the Modern Fact: Problems of Knowledge in the Sciences of Wealth and Society*. Chicago, IL: University of Chicago Press.

Porter, M.E. (1998) 'Clusters and the new economics of competition', *Harvard Business Review* (November–December), 77–90.

Possehl, G.L. (1998) 'Sociocultural complexity without the state: the Indus civilization', in G.M. Feinman and J. Marcus (eds) *Archaic States*. Sante Fe, NM: School of American Research Press, pp. 261–92.

Postgate, J.N. (1992) *Early Mesopotamia: Society and Economy at the Dawn of History*. London: Routledge.

Powell, W.W. (1990) 'Neither markets nor hierarchy: network forms of organization', *Research in Organizational Behavior* **12**, 295–336.

Pred, A. (1966) *The Spatial Dynamics of US Industrial Growth*. Cambridge, MA: MIT Press.

Previts, G.J. and R. Murwanto (2003) 'Accounting and bookkeeping', in J. Mokyr (ed.) *The Oxford Encyclopedia of Economic History*. Volume 1. Oxford: Oxford University Press, pp 1–5.

Price, B. (1978) 'Secondary state formation: an explanatory model', in R. Cohen and E.R. Service (eds) *Origins of the State: The Anthropology of Political Evolution*. Philadelphia, PA: ISHA, pp. 165–90.

Pyburn, K.A. (1997) 'The archaeological signature of complexity in the Maya lowlands', in D.L. Nichols and T.H. Charlton (eds) *The Archaeology of City-states: Cross-Cultural Approaches*. Washington, DC: Smithsonian Institution Press, pp. 155–68.

Reclus, E. (1895) 'The evolution of cities', *Contemporary Review* **67**, 246–64.

Reid, A. (2000) 'Negeri: the culture of Malay-speaking city-states of the fifteenth and sixteenth centuries', in M.H. Hansen (ed.) *A Comparative Study of Thirty City-State Cultures*. Copenhagen: Historisk-filosofiske Skrifter 21 (Royal Danish Academy of Sciences and Letters), pp. 417–29.

Renfrew, C. (1975) 'Trade as action at a distance: questions of integration and communication', in J.A. Sabloff and C.C. Lamber-Karloversusky (eds) *Ancient Civilization and Trade*. Albuquerque, NM: University of New Mexico Press.

Renfrew. C. and Bahn, P. (2008) *Archaeology: Theories, Methods and Practice*. London: Thames & Hudson (fifth edition).

Renger, J.M. (2003) 'Banking', in J. Mokyr (ed.) *The Oxford Encyclopedia of Economic History*, volume 1. Oxford: Oxford University Press, pp 220–21.

Rennstich, J.K. (2006) 'Three steps in globalization', in B.K. Gills and W.R. Thompson (eds) *Globalization and Global History*. London: Routledge.

Rice, M. (1994) *The Archaeology of the Arabian Gulf, c. 5000–323 BC*. London: Routledge.

Roach, J. (2008) 'Ancient Amazon cities found; were vast urban network', *National Geographic News*, online at news.nationalgeographic.com/news/2008/08/080828-amazon-cities (accessed 15 July 2009).

Robson, B.T. (1973) *Urban Growth: An Approach*. London: Methuen.

Robson, B.T. (1986) 'Coming full circle: London versus the rest, 1890–1980', in G. Gordon (ed.) *Regional Cities in the UK: 1890–1980*. London: Harper & Row, pp. 217–42.

Rodseth, L., R.W. Wrangham, A. Harrigan, and B.B. Smuts (1991) 'The human community as a primate society', *Current Anthropology* **32**, 221–54.

Rudgley, R. (1998) *Lost Civilizations of the Stone Age*. London: Century.

Sabloff, J.A. (1989) *The Cities of Ancient Mexico*. London: Thames & Hudson.

Sack, R.D. (1986) *Human Territoriality: Its Theory and History*. Cambridge: Cambridge University Press.

Sahlins M. (1972/2004) *Stone Age Economics*. London: Routledge.

Sanderson, S.K. (1995) 'Expanding world commercialization: the link between world-systems and civilizations', in S.K. Sanderson (ed.) *Civilizations and World-Systems*. Walnut Creek, CA: AltaMira.

Sassen, S. (1991) *The Global City*. Princeton, NJ: Princeton University Press.

Sassen, S. (1999) 'Whose city is it? Globalization and the formation of new claims', in J. Holston (ed.) *Cities and Citizenship*. Durham, NC: Duke University Press, pp. 177–94.

Scarre, C. (ed.) (1988) *Past Worlds. The Times Atlas of Archaeology*. London: Times Books.

Schama, S. (1987) *The Embarrassment of Riches*. London: Collins.

Schattschneider, E.E. (1960) *The Semi-Sovereign People*. Hinsdale, IL: Dryden.

Schmidt, K. (2008) 'When humanity began to settle down', *German Research* **30**, 10–13.

Scott, A.J. (ed.) (2001) *Global City-Regions*. Oxford: Oxford University Press.

Scott, J.C. (1998) *Seeing Like a State*. New Haven, CT: Yale University Press.

Shane, O.C. III and M. Küçük (1998) 'The world's first city', *Archaeology* **51** (2), 43–47.

Shen, C. (2003) 'Compromises and conflicts: production and commerce in the royal cities of Eastern Zhou, China', in M.L. Smith (ed.) *The Social Construction of Ancient Cities*. Washington, DC: Smithsonian Books, pp. 290–310.

Shy, O. (2001) *The Economics of Network Industries*. Cambridge: Cambridge University Press.

Simonsen, J.B. (2000) 'Mecca and Medina: Arab city-states or Arab caravan-cities?', in M.H. Hansen (ed.) *A Comparative Study of Thirty City-State Cultures.* Copenhagen: Historisk-filosofiske Skrifter 21 (Royal Danish Academy of Sciences and Letters), pp. 241–9.

Sklair, L. (2002) *Globalization: Capitalism and its Alternatives.* Oxford: Oxford University Press.

Small, D. (1997) 'City-state dynamics through a Greek lens', in D.L. Nichols and T.H. Charlton (eds) *The Archaeology of City-states: Cross-Cultural Approaches.* Washington, DC: Smithsonian Institution Press, pp. 107–18.

Smart, B. (1999) *Facing Modernity: Ambivalence, Reflexivity and Morality.* London: Sage.

Smith, M.E. (2000) 'Aztec city-states', in M.H. Hansen (ed.) *A Comparative Study of Thirty City-State Cultures.* Copenhagen: Historisk-filosofiske Skrifter 21 (Royal Danish Academy of Sciences and Letters), pp. 581–95.

Smith, M.L. (ed.) (2003a) *The Social Construction of Ancient Cities.* Washington, DC: Smithsonian Books.

Smith, M.L. (2003b) 'Introduction: the social construction of ancient cities', in M.L. Smith (ed.) *The Social Construction of Ancient Cities.* Washington, DC: Smithsonian Books, pp. 1–36.

Smith, M.L. (2003c) 'Early walled cities of the Indian subcontinent as "small worlds"', in M.L. Smith (ed.) *The Social Construction of Ancient Cities.* Washington, DC: Smithsonian Books, pp. 269–89.

Smith, M.L. (2005) 'Networks, territories, and the cartography of ancient states', *Annals of the Association of American Geographers* **95**, 832–49.

Smith, M.L. (2007) 'Territories, corridors, and networks: a biological model for the premodern state', *Complexity* **12**, 28–35.

Smith, W.D. (1984) 'The function of commercial centres in the modernisation of Europe: Amsterdam as an information exchange in the seventeenth century', *Journal of Economic History* **44**, 985–1005.

Snow, C.P. (1959) *The Two Cultures.* Cambridge: Cambridge University Press.

Soja, E.W. (2000) *Postmetropolis: Critical Studies of Cities and Regions.* Oxford: Blackwell.

Soja, E.W. (2010) 'Cities and states in geohistory', *Theory and Society* **39** (3–4), 361–376.

Southall, A. (1998) *The City in Time and Space.* Cambridge: Cambridge University Press.

Spencer, C.S. (2010) 'Territorial expansion and primary state formation', *Proceedings of the National Academy of Sciences of the United States of America* **107** (16), 7119–26.

Spruyt, H. (1994) *The Sovereign State and its Competitors*. Princeton, NJ: Princeton University Press.

Spufford, P. (2002) *Power and Profit: The Merchant in Medieval Europe*. London: Thames & Hudson.

Steans, J., L. Pettiford, T. Diez and I. El-Anis (2010) *An Introduction to International Relations Theory*. Harlow: Pearson.

Steel, C. (2008) *Hungry City: How Food Shapes our Lives*. London: Chatto & Windus.

Stein, G.J. (1999) *Rethinking World-Systems: Diasporas, Colonies and Integration in Uruk Mesopotamia*. Tucson, AZ: University of Arizona Press.

Stouffer, S.A. (1940) 'Intervening opportunities: a theory relating to mobility and distance', *American Sociological Review* **5**, 845–67.

Strange, J. (2000a) 'The Palestinian city-states of the Bronze Age', in M.H. Hansen (ed.) *A Comparative Study of Thirty City-State Cultures*. Copenhagen: Historisk-filosofiske Skrifter 21 (Royal Danish Academy of Sciences and Letters), pp. 67–76.

Strange, J. (2000b) 'The Philistine city-states', in M.H. Hansen (ed.) *A Comparative Study of Thirty City-State Cultures*. Copenhagen: Historisk-filosofiske Skrifter 21 (Royal Danish Academy of Sciences and Letters), pp. 129–39.

Sweezy, P. (1976) 'A critique', in R. Hilton (ed.) *The Transition from Feudalism to Capitalism*. London: Verso, pp. 33–56.

Taaffe, E.J., H.L. Gauthier and M.E. O'Kelly (1996) *The Geography of Transportation*. Upper Saddle River, NJ: Prentice Hall.

Taylor, P.J. (1994) 'The state as container: territoriality in the modern world-system', *Progress in Human Geography* **18**, 151–62.

Taylor P.J. (1996a) 'Embedded statism and the social sciences: opening up to new spaces', *Environment and Planning A* **28**, 1917–28.

Taylor, P.J. (1996b) *The Way the Modern World Works: From World Hegemony to World Impasse*. New York: Wiley.

Taylor, P.J. (1997) 'Hierarchical tendencies amongst world cities', *Cities* **14**, 323–32.

Taylor, P.J. (1999a) *Modernities: A Geohistorical Interpretation*. Cambridge: Polity.

Taylor P.J. (1999b) 'Places, spaces and Macy's: place–space tensions in the political geography of modernities', *Progress in Human Geography* **23**, 7–26.

Taylor, P.J. (2000) 'World cities and territorial states under conditions of contemporary globalization', *Political Geography* **19**, 5–32.

Taylor, P.J. (2001) 'Specification of the world city network', *Geographical Analysis* **33**, 181–94.

Taylor, P.J. (2002) 'Relocating the demos?' in J Anderson (ed.) *Transnational Democracy. Political Spaces and Border Crossings.* London: Routledge, pp. 236–44.

Taylor, P.J. (2004) *World City Network: A Global Urban Analysis.* London: Routledge.

Taylor, P.J. (2005) 'Leading world cities: empirical evaluations of urban nodes in multiple networks', *Urban Studies* **42**, 1593–1608.

Taylor, P.J. (2006) 'Development as a "monstrous hybrid": an essay on the primacy of cities in the expansion of economic life', *Environment and Planning A* **43**, 793–803.

Taylor, P.J. (2009) 'Urban economists in thrall to Christaller: a misguided search for city hierarchies in external urban relations', *Environment and Planning A* **41**, 2550–55.

Taylor, P.J. (2011a) 'Thesis on labour imperialism: how communist China used capitalist globalization to create the last great modern imperialism', *Political Geography* **30**, 175–7.

Taylor, P.J. (2011b) 'Spatial planning in the age of globalization', *Built and Environmental Studies* **4**, 153–168.

Taylor, P.J. (2012a) 'On city cooperation and city competition', in B. Derudder, M. Hoyler, P.J. Taylor and F. Witlox (eds) *International Handbook of Globalization and World Cities.* Cheltenham, UK and Northampton, MA, USA: Edward Elgar, pp. 56–63.

Taylor, P.J. (2012b) 'Transition towns and world cities: towards green networks of cities', *Local Environment* **17**, 495–508.

Taylor, P.J. and R. Aranya (2008) 'A global "urban roller coaster"? Connectivity changes in the world city network, 2000–04', *Regional Studies* **42**, 1–16.

Taylor, P.J., M. Hoyler, and D.M. Evans (2008) 'A geohistorical study of "the rise of modern science": mapping scientific practice through urban networks, 1500–1900', *Minerva* **46**, 391–410.

Taylor, P.J., A. Firth, M. Hoyler and D. Smith (2010a) 'Explosive city growth in the modern world-system: an initial inventory derived from urban demographic changes', *Urban Geography* **31**, 865–84.

Taylor, P.J., Hoyler, M. and Verbruggen, R. (2010b) 'External urban relational process: introducing central flow theory to complement central place theory', *Urban Studies* **47**, 2803–18.

Taylor, P.J., P. Ni, B. Derudder, M. Hoyler, J. Huang and F. Witlox (eds) (2011) *Global Urban Analysis: A Survey of Cities in Globalization.* London: Earthscan.

Taylor, P. J., B. Derudder, M. Hoyler and P. Ni (2013) 'New regional geographies of the world as practised by leading advanced producer service firms in 2010', *Transactions, Institute of British Geographers* **38**.

Tellier, L-N. (2009) *Urban World History: An Economic and Geographical Perspective*. Québec, QC: Presses de l'Université de Québec.

't Hart, M. (1989) 'Cities and statemaking in the Dutch Republic, 1580–1680', *Theory and Society* **18**, 663–87.

't Hart, M. (1993) *The Making of a Bourgeois State*. Manchester: Manchester University Press.

Thompson, G.F. (2003) *Between Hierarchies and Markets: The Logic and Limits of Network Forms of Organization*. Oxford: Oxford University Press.

Thompson, W. R. (ed.) (2009) *Systematic Transitions: Past, Present, and Future*. New York: Palgrave Macmillan.

Thowsen, A. (2003) 'Maritime insurance', in J. Mokyr (ed.) *The Oxford Encyclopedia of Economic History*, volume 1. Oxford: Oxford University Press, pp. 87–91.

Thuesen, I. (2000) 'The city-state in ancient western Syria', in M.H. Hansen (ed.) *A Comparative Study of Thirty City-State Cultures*. Copenhagen: Historisk-filosofiske Skrifter 21 (Royal Danish Academy of Sciences and Letters) pp. 55–65.

Tilly, C. (1990) *Coercion, Capital, and European States, AD 990–1990*. Oxford: Blackwell.

Tilly, C. (2010) 'Cities, states and trust networks: chapter 1 of *Cities and States in World History*', *Theory and Society* **39**, 265–80.

Tracy, J.D. (2000) *City Walls: The Urban Enceinte in Global Perspective*. Cambridge: Cambridge University Press.

Turok, I. (2009) 'The distinctive city: pitfalls in the pursuit of differential advantage', *Environment and Planning A* **41**, 13–30.

Tyner, J.A. (2008) *The Killing of Cambodia: Geography, Genocide and the Unmaking of Space*. Aldershot: Ashgate.

UNCSD (United Nations Conference on Sustainable Development) (2012) 'Sustainable cities', Rio 2012 Issues Briefs No. 5, http://www. uncsd2012.org/rio20/index (accessed 13 June 2012).

UN-Habitat (2003) *The Challenge of Slums: Global Report on Human Settlements 2002*. London: UN-Habitat.

UN-Habitat (2010) *The State of China's Cities 2010/2011: Better City, Better Life*. Beijing: Foreign Languages Press.

United Nations Population Fund (2007) *Unleashing the Potential of Urban Growth,* www.unfpa.org/swp/2007/english/ (accessed 12 October 2011).

Urry, J. (2003) *Global Complexity*. Cambridge: Polity.

Uytven, R., van (1995) 'Stages of economic decline: late medieval Bruges', in J-M. Duvosquel and E. Thoen (eds) *Peasants and Townsmen in Medieval Europe*. Gent, Belgium: Snoeck-Ducaju & Zoon, pp. 259–69.

Valente, M.A. (1998) 'Reassessing the Irish "monastic town"', *Irish Historical Studies* **31** (121), 1–18.

Vance, J.E. (1986) *Capturing the Horizon: The Historical Geography of Transportation*. New York: Harper & Row.

Vanhaute, E. (2008) 'The end of peasantries? Rethinking the role of peasantries in world-historical view', *Review* **31**, 29–59.

Wagner, P. (1994) *A Sociology of Modernity: Liberty and Discipline*. London: Routledge.

Waley, D. (1969) *The Italian City-Republics*. London: Weidenfeld & Nicolson.

Wall, R., B.V.D. Knaap and W. Sleegers (2007) *Towards Network Sustainability: Between Corporate Network Analysis and Development Indicators* (Final Report for The Netherlands Environment Assessment Agency). Rotterdam, Netherlands: Faculty of Applied Economics, Erasmus University.

Wallerstein, I. (1974) *The Modern World-System: Capitalist Agriculture and the Origins of the European World-Economy in the Sixteenth Century*. New York: Academic Press.

Wallerstein, I. (1979) *The Capitalist World-Economy*. Cambridge: Cambridge University Press.

Wallerstein, I. (1983) *Historical Capitalism*. London: Verso.

Wallerstein, I. (1984) *The Politics of the World-Economy*. Cambridge: Cambridge University Press.

Wallerstein, I. (1991) *Unthinking Social Science: The Limits of Nineteenth-Century Paradigms*. Cambridge: Polity Press.

Wallerstein, I. (1992) 'The West, capitalism, and the modern world-system', *Review* **15** (4), 561–619.

Wallerstein, I. (1993) 'World system versus world-systems: a critique', in A.G. Frank and B.K. Gills (eds) *The World System: Five Hundred Years or Five Thousand?* London: Routledge, pp. 292–6.

Wallerstein, I (1999) *The End of The World As We Know It: Social Science for the Twenty-First Century*. Minneapolis, MN: University of Minnesota Press.

Wallerstein, I. (2004) *World-Systems Analysis: an Introduction*. Durham, NC: Duke University Press.

Wallerstein, I. (2011) *The Modern World-System IV: Centrist Liberalism Triumphant, 1789–1914*. Berkeley, CA: California University Press.

Wallerstein, I., C. Juma, E.F. Keller, J. Kocka, D. Lecourt, V.Y. Mudimbe, K. Mushakoji, I. Prigogine, P.J. Taylor and M-R. Trouillot (1996) *Open the Social Sciences*. Stanford, CA: Stanford University Press.

Webb, M.C. (1975) 'The flag follows trade: an essay on the

necessary interaction of military and commercial factors in state for-mation', in J.A. Sabloff and C.C. Lamber-Karloversusky (eds) *Ancient Civilization and Trade*. Albuquerque, NM: University of New Mexico Press.

Weber, A.F. (1899) *The Growth of Cities in the Nineteenth Century: A Study in Statistics*. Ithaca, NY: Cornell University Press (1963 reprint).

Weber, M. (1958) *The City*. New York: Free Press.

Weber, M. (1978) *Economy and Society*, volume 1. Berkeley, CA: University of California Press.

Webster, D. (1997) 'City-states of Maya', in D.L. Nichols and T.H. Charlton (eds) *The Archaeology of City-states: Cross-Cultural Approaches*. Washington, DC: Smithsonian Institution Press, pp. 135–54.

Wenke, R.J. (1997) 'City-states, nation-states, and territorial states: the problem of Egypt', in D.L. Nichols and T.H. Charlton (eds) *The Archaeology of City-states: Cross-Cultural Approaches*. Washington, DC: Smithsonian Institution Press, pp. 27–49.

Whitehouse, R. (1977) *The First Cities*. Oxford: Phaidon.

Wickham, C. (2009) *The Inheritance of Rome: A History of Europe from 400 to 1000*. London: Allen Lane.

Wilkinson, D. (1992) 'Cities, civilizations and oikumenes: I', *Comparative Civilizations Review* **27**, 51–87.

Wilson, D.J. (1997) 'Early state formation on the north coast of Peru: a critique of the city-state model', in D.L. Nichols and T.H. Charlton (eds) *The Archaeology of City-states: Cross-Cultural Approaches*. Washington, DC: Smithsonian Institution Press, pp. 229–44.

Wójcik D. (2011) 'The dark side of NY-LON: financial centres and the global financial crisis', working papers in employment, work and finance 11–12, School of Geography and the Environment, Oxford University, http://ssrn.com/abstract=1890644 (accessed 28 November 2011).

Wolf, E. (1982) *Europe and the People without History*. Berkeley, CA: University of California Press.

Wolmar, C (2007) *Fire and Steam: How the Railways Transformed Britain*. London: Atlantic Books.

World Bank (2000) *World Development Report 1999–2000. Entering the 21st Century*, web.worldbank.org/WBSITE/EXTERNAL/EXTDEC/EXTRESEARCH/EXTWDRS (accessed 12 October 2011).

Wright, E.O. (2000) *Class Counts*. Cambridge: Cambridge University Press.

Yates, R.D.S. (1997) 'The city-state in ancient China', in D.L. Nichols and T.H. Charlton (eds) *The Archaeology of City-states: Cross-Cultural Approaches*. Washington, DC: Smithsonian Institution Press, pp. 71–90.

Yoffee, N. (1997) 'The obvious and the chimerical: city-states in archaeological perspective', in D.L. Nichols and T.H. Charlton (eds) *The Archaeology of City-states: Cross-Cultural Approaches*. Washington, DC: Smithsonian Institution Press, pp. 255–63.

Yoffee, N. (2005) *Myths of the Archaic State: Evolution of the Earliest Cities, States, and Civilizations*. Cambridge: Cambridge University Press.

Yunis, M. (2007) *Creating a World Without Poverty*. New York: Public Affairs.

Zeder, M.A. (2003) 'Food provisioning in urban societies: a view from northern Mesopotamia', in M.L. Smith (ed.) *The Social Construction of Ancient Cities*. Washington, DC: Smithsonian Books, pp. 156–183.

Zhang, L-Y. (2003) 'Economic development in Shanghai and the role of the state', *Urban Studies* **40**, 1549–72.

Zolberg, R. (1986) 'Strategic interactions and the formation of modern states: France and England', in A. Kazancigil (ed.) *The State in Global Perspective*. Aldershot: Gower.

Cities index

Aachen 215, 219
Abu Dhabi 313, 321
Abu Gosh 113
Abu Hureyra 113
Abydos 151, 153
Acre 241, 242
Adab 114, 148
Adrianople 242
Aegina 193
Agades 166
Agrigentum 155
Ahmedabad 242
Akkad 114, 128, 131
Akshak 114
Ain Ghazal 113
Al Ahsa 211
Alep 148
Aleppo 241, 242
Alexandria 154, 155, 202, 209, 210,
    211, 214, 221, 241, 242
Ali Kosh 113
Alkalawa 167
Allada 166
Almaty 313
Amida 241
Amman 313
Amsterdam 11, 74, 165, 250–55, 257,
    259–60, 264, 265, 267–72, 274,
    276, 287–9, 303, 313, 355, 381,
    393, 395, 399
Angkor 241, 242
Anhilvada 241, 242
Ani 241
Anshan 148
Antioch 155, 210, 211, 214
Antwerp 11, 79, 191, 243, 246–52,
    258–60, 264, 265, 268, 274, 314,
    383, 393, 395
Anyi 206
Ao 163
Apamea 210, 211

Aquila 79
Aram 148
Arles 214
Argos 155
Arvad 156
Asikli Hüyük 113
Assur 148, 149–51
    governance of 150
Asunción 17
Athens 4, 154, 155, 193, 201, 214, 314
Atlanta 74, 270, 271, 282, 285, 312,
    314, 316, 365, 392
Auckland 313
Augsburg 79, 265, 268
Ava 242
Avaris 152, 204
Awdaghost 166
Axum 176
Ayutia 242
Azcapotzalco 170

Babylon 57, 148, 149–50, 157, 186, 193,
    204, 391, 392
Badtibira 118, 148
Baghdad 194, 198, 201, 210, 211, 220–
    21, 227, 241, 242, 258
Balasaghun 241
Baltimore 265, 266, 269, 270, 273, 282,
    283, 284, 285, 310, 312
Bangalore 4, 304, 314, 325
Bangkok 270, 314, 336
Barnsley 377
Barcelona 265, 269, 270, 314, 362
Bar-sur-Aybe 224
Basrah (Basra) 211, 241
Bath 86
Beidha 113
Beijing (see also Peking) 57, 77, 266,
    270, 303, 304, 305, 311, 312, 314,
    315, 318–19, 321, 329, 339, 340,
    341, 343, 374, 381, 392, 402

Beirut 314
Belgrade 314
Benares 241
Benevento 217
Benin 165, 166
Berlin 57, 108, 119, 130, 263, 265, 269, 270, 271, 304, 314, 386
Bidar 242
Biram 167
Birka 218
Birmingham (UK) 3, 21, 32, 265, 268, 269, 270, 277–8, 280, 290, 304, 314, 323
Birmingham (USA) 366
Blackburn 277, 278, 280
Blackpool 86
Bo (Yanshi) 163
Bogotá 174, 314, 318
Bokhara 211, 241, 242
Bologna 226, 237, 241, 242
Bolton 277
Bombay (see also Mumbai) 265, 269, 270
Bordeaux 265, 267, 268
Boston 38, 84, 265, 269, 270, 271, 282, 283, 284, 285, 300, 312, 314, 316, 321, 323, 325, 365, 389
Bougie 241, 242
Bouqras 113
Bradford 277, 279, 280
Brasilia 59, 304, 312, 318
Bratislava 314
Brescia 226
Brill 257
Brisbane 314
Bristol 265, 268, 269, 278, 290, 304, 361–2, 364
Bruges 224–7, 242, 243, 247–9, 258, 274, 283, 402
Brussels 265, 269, 270, 274, 303, 312, 314, 315
Bubastis 152
Bucharest 314
Budapest 265, 314
Buenos Aires 17, 264, 265, 269, 270, 283, 303, 314, 318, 329
Buffalo 282, 284, 285
Bursa 242
Bussa 166
Buto 151

Byblos 156
Byzantium 155

Cadiz (Gadir) 155, 156, 265, 269
Caesarea 211, 214, 241
Caesarea Mazaca 211
Caffa 225, 242
Cahokia 26, 137–8, 142–4, 391, 396
    population growth of 143–4
Cairo 194, 198, 311, 221, 228, 241, 242, 269, 270, 314, 329
Cajamarquilla 174
Calcutta (see also Kolkata) 265, 269, 270, 304, 314
Calgary 314, 323
Calicut 242
Cambay 241, 242
Cambridge 85, 86
Canterbury 85
Canberra 57, 86
Canton (see also Guangzhou) 208, 209, 241, 242
Cape Town 313, 323
Capua 155, 210, 211
Caracas 18, 313
Carchemish 148
Cardiff 277, 279, 280
Carthage 57, 155, 157, 204, 210, 211, 214
Casablanca 313
Çatalhöyük 26, 96–113, 131, 133, 135, 136, 137, 178, 386, 389
    excavations at 97, 103, 105, 109
    external relations of 105–6
    fall of 136
    house-based organization of 111
    Jacobsean size of 101
Catania 265, 268
Çayönü 113
Chakanputun 171
Chanchán 174
Changan 207
Charlotte 312, 314
Chengdu 207, 208, 209, 241, 242, 339, 340
Chennai (see also Madras) 304, 314
Chicago 11, 57, 264, 265, 269, 270, 271, 282, 284, 285, 303, 304, 308–11, 314–16, 318, 325, 365, 374
Chichen-Itzá 170

Chitor 242
Cholula 170
Chongqing 339
Chuanchow 208, 241, 242
Chunar 241
Cibyra 210
Cincinatti 282, 284, 285, 314
Cirta 155
Ciudad Juarez 355–6
Cleveland 282, 284, 285, 313
Coapexco 143
Cologne 217, 218, 225, 226, 227, 237, 241–2, 314
Columbus 282, 285, 312
Constantinople 58–9, 74, 210, 214, 227, 241, 242
Copán 170
Copenhagen 74, 263, 265, 269, 270, 314, 321
Corcyra 155
Cork 265, 269
Cordova 211, 220–21, 225, 240, 241
Corinth 155, 193
Cremona 226, 237
Crewe 85
Croton 155
Cuenca 265, 268
Cueta 241, 242
Cuicuico 170
Curitaba 304
Cuttack 241, 242
Cuzco 174, 175
Cyrene 155

Dacca 84, 356
Daliang 206
Dallas 265, 270, 271, 292, 313, 316, 365–6
Damascus 198, 214, 241, 242
Damietta 242
Dar es Salaam 85
Daura 167
Delft 255, 257, 276, 287, 289
Delhi (see also New Delhi) 241, 242
Denver 282, 285, 314
Derby 277, 280
Detroit 178, 265, 270, 271, 282, 284, 285, 312, 314
Deventer 272
Dhaka 329, 356

Dholavira 159–60
Dilmun 131, 148, 149
Dobrovody 140
Doha 314
Domberg 218
Dongtan 374
Dordrecht 249, 257, 276
Dorestad 218
Dresden 265, 269, 270, 271
Dubai 303, 308, 314, 321
Dublin 140, 263, 316
Dundee 277
Durbi 166
Dur-Kurig 148
Durrington Walls 141
Dur Untash 148
Düsseldorf 304, 314

Ebla 148
Edam 289
Edessa 214
Edinburgh 214
Emerita 210, 211
Enkhuizen 255, 257, 276
Ephesus 155, 210, 211
Erfurt 237
Eridu 99, 114, 118
Erlitou 163, 164
Eshnunna 148

Fez 240, 241, 242
Florence 3, 80, 225, 226, 237, 242, 245
Foshan 209
Fostat (see also Fustat, Cairo) 221
Frankfurt 76–7, 270, 301, 303, 304, 315, 319, 381
Fuchow 208, 209, 241, 242
Fustat (see also Fostat, Cairo) 211
Fuzhou (see Fuchow)

Galway 272
Ganweriwala 159
Gao 166, 168
Gaur 241, 242
Gbara 166
Gela 155
Gelonus 204
Geneva 270, 314
Genoa 79–80, 191, 224–6, 237, 241, 243–7, 258–60, 258, 259, 260, 286

Ghana 166
Ghazni 241
Ghent 212, 225–8, 242, 243, 274
Girsu 114, 127, 148
Glasgow 84, 265, 268, 269, 270, 277,
 304, 314
Göbeki Tepe 113
Gobir 166, 167
Gouda 376
Granada 226, 228, 241, 242
Great Zimbabwe 26, 141
Groningen 275, 276
Guangzhou (see also Canton) 207, 304,
 314, 329, 340, 341, 356
Guatemala City 314

Haarlem 254, 257, 265, 267, 268, 276,
 287, 289
Hamburg 74, 264, 265, 268, 269, 270,
 271, 304, 314, 362
Hamwic 218
Handan 206
Hangchow (see also Hangzhou) 208,
 209, 240, 241, 242
Hangzhou (see also Hangchow) 340,
 341
Hanoi 314
Haoqing 163, 204
Harappa 139, 159–61, 178, 391
Hattusah 148
Havana 18
Hazor 148
Heart 242
Hedeby 218
Heliopolis 152
Hellevoetsluis 288
Hierakonpolis 151, 153
Hippo 214
Ho Chi Minh City 314, 356
Hong Kong 74, 77, 265, 270, 302, 303,
 305, 308, 314, 321, 323, 337, 392
Hoorn 255, 274, 276, 289
Hormuz 241, 242
Houston 365, 270, 271, 282, 285, 314,
 365, 366, 369
Hsuchow 242
Huddersfield 290
Huari 174

Ife 166

Ijebu 166
Ipswich 218
Indianapolis 282, 285
Isfahan 211, 241, 242
Isin 114, 148
Istanbul 270, 312, 314, 329
Iximche 171
Izapa 170

Jakarta 314, 329
Jarkutan 148
Jarmo 113
Jaunpur 242
Jeddah 314
Jenné 166, 167
Jerez 265, 268
Jericho 102–3, 108–9, 113, 131, 134–5,
 188
 excavations at 102–3, 129–30
Jersey City 282, 285
Jerusalem 210, 214, 241
Jima 166
Johannesburg 302, 312, 315, 319, 323

Kaifeng 207, 208, 209, 240, 241, 242
Kairouan (also Kairwan) 211, 241
Kamakura 208, 241, 242
Kampen 275, 276
Kanauj 241
Kanesh 149–50
Kano 166, 167
Kansas City 282, 285, 314
Karachi 84, 159, 314, 329, 331
Karaman 242
Kashgar 241, 242
Katsina 166, 167
Kayseri 241, 242
Kazargamu 166
Kebbi 166
Kesh 114
Khajuraho 241
Khartoum 84
Kiama 167
Kiawa 167
Kiev 241, 314
Kikiwhary 166
Kilwa 166
Kingtechen 209, 241, 242
Kinshasa 84, 331
Kish 114, 120, 127

Knoxville 84
Konia 241, 242
Krenik 166
Kolkata (see also Calcutta) 329, 356
Kuala Lumpur 303, 314
Kumasi 167
Kuwait 314
Kyoto 207, 208, 209, 242, 242

Lagash 114, 127, 186
Lagny-sur-Marne 224
Lagos 84, 313, 329
Lanchow 209
Larak 114, 118
Larsa 114, 148
Las Vegas 86
Lecce 265, 268
Leeds 277–8, 280, 290
Leeuwarden 276
Leicester 32, 277, 280
Leiden 189, 254, 265, 267, 268, 287, 289
Leipzig 79, 265, 269, 270, 271
Leon 225
Leptis 214
Liaoyang 241
Lima 18, 313
Linzi 204, 206
Lisbon 84, 212, 226, 242, 243, 264, 265, 268, 270, 314
Liverpool 84, 264, 265, 268, 269, 270, 277, 278, 280, 290
London 3, 11, 18, 21, 32, 57, 62, 74, 76–80, 191, 201, 212, 225–6, 242, 243, 259–61, 264, 265, 268, 269, 270, 272, 276, 278, 280, 290–91, 300–304, 310–11, 312, 313, 314–16, 318–19, 321, 323, 325, 327, 329, 331, 334, 350, 361
Los Angeles 57, 264, 265, 270, 271, 282, 283, 285, 292, 303, 304, 308, 312, 314, 319, 329, 365
Louisville 282, 284, 285
Lsasa 207
Luoyang (Loyang) 203, 204, 206, 207, 241
Luxembourg City 313
Lydia 193
Lyon 79, 226, 265, 267–8, 269, 270

Maastricht 272
Macclesfield 290
Madras (see also Chennai) 265, 266, 269, 270
Madrid 212, 245, 266, 270, 303, 314, 318, 321
Madurai 241, 242
Magdeburg 265, 268
Mainz 218
Mali 166
Manama 314
Manan 166
Manchester 264, 265, 268, 269, 270, 277–8, 280, 290, 303, 304, 305, 314, 355
Mandu 242
Manila 314, 329
Mani 171
Manyakheta 241
Manzura 241
Mari 148
Marrakesh 241, 242
Marseille 218, 265, 267
Masenya 166
Masham-Sha 148
Mayapán 170
Maydanets 140
Mecca 149, 176, 399
Medina 149, 176, 399
Mehrgarh 139
Melbourne 11, 81, 266, 270, 313, 314, 319, 323, 327
Memphis (Egypt) 152, 204
Memphis (USA) 366
Messina 155
Metz 217, 237
Mexico City 18, 303, 314, 315, 329
Miami 270, 310, 312, 314, 316, 318–19, 325, 356, 365
Middelburg 249, 276
Middlesbrough 277, 280
Milan 79–80, 155, 210, 211, 212, 214, 217, 225, 226, 227, 237, 240, 241, 242, 243, 244, 245, 265, 268, 269, 270, 303, 308, 312, 314, 321
Miletus 157
Milford Haven 85
Milwaukie 282, 284, 285
Minneapolis 266, 270, 282, 285, 314
Mitla 171

Moche 174, 175
Mohenjo-daro 99, 139, 159, 178
Monnikendam 289
Monte Albán 143, 170
Monterrey 314
Montevideo 18, 314
Montgomery 272
Montréal 81, 265, 270, 314, 327
Mopsuetia 211
Mosul 241, 242
Moscow 264, 265, 269, 270, 303, 314,
    319, 321, 329, 338
Mumbai (see also Bombay) 303, 304,
    305, 310, 312, 313, 321, 323, 325,
    329, 356–7
Mundigak 148
Munich 265, 269, 270, 271, 304, 312,
    314
Mureyra 113

Nagada (Naqada) 151, 153
Nagoya 209, 265, 270
Nairobi 314, 323, 377
Nanking 208, 241, 242
Nanning 241
Naples 79, 212, 217, 225, 226, 242, 243,
    224, 266, 270
Nara 207
Nashville 366
Naya 166
Newark 282, 284, 285
New Delhi 241, 242, 304, 310, 323,
    325, 329
New Orleans 282, 284, 285, 291, 356–7
New York 10, 18, 21, 57, 65, 74, 79–80,
    259–61, 264, 265, 270, 271, 280
    282–3, 284, 285, 291–2, 300, 302,
    303, 304, 308, 309, 311, 312, 314–
    16, 318, 319, 323, 327, 329, 331,
    334, 356, 364–5
Newcastle 265, 268, 269, 270, 278, 291,
    292
Ngala 166
Nicomedia 210
Nicosia 314
Nijmegen 276
Nimes 155
Nina 114, 148
Ningbo (see also Ningpo) 356
Ninghsia 209, 241, 242

Ningpo (see also Ningbo) 209, 242
Niniveh 148
Nippur 114, 118, 119, 148
Nishapur 211, 241
Nisibis 155, 214
Njimye 166
Nottingham 277, 279, 280
Novgorod 242
Nufi 166
Nupé 166

Oakland, 282, 285
Ochrida 241
Oklahoma City 366
Olbia 155
Osaka 208, 209, 266, 269, 270, 314,
    327, 329, 374
Oslo 312, 314, 321
Ostia 155
Ottawa 86
Ouagadougou 166
Oxford 85
Oyo 166
Ozkend 241

Padua 237
Pagan 241, 242
Palermo 212, 241, 242
Palma Nuova 189
Palo Alto 310, 314–15, 316,
Pampa de las Llamas-Moxeque 142
Panama City 314
Paris 18, 21, 57, 212, 217, 224, 225,
    226, 227–8, 240, 241, 242, 243,
    265, 267–8, 269, 270, 303, 308,
    312, 314, 315–16, 319, 329, 356,
    374
Pátzcuaro 171
Pavia 217, 237, 244
Pegu 242
Peking (see also Beijing) 207, 208, 228,
    241, 242, 258
Pergamum 155, 210, 211
Perth 314
Philadelphia 265, 269, 270, 271, 282,
    283, 284, 285, 312, 314, 318
Phoenix 313
Piedras Negras 170
Pi-Ramses 152, 204
Pisa 237, 241, 242

Pittsburgh 265, 269, 270, 271, 282, 284, 285, 312, 314
Portland 282, 285, 314
Port Louis 314
Porto Alegre 304, 355
Potosi 212
Poundbury 350
Prague 212, 225, 226, 242, 243, 265, 269, 270, 314
Prambanan 241
Preston 277, 278, 280
Provins 224
Puje 166
Purmerend 289
Pyonyang 241

Qatna 148
Qiyi 163
Quanzhou (see Chuanchow)
Quentovic 218
Qufu 206
Qus 241, 242
Quito 174
Quilon 241, 242

Rakhigarhi 159
Rano 167
Rao 166
Ras Shamra 113
Ravenna 214
Ravy 211, 241
Reims 217
Rhodes 155
Rhondda 280
Ribe 218
Riga 313, 323
Riobamba 174, 242
Rio de Janeiro 81, 265, 269, 270, 304, 313, 318, 329, 368
Riyadh 313
Rochdale 277
Rochester 282, 284, 285
Rome 79, 134, 154, 157, 184, 209, 210, 213, 214, 215, 231, 258, 265, 270, 293, 321
Rotterdam 254, 255, 257, 265, 267, 268, 289, 292
Rouen 225, 226, 241, 242, 264, 265, 268

Sale 241, 242

Samarkand 198, 211, 241, 242
Samarra 211
San Diego 314, 369
San Francisco 265, 270, 271, 282, 284, 285, 304, 314, 315
Sangha 167
San José 314
San Juan 314
Sannai-Maruyama 26, 135, 138
Santiago 18, 265, 270, 314, 318
Santo Domingo 314
São Paolo 76, 80, 81, 265, 270, 303, 304, 305, 312, 314, 318–19, 321, 327, 329
Sapinuwa 148
Sarai 241, 242
Sardis 155
Seattle 265, 270, 271, 282, 285, 314
Seoul 208, 209, 242, 265, 270, 303, 312, 314, 319, 329
Seville 155, 241, 242, 245–6, 263–4, 265, 268, 396
Shabat-Enlil 148
Shackenwald 79
Sanxingdui 163
Shang 162, 163, 164, 193
Shanghai 77, 201, 209, 264, 265, 269, 270, 301, 303, 304, 305, 308, 312, 314, 318, 321, 329, 340, 341, 343, 356, 374
Shangqiu 206
Sheffield 32, 277, 280
Shenzhen 312, 314
s-Hertogenosch 272
Shiraz 198, 241, 242
Shuruppak 114, 118
Smolensk 226
Smyrna 211, 214
Sian 208, 241, 242
Siangyang 241, 242
Sidon, 154, 155, 156
Singapore 80, 265, 270, 303, 308, 312, 314, 316, 319, 323, 327, 337
Sippar 118, 150, 151
Sofia 314
Somnath 241
Songdo 241
Soochow (see also Suzhou) 208, 209, 241, 242
Sparta 155

Speyer 237
St Louis 282, 284, 285, 314
Stockton 280
Stoke-on-Trent 277
Stockholm 270, 312, 314, 321
Stuttgart 266, 270, 314
Suheri 114
Sultaniya 198
Sumpu 208
Suramé 166
Susa 148, 151
Suzhou (see also Soochow) 206, 207
Sydney 81, 266, 270, 301, 303, 308,
    311, 312, 314, 316, 319, 323, 327
Syracuse 155, 210, 214

Tabriz 242
Tademekka 166
Taiyuan 242
Tali 241, 242
Tallyanky 140
Taipei 314
Tajin 170
Tampa 314
Tanis 152
Tanjore 241
Tarentum 155
Tehran 329
Tel Aviv 314
Tenayuca 170
Teotihuacán 170, 172, 173
Texcoco 170
Thaneswar 241
Thebes 204
The Hague 86, 253, 257, 272, 276,
    289
Thessalonica 155, 242, 242
Tiahuanaco 174
Tientsin 209, 265, 269, 270
Tiho 171
Tikal 170, 172
Tilantongo 170
Timbuktu 166, 167, 168
Tinnis 211, 241
Tlapacoya 143
Tlatilco 143
Tlaxcala 171
Tlemcen 241, 242
Tokyo (see also Yedo) 4, 21, 65, 81,
    265, 269, 270, 300, 303, 308, 310,

311, 312, 314, 315, 318–19, 327,
    329
Tollan (see also Tula) 170
Torino (see also Turin) 265, 268
Toronto 81, 84, 265, 270, 303, 310, 311,
    312, 314, 316, 319, 321, 323, 327
Totnes 359, 360, 361, 362
Tours 217
Trebizond 241, 242
Tres Zapotes 170
Trier 210, 211, 214, 217
Trieste 312
Trnovo 241, 242
Troki (Vilnius) 226, 242, 243
Troy 148
Troyes 224
Tula (see also Tollan) 172
Túmbez 174
Tunis 241, 242
Turin (see also Torino) 312
Turunku 166
Tyre 148, 154, 155, 156, 157
Tzintzuntzán 171

Ugarit 148, 155
Ujjain 241
Umma 114, 127, 148
Ur 99, 114, 129, 131, 145, 148, 203, 204
Uruk 98, 99, 101, 108, 114, 119–20,
    122–5, 128, 131, 133, 144–5, 148,
    151, 168, 186, 190, 201–5, 249, 380
  city development of 122, 168, 202
  city wall of 125, 168
  population level of 114, 202–3
  world-system of 124
Utatlán 171
Utrecht 275, 276, 289
Uxmal 170

Valencia 226
Valladolid 226
Vancouver 314, 323
Yangchow 208, 241, 242
Yangzhou (see Yangchow)
Verona 217, 237
Venice 74, 79–80, 86, 212, 218, 220–23,
    225, 226, 227–8, 240, 241, 242,
    243, 245, 253, 254, 258, 259, 260,
    265, 268, 274
Vicenza 265, 268

Vienna 79, 214, 226, 263, 265, 269, 270, 314
Vienne 214
Vijaya 241, 242
Vijayanagar 228, 242

Waddinxveen 288
Wakefield 290
Walata 166
Warangal 241, 242
Warsaw 265, 269, 270, 314
Washington DC 57, 86, 265, 270, 271–2, 282, 284–005, 304, 312, 314, 315, 332, 354, 365
Washukhani 148
Wuchang (see also Wuhan) 207, 208, 241, 242
Wuhan (see also Wuchang) 339, 340
Wuxi 340

Xiang 163
Xiatu 165, 204, 206
Xi'an (see Sian)
Xin Jang 207
Xinzheng 206
Xochicicalco 170

Yamagushi 208
Yangchow (Yangzhou) 241
Yedo (see also Tokyo) 209
Yenhsiatu 206
Yianyang 206
Yin 163, 204
Yiyang 206
Yong 206
York 85, 218
Youzhou 207
Yunnanfu 242

Zaachila 171
Zabalam 114, 148
Zagha 166
Zagreb 314
Zamfara 166
Zampoala 171
Zanzibar 85
Zaria 166, 167
Zawi Chemi 113
Zhengzhou 163
Zurich 270, 312, 314, 316
Zutphen 375, 376
Zwolle 272

General index

Abu-Lughod, Janet
  Before European Hegemony (1989)
    227
Agnew, John
  territorial trap argument 12, 18
Algaze, Guillermo 98, 100–101, 121–4,
    128, 205
  concept of 'technologies of the
    intellect' 123
Algeria 83
Amin, Samir 84
Anatolia 26, 102, 105–6, 113, 124, 129
  copper production in 150
  early urban settlements in 110
  metal production in 122
Arrighi, Giovanni 46, 244–5, 257,
    347–8, 376
  social space model 53
  systematic cycles of accumulation
    261
Arup Report (2011)
  findings of 368
Assyrian Empire 115, 149, 151, 156–7
  law code of 186
Australia 181
  product supply identity of 82
Aztecs 173, 177

Bahn, Paul
  *Archaeology: Theories, Methods and
    Practice* (2008) 94–5
Bairoch, Paul
  Cities and Economic Development
    (1988) 11
Bangladesh 42
Belgium 20
Belich, James
  Replenishing the Earth (2009) 11, 178
Blaut, Jim
  Eight Eurocentric Historians (2000)
    236

Bonaparte, Napoleon 215
Brand, Stuart 9
Braudel, Fernand 31, 46, 54, 59, 89,
    184, 215, 223–4, 228, 240, 247,
    249, 252, 264, 275, 297
  concept of world-economy 203, 257
  social time theory of 51
  society model of 47–8
Brazil 347
Bretton Woods 261
Brenner, Neil 6, 57
BRIC countries 347
  shortcomings of concept 337
Brown, Gordon
  British Chancellor of the Exchequer
    333
Brugmann, Jeb
  Welcome to the Urban Revolution
    (2009) 10
Buddhism 161
Byzantium Empire 222
  Fall of Constantinople (1453) 58–9

Calthorpe, Peter 350, 357–8, 364,
    366–8
Cambodia 84–5
Canada
  rank-size rule of 17
capitalism 40, 48, 89, 184, 201, 207,
    230, 235, 238, 257, 260, 332–3, 375
  cycles 50
  free market 60
  market-led 47
  world-economy 28–30, 46–7, 50,
    55–6, 200, 207, 229, 250, 293,
    332–3, 335, 338, 341, 348, 353–5
Carneiro, Robert L.
  non-urban 'circumscription
    hypothesis' 125
Carolingian Empire 215–16, 220–22
  economy of 218–19, 221

Castells, Manuel 54, 300
  The Rise of Network Society 52
  theories of 25, 31, 53, 305, 332
Castle, Stephen
  The Age of Migration (2003) 20
Catholic Church 231
central flow theory 78, 107–9
  as interlocking network 80
  city-ness based on 108
central place theory 107, 117, 126
  impact on national urban systems
    17, 75
Chad
  slum-dwelling population of 331
Champagne fairs 224
Chandler, Tertius 99–100, 113, 146,
    151, 155, 165, 167, 169, 173, 174,
    175, 206, 207, 208, 209, 210, 211,
    212, 214, 217, 221, 224, 226, 227,
    228, 237, 240, 262, 328
Charlemagne 215
  territory conquered by 222
Charlton, Thomas
  The Archaeology of City-States
    (1997) 146
Chase-Dunn, Christopher 205
  analysis of inter-city relations 198–9
  *Rise and Demise: Comparing World-
    Systems* (1997) 192
Childe, Gordon 102–3, 115
  city development theories of 96–7
Chile
  government junta of 334
China 20, 28, 54, 62, 134, 139, 154,
    162, 176, 186, 188, 203, 206, 213,
    228–9, 233, 299, 328, 336–8, 347,
    366, 373, 376
  city growth rates of 339–40
  Cultural Revolution 338
  GDP of 339
  globalization process of 341, 344–5
  government of 342
  Great Leap Forward 338
  member of WTO 332–3
  Ming dynasty 207
  national plan of (2010) 346
  Shang dynasty 162
  Tang dynasty 206
  urban-rural migration in 83
  Warring States period 165, 197

Xia dynasty 162, 164
Yan state 165
Zhou dynasty 162, 205
Christianity
  Bible 154
  Irish 140
cities 4, 25, 31–2, 56, 86–7, 102, 116,
    129, 145, 162, 172
  agglomeration process of 81
  as process 26
  as social institution 56–7
  as social phenomena 12
  economic discovery of 5–7
  economic processes of 10
  impact of globalization on 5–6
  network externalities 74–5, 79
  political elements of 8
  relationship with state-istics 20–21
  relationship with states 22, 286,
    302
city-ness 98, 100, 102, 121, 163, 288
  based on central flow theory 108
  commercial 368
  process of 101, 124–5, 141, 144
  relationship with town-ness 108–9,
    167
city network 8, 26, 64, 76, 106, 113,
    116–17, 126–7, 129–31, 133, 138–
    40, 142, 144, 149, 154, 156, 160,
    164, 177–8, 183, 198–9, 221, 248,
    258, 288, 347, 357
  American 280, 283
  collapse of 28, 73, 136–7
  commercial 78
  development of 130, 319
  externality 74–5, 79
  formation of 29–30, 73, 157–8, 305,
    328, 331
  governance of 119
  growth of 30, 50
  process of 275, 302
  sustainable 351
  world 6, 30, 74, 78–82, 89, 201–7,
    209–10, 212, 214, 230, 298–9,
    301–3, 305, 319, 321, 327–8,
    331, 333–7, 370, 372–5
city-states 8, 29, 54, 58, 63, 95, 115–16,
    119, 123–4, 145, 153, 161–2
  commercial practices 95, 118, 120–21
  development of 167–8

formation of 102, 117, 125, 127, 129, 132
guardian practices 95, 118, 120–21, 126, 146–7
civilizations
concept of 93–4
relationship with states 94
clustered cities
concept of 141–2
Cold War 16, 321, 358
colonization 165
Concert of Europe 261
Congo
product supply identity of 82
de la Court, Peter
estimation of population in different economic sectors 251–2
The True Interest and Political Maxims of the Republic of Holland 256

Darwin, Charles 95
Davis, Mike
Planet of Slums (2006) 338
research on mega-slums 330–31
delinking 84-5
Democracy, Citizenship and the Global City 8
development theory
classic 83
Dobb, Maurice
debate with Paul Sweezy (1979) 237–8
Studies in the Development of Capitalism (1946) 238
Dutch Revolt (1568–1648) 250, 287
events of 274–5

early settlements 108
hunter-gatherer 58, 94, 99, 101, 103–5, 111–12
size estimation methods 98–101, 112
economies 131, 214, 223, 274
as global city-regions 81–2
development 64, 66
import replacement 66–8, 72–3, 327, 371
of mega-slums 331–2
processes of 63–6, 68–73

Egypt 28, 73, 151, 197, 203
population estimate of cities of 152–3
embedded statism
concept of 12–13
Ethiopia 73, 174, 375
slum-dwelling population of 331
European Central Bank
location of 76–7
European Union (EU)
Council of Ministers 77
launch of Euro (2001) 76
regional policy of 9
spatial policies of 9

Feinman, Gary
Archaic Studies (1997) 146
feudalism 231
definitions of 238–9
First World War (1914–18) 259, 283
France 253, 261
Revolution (1789–99) 43, 60
Frank, Andre Gunder 48, 183, 193–5, 207, 215, 347
development of underdevelopment 82
The World System: Five Hundred Years or Five Thousand? (1993) 192
Friedmann, John
world city hierarchy of 18–19
Fukuyama, Francis 60

Gamble, Clive 34, 45, 95
Gaul 215, 217
economy of 215
Germany 247, 261, 303, 305
Third Reich (1933–45) 62
Turkish migrant population of 83
Ghana
product supply identity of 82
Volta dam 84
Gills, Barry 48, 183, 215
The World System: Five Hundred Years or Five Thousand? (1993) 192
Glaeser, Edward 3–4, 32, 39, 349–51, 369
estimation of carbon emissions for US cities 364–6

Triumph of the City (2011) 7,
    364
global financial crisis (2007–9) 337
globalization 5, 24, 79–80, 293, 300,
    302, 327, 372
    China 341, 344–5
    contemporary 52, 230, 297, 299, 303,
        305, 331, 343, 371
    impact on cities 5–6
    neoliberal 333
    processes of 302, 305, 334–5, 343
    strategies of 315–16, 318–19, 323,
        325
Globalization and World Cities
    (GaWC) Research Network
    establishment of (1978) 21
    research conducted by 299, 302
Graeber, David 185-6
Greece 134, 209
Grimal, Pierre 209-10, 213
Gulbenkian Commission on the Crisis
    of the Social Sciences 13

Hall, Peter 3
    Cities in Civilization (1998) 11, 201
Hall, Thomas 193–5
    *Rise and Demise: Comparing World-
    Systems* (1997) 192
Hansen, Mogens
    *A Comparative Study of Thirty City-
    State Cultures* (2000) 146
Hapsburg Empire 253, 259, 274–5
    territory of 245–6, 249–50
Harvey, David
    time-space compression 293
    neo-liberalism 332
Hausaland 176
    city-state development in 167–8
Havighurst, Alfred
    *The Pirenne Thesis: Analysis,
    Criticism, and Revision* (1976)
    216
hegemony 173, 275, 285, 291–3, 299,
    348, 355
    American 62, 268–9, 273, 280–82,
        284, 337, 341, 345–6
    British 268, 272–3, 280, 290–91
    cycles of 30, 55, 230, 234, 250,
        258–9, 261–2, 267–8, 271–4,
        276, 278, 280, 284, 286–7, 293,

    345, 347
    definitions of 260–62
    Dutch 212, 267, 273–5, 287, 291
    economic 271–2
    guardian phase of 284
    high 261, 267, 271–3, 278, 281–6,
        291
    modern 289
    network 273
    states 55, 261, 264, 267, 272, 284,
        345, 347–8, 378
history
    Abnormal 27, 29, 229, 231
    Early 161
    gender 186
    Normal 27, 29–30, 132, 145, 157,
        177, 181–5, 187–9, 191–2,
        195–9, 201, 203, 205, 207, 213,
        216, 221, 228–36, 238–9, 258,
        298, 347, 375
Hodder, Ian 99, 111
    town theories of 107, 109–10
Holy Roman Empire 236
Hopkins, Rob 359, 362–4, 370–71, 373
    concept of 'relocalisation' 360
    concept of transition towns 361, 366
Hunt, Tristram 5, 349

imperialism 15, 59, 162, 165
    American 62
    British 323
    economic 131
    labour 342–3
    political 132
Inca
    cities of 174–5
India 134, 154, 186, 328, 366
    caste system of 43
    rank-size rule of 18
indisciplinarity 22-4, 177
Indus Valley 160–61
industrialization 14, 17, 83, 202, 261–2,
    277, 336, 341–2, 349
    large-scale 328
    modern 210
inter-city relations 18, 21, 75–7, 80, 198
    networked 199
    non-local 78
International Monetary Fund (IMF)
    335

international relations (IR) studies
view of state formation processes
62
Iran 139
cities of 124
metal production in 122
Ireland
monastic towns of 140–41
Islam 142, 222
rise of 210, 212, 215–16
Islamic Caliphate 258
decline in 227
expansion of 220
territory of 210, 218–19
world-economy of 221, 223
Islamism 62
Italy 47, 214, 217–18, 240, 246, 264
French invasion of (1494) 246
Lombardy 222
podestà 244–5
Treaty of Lodi (1454) 245
Ivory Coast
product supply identity of 82

Jacobs, Jane 3, 24, 31–3, 42, 46, 51, 84,
98, 101–5, 107, 110, 112–13, 121,
134, 177–8, 215, 227, 257, 278,
299, 327, 332, 351, 371–2
city growth process of 262–3
concept of 'economic grotesques'
82
concept of 'knowledgeable flexibility'
43–4
Dark Age Ahead (2004) 23–4
division of labour interpretations
109–10
moral syndrome theory of 34–40, 54,
56, 233–4, 239, 376
Systems of Survival (1992) 33–4, 44,
46
*The Death and Life of Great
American Cities* (1960)
106
The Economy of Cities (1969) 7, 106,
285–6
theory of cities 25, 65, 72–3, 176
theory of economies 63–8, 70, 72–3,
331, 351, 374–5, 378
view of Çatalhöyük 98
view of company towns 175

Jacobsen, Thorkild 118–20
Janelle, Donald
concept of 'time-space convergence'
293
Japan 135, 321, 328
economy of 65
financial sector of 318
Jomon culture of 138

Keynes, John Maynard
economic theories of 332–3
Khan, Matthew
estimation of carbon emissions for
US cities 364–6
King, Anthony
Global Cities 5
Knox, Paul
concept of 'New Urbanism' 366
Krugman, Paul 6–7, 121
Kuznets curve 339, 346
concept of 336

Lattimore, Owen 54
Leick, Gwendolyn
*Mesopotamia: The Invention of the
City* (2001) 96
Low Countries 11, 82, 235, 247, 249,
252, 264, 286–7
political division of 253

macro-social change 4, 15, 19, 51
forms of 13–14
nationalization of 13
reproduction methods 49
transitions 50
Malaya
product supply identity of 82
Mann, Michael
'social caging' 124
Sargon of Akkad 128
Marcus, Joyce
Archaic Studies (1997) 146
Marshall, Alfred 22, 277
Principles of Economics (1890) 6
Martin, Hans-Peter
The Global Trap (1997) 343
Marx, Karl 345, 354
Maya 142–3, 169, 197
political economy of 172
population growth of 173

McAdams, Robert
  The Evolution of Urban Society
    (1966) 116
McCormack, Michael 222
  *Origins of the European Economy:
    Communication and Commerce
    AD 300–900* (2001) 218–19
mega-city 330, 346, 368
  examples of 328
  formation of 328–9
  mega-slums 10, 330–32, 367
  origin of term 9
Mellaart, James
  excavations conducted by 105–6,
    109–10
mercantilism 262
Mesopotamia 28, 93–4, 118, 129, 133,
    160, 173, 177, 187–8, 197, 237,
    379
  cities of 96, 102, 105, 113–15, 118–
    19, 124, 127, 144–5, 153
  city-ness of 121
  states originating in 115
Mexico 28, 177, 197
  city-state cycles in 172–3
  Olmec city sites in 143
military
  city defences 188–9
Mill, John Stuart 22
Miller, Mark
  The Age of Migration (2003) 20
mini-systems 50
  reproduction of 49
Moche 175
  urban societies of 174
Modelski, George 99–100, 113, 114,
    139, 140 146, 148, 153, 159, 163,
    164, 202, 203, 204, 206, 207, 209,
    210, 211
  World Cities: – 3000 to 2000 (2003)
    202–3
modernity 44, 233, 235–6, 238, 261,
    289
  consumer 262
  industrial 262
  mercantile 262
moral syndrome 34, 37–40, 56–7, 88,
    185, 233, 239, 376
  Action Cluster 36
  Basic Cluster 36

commercial 35, 39–42, 47, 54, 88–9,
    95, 121, 187, 243
  Enterprise Cluster 36
  guardian 35, 41, 47, 53–4, 59–60,
    88–9, 95, 112, 186, 243
  Life Cluster 36
  monstrous hybrids 41–2
  Operating Cluster 36
  role in modern-world system 234
Morocco 156
Mozambique 176

national urban systems 17, 75
nationalization 17
  of institutions 13
  of macro-social change 13
  of social knowledge 75
neoliberalism 344
  concept of 334
  growth of 332–3
  impact of 334–7
Netherlands (United Provinces) 267
  beurtveren 287–8
  hegemony of 212, 267, 273–5, 287,
    291
  Holland 250, 253, 255, 262, 274–5,
    288, 292
  States General 253–4
  trekvaart network 287–8
  Zeeland 255, 275
network
  concept of 76
  formation of 78
  interlocking 78
Nissen, Hans
  concept of 'territorial state' 128
Norwich, John Julius 3
  The Great Cities in History (2009)
    11, 201
Nyerere, Julius 85

O'Brien, Patrick
  *Urban Achievement in Early Modern
    Europe* (2001) 11
oppida
  concept of 140
Organisation for Economic Co-
    operation and Development
    (OECD) 336
  working papers of 356–7

Orientalism 14
  concept of 15
Owen, David 9
  Green Metropolis (2009) 10, 364

Pacioli, Luca
  Summa de Arithmetica, Geometrica,
    Proportioni, et Proportionalita
    (1494) 191
Pakistan 139
Palestine 177
permaculture
  concept of 363
Persian Empire 157
Peru 28
  Casma Valley 142
Philistines 149
  cities of 176–7
Phoenicians 154–5, 209
  elite economy of 157–8
  territorial expansion of 156
  xenia 158–9
Pirenne, Henri 223, 227, 238–9, 257
  Medieval Cities: Their Origins and
    the Revival of Trade (1969) 215,
    235
'Pirenne thesis' 216–19, 222
Plato 42
Portugal 247
prehistory
  Abnormal 26–8
  examples of 26
  Normal 26–7, 29
principal components analysis (PCA)
  311
  concept of 306–8
Pyburn, Anne 169, 172

rank-size rule 199
  examples of 17–18
Reagan, Ronald 62
  economic policies of 332
Renfrew, Colin 108
  Archaeology: Theories, Methods and
    Practice (2008) 94–5
  concept of 'early state modules'
    126
Republic of Ireland 55, 262, 277
Robson, Brian
  analysis of UK urban growth 277–8

Roman Empire 157, 209, 258
  as example of world-economy 184
  fall of (476 AD) 213, 231, 293
  world city network of 210, 214–15
Roman Republic 209
  cities of 210
Roosevelt, Franklin D
  New Deal 337
Rudgley, Richard 97, 135-8
Russia 328, 347

Sahlins, Marshall 111
  theory of value in nonexchange
    112
Sargon of Akkad 128, 129, 256
Sassen, Saskia 3
  The Global City (1991) 5, 300, 302,
    327
Schattschneider, E.E. 60–61
Schuman, Harald
  The Global Trap (1997) 343
Scott, Allen
  Global City-Regions (2001) 12
Scott, James
  Seeing like a State (1998) 58–9
Second World War (1939–45) 15, 259,
    292, 337
  belligerents of 62
  decolonization following 16
shallowness 22–3
Smith, Adam 34
Smith, Monica 63, 115
  The Social Construction of Ancient
    Cities (2003) 146
Soja, Edward W. 95, 101, 103–6
  concept of 'regionality of cityspace'
    98
  concept of 'synekism' 98
  division of labour interpretations
    109–10
  T-shaped region 113, 129, 131, 135
South Africa
  apartheid 62
  product supply identity of 82
South Korea 337
Soviet Union (USSR) 60, 70, 83, 334
  as example of monstrous hybrid
    41
space
  construction of 53

spaces of flows 6, 52–3, 58, 63, 74, 85, 198, 202, 203, 285, 299, 300, 351, 358
spaces of places 6, 52–3, 54, 56, 58, 59, 62, 126, 234, 351, 356
Spain
Castile 246
military of 250
Sri Lanka
product supply identity of 82
state simplification 59
state-istics 18–19
relationship with cities 20–21
states 13, 16–17, 19–20, 24–5, 29–32, 56, 102, 145, 172
as process 26
as social institution 56–7
as spatial organization 57–8
creation of 26, 61, 116–17, 188
relationship with cities 22, 286, 302
relationship with civilizations 94
Sumer 94, 124, 127–8, 131, 134, 151, 176, 249
cities of 98, 108, 113–14, 125, 132, 149, 160, 204
city-empires of 128–9, 149
city-states 127–8
Kings List 120
language of 123
metal-processing industries of 122
religious culture of 118–19
state formation process in 130–32
Sweezy, Paul 238, 240
debate with Maurice Dobb (1979) 237–8
Syria 129, 177

Taiwan 337
Tamerlane
military conquests of 198, 232–3
Tanzania 85
territorial state
formation of 132
Thatcher, Margaret
economic policies of 332
Thirty Years' War (1618–48)
Treaty of Westphalia (1648) 29, 189, 261, 275, 356
Thompson, Grahame 76, 88–9

Thompson, William 192, 195-7
TimeSpace 32, 53, 57, 137, 196, 228
concept of 31, 51–2
Structural 52
variants of 53–5
town-ness 121, 163
relationship with city-ness 108–9, 167
Transition Initiative
development of 359–62
The Transition Handbook (2008) 359, 361, 363

Ukraine
South Bug-Dnepr region of 139–40
United Kingdom (UK) 30, 55, 85, 262, 267, 305, 348
class system of 43
hegemony of 268, 272, 276, 278, 280, 290–91, 303
space-economy of 290
transport network of 289–91
United Nations (UN) 9–10, 261, 328, 330
Human Settlement Programme (UN-HABITAT) 330, 339–40
members of 342
Population Fund 9
United States of America (US) 30, 55, 83, 134, 262, 267, 299, 305, 347, 373
carbon emissions in 364–6
economy of 18
government of 292
hegemonic city growth rates of 281–5
hegemony of 268, 271, 273, 280–82, 284–5, 337, 341, 345–6
Hurricane Katrina (2005) 356
Interstate Highway System 292
rank-size rule of 17
transport network of 291–2
urban hierarchy 76, 198
concept of 75, 77–8
national 17, 59, 198
world 25
urbanization 10, 121, 162, 167, 175, 201, 230, 277, 298, 328, 339
increase of 101, 183, 238, 331
New World 173

process of 153–4, 330
structures of 274
Urry, John
size and complexity 100

de Vries, Jan 288
Barges and Capitalism (1981) 287
city population database 262

Wallerstein, Immanuel 24, 55–6, 60–61,
    89, 235–6, 239–40, 243, 257, 260,
    273, 284, 332, 348, 358, 376, 379
concept of 'world-economies' 182,
    184
concept of 'world-empires' 182
core-periphery model of 258
criticism of Braudellian society
    model 48
definition of hegemony 260–61,
    264
theories of 23–4, 31
world-systems analysis 44–6, 55, 183,
    192, 200, 234–5, 237, 267, 352–5
Weber, Max 22, 125, 235–7
concept of 'monopoly of legitimate
    violence' 58
theories of 25
Wickham, Chris 222
    The Inheritance of Rome (2009) 213
Wolf, Eric 14
World Bank 335
    Gross External Debt Position
        statistics 344
    World Development Report (2009) 9
World Economic Forum 355
world-economy 9, 18, 45–6, 48–50, 54,
    73–4, 84–5, 124, 154, 182, 184,
    221–3, 234, 247, 257, 259, 268,
    272, 283, 305, 310–11, 316, 318,
    332, 336, 355
capitalist 28–30, 46–7, 50, 55–6, 200,
    207, 229, 250, 293, 332–3, 335,
    338, 341, 348, 353–5
commercial practices of 177
concept of 182, 203, 257–8
contemporary 20–21
core zones of 85, 258, 260, 321,
    327–8, 330
growth of 67, 271, 345, 353

peripheralization in 82–3
processes of 46
reproduction of 49
settlements within 67–8
transition from mini-system to 49–50
USA plus London (USAL) 310–11,
    314–16, 318, 325, 327
world-empires 48, 52, 56, 184, 192, 203,
    205, 207, 213, 231, 258–9, 261,
    350, 379
commercial practices in 118, 121,
    183, 234
concepts of 45–6, 182
guardian practices of 47, 95, 118,
    120–21, 177, 234, 353, 378
predominance of TimeSpace I 54
reproduction of 49, 54, 187, 229
structures 231, 236
transition from mini-system to 49–50
transition to mini-system from 49–50
World Social Forum 355
World Trade Organization (WTO)
    establishment of (1995) 332
    members of 332–3
world-systems 44, 46, 192, 198, 229,
    234–5, 237, 267, 350, 352–5, 378
commercial processes 55, 129, 144,
    154, 156–7, 183–4, 187, 196,
    198–200
conversion into world-empires 261
core-periphery structure of 367
geohistorical systems 45
guardian processes 55, 60, 76, 119,
    125, 129–31, 167, 178, 182, 184,
    197–201, 236, 254
Islamic 222
modern 63, 230, 243, 246, 258, 260–
    62, 264, 299, 348, 358
role of moral syndromes in 234
systemic properties of 45

Xiaoping, Deng 338, 344

Yates, Robin
    definition of city-states 162–3
Yoffee, Norman 51, 93, 95, 116-8, 121,
    124-9, 151-3
Yunis, Muhammad
    Grameen Bank 42